THE NEW NATURALIST LIBRARY

A SURVEY OF BRITISH NATURAL HISTORY

LAKES, LOUGHS AND LOCHS

D1069324

THE NEW NATURALIST LIBRARY

LAKES, LOUGHS AND LOCHS

BRIAN MOSS

WILLIAM
COLLINS

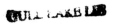
This edition published in 2015 by William Collins,
An imprint of HarperCollins Publishers

HarperCollins Publishers
1 London Bridge Street
London SE1 9GF
WilliamCollinsBooks.com

First published 2015

© Brian Moss, 2015

A CIP catalogue record for this book is available
from the British Library.

Set in FF Nexus, designed and produced by
Tom Cabot/ketchup

All photos by the author unless otherwise credited.

Printed in Hong Kong by Printing Express

Hardback
ISBN 978-0-00-751138-9

Paperback
ISBN 978-0-00-751139-6

All reasonable efforts have been made by the author to trace the copyright
owners of the material quoted in this book and of any images reproduced
in this book. In the event that the author or publishers are notified of any
mistakes or omissions by copyright owners after publication of this book,
the author and the publisher will endeavour to rectify the position
accordingly for any subsequent printing.

Contents

Editors' Preface

OUR UNDERSTANDING OF THE FUNCTIONING of freshwater habitats has made great advances in the more than 60 years since the publication of Macan and Worthington's New Naturalist *Life in Lakes and Rivers* was published. Brian Moss brings us a vivid account of the current state of subject, to which he has himself made a very substantial contribution. He shows how landscape, geology, chemistry and weather, as well as living organisms of many different groups, contribute to the functioning of the system, and help to determine whether we have a clear lake with submerged plants or a smelly soup of cyanobacteria; and he takes us on a tour of Britain and Ireland to introduce us to a diversity of lakes and to show how geographical variation in lake types depends on climate and geological history. He shares his delight in pristine waters, and tells sorry tales of the results of human intervention, whether inadvertent due to changes in the catchment, or resulting from 'management', which has often resulted in unexpected and unwanted effects.

These freshwater ecosystems appeal particularly to broad-minded naturalists because so many different groups of organisms interact here, and because with a pond net and a microscope a wonderful range of organisms can be studied throughout all seasons of the year. This book will surely attract new devotees to the subject and act as a launching pad for further advances in our understanding of these very interesting and accessible ecosystems.

Author's Foreword and Acknowledgements

BOOKS SHOULD SPEAK FOR THEMSELVES and long prefaces are indulgent, but there are a few things to be said. First, writing this was no chore. I have worked with freshwaters and particularly lakes since the accidents of fate and personality, completely uninfluenced by a bureaucracy of professional careers advice, led me to a PhD project on two small ponds near Bristol. The background to that came in 1960 from the inspiration of a course at Preston Montford Field Centre on 'Meres and Mosses', run by Charles Sinker, leavened by a parallel course from the then all-female Bedford College, taught by Francis Rose, and his demonstrator, David Bellamy, onto which we were co-opted when Charles was administering the Centre. The key influences after that were the second-year limnology lectures in 1963, concocted as he went along from a pile of reprints, by Frank Round at the University of Bristol. I still remember the complete fascination of thermal stratification and the phytoplankton spring growth. Since then, lakes have been a continuous part of my life and still are. If the writing in this book occasionally touches on the acid, it is because both freshwaters and freshwater ecologists have been sorely tried, in Britain at least, over the past several decades. But in a book written mostly for a British and Irish audience, you may put it down also to dry humour. It was a pleasure to write specifically for the natives and not to have to sanitise everything for a global clientele.

The second point is an apology to Wales and the Welsh. There was no way that I could work *Llyn* or *Llynoedd* into a title that needed to look attractive and sound lilting. And yes, I know that *Loughs* is pronounced in Gaelic with a hard ending, like *Lochs*, but many people use the soft ending, and that served my purposes well. I have at least taken a very pro-Welsh standpoint in the body of the text.

Lastly, an explanation for some of the approach I have taken. The New Naturalist series has an admirable policy of minimising clutter in the text by avoiding too many references and spurning scientific names, in favour of common ones. I have dealt with the first issue by using a system of notes at the end in which to give the references. The background evidence for any ecological subject is now extensive and the 400 or so I have had to quote really does represent a minimum in an area where at least 5,000 new papers emerge every year. I have used British and Irish work where I could, but science is an international endeavour and it would be foolish to be parochial. The number of authors on scientific papers has increased steadily, indeed logarithmically, over the past fifty years, from a mean of 1.5 in the 1960s to around four in the last 5 years with sometimes as many as 50. There are interesting reasons for this, mostly concerned with the organisation and sociology of science (see Moss, 2013), but from the point of view of printing costs it means that many references now take up much more space than former ones did. Consequently, in the list of references I have quoted all authors for papers with four or fewer, but simply the first author 'and others' for the rest. That makes for some injustice, especially in areas where the convention is that the last author is the most important (because he or she raised the funds to do the work, whilst the first author is often the graduate student who was supervised to carry it out) but the full list will be available in the original reference. Some of the original papers may require access to a university library because journal subscriptions are high, but the trend now is for free and open access on the web and a little searching will often produce free copies of many that were previously inaccessible to a general readership.

I have had to take a hybrid approach to the issue of common versus scientific names. There are well-known common names for higher plants, fish, birds and mammals, but the natural history of lakes depends also on a great many microorganisms and invertebrates, for which there are none. I have minimised lists of names, but sometimes have had to use scientific ones. The consolation is that the scientific names tell a great deal more than the common names once the system, which is very straightforward, is understood. A little dalliance with Latin improves appreciation of the meanings, but is not essential. I have given both scientific (in italics) and common names where available in the Index. To my regret, I could not find a way of mentioning *Micrasterias mahabuleshwarensis* var *wallichii*, a green algal desmid with a hint of exotic connections that is said to be found in some English lakes, but I hope that you will enjoy the book nonetheless.

Brian Moss, Liverpool, February 2015

CHAPTER 1

Romance and Reality: Limnology in Britain and Ireland

W E START EARLY, BUT, OF course, long after the true beginning …
The sun, setting behind the mountain ridges to the west,
darkened the shoreline of the loch yet still blazed on the palisade
surrounding the island; the dip of a paddle disturbed the heron that had been
fishing from the submerged rock causeway, which, if you knew its zigzags, would
lead you to the crannog gate (Fig. 1).[1] The shoal of small perch, which the heron
had been stalking by the causeway's edge, began to move into the open waters.
Copepods, their day spent in the deep waters, were on their way upwards to filter
their food near the lake's surface, but in the twilight also to risk their lives to the
hungry perch. The boatman felt no particular significance of the times; we would
call it the Iron Age; he was about his daily routine.

Nightly he returned, from penning his cattle in a compound of gorse and
thorn on the nearby shore, to the small island of timbers and boulders. It
had been built long ago, and his family felt safe surrounded by water and the
palisade. The heron settled in an oak, part of the forest that gave way to alders

FIG 1. Reconstruction of a crannog. Etching from Wood-Martin (1886), *The Lake Dwellings of Ireland.*

FIG 2. Distribution of wetlands in England in the prehistoric period, about 7,000 years ago and at present. Based on maps made by Wetland Vision (2008).

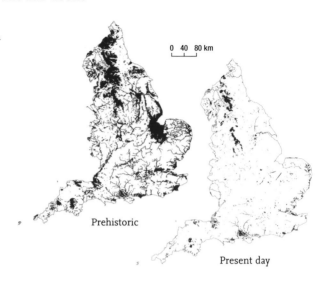

0 40 80 km

Prehistoric

Present day

near the lake's edge, and studied the small fields that had been wrested from the woodland. The movements of the fish away from the shore had frustrated her fishing but there might be an eel slithering through the grass, or a snake. The man had brought some lapwings he had snared, and pots he had bartered for fish, and the smoke of his family's fire merged in the wind with that of the dozen other crannogs set around the loch.

To the southwest, in Ireland, his distant Gaelic relatives also heard the harsh call of a heron during their evening routine but young sea trout took the place of perch in the lough; perch had not reached Ireland before the rising seas had cut it off as an island, 6,000 years previously. The copepods were there though, easily transported as eggs in the damp crevices of birds' feet, and had long made their day-and-night migrations. To the south, in what was to be called England, a warmer, drier landscape harboured fewer lakes and wetlands, though the land was still well watered (Fig. 2). The floodplains bordering the Severn estuary saw the movements of boats back to lake islands[2] in waters close to what was to become, in later centuries, the town of Glastonbury. The living was richer, the game more varied, the fields wider than in the north. But the links with the water were just as strong (Fig. 3). As everywhere and always, human settlements were drawn by need to lakes and rivers, springs and streams. The water stitched the landscape together; it was (and is) as the bloodstream is to the body.

The bloodstream was then pulsing and vigorous. As now, the west winds brought in gouts of wet air from the Atlantic to douse the north and west. The east got northeasterly continental air, which had passed over so much land that it was dry and cold in winter but hot in summer. Nonetheless it still rained a lot. The lakes were brim full, the rivers rose with the winter floods, spreading the water from the mountains into lowland floodplains where a mosaic of open water and wetlands provided a living for small groups of marsh dwellers, as they had for the thousands of years since the ice had retreated. They were also to hide those outlawed by the continental conquerors and colonisers that were to covet the islands in the coming centuries.

From AD41 until the twelfth century, Romans, Saxons, Vikings and Normans speeded the already begun conversion of a gushing lowland of wildwood and scattered pastoralists towards the present thirsty fields, pastures, embanked rivers and drained floodplains of our day. Only isolated patches of semi-natural woodland, heath and wetland (Fig. 2) remain, as tiny monuments, now so infrequent as needing to be glorified as nature reserves and Sites of Special Scientific Interest. Even in the uplands, the continuous forest, with its spongy organic soils, has almost gone; many upland lakes are regulated by dams to check flooding in the lowlands, divert the water to the cities, or provide irrigation for the fields. The lowland floodplain lakes have been drained and replaced by reservoirs, embanked and intrusive, with sterile drawn-down shores. Our population is concentrated into towns and cities that have eased themselves into habits and lifestyles whose demands strain the water supply, particularly in central and southern England. The water has variously become acidified from

FIG 3. Glastonbury lake village excavations in 1897 (left) and a reconstruction of the village from Bulleid (1924) (right).

FIG 4. Glen Affric, an attractive Scottish lake landscape, but one bearing, in its paucity of forest, the evidence of severe human disturbance. (Scottish Tourist Board)

FIG 5. *Ullswater from Gobarrow*, J. M. W. Turner, 1819. (Whitworth Art Gallery, Manchester)

air pollution, sullied by fertilisers wasted from agriculture or the sewage works, or polluted by the chemicals and by-products of myriad industries, at first heavy and now from pharmaceuticals, bathrooms and beauty parlours. The availability of water is changing still as the climate changes from the consequences of our profligate energy use.

The picture is not always depressing. The Scottish Highlands and Islands, the edges of Ireland, Snowdonia, Cumbria and other uplands, and patches in the lowlands, still provide landscapes that are interesting and attractive, even beautiful because the historic influence of human toil coupled with a ruggedness that has prevented intensive use (Fig. 4). The lakes still inspired the painters and poets[3] of the romantic artistic tradition of the nineteenth century (Fig. 5). Despite a population of nearly 70 million people, in an area of only 314,000 km^2, Britain and Ireland might be said to have coped well in the compromise between preserving natural features and giving people comfort and security.

The excesses of nineteenth-century industrial and urban development (Fig. 6), when factories, slaughterhouses and domestic dwellings released their wastes into rivers that became grey and foetid sources of cholera and typhoid, have been dealt with by increased understanding of public health, and appropriate legislation, but

FIG 6. 'Monster Soup', a cartoon comment in 1828 by William Heath on the state of the water of the River Thames seen through a microscope. (Wellcome Library)

all is not entirely well. There is still the bloodstream of freshwater; there has to be, because neither natural land vegetation, nor agriculture, nor people can exist without it; but the arteries are constrained, the veins diseased and the capillaries less rich. We understand the structure and function of this bloodstream better than ever before, but the patient lies in the emergency room.

LIFE IN LAKES AND RIVERS

The New Naturalist predecessor (Fig. 7) to this book, *Life in Lakes and Rivers*, by Thomas Macan and Barton Worthington,[4] published in 1951, came at pivotal time in this history of our freshwaters. Agriculture was intensifying, following the deprivations of the Second World War, when food supplies had been scarce, but was yet far from the excesses that subsidies were later to encourage. Engineers were only just beginning a phase of deepening and straightening the rivers, and confining them within banks riven of trees that might fall into the water and block

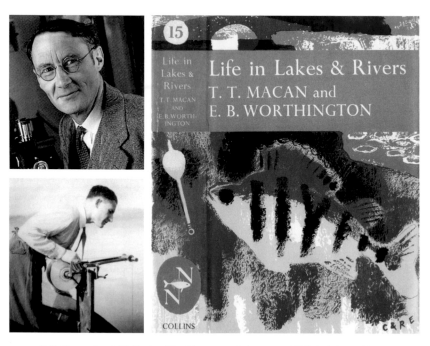

FIG 7. T. T. Macan (top left), Barton Worthington and the cover of *Life in Lakes & Rivers*. (Freshwater Biological Association and Dr R. Lowe-McConnell)

the flow. The floodplains had been under attack since Roman times but many were still intact, and the silt-fertilised river meadows bore swards of fritillaries, orchids and meadowsweet. Many ponds, dug or dammed for stock or other rural needs, still lay in the corners of the fields; the severer pressures of drawdown of lakes and reservoirs for irrigation and domestic supply, of conversion of pasture to arable and consequent greater nutrient pollution from fertiliser, and the massive burning of fossil fuels in the later twentieth century, were still to be felt.

Moreover the times were optimistic. The Second World War was six-years over; during it, science had advanced greatly in many ways that could be harnessed in peacetime, including aerial photography, radar, medicine and instrumentation. Government was seeing the advantages of investing further. Talented people were eager to resume their pre-war careers, not least the newly appointed staff of the Freshwater Biological Association Laboratory on Lake Windermere, including Macan and Worthington. There were major social changes. The education system, previously favouring the well-off, was being reformed to allow free access for everyone to have a secondary schooling, and for increasing numbers to move on to university. The universities were packed with ex-servicemen avid to learn and unwilling to tolerate a stuffy authoritarian regime. Seeds sown by social unrest in the 1930s had germinated into the National Parks and Access to the Countryside Act of 1949, which not only opened up swathes of countryside to walkers but also preserved tracts as Sites of Scientific Interest and the best of them as National Nature Reserves. The National Health Service was born in a welfare state that was raising hopes and expectations for people who had previously struggled. It was the new Elizabethan Age. My parents and I were among the first to benefit. I would not now be writing this book at the age of over seventy had it not flowered; I would be long dead from an infectious disease, disheartened from some mundane job, or, I hope, fighting, from the wrong side of the tracks, the social injustices that were swept away but alas are beginning now to creep back.

In the late 1940s, Barton Worthington, the Director of the Freshwater Biological Association, had been asked by the editors of the New Naturalist series to write a book on freshwaters. He was taking up new responsibilities in Africa, however, where he had much previous experience of its freshwater fisheries, so he asked Tommy Macan to help. In the end the book perhaps reflected Macan's love of invertebrates more than Worthington's concern with fish, but it was nonetheless the most accessible and broad coverage of freshwater ecology available in English for the next few decades, and was even adopted as a text-book by the Open University.

But that is to get ahead of an account of freshwater science in Britain and Ireland. Our ancestors, of the prehistoric and mediaeval crannogs, doubtless acquired intimate knowledge of natural history (indeed perhaps to an extent that we have now lost) and, being no less human and feeling than us, appreciated, as we do, the aesthetic qualities of the waterscapes. But they had neither time nor facilities to investigate freshwaters in the systematic way that the more privileged people of the nineteenth century began to do, and which flourished after the Second World War.

UNDERSTANDING INCREASES: THE BATHYMETRICAL SURVEY OF THE SCOTTISH LOCHS

Scientific effort in understanding freshwaters, indeed ecology in general, began with the improvement of microscope lenses by Antonie van Leeuwenhoek in Delft in the mid-seventeenth century and his early observations on bacteria and single-celled animals.[5] The eighteenth and nineteenth centuries saw a rise in the number of people, often clerical and with private means, who became expert in particular groups of animals and plants, and kept notes on where they grew, when and in what abundance. They benefited from the standard system of naming, using genus and species names, that Carl von Linné (Linnaeus), in Sweden, had proposed, in several editions of *Systema Naturae* published between 1735 and 1758. Eventually, what at first had seemed a study of random curiosities, created by a whimsical God, was given meaning by Charles Darwin's and Alfred Russell Wallace's revelation in 1858 of the main mechanism of evolution, and the processes of speciation. It gradually dawned that there was some sort of organisation of organisms in their habitats. In the United States, Stephen Forbes produced a famous paper 'The lake as a microcosm' in 1877,[6] which pointed out that there were preferences for different parts of the habitat by different species and that they were interlinked through what eventually came to be known as food chains. Towards the end of the nineteenth century there were field stations in mainland Europe and America, employing scientists to look at lakes and rivers systematically, but Britain and Ireland remained served largely by the gifted amateurs working alone.

The turning point came by a curious route. In the latter half of the nineteenth century, the needs of the British Admiralty for charting the oceans had led to the Challenger expeditions, which took place under the direction of Charles Wyville Thomson, between 1872 and 1876. A Scots-Canadian émigré, John Murray (Fig. 8), was appointed Thomson's assistant and eventually directed the publication, in a series of book-length reports, of many of the results, which included physical, chemical and biological observations as well as depth surveys. Murray, later knighted, became interested in the Scottish sea lochs and surveyed these in 1897. He then sailed into the freshwater lochs, Lochy, Oich and Ness, using the Caledonian Canal, and noted how very different these were from the sea lochs,

FIG 8. Frederick Pullar (left) at the time of the survey of the Scottish lochs, and Sir John Murray, in later life.

because of the contrasts in chemistry and density of fresh and salt water. Soon afterwards he persuaded a friend and philanthropist, the businessman Laurence Pullar, to provide funds for the start of a survey of the freshwater lochs.

Murray was an energetic man. He sought support from the Admiralty and the Ordnance Survey for a fuller survey of the freshwater lochs, but the Admiralty thought mostly of the ocean (it had, however surveyed the depths of Lochs Lomond and Awe) and the Ordnance Survey confined its interests, it said, to the land. Eventually it made two copies of its six-inches-to-the-mile maps available to Murray, provided he returned one copy with the contours of the lochs marked in. Since then the Survey has shown these on its maps. Murray, though, still needed funds to survey the lochs, and Laurence Pullar obliged. His son, Frederick (Fig. 8), an enthusiastic young amateur meteorologist, engineer and scientist, had become involved. Tragically, Frederick, who developed many of the instruments used in the surveys, was drowned, aged 25, in February 1901 attempting to rescue a woman from the icy waters of Airthrey Loch, now part of the University of Stirling, near his home in Bridge of Allan. He had previously rescued three other skaters in difficulties. Murray was deeply distressed by this and almost gave up the project. Laurence Pullar persuaded him to continue and set up trust funds for the work, in memory of Frederick, and the fieldwork was completed between 1902 and 1907.

By 1909, bathymetric (depth) maps of some 562 lochs had been made and a wealth of other information collected. *The Bathymetrical Survey of the Fresh Water Lochs of Scotland under the direction of Sir John Murray KCB, FRS and Laurence Pullar FRSE* [7] endures as the most substantial early contribution to the freshwater sciences in Britain. It comprises six volumes, the first an introduction and report on the scientific results, the second a set of descriptions of the lochs and the third to sixth the bathymetric maps (Fig. 9), from the 25.47 mile length of Loch Awe (Etive) to the 0.1 mile of the Rainbow Loch, the 27.45 square miles of Lomond

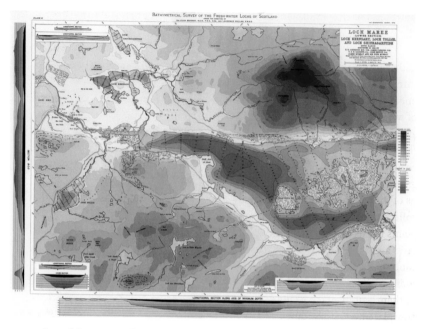

FIG 9. One of the maps made as a result of the survey of Scottish lochs by Murray and Pullar.

to the 0.003 of Allt na Mult, and the 1,017 ft maximum depth of Morar to the 2 ft of Setter. Murray loved numbers. Many of the maps are available online from the Scottish National Library, which continues Murray's predilection by being unable to stop itself from pointing out that Loch Ness has more water than the sum total of all water bodies in England and that the Eiffel Tower could fit into Loch Morar with 33 feet to spare. Volume 1, however, is a rich account of the survey, the people concerned and the results other than the maps themselves.

My copy is still in its original brown leather bindings, the corners reinforced, the title in gold leaf: a very solid book, worthy of the seriousness of the work. Vol. 1 has an account of many aspects of the lakes, a survey of limnology (the science of lakes) to date and a bibliography of the papers and books then available worldwide on limnology. What comes through is something denied in most of the modern scientific literature: a description of the problems, of how the work was done, even pictures of Murray, having lunch, a cigarette between his lips and of Frederick Pullar, a cigar between his, both against a background of a boat and boatman, with Pullar's sounding device mounted on the gunwale. There is an account of the difficulties of knowing where in the lake the soundings were being made, resolved in the end by the simplest of all methods: steady rowing along a line between shore markers and stopping at set numbers of oar strokes.

The survey looked at several aspects of lakes, using the experts of the day to gather and interpret the information. E. M. Wedderburn's enthusiasm for the minutiae of water temperature comes through in an account of the exchange of energy in the lakes that was one of the foundations of our modern understanding of water mixing, though, as always in early work, he had some misconceptions. We are introduced to the splendid, if now archaic word 'denivellation', for changes in the height of the water surface and 'embouchure' for the mouth of an inflowing river. George West, then Professor of Botany at Birmingham, but having figured greatly with his father, William West, in describing the British algal flora, tells us of the aquatic plants. After deriding previous botanists for merely making collections and lists, he quotes Herbert Spencer[8] to the effect that the structures of plants tell us of their functions and his insights stand up well today. W. A. Caspari gives a short account of the water chemistry, recognising the importance of the commoner ions in telling how waters to the west of Scotland tend to be richer in sodium and chloride, because of the effects of gales and the sea spray drawn up by them, but barely mentions nitrogen and phosphorus, elements on which we now place huge importance. James Murray gives an account of the plankton, again recognising fundamentals that we misbelieve are much more recent: for example the overall uniformity, even in a large loch, owing to wind mixing, the existence of vertical movements and the low diversity compared with the ocean plankton. Somewhere, John Murray must have met the prominent Danish limnologist Carl Wesenberg-Lund and persuaded him to review the state of limnology at the time and give his views on where limnology was heading.

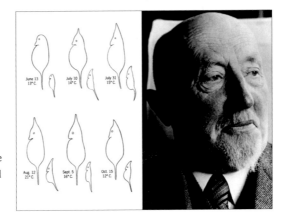

FIG 10. Prof. Wesenberg-Lund and some drawings of a Daphnia species from one of his studies on changes in shape of the animals (adults and new-born) during the year. The temperatures of the water testify to his belief that this was the cause of the changes, but we now know that they are induced chemically by the presence of fish predators.

Wesenberg-Lund gives many diagrams of the changes in shape of particular zooplankton species (Fig. 10) that occur during the year, and speculates on the reasons, which he thinks are due to changes in physical conditions like temperature. He suggests that solution of this problem needs studies on lakes with less seasonality in the tropics. Indeed those studies, now carried out, show that it is not temperature that is directly responsible but the chemical influences of predatory fish. But at that time fish and fisheries were seen as somewhat separate and indeed it took well into the twentieth century for fisheries and limnology to become integrated. There are still separate societies and even government departments for fisheries and the water environment in many countries. It is fascinating though to see the spirit of enquiry coming through in the writing, though not without a good dose of dogmatism.

Later in Volume 1, John Murray shows an excellent command of their origins and curiosities in presenting an account of the lakes of the world, before James Chumley, who, in the Challenger Office, had ably managed the data being collected, attempts to compile a complete bibliography of limnological papers then published. There were some 3,000 of them, mostly since the 1860s, a figure that is exceeded by far in every year now, so that his final word is a quotation from Elliott Coues (a nineteenth-century American army surgeon and ornithologist): 'If you are troubled with a pride of accuracy, and would have it completely taken out of you, print a catalogue.'

Experimentation, as opposed to deduction from observation, had not yet reached the environmental and biological sciences from chemistry and physics, and Murray and his collaborators deigned to use much in the way of statistical or graphical techniques for summarising their data, but this is still a landmark book, and the survey something to be greatly admired. It was unparalleled in the other countries of Britain and Ireland, though limnology was advancing in North America and mainland Europe, not least because of the field stations that were being set up. In the USA, the state lake surveys, documenting the water and fish resources, had been in operation for decades.

AMATEUR NATURALISTS AND THE NEW GENERATION OF SCIENTISTS

Amateur naturalists had been at work in Britain and Ireland for some time. Roderick O'Flaherty (1629–1718), Patrick Browne (1720–90) and John Templeton (1766–1825) catalogued the Irish fish. Richard Barton had given an account of the natural history of Lough Neagh in the mid-eighteenth century. In the nineteenth century, John Hood, a metal turner, was working on rotifers, William Frederick Johnson on dragonflies and the doyen Irish naturalist, Robert Lloyd Praeger, on water plants. Scotland too has had its share, and there were some early accounts of the lake basins themselves, particularly the larger ones. The more prominent naturalists ranged widely and William West and his son George sought samples from all over the archipelago for their accounts of the British freshwater algae and particularly the desmids, a group of green algae particularly diverse in acid lakes.

The Wests reflected the emerging scientific spirit, though they were not of typical background. William West (1848–1914) began life as a pharmacist in Yorkshire, taught himself botany, and later was lecturer in botany and *materia medica* at Bradford Technical College. His younger son, George Stephen (1876–1919), who co-authored many papers and several books with him, went straight into the academic profession after graduating at Cambridge and became Professor at Birmingham University. The previous gentlemanly tradition continued however, and Eustace and Robert Gurney, scions of a philanthropic Quaker banking family in Norfolk, founded, in 1901, a small laboratory in a cottage (Fig. 11) next to Sutton Broad in Norfolk.[9] They fitted out a solid commercial boat, a wherry, for sampling, and invited others to work there, but were not always complimentary about their conclusions. Two of them, Benjamin Millard Griffiths and Frank Balfour-Browne, who worked respectively on algae and beetles, were to figure significantly in later events. The laboratory was closed at the outbreak of the First World War, but Robert Gurney remained a prominent expert on the crustaceans for several decades afterwards.

In the first decade of the new century, William Pearsall and his son William Harold Pearsall (1891–1964) became interested in the aquatic plants of the Cumbrian Lake District and particularly in the processes of succession on the

FIG 11. The house at Sutton Broad in Norfolk, built for use as the first British freshwater field station by the Gurney brothers in 1901.

FIG 12. W.H. Pearsall, in a drawing displayed at the Freshwater Biological Association, and Esthwaite Water. Some of Pearsall's earliest work was on the vegetation that straddles the small lake, Priest Pot, in the foreground, and in the main lake. (English Heritage)

delta where the Black Beck enters Esthwaite Water (Fig. 12). Pearsall Senior was a teacher commanding high respect in the area and imbued his son with a spirit of independent enquiry. 'Think, try, ask' read a maxim on his parlour wall. Even before W.H. Pearsall entered the University of Manchester, he and his father were busy with bicycles and rowing boats, sampling the plants of the major lakes and W.H. was formulating theories which were to dominate thinking in British limnology for decades as to how the communities were related to the water chemistry and ageing of the lake basins. The transition from listing species to contemplating how the ecosystems worked, begun in the nineteenth century, was accelerating.

In London, yet another middle-class family of teachers had spawned one of the greatest algologists, who in 1902, as a lecturer in botany to the trainee gardeners of the Royal Botanic Gardens, Kew, wrote a paper on the plankton of the Thames and lamented the lack of a field station in the British Isles for the study of freshwaters. Frederick Fritsch (1879–1954), British born but with German connections, knew of the stations founded at Plön im Holstein in 1892, and Madison, Wisconsin, in 1896 and later visited that built in 1906 at Lunz am See, in Austria. Methodical, affable but asthmatic, he was unable to indulge in extensive fieldwork but built up a knowledge of algal biology unrivalled until electron microscopes, widely used after his death, gave many new dimensions, but did not undermine his careful observations of structure and life history. Often I have been excited to find some interesting 'new' feature of an alga that I had not seen before, only to discover an accurate picture of it in one of Fritsch's two 1945 volumes on *The Structure and Reproduction of the Algae*.

Another Norfolk Quaker family, the Buxtons, with an ancestry of country gentlemen, collectors, keen naturalists and bankers, and an aversion to academia and the arts, but with intermarriage to farming families, produced Patrick Alfred Buxton (1892–1955), a boy initially shy and the butt of jokes as he made his way through Rugby School to become a medical doctor at Cambridge. Whilst serving in Mesopotamia in the First World War, he became an expert on desert animals, an accomplished anthropologist, making notes on the marsh arabs, and notably the habits of mosquitoes and various other vectors of disease. As Head of the Department of Entomology at the London School of Hygiene and Tropical Medicine, he extended this work to pioneer areas of physiology and its use in development of insecticides, and the concept of applied biology. Physiology was very much the rising subject in biology and at Cambridge University a centre was growing around J. T. Saunders, who was interested in the physiology of protozoa and other aquatic animals. Saunders established, in the 1920s, the first course in freshwater biology in the UK (though such courses began in the USA with Joseph Needham at Cornell University in 1908). Saunders figures less in the pantheons of scientific publication than the giants of Fritsch, Pearsall, Gurney and Buxton,[10] but his strengths were teaching and organisation. The former is seen in the next generation of freshwater biologists, many of whom he trained, and the latter in the setting up of the Freshwater Biological Association (FBA) in the early 1930s (with many of the early staff members having been his students) and in his principalship of the University College at Ibadan in Nigeria, following his mastery as Secretary of the Faculties at Cambridge.

THE FRESHWATER BIOLOGICAL ASSOCIATION

Pearsall met Saunders in 1924 and they talked of the need for a national freshwater laboratory. Fritsch became involved, and made it the subject of his presidential address to the British Association for the Advancement of Science (BA) in 1927. The BA was then much more prominent than it is now, and it was at the BA meeting the next year that a committee emerged to look into the idea of a laboratory. The Committee met in December 1928 and January 1929. Fritsch was chairman, Balfour-Browne secretary and Pearsall, Saunders and Gurney were prominent members. Also on it, though with perhaps lesser influence, were Benjamin Millard Griffiths, from Durham University, and H. S. Holden, an expert in ferns. The last member was Edward Stuart Russell, a Scottish fisheries scientist, who made a singular contribution to the management of fisheries in his famous equation stating that the annual catch must be no greater than the annual growth of the fish population if the fishery were not to go into the decline of overfishing. Patrick Buxton became involved later.

The committee wrote a document, floating the idea of a field station to interested parties such as water companies and fishery organisations. It gave four main reasons for such a need: the many questions concerning the annual cycles of flora and fauna in lakes and the relationships between what was going on at the edges and in the main water mass; the need for scientific knowledge in solving problems of water pollution and purification; the opportunities for understanding more about fish and fish culture for food; and likewise those for solving biological problems of domestic water supply. It gave some details of cost of site and building (£1,500), of annual maintenance and paying a botanist, a zoologist, a laboratory assistant and a laboratory boy (total £1,250) because the circular was designed to attract offers of private support in the hope that government funds might then be provided. To focus all this, it proposed the setting up of a Freshwater Biological Association (FBA). There was dissent from Robert Gurney[11] who thought that the wording of the third aim (fish and fisheries) was explicitly offering to increase the economic contribution of fish culture but in the end he was persuaded not to resign, which might have undermined the project, so prominent was his reputation.

The idea caught on and there were contributions from individual subscriptions, the Fishmonger's Company, water undertakings, universities and a small grant from the government Development Commission. These were times of depression and doubtless much in the way of personal contacts and friendships was at work in raising enough to begin a laboratory. There was not enough money to buy land for building, but in 1931 the National Trust leased part of a Victorian folly, Wray Castle (Fig. 13), on the shores of Windermere, to the Association. Two former students of Saunders, Phillip Ullyott and R.S.A. Beauchamp were appointed, and Penelope Jenkin[12] used a grant for graduate work from Newnham College to base her fieldwork there, indeed arriving first. W.H. Pearsall was appointed part-time, unpaid Director, maintaining contact from his department at the University of Leeds, where he was Reader in Botany. The laboratory assistant, appointed straight from school, was the sixteen-year old

George Thompson, who became a redoubtable figure, immensely important in the organisation, until his death in 1972.

The work went well; the annual Easter class, designed to give practical experience for students from the universities, began in 1932 and was probably the single most influential course in training the next generation of freshwater scientists in the UK. An inspection by the Development Commission, eager to know how its funds were being spent, resulted in a bigger grant in 1937. The condition for this was that a permanent director should be appointed. This was to be E. Barton Worthington, another student of Saunders. At the outbreak of war in 1939 there was a staff of seven, and though most of these were called away to the armed forces, evacuated staff, too old for military service, from the British Museum (Natural History) and the Fisheries laboratory at Lowestoft maintained research. One wartime project was to catch and can perch from the lake as food (perchines). This began a long-term study of the changes in fish populations of the lake.[13]

FIG 13. Laboratories of the Freshwater Biological Association on Lake Windermere at Wray Castle (above left) and the Ferry House (left). Wray Castle is owned by the National Trust and now let as holiday accommodation. The Ferry House has been converted into flats but the newer Pearsall Building, behind it, still houses the offices of the Freshwater Biological Association.

After the War, many of the early staff resigned to take up posts elsewhere. Worthington became involved in colonial administration but new people were appointed in numbers that required a move to a bigger building, the Ferry Hotel (Fig. 13), four miles down Lake Windermere. Yet another of Saunders' students, Hugh Carey Gilson, became Director and stayed for many years, whilst a nucleus of people who have become 'household names' in the world of freshwater science, including T. T. Macan, made the FBA laboratory the centre of freshwater research in Britain and Ireland for the next 40 years. At one stage, in the 1970s, there were four Fellows of the Royal Society on the staff (J. W. G. Lund, J. F. Talling, Geoffrey Fryer and Winifred Pennington), whilst Clifford Mortimer, who had worked extensively with Lund at the FBA in earlier years, but left to work in the USA, was also a Fellow.

POST-WAR SCIENCE, REGULATORY AND CONSERVATION ORGANISATIONS

Freshwater science flourished in the post-war period. Most British universities had at least one freshwater biologist on their staff and the establishment of the Natural Environment Research Council in 1965 helped target funds that would have been competed for more widely under the previous Department of Industrial and Scientific Research, although the latter had been generous in its support. The FBA expanded to over 100 staff by the 1970s and many university scientists served on its Council and Science Advisory Committee. Conservation and management of freshwaters were changing too.

In 1949, the National Parks and Access to the Countryside Act had established the concept of Sites of Special Scientific Interest (SSSI) and freshwaters were included as parts of many of these. The problem was, however, that a lake cannot be managed without attention to the water sources in its catchment and the boundaries of SSSI rarely extended to these. The Nature Conservancy was set up by the 1949 Act to look after the designated sites and was dominated by scientific expertise.[14] The Royal Society for the Protection of Birds, the Wildfowl and Wetlands Trust, the County Naturalists Trusts and the National Trust had major parts in acquiring sites and managing them as best they could.

Management of the freshwater system as a whole had its problems. In Scotland, the River Purification Boards had a relatively easy time, for Scottish freshwaters were less sullied by human activities than those in England and Wales, where, in 1984, reform of the water industry at least placed management notionally on a catchment basis, though the new Water Authorities could do no more to manage the catchments than the various local bodies they replaced. At first the Authorities were responsible for all of regulation of water quality, provision of domestic supply and treatment of domestic and industrial wastewater, but were themselves major polluters (through poorly functioning sewage treatment works). In 1989, the regulatory function was passed to the National Rivers Authority (NRA) in England and Wales, and water supply and wastewater treatment became the purview of private companies. The name of the NRA reflected an emphasis on rivers in England and Wales though its responsibilities extended to lakes, and it had a publicity fillip when a hot summer in the year of its foundation led to problems of algal growths on some reservoirs that led to deaths of sheep and dogs. Meanwhile, in Scotland, the River Purification Boards had had similar roles since 1951 to the Water Authorities.

The Nature Conservancy was made into a regulatory body, the Nature Conservancy Council (NCC), without responsibility for the scientific research needed for conservation, in 1973, but still with United Kingdom coverage. It retained a strong scientific base however, and was highly critical of moves on the parts of landowners to manage peatlands in Scotland for commercial forestry, which gave short-term profit (but only from government grants), but was far from wise in the long term. A peevish government broke up the NCC in 1991 and created separate conservation bodies for England, Scotland and Wales, those in the latter two countries responsible for the wider countryside as well as the SSSI system. In England, English Nature and the Countryside Commission, later Countryside Agency, separated these functions until they were combined as Natural England in 2006. At every stage the bodies were weakened, their scientific capacity reduced and their annual reports increasingly determined by their publicity departments rather than by their scientists.

DECLINE

Meanwhile, the governments of the 1980s, led by Margaret Thatcher, transferred funds formerly allocated for fundamental research to government departments, to be reallocated in response to 'customer needs' whilst also reducing their total amount. It became more and more competitive to acquire funds for curiosity-driven research, though there was still no shortage of good ideas and the intellectual ability to follow them up. The quality of the freshwater SSSI and nature reserves has steadily declined as intensive farming, acidification from the burning of fossil fuels, river engineering and drainage, and invasion by exotic species have had their effects uncountered by serious government concern. The European Union has been a boost to research funds, but it too has been largely concerned with finding palliatives for emerging problems rather than increasing fundamental understanding.

In 1996 the National Rivers Authority was combined with agencies responsible for air pollution control and solid waste disposal, into the Environment Agency in England and Wales with fanfares that it was the most powerful regulatory agency in Europe. In Scotland the Scottish Environment Protection Agency was formed as a parallel body. Together with their predecessor Water Authorities, River Purification Boards and NRA, the environment agencies have done much to solve the essentially nineteenth-century problem of gross organic pollution by factories and sewage works, but are faced with a general decline in freshwater habitat quality caused by the effects of farming and urban development. Similar trends, with an equally tedious detailed history of organisation and reorganisation of government bodies, pertain in Northern Ireland and Ireland.

The European Union has produced Directives that have done much to improve habitats and waters but the principle of subsidiarity that gives member states a great deal of discretion and time, has frustrated many of them. The latest, the Water Framework Directive in 2000 promised a revolution in the state of both freshwater and coastal habitats in the European Union.[15] Ecological quality rather than simply water chemistry was to be the important criterion but political compromises have downgraded the Directive's impact to the state of a 'toothless tiger' (Chapter 10). Meanwhile, the number of people working in freshwaters in British and Irish universities has steadily declined since the 1970s. Government policy changes, from the 1980s onwards, have interfered greatly with universities and research institutes, placing emphasis on the amount of money raised from non-government sources and pushing business and economic issues rather than understanding and care for the environment. Biotechnologists, biochemists and geneticists, who are able to command greater funds from industrial sources, have often replaced ecologists.

The Freshwater Biological Association, an independent organisation but supported largely by government funds from 1931 until 1989, was completely taken over by government in the 1970s, renamed the Institute for Freshwater Ecology, and progressively reduced in size and influence, until it is now only a quarter of its former size. It lost its individual ethos by being merged in 2000 into a larger organisation, the Centre for Ecology and Hydrology, itself under pressure to raise more and more funds from industrial and commercial contracts, or from government departments concerned with specific problems.

The decline in British freshwater biology can be seen in the number of papers published in a very successful journal, *Freshwater Biology*, founded as a medium particularly for British publications in 1971.[16] Though the journal has expanded greatly, the number of papers originating from the Britain and Ireland is now vanishingly small, yet the quality of what is produced is very high indeed and its international influence is considerable.

MODERN APPROACHES

Happily, this declining picture of the extent of work in Britain and Ireland is not shared by the rest of the world, nor by the vigour of British and Irish freshwater science. New ideas abound and understanding of lakes since the days of Macan and Worthington has benefited from new techniques using stable isotopes and molecular biology, from ambitious approaches using whole lakes or large arrays of experimental ponds for experiments, from advances in chemical methods that can detect tiny traces of nonetheless important organic substances, and from the development of many new electronic instruments. Geographical information systems, based on satellite information, have replaced endless wanderings with Ordnance Survey maps (though maybe do not give quite the same pleasures). The natural development of Darwin's original understanding of the connections between evolution, adaptation and ecology has led to rational meaning being given to the many detailed and perceptive observations of naturalists. The fruits of these will emerge in the following pages.

Science is now much more strongly international; communication between scientists on different continents is very easy, access to the burgeoning literature has become a matter of pressing a few buttons on a computer rather than hours turning through the pages of books and journals in the library. Where unsullied by man, and often where the influence has been modest, the world is still a wonderful place. We have enough technical understanding to ameliorate all of the world's environmental problems. The blockage is elsewhere.

LIFE AS A LIMNOLOGIST, THEN AND NOW

From Macan to Moss, life as a limnologist has changed a great deal in detail, but not in principle. The first workers at Wray Castle adapted themselves to a building made for other purposes, in which, at first, they also lived. It had interesting nooks and crannies, cellars and attics, and impressive views of the mountains from the windows; pond nets were stacked in corners, open shelves housed the increasing number of samples before they were eventually archived in the cellars. Many hours were spent sampling in the field; cars had taken over from bicycles, but rowing boats still sufficed. Long hours were worked but somewhat irregularly. A good sunny day might be better used exploring the hills, whilst a winter gale could be profitably endured, from breakfast until late in the evening, by sorting and identifying samples of invertebrates from streams or lake edges. Curiosity drove most of the projects, and living by the lake stimulated the regular sampling of water and plankton that has produced, since the 1940s, an extremely valuable record of changes in Lake Windermere. Similar records were kept for Blelham Tarn and Esthwaite Water, both very close to the laboratory.

Being in the midst of the Lake District offered many opportunities for casual observations of natural history to be turned into proper investigations. Macan wrote an extremely fine account[17] from his close observations of the habits and movements, the risks and opportunities, of the animals he found on the bottom of Hodsons Tarn, up the hill from the FBA. He imagined himself as Gulliver, reduced in size and exploring the weedbeds, with their huge and often fearsome invertebrates. Over morning coffee, lunch or afternoon tea, when everyone would assemble in a library annexe of the new laboratory in the Ferry House, there was a great deal of discussion. The library was becoming increasingly well stocked and long hours were spent browsing. The outside world of limnology was encountered at scientific meetings, but perhaps only once every year or two, or when visiting scientists spent a few weeks at the laboratory. The metal and wood workshop was as important as the library. Most equipment was hand-made and adeptness with the soldering iron, saw, lathe or sewing needle was a great advantage.

Brass was pre-eminent. I well remember, in the 1960s, carrying a brass light-meter, a relic of the early days, across the cloying soils of a muddy field to reach the boathouse on Esthwaite Water. The meter was extremely heavy. There was administration to be done, of course. Accounts had to be kept, data properly stored, staff paid, materials ordered, but it took up much less time than now. The organisational needs were small, those of a mouse not an elephant. The same was true of the small clusters of people working in the universities, though they had larger teaching loads than are now common. The energy required to maintain a mouse is small, leaving a large surplus for the production of more mice. An elephant spends much more of its energy maintaining itself and far less on new production.

Life for a limnologist in the early years of the twenty-first century is, on the face of it, very different. There is less emphasis on fundamental, more on applied work.

Much more time is spent in raising and managing funds, for the amount of external income brought in is enforced as a measure of achievement. Administrators rule. Much more time is spent on making applications, most of which fail, for grants and contracts, filling in forms accounting for how time is spent, and making interim reports on contracts. There is also more pressure to publish papers. An enormous and expanding number of journals exists but some journals are prized (by promotions and appointments committees) more than others and the competition to get into these is intense, involving often many resubmissions and revisions to meet the requirements of increasingly critical referees.

Statistics and mathematics figure prominently in biology and it is rarely now enough just to use the leisured hands and quiet eyes of the traditional naturalist to make observations and report them. They must be put onto a quantitative basis. Sophisticated and specialist measurements need skilled technicians and the scope of modern investigations needs graduate students and postdoctoral workers to form research teams. They do most of the practical work. The poor principal is stuck in his or her office most of the time, mesmerised by the computer, raising the resources to keep the elephant ticking over. A rare day might be spent in the field, but the freedoms of the 1930s are scarcer. The office is likely to be simpler and bleaker, with few shelves as books are replaced by computer files, and no benching for practical work. The modern scientist must use his or her security swipe card, dangling on a ribbon around the neck, to enter a separate, secure laboratory, where space is shared, and the cluttered nooks of the ancestors are swept clear of character, and even of the occasional potted plant, by assiduous safety officers. New ideas are still generated, though more often perhaps from the welter of scientific information produced elsewhere than from the casual inspection of a sample of pond water, the musings on a walk in the hills, or the flight of the birds to roost.

But the copepod, the fish and the heron remain, still holding many secrets of their behaviour to be wondered at and probed. The bloodstream of the waters

FIG 14. The author sampling experimental ponds at the University of Liverpool's Ness Gardens in 2004.

and the tissues of the land are showing new links even as the destruction of these relationships reveals their former importance. The curiosity of the human mind (or at least of some human minds, for conformity is increasingly the order of the day for many societies) remains and young scientists entering the field are as enthusiastic as ever. No longer do we paddle to the crannog at night, noting the flight of the heron or the jump of the fish. More rarely do we row our boat to pull a plankton net through some remote tarn. Instead we muse on a scatterplot of data, a table of figures, or the analyses of water taken with an expensive and intricate sampler from some carefully designed experiment. But deep down, Murray and Pullar, the Wests, Pearsall, Saunders, Fritsch and Macan are still within us (Fig. 14).

CHAPTER 2

The Nature of Lakes

THE BACKDROPS TO OUR LAKE basins are the rocks – progeny of the violent and varied geological history of Britain and Ireland. Over millions of years, great blocks of the Earth's crust have drifted on an underlying sea of semi-liquid magma. They collided and reared as mountains, then eroded back to hills and plains. New sedimentary rocks formed from the debris of erosion, squeezed by its own weight into layers that skirted the seas around the continents. Plumes of molten rock, from below the crust, injected lavas to the surface or between the layers of sediments. Sometimes these were

FIG 15. Britain and Ireland are made up of fragments of former continents, called terranes, shown here in different colours. Those in greenish tones are from the former Laurasian continent, from which much of North America is derived. Those in warmer tones are from Gondwana, which gave rise to South America, Africa, Antarctica and much of Asia. Major fault lines mark the junctions of the terranes and the Iapetus suture runs along the line where the Iapetus Ocean was obliterated when Laurasia and Gondwana collided.

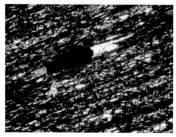

FIG 16. Thin sections of rocks: upper, igneous (granite, upper, 10 mm width), middle, sedimentary (sandstone, 8 mm width) and lower, metamorphic (slate, 2.5 mm width). (Courtesy of Cambridge Earth Sciences Image Store)

pushed upwards again, sometimes baked and metamorphosed by the lavas, and often they collided with pieces of other continents. There are bits of an ancient continent of Laurasia, now forming Scotland and part of northern England and Ireland, and of former Avalonia and Gondwana joined on as southern England (Fig. 15). These continents were once separated by an ocean, the Iapetus Ocean, before they broke up and drifted willy-nilly over the globe. The geological structure of our islands is unbelievably complicated, and unravelling it, and the changes that have occurred in tandem in the atmosphere and the oceans, has preoccupied earth scientists for over two centuries.[1]

There is now a nearly 4 billion year history of our islands, laid out in the outcropping of countless rock types, made up of thousands of minerals, its chapters and pages sometimes ordered by fossils that recount the parallel story of the evolution of life. For the current inhabitants of lakes, both the stratigraphical and evolutionary stories are of great importance. Beyond a degree of accident in what species have managed to recolonise a set of disturbed islands, what thrives in our waters is determined by the nature of the organisms, and the water chemistry that bathes them. Chemistry selects some for the uplands, others for the lowlands; it changes with the varying catchment mixtures of hard igneous rocks, resistant to weathering, softer sedimentary ones, easily broken, dissolved and leached by rainwater, or metamorphic rocks intermediate in character (Fig. 16).

The long-term rhythms in the shape of the Earth's orbit around the sun, the slow but regular wobbles in the angle of its daily spin, and the particular distribution of continent and ocean, have, on occasions, brought sufficient

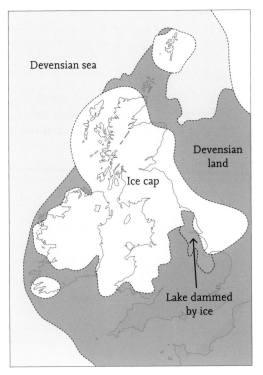

FIG 17. Extent of the last phase of the most recent glaciation, the Devensian, in Britain and Ireland. There was a land connection with what is now mainland Europe and isolated ice caps over Shetland and southwestern Ireland. A large lake was dammed in eastern England at the foot of the main ice cap.

cooling for ice to spread from the poles over much of its surface. Glaciation obliterates most past landforms and greatly changes the bigger ones that survive it. Virtually all the lake basins in Britain and Ireland are children of the glaciation that ended less than 20,000 years ago, or of later events. The to-ing and fro-ing of the ice smoothed the landscape, removed or reshaped all previous lakes, killed most of their living organisms or drove them southwards, sometimes temporarily to return in the warmer interglacials (interstadials). It reset the freshwater stage many times. Only with the retreat of the final Devensian ice, around 13,000 to 17,000 years ago, could the warming climate start to build a modern history of the landscape on the palimpsest of the old (Fig. 17). It was a fresh new world, a bare and almost empty stage onto which refugee freshwater actors swam or crawled. They came from the south and east, through rivers that crossed lands that are now the Irish and North Seas, or flew, or were transported on the winds, to repopulate the new lake basins, before the rising oceans, fed by the melting glaciers, isolated the islands only a few thousand years ago.[2]

G.E. HUTCHINSON AND THE ORIGINS OF LAKES

FIG 18. G.E. Hutchinson.
(Yale University)

George Evelyn Hutchinson (1903–91) was a man of charm and learning (Fig. 18).[3] He had been educated at Cambridge, travelled to South Africa then Ladakh, to study their lakes, and eventually settled at Yale in the USA to become the doyen of limnologists. In 1957 he published the first volume of his *Treatise on Limnology*,[4] which was to became the reference book of limnology for several decades, and is still of great value. In the first volume, Hutchinson laid out 75 ways in which lake basins are formed, of which 25 (Table 1, overleaf) are found in Britain and Ireland, with more than half directly related to the action of the ice (Fig. 19).[5] The rest come from usually more recent geomorphological processes, such as the blocking of estuaries by shingle or sand dunes, the solution of limestone rock by rainwater, the cutting off of oxbows by meandering rivers, or when we build dams.

The sundering of the Earth's plates that created the rift valleys, in which lie Lake Baikal and the Great Lakes of Africa, has little role here, though Loch Ness (Fig. 20) partly owes its origin to a great fault between the rocks. Nor does the depression of a huge land area by earth movements, which has created Lake

FIG 19. Wastwater, in Cumbria (left), was formed by a glacier moving down a pre-existing valley and Rostherne Mere (right) by melting of a large ice block buried in gravel and sands washed out from the glacier as it melted back.

FIG 20. Loch Ness (left: courtesy, Platinum Golf) and Lake Malawi (right: NASA) are both associated with rifts in the Earth's crust caused by the collision or separation of plates.

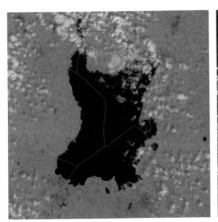
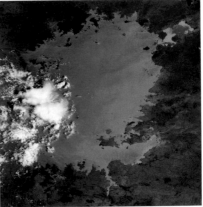

FIG 21. Lough Neagh (left) and Lake Victoria (right) both have underlying basins formed by sinking of the crust associated with major movements of the Earth's plates. (NASA)

Victoria, though there is a hint that Lough Neagh may be underlain by such a depression, albeit very shallow (Fig. 21). We have no lakes in volcanic craters, nor dammed by lava flows, nor landslides created by earthquakes; no basins have arisen from meteorite impact, coral atolls, nor even created by beavers. But there is still a rich variety, not least in the ways of the ice, and for the reasons that reservoirs or ponds have been created by human activity (Fig. 22).

Freshwater biologists are often asked the difference between a pond and a lake. Some will unwisely attempt a firm distinction but every definition crumbles when some exception is found. The general understanding is that ponds are small (less

TABLE 1. Origins of lake basins in Britain and Ireland. Based on Hutchinson, 1957.

No.	Origin	Examples
1	Peat bog sliding down a slope across a narrow valley	Occurred in 1745 in Galway, but the lake is now drained for agriculture
2	Lakes dammed by landslides, mudflows, or rockfalls	Goatswater (below Coniston Old Man) and Hard Tarn (Helvellyn) may be formed by scree dams
3	Lakes in or on ice	Ancient examples in the UK Midlands near the former edges of the ice sheets and recognised by lake silts overlain by more recent glacial drift
4	Glacier-dammed lakes	Ancient case of Glen Roy, northeast of Ben Nevis. Parallel 'roads' on the hillsides are terraces from different levels of such a lake
5	Moraine damming of lateral valleys	Some examples in the West Midland Plain and Scotland
6	Ice-scour lakes where the moving ice sheets carved out a basin from the underlying rocks	Trealaval, Isle of Lewis; many examples in western Scotland and Ireland. The lakes have irregular bottoms and shapes. The landscapes of Finland and Canada have many such lakes
7	Cirque lakes, cwms, corries and tarns formed at the head of a glacier by ice freezing and thawing and plucking rock from the mountain wall. May be held by moraines or a rock lip.	Many examples in the English Lake District, Scotland, Snowdonia, the Brecon Beacons and Co Kerry
8	Valley rock basins or paternoster lakes in which a glacier has scoured out a sequence of basins, separated by harder rock ridges down a valley	Ireland and Wales
9	Glint lakes where a mass of ice (a cauldron) occupied a pre-existing depression and deepened it, often breaking down the previous passes and joining several basins into a much more irregular and complex new basin	Many examples in Scotland around the former Rannoch moor ice cauldron: Rannoch, Ericht, Ossian, Treig
10	Fjord and piedmont lakes. Large glaciers passed through and deepened long valleys (may be fault determined), often close to the sea. They may be scoured rock basins or moraine or drift dammed	Loch Ness was so formed in the Great Glen fault. The main lakes of the English Lake District were formed in pre-existing valleys and described as 'spokes from the nave of a wheel' by Wordsworth in his introduction to Joseph Wilkinson's (1810, 1820) *Views of the Lakes*. Wastwater is a rock basin, the others are mainly moraine-dammed. In Scotland moraine dams are less common than rock basins, with moraine dams more likely in the lowlands
11	Damming by drift	Lough Neagh. There is a ravine of a former river in the bed of the lake
12	Irregularities in ground moraine	Very common, probably the most common of all glacial types. Many in Ireland, a few in Scotland

13	Kettle holes formed by the burial of ice blocks falling from a glacier as it melted back	The West Midland meres and small basins in the Scottish lowlands and central Ireland
14	Glacial tunnel lakes, excavated by melt water under the ice	A few examples in Scotland
15	Dolines, in which limestones are dissolved by percolating rainwater (which is naturally acid) but which may be initiated by organic decay at the surface	Some in the Pennines. Many turloughs in Ireland, which have a greatly changing water level and which may dry out completely in summer may be formed in this way, also the similar Breckland Meres and one example in Wales
16	Underground solution of limestone or salt deposits then collapse of the cavern roof	The Cheshire flashes, though the solution is the result of salt mining rather than natural processes
17	Underground lakes in caverns	Examples in cave systems in the Pennines, though accessible only to speleologists
18	Fluviatile dams in lakes. A delta from an inflowing river builds up across a basin formed in some other way and splits it into two new basins	Good examples are the separation of Derwent Water from Bassenthwaite Lake, and Buttermere from Crummock, in the English Lake District. Llyn Peris is similarly separated from Llyn Padarn in Snowdonia
19	Strath lakes, formed as a small separate basin at the head of a pre-existing lake by build up of sediment deposited by wave action and levees (floodbanks of the stream)	Loch Geal (upper end of Lomond), and Loch Buidhe at head of Loch Lubnaig. Priest Pot at the head of Esthwaite Water
20	Floodplain levee lakes	Possible originally in the East Anglian fens where rivers may have been dammed by marine sediment. Subsequent drainage for agriculture has obliterated most of the evidence. Red Mere (now the site of a jam factory). Willingham, Streatham, Ramsey, Benwick and Soham meres. Marton Mere maybe.
21	Oxbow lakes	Many residual examples where floodplains have not been fully drained, but many damaged by drainage
22	Valleys dammed by sand dunes	Llyn Maelog and Llyn Coron, Anglesey
23	Lakes formed between dunes	Kenfig pool. Many slacks in sand dune systems. Little Sea
24	Lagoons, where streams are dammed by shingle bars formed along the coast and favoured by rising then falling sea level	Slapton Ley, small lakes on Dungeness
25	Human construction	Many examples include the Norfolk and Suffolk Broads (ancient peat cuttings), abandoned gravel workings, lakes constructed as part of the landscaping of great estates, thousands of small ponds and a very large number of lakes formed by concrete or earth dams, constructed in the last two centuries

than a hectare or two), shallow (2 m or so) and sometimes dry up, but have water at least for several months each year. On the other hand there are huge shallow lakes, particularly in arid regions, and very small deep lakes in volcanic craters. Ponds are often manmade, but there are millions of natural equivalents, created by the action of freezing and thawing in the Arctic tundra. Ponds often lack fish and provide havens for amphibians, whose tadpoles are otherwise eaten, but there are plenty of ponds with fish, many lakes where fish and amphibians coexist, and numerous high-altitude lakes that fish have not yet reached. The word 'pond' is used in New England for quite large lakes and the word 'lake' even for streams in parts of Pembrokeshire in West Wales.

FIG 22. Ponds can be made for many reasons. This example, complete with the clutter of countryside management, was dug from the foredunes at Ainsdale to encourage breeding of natterjack toads, which do not compete well with common toads in well-vegetated ponds.

Moreover there is a continuum in the nature of standing waters and even among standing and flowing waters. Continua have no discrete types and no boundaries, only steady and uninterrupted change between two extremes. There are lakes whose water mass is replaced so rapidly by their inflows that they are effectively very slow-flowing rivers, and lowland rivers that almost cease to flow for part of the year, and behave as lakes. It is much more useful to think of a continuity of aquatic habitats, from the smallest rivulets and springs that flow down hillsides in rainstorms, to the headwater streams, the unseen, but nonetheless extensive network of groundwater movements, bigger streams, rills, becks, brooks, runnels, braes, creeks and flows, to the floodplain rivers, lagoons and estuaries and the inshore seas and deep oceans. Nodes in the network are where the accidents of geology have placed a basin where water can collect for a time: the puddles, pools, ponds, lakes, lakelets, loughs, lochans, lochs, llyns, tarns, reservoirs, meres, leys, inland seas and waters.

Think of the continuous thread of water molecules as they move from the raindrop to the middles of the oceans and are cycled back by evaporation, then rain and snow. Think of a bloodstream moving through the tissues of the land. Those who classify habitats into such as forests, grasslands, heaths, marshes, bogs … and freshwaters, have hindered nature conservation and wise management of our landscape. Such classification emphasises boundaries and separation; it is the affliction of living in a land divided by human activity for millennia, but it is not the setting in which freshwater animals and plants evolved, nor in which ecological processes operate. The logical unit is the entire catchment, with its continuum of land, the air, groundwater, streams and lake. But to keep matters under control, I need, for the purposes of this book, a simple definition of a lake. Lakes in Britain and Ireland are big enough to be called Lake, Lough, Llyn, Loch, Lochan, Water, Ley, Broad or Mere; they have a mass of water that is not replaced by the inflows in less than a week or so, and they do not dry out, although in turloughs they may drain.[6] It is not a perfect definition (I do not include the sea lochs), but it will have to do and in any case I will frequently offend against it by emphasising the connections rather than the entities.[7]

SHAPE AND STRUCTURE, ORIGINS AND REGIONS

Each lake basin differs from the next in basic ways. These include origin, shape, depth, volume, light penetration, local weather and water chemistry. The latter is strongly influenced by the catchment geology and consequent land use. The weather determines the amount of water that flows through the lake, and, with the volume, how long it stays (the residence time). A limnologist must have some

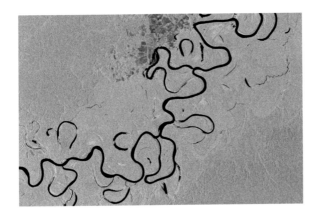

FIG 23. Oxbow lakes along the Jurua River in Brazil. (ESA)

command of geology, physics, chemistry and hydrology before he or she can contemplate the intricacies of natural history and ecology, for this background is the stage on which proceeds the play that the lake organisms enact. Hutchinson first coined the analogy of the ecological theatre and the evolutionary play, which infuses this book, to describe an understanding that ecology and evolution are two sides of the same coin.

Origin (Table 1) determines the morphometry of the basin; morphometry means its shape and size, both in the two-dimensions of its appearance on a map, and the way that the edges slope down to the deepest point, giving the contours of its bottom. Some lakes are reasonably regular in shape. Those formed by glaciers moving down pre-existing valleys (Type 10) often have nearly parallel edges, whilst those formed in kettle holes by the melting of ice blocks (Type 13) and those formed in corries at the heads of glaciers (Type 7) are broadly isodiametric. Oxbow lakes (Type 21, Fig. 23) are curved or kidney-shaped.

Beyond these, there is no particular relationship between origin and plan shape, and the irregularities of origin may be changed by silting and the ingrowth of vegetation at the edges, and on the deltas where inflow streams enter. Lakes formed in ice cauldrons (great bowls spanning several valleys) or by glacial scour (Types 6, 8 and 9) may be very irregular. Maps of the Scottish Highlands (Fig. 24) or western Ireland compared with those of Finland or eastern or northern Canada (Fig. 25) are revealing. The former areas were mountainous before the ice advanced; the mountains constrained the ice, forcing it down valleys formed by previous erosion, so that the lakes are smooth-edged, often with parallel sides and discrete from one another. Finland and eastern Canada are set on very ancient rocks that had been previously worn down to comparative flatness by millions of years of erosion. The landscape offered little resistance, and the glacier moved rapidly over a broad front, like a huge bulldozer, leaving lumps of harder rock and removing the softer beds between, giving a modern landscape of lakes with jagged shapes and many interconnections.

A distinctiveness is often seen in lakes formed behind dams created by man (Fig. 26). These have generally been made by damming rivers with a previous drainage network of tributary streams that entered in a quasi-orderly pattern. The network is called dendritic, like the branches emerging from the trunk of a tree. In an artificially dammed lake, it shows up in a system of sharply tapering bays, often roughly matched to either side of the length of the lake if it is big enough. In contrast to natural lakes, where forces like ice have obscured the details of any former drainage network, artificial reservoirs can easily be picked out from the evidence of this pre-existing network. Lakes formed recently by shingle deposition, such as Slapton Ley, may also show strong signs of the stream network that they drowned (Fig. 26).

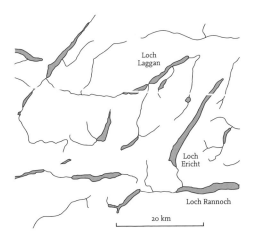

FIG 24. Lakes in the Scottish Highlands were formed in a relatively young landscape by ice constrained by the mountainous terrain

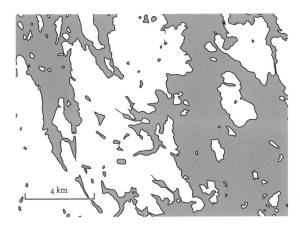

FIG 25. The ancient, eroded, flat landscape of Finland offered little resistance to ice movement, which scraped out irregular basins in which both large and small lakes have formed.

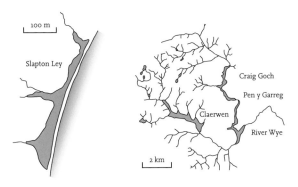

FIG 26. Lakes formed by recent damming of river systems, such as Slapton Ley, in Devon, behind a shingle barrier (far left); and the Elan Valley reservoirs, in mid-Wales, behind man-made dams. Both show evidence of the previous rivers in the patterns of their triangulate bays.

FIG 27. The Norfolk Broads were dug out as peat pits. The evidence of this can be seen in a 1940s aerial photograph of Barton Broad, as parallel lines of baulks. These have now been largely eroded away by boats or destroyed by flood defences.

The Norfolk Broads in East Anglia (Fig. 27), at least until heavy boat activity eroded the margins into smoothness, showed peculiar edges with parallel straight fingers of land alternating with fingers of water. The Broads were originally peat diggings, excavated between the ninth and thirteenth centuries in the floodplains of the rivers Ant, Thurne, Bure, Yare and Waveney and the valley peat was dug out in strips so that the wet turves from the excavated 'rooms' could be piled on intervening 'baulks' to dry and later to be carted away. Following flooding of the pits since the thirteenth century, the baulks remained, projecting into the new lake and often continue as ridges along the bottom.[8]

DEPTH

Plan shape and area tell us little about depth. Small lakes, for example some of the northwest Midland meres, formed in kettle holes, can be relatively deep (say ten or more metres); large lakes may be very deep or, like Lough Neagh, very shallow. Some clue to depth can be had from the surrounding land. Mountainous areas have deep valleys, which ice further deepened, and thus have deep lakes; the bigger the mountains, the deeper the lakes, as in the sequence from Snowdonia to the English Lake District and the Scottish Highlands. The lowlands everywhere, bar kettle holes and an occasional artificial reservoir, bear lakes only a few metres deep. The pattern, in Britain, of old, hard, igneous and metamorphic rocks to the north and west, and soft, young rocks in the south and east, of mountains and plains

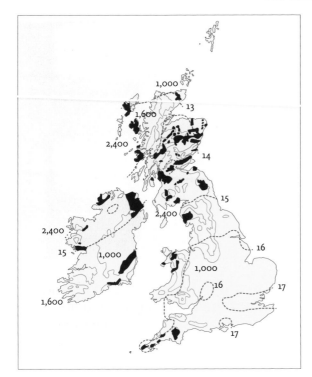

FIG 28. Three trends, which separate the north and west from the south and east underlie the limnology of Britain and Ireland: the geology, epitomised here by the occurrence of igneous rocks in purple, the annual rainfall (blue lines, values in mm, with the lowest contour at 1,000 mm and others at 1,600 and 2,400 mm), and temperature (red lines, July mean values °C).

(Fig. 28), leaves its mark. Soft rocks are often porous and it is more difficult for impervious lake basins to form, whilst low altitudes have lower rainfall and drying streams. In the richness of its waterways, if not in those of human opportunity and luxury, the southeast is deprived and the north is replete. No wonder that many of our most prominent limnologists have been northerners and Scots.

A deep lake is usually voluminous and stores a lot of water. The amount of water entering, the discharge, can be calculated by multiplying the area of the catchment by the net run-off (the difference, in units of depth, between total precipitation (rain and snow) and actual evaporation) for a given period. If the annual discharge is divided by the volume of the lake, the number of times that the mass of lake water is replaced in a year can be calculated, and this is known as the turnover rate. Alternatively, the reciprocal of the turnover rate is the residence time, the average length of time that a water molecule spends in the lake before it is washed out. It is an average because the movement of water through lakes is not even. Some water may pass rapidly through the middle, whilst the rest may be retained in the edges and bays, and in beds of water plants, for much longer than the average.

The residence time is important because if it is very short, perhaps only a few days, there will not be time for a plankton community (see below) to develop before the water is lost to the outflow. Rivers have very short residence times, from minutes in sections of streams, to a few days over a few kilometres in large rivers. Plankton does not develop at all in streams and theoretically should not develop in the few days' residence in big rivers. In practice, because the residence time is an average and there are 'dead zones',[9] associated with backwaters and on large bends, where water stays for rather longer, such rivers do develop plankton and illustrate the continuum between flowing and still waters.

DEPTH AND THE ABSORPTION OF LIGHT AND OTHER SOLAR RADIATION

The second influence of depth concerns the penetration into the lake of energy from the sun. Solar energy comes in a continuous band of wavelengths of electromagnetic radiation. The most energetic, shortest-waved radiation includes the ultraviolet, with wavelengths of 3,000 to 4,100 nanometres. A nanometre (nm) is one thousand millionth of a metre. Then there is the band from violet to red (about 4,100 to 7,000 nm), which is that which our eyes can detect, and which powers photosynthesis, and beyond that the infrared (7,000 to 8,000 nm), and longer wavelengths, into the bands of radio waves.

Some solar energy is reflected from the top of the atmosphere into outer space and some is absorbed by the atmosphere, but about half of the band from ultraviolet to infrared reaches the land and water surfaces (Fig. 29). Infrared penetrates a little way into lakes and warms the surface layers. Shorter wavelengths should penetrate deeper and sometimes do in very clear waters, but they are often quickly absorbed by coloured substances and particles in the water, so that blue light is absorbed as quickly as the infrared and red, whilst green and yellow light penetrate deepest. This creates a 'light climate' in which the colour experienced changes with depth.

The effects of the infrared heat absorbed do not necessarily stay in the surface layers because wind mixes the warmer surface water downwards, overcoming its lower density compared with that of the colder, deeper layers. From autumn to spring, unless ice interrupts the process, the wind is usually strong enough to mix the water to the bottom even of deep lakes. We refer to the water mass then as mixed or isothermal, with the same temperature from top to bottom. In turn this keeps the water well oxygenated, because oxygen diffuses into the water at the surface and the surface water is circulated down

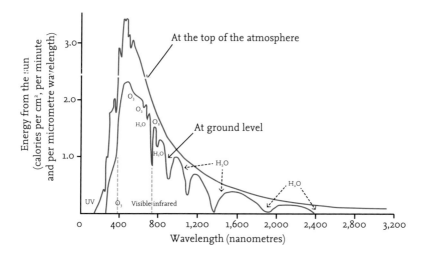

FIG 29. Energy is received from the sun over a spectrum of wavelengths, the most important for life being from around 150 to 2,400 nm (a nanometre is one-billionth of a metre). Gases in the atmosphere (primarily ozone, oxygen and water vapour) selectively absorb this energy so that the amount received at ground level is just over half that which enters at the top of the atmosphere. Ultraviolet, which can be damaging, is efficiently removed by ozone. Other gases (carbon dioxide, methane) also remove infrared radiation.

to the bottom by the winds. Water is a peculiar substance, however, and in a cold winter a point may be reached when the lake water is at 4°C and some remarkable properties are shown.

THE PECULIAR PROPERTIES OF THE WATER MOLECULE

The density of pure water is greatest at 4°C, or strictly 3.94°C. This is because water has features of both electrically charged and non-charged substances. Each molecule comprises one oxygen atom and two hydrogen atoms, the familiar H_2O. By the rules of chemical combination, the single electrons that are associated with each hydrogen and the six electrons in the outer part of the oxygen should balance the eight protons in the molecule, one each for the hydrogen atoms and six for the oxygen, to give a compound with electrical neutrality, a covalent compound. However, the combined electron cloud, instead of evenly circulating among the three atoms, tends to rest

FIG 30. Water has peculiar properties because oxygen has a greater affinity for shared electrons in the molecule than hydrogen. This causes molecules to attract one another and form a degree of structure even in liquid water but the network is eventually most rigid in ice.

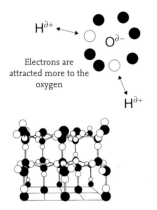

Ice has a crystalline structure

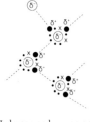

Hydrogen and oxygen on different molecules are attracted to each other

longer on the hydrogens, making them slightly negative and the oxygen atom consequently slightly positive. The consequence is that water molecules link to one another, the slightly negative hydrogen of one molecule being attracted to the slightly positive oxygen of the next, so that a network is formed (Fig. 30).

In ice, the network is very orderly; ice is a crystal and the tendency (their heat content) that causes molecules to move apart is low at low temperatures. The attractive forces between the molecules can organise them into a rigid geometric framework. Ice forms at 0°C and becomes more and more stable as the temperature falls below this. In cold winters, ice will form at the surface of lakes because the density of ice is lower than that of liquid water at the freezing point: the spacing of the molecules in the crystal is wide compared with that in the liquid water. As ice melts, the crystal starts to collapse in on itself, so that the density of the melt water is slightly higher than that of the ice. It is like a building in which the walls are at first held apart to enclose the spaces of the rooms, but which collapses into a pile of dense rubble when it is demolished. The molecular collapse of icy water goes on until a temperature of 3.94°C is reached when it is overcome by the tendency of the molecules to fly apart as they warm. But even above 3.94°C, some attraction between the molecules persists, and liquid water retains remnants of the crystalline structure in ice.

The tendency to fly apart, however, becomes stronger, and the density decreases steadily, up to the boiling point, when liquid water changes to vapour. That it takes quite a lot of energy to raise the temperature of water to the boiling point (and thus that electric kettles are expensive devices to run) is due to the need to break down the residual crystal structure in the water. Conversely, freezers are relatively cheap to run as the crystal structure is already partly formed in liquid water and it takes little loss of energy to encourage ice to form once the freezing point has been reached.

As our northernmost lakes cool in winter and reach just under 4°C, further cooling tends to leave less dense colder water at the surface. The wind may continue to mix this downwards on windy nights, but on still, cold, clear nights, rapid falls in temperature lead to cooling to zero and ice begins to form, floating on denser water below at temperatures of up to 4°C in deeper and deeper water. These temperature properties of water are crucial, not only to lake organisms, which can almost always find liquid layers below even a thick ice cover (only very shallow puddles freeze solid) but to the whole of the biosphere.

The closest relatives to water among other compounds, the hydrides of sulphur (H_2S), selenium (H_2Se) and tellurium (H_2Te), do not have the slight polarity of electrical charge between their hydrogens and their other atom, and are all gases at Earth temperatures. The lack of polarity means that their molecules do not associate and their liquids boil to vapour easily at very low temperatures. Water would also be a gas at Earth temperatures were it not for the quirks of oxygen and the electrical attraction that makes so much energy necessary to convert liquid water to vapour. Liquid water is absolutely essential for life. We owe our existence on Earth to the oddity of the oxygen atom.

STRATIFICATION

Because wind cannot penetrate below ice, and because of the increase in density of liquid water from 0 to 4°C, there is a layering of the water below an ice cover in lakes. This is called stratification and because the warmest water is at the bottom, it is known as inverse stratification. Further north than Scotland, in Scandinavia, Iceland, Canada and Russia, freezing of the lakes in winter and inverse stratification under the ice is usual, even in shallow lakes. In northern Scotland it is also usual, but for a much shorter period. Then as we move southwards it may only occur in some years and for short periods. In southern England it is infrequent, though not entirely absent; the presently warming climate, however, is decreasing the frequency and period of freezing. Below the ice, with no access of the water to the atmosphere and especially if there is snow (which is opaque) over the ice, so that little or no light can penetrate to support photosynthesis, bacteria in the sediment and water will use up oxygen and anaerobiosis (life without oxygen) will increase as winter progresses. Anoxia (complete lack of oxygen) may be reached. This is rare in deep lakes, with a large water mass, but not uncommon in shallow ones.

Spring brings rising temperatures and the melting of ice if it has formed. The winds are still vigorous and the ice, as it breaks into small pieces, is piled up, with a pleasant tinkling sound, on the lee shores. The water mass warms and remains mixed but as spring progresses the winds, variable anyway, eventually lessen so that they can no longer mix the water fully to the bottom in a deep lake, and are only able to disturb the surface layers. In a shallow lake (say less than 3 m, or a little more if the lake is large and the wind fetch long) even the light breezes of summer may be enough to maintain the water column isothermal throughout the year.

The sun's energy is absorbed exponentially, which means that as one layer absorbs its proportion, there is less to be absorbed, in the same proportion in the one below, and even less in the one below that, until there is virtually nothing left. The graph of absorption and thence that of water temperature with depth is thus theoretically one that obeys the laws of logarithms. The winds of early summer, however, destroy this by mixing the surface layers, giving an isothermal upper layer, then a discontinuity in temperature, called the thermocline, then a lower set of layers in which the exponential decline in temperature is resumed in water that has barely warmed from its winter temperature. It may even remain at 4°C in the deepest lakes.

This process divides the lake into an upper, well-illuminated, mixed epilimnion, a middle layer where the temperature declines rapidly in the thermocline, called the metalimnion, and a deep, cold and dark layer, the hypolimnion (Fig. 31). The epilimnion remains well oxygenated, for it is mixed and in contact with the atmosphere and bears photosynthetic algae in the plankton. The hypolimnion is isolated and as materials fall into it from the plankton above, its bacteria progressively use up its winter store of oxygen, and deoxygenation and perhaps anoxia may soon ensue. There are also linked chemical processes dependent on this depletion of free oxygen that will be considered later, and which are of great consequence for the lake's organisms.

By summer, the direct stratification (warmest water at the top) strengthens as the winds become less vigorous and the sun's angle increases, delivering more and more energy to the lake's surface. The contrast between the surface, perhaps at around 20°C and the bottom, minimally around 4°C, but perhaps as high as 9°C or 10°C, depending on the latitude and how vigorously the water was mixed in late winter and early spring, may be very large. Autumn brings lower solar radiation, rising winds and cooling of the surface. The thermocline is progressively deepened as the winds mix deeper, and eventually, perhaps in late October or November, the stratification is completely overturned and the lake becomes completely isothermal again, with dissolved oxygen present throughout. The year's cycle has been completed.

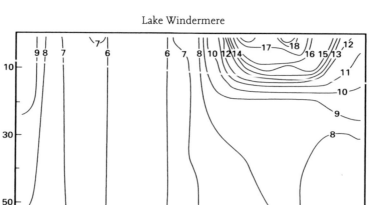

FIG 31. The seasonal changes in temperature (or any other feature) in relation to depth in lakes are best shown as a depth–time diagram. Individual values are plotted at co-ordinates of depth and date and then 'contour' lines are drawn joining similar values. The more vertical the lines, the greater the degree of mixing; the greater the horizontal component, the stronger the stratification. This diagram is for water temperature in Windermere and shows the winter and spring mixing and direct summer stratification. There was a disturbance in July caused by a cooler period. The original data were collected by Penelope Jenkin in 1941.

MONOMICTIC AND DIMICTIC STRATIFICATION

The lakes in the coldest parts of our islands thus have two periods of stratification, one of inverse stratification under ice in winter, one of direct stratification in summer, and two intervening periods of complete mixing, in autumn and in spring. These are called dimictic (twice-mixing) lakes. To the north, in the Arctic, a state of cold monomixis (an alternation of inverse stratification under ice, and summer mixing, in a climate where the winds are always strong and the sun too weak to warm the water enough to directly stratify the lake) is usual. This might also occur in Scotland in shallow lakes that freeze in winter but are too shallow to stratify in summer. To the south, lakes are increasingly likely to be warm monomictic with circulation from autumn to spring and a summer direct stratification. There may be short periods (a few

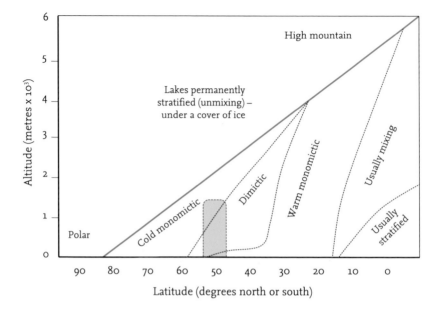

FIG 32. The pattern of stratification in lakes deeper than a few metres is determined by the climate, which in turn is a function of altitude and latitude. Polar and very high mountain lakes are permanently covered by ice and do not mix. With decreasing altitude and latitude, there is a sequence from cold monomictic to states of continuous mixing (at high altitude) or permanent stratification as the Equator is reached. The coloured rectangle covers possible conditions in Britain and Ireland.

days or a couple of weeks) of ice cover and inverse stratification, and, in summer, cold windy periods may temporarily deepen the thermocline or even destroy it, for it to re-form in warmer quieter periods. Shallow lakes to the south will mix throughout the year, though on hot still days there may be hints of stratification by day that break down overnight. And if we extend the sequence to the warm temperate lakes in regions of Mediterranean climates and to tropical climates, we find a variety of seasonal mixing and direct stratification, culminating in deep lakes near the Equator that never mix and have a permanent direct stratification (Fig. 32). Mixing and stratification are very important in determining the behaviour of the plankton (Chapter 6).

DISSOLVED SUBSTANCES

The next element of the stage on which the microorganisms, plants and animals of lakes act out their play, is what is dissolved in the water. The concentrations of dissolved substances in freshwaters are comparatively low, but their variety is immense. No one has ever fully analysed any natural sample of water, and until the mid-twentieth century just a handful of substances, mostly inorganic ions, were measured. Typically these included: calcium, magnesium, sodium, potassium, hydrogen, bicarbonate, chloride and sulphate (called the major ions but only because their concentrations are generally the greatest among the substances found); some other ions (nitrate, ammonium and phosphate) that are important nutrients for lake organisms (and all others too); and some metals found in trace quantities, like iron, manganese, copper, cobalt and zinc. Silicate, needed by an important group of algae, the diatoms, plus dissolved oxygen and carbon dioxide, some measure of total dissolved organic matter and a handful of substances resulting from industrial pollution were often included and this collection was all that was thought to be important, a slate fewer than 50 in all.

The development of new analytical techniques after about 1970, particularly the gas chromatograph coupled with mass spectrometry, widened the list to include many organic compounds, at first pollutants like pesticides, but then a host of different natural organic compounds, often washed in from the catchment area, but also secreted into the water by the lake organisms themselves. Probably there are hundreds of thousands to millions of substances present in any natural water, all of them with some meaning for the functioning of the lake.

Three things are particularly important in considering the dissolved content: first, the reason why water is so versatile in dissolving substances; and, second, the understanding that the lake is not isolated. It must always be considered in the context of its catchment (watershed) and its airshed, from both of which come its water and many of the substances dissolved in it. The airshed, the part of the atmosphere influencing the lake, which may extend over a vastly greater area than the watershed, is also linked with the third important issue, the influence of climate, which provides the water but may bring in sea salts and dust on the wind, and in hot climates may concentrate the substances through evaporation.

DISSOLUTION AND THE PROPERTIES OF WATER

Water dissolves many things because of the same molecular oddity that gives its density and temperature properties, and its both covalent and polar nature. True solution involves a chemical reaction between the water molecule and the solute (the thing that is dissolved). An electrically charged solvent (in this case water) will react readily with other electrically charged substances, such as the cations (metals like sodium and calcium and many others), which are positively charged, having lost one or more electrons, and the anions, like sulphate and chloride, which have gained electrons.

Water will not react (because it is charged) with completely uncharged substances, such as oils and fats, and gases like oxygen, nitrogen, neon and argon, but it is possible for physical mixtures, rather than true solutions, to be formed, though the amount of substance that can remain in the mixture is generally very small because it is repelled by the charged medium of the water. Water therefore 'dissolves' very little oxygen or nitrogen, a few mg/L compared with a capacity to dissolve a hundred thousand times more sodium ion, and hundreds of times more carbon dioxide, which is also charged. This repulsion by water of completely covalent compounds might seem to imply that not much organic matter (the compounds based on carbon and hydrogen, often with other elements, particularly oxygen) will dissolve, but the converse is true.

There are many organic substances with groups such as hydroxide (–OH) or amino ($-NH_2$) that are also slightly polar, and allow true solution. Many of these, the sugars, alcohols, amides and amino acids, are important for living organisms and they account for much of the diversity of substances that water dissolves. Lake organisms are bathed in a solution and mixture of very great complexity and use the various components as nutrients, as keys to release energy and as signals by which they may detect mates or prey, repel predators or indicate to others the existence of hazards. In this chapter we will consider largely the substances that come into the lake from outside and leave those organic substances produced within the lake by the organisms themselves until later.

MAJOR IONS

The concentrations and balance of the major ions help determine which organisms inhabit particular lakes, especially the invertebrates like molluscs and crustaceans that need large amounts of calcium for their shells and carapaces, and some water

TABLE 2. Chemistry of rain and lake waters in regions of Britain and Ireland. Values in mg/L, except for conductivity (µS/cm) and pH. Mean values are given.

Region	Geology	Cond.	pH	Na+	K+	Ca++	Mg++	HCO3-	Cl-	SO4 --	Reference
Rain, Ireland		62	5.3	7.4	0.38	0.98	0.86	1.5	12.4	4.9	Jorlan, 1997
Rain, eastern England			4.6	3.9	0.8	3.7	0.5				Moss, 1983
Scottish lochs	Granite & gneiss		6.6	1.9	0.4	1	0.6	8.1		2.1	Harriman & Pugh, 1994
	Sandstone		6.8	1.2	0.8	1.8	0.8	7.6		4.6	
	Limestone		7.9	0.8	0.5	51.2	8.3	195		4.1	
Western Ireland, small headwater lakes	Generally igneous & metamorphic	100	5.1	7.5	0.6	2.4	3.8	0.6	22.9	7.1	Burton & Aherne, 2012
Upland streams, English Lake District	Borrowdale volcanic (igneous) rocks		6.5	3.8	0.3	3.4	0.9	4.1	6.3	5.2	Sutcliffe, 1998
Upland tarns, English Lake District	Silurian slates (metamorphic)		7.3	6.1	0.8	11	2.1	28	13	10	Sutcliffe, 1998
Upland tarns, northern England	Sedimentary rocks Carboniferous, Permian and Triassic periods		7.7	8.8	2.6	57	8.3	183	17	17	Sutcliffe, 1998
Snowdonia lakes	Slates	32	6.5	3.3	0.2	1.9	0.5	3.1	5.3	3.5	Duigan et al., 1998
West Midland meres	Glacial drift overlying largely sedimentary rocks	429	8.0	13	5.8	41.7	8.4	202	23	40	Reynolds, 1979
Lakes around London	Sedimentary chalks & sandstone	563	7.6	41	8.7	82.8	10	201	75.1	86.2	Bernion et al., 1997

plants that have restrictions, determined by pH and bicarbonate concentrations, on the nature of the carbon compounds that they can absorb for photosynthesis. The geology of the catchment determines the major ion concentrations in lakes. Igneous rocks are hard and crystalline. Freezing and thawing break them into smaller particles, and rain, with its natural acidity, and the substances secreted by lichens and mosses that live on exposed rocks, will attack the mineral crystals from which the rocks are made. Ions are released to dissolve and run into the rivers and lakes, and clays are formed as by-products, but the process is slow.

On catchments of some igneous rocks, such as the Borrowdale volcanics that make up the heart of the English (Cumbrian) Lake District, the waters of the streams and high tarns are essentially little changed rainwater (Table 2). Rain picks up dust, and droplets of seawater spumed upwards in storms, as well as dissolving gases like carbon dioxide from the air. Its ionic content is dominated by sodium, magnesium and chloride, from the sea, and hydrogen ions from the formation of carbonic acid when carbon dioxide is dissolved. The pH, a measure of the hydrogen ion concentration, or acidity, will be around 5.5, unless, as often now, industrial pollutants, like sulphur gases, and nitrogen oxides released by vehicle engines and from oxidation of the ammonia produced by intensive stock husbandry, have made it even more acid. pH values down to 2.5 are not unknown.

The total ionic content is measured by the water's ability to conduct electricity, its conductivity, which is measured in microSiemens per centimetre (μS cm^{-1}). Siemens are the reciprocals of the more familiar unit of resistance, the ohm. Upland tarn waters may have conductivities around 50 μS cm^{-1}, just like rain. As the water flows downhill and is joined by water that has percolated through deeper soils than those at the mountaintops, it will acquire more ions because soil weathering will release more substances, particularly calcium and bicarbonate, but there will never be much. Moreover, where the catchment is covered by natural ecosystems, usually some form of forest in the north-temperate region, the forest vegetation will take up and hold many of the weathered ions, for they are important as plant nutrients. Removal of the forest when the land is converted to grassland, as in much of Britain and Ireland, will destroy these mechanisms of retention and enrich the run-off water, but on igneous and many metamorphic rocks, such as slates, a conductivity of only a hundred or so μS cm^{-1} is to be expected.

Sedimentary rocks weather much more easily and release many more soluble ions (Table 2). Limestones and chalks are particularly easy to weather as they dissolve readily in acidic rainwater. Lakes fed by water from sedimentary catchments will thus have conductivities of several hundreds of μS cm^{-1} and the balance of their major ions will swing towards calcium and bicarbonate. The

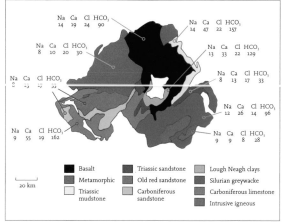

FIG 33. Geology determines the concentrations of major ions, here in Northern Ireland. Values are in mg/L. Based on Gibson *et al.*, 1995.

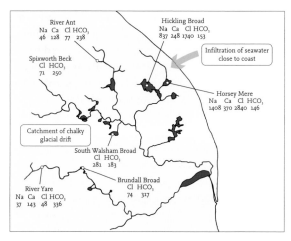

FIG 34. Major ion concentrations in areas with softer, more permeable rocks and glacial drift, like the Norfolk Broadland, may also be influenced by penetration, both ancient and contemporary, of seawater.

compositions of the West Midland Meres, the Norfolk Broads and many waters in southeast England, which include catchments of chalky rocks and fine sandstones, contrast very greatly with those of the Scottish Highlands, and the tarns of the igneous and metamorphic rocks of the English Lake District (Table 2).

An inspection of the water chemistry of two contrasted areas, Northern Ireland (Fig. 33) and the Norfolk Broadland (Fig. 34), illustrates the generalities that are shown in Table 2. Northern Ireland has a great variety of rocks, but they divide into the intrusive igneous granitic rocks and the sandstones with low calcium and bicarbonate levels and the mudstones, clays and limestones with much higher levels in the waters. Basalts are igneous but intermediate in character. Sodium and chloride are largely supplied from the rain and much less influenced by the geology. In contrast, the Norfolk Broadland, fed by rivers, particularly the Yare and Bure, that take groundwater from the chalk and from chalky boulder clay, have overall higher levels of all four ions shown. The underlying geology is very porous so there has been a great deal of ancient infiltration of seawater so that sodium and chloride levels are high, exceptionally so to the east where seawater is actively sucked into the system by drainage pumping.

ORGANIC MATTER

The nature of the catchment is equally important for two further features: the supply of organic matter and of nutrients to a lake. Conventional wisdom has it that the food webs of ecosystems are supported entirely by the photosynthesis of the plants and algae that live within them, but that is not necessarily so. For several decades we have understood that in natural streams, particularly where the surrounding forest vegetation is intact, most of the energy to support the food webs comes from leaf and twig debris that falls or is washed into the streams from the forest.[10] Water plants and algae provide rather little until far downstream, where the channel widens and more light can reach the bed. Even then much of the energy still comes from the forest, in the form of fine organic material shredded and defaecated from the soggy leaves by invertebrates in the stream, or washed in from the forest soils. As the river widens into a floodplain, the main channel may be so turbid with suspended silt that photosynthesis is inhibited, and organic matter, washed in from upstream, or from the swamps, grasslands and forests of its floodplain, to a large extent feeds the invertebrates that live in its sediments and the fish that eat them.

Lake ecosystems, in contrast, were thought, until recently, to be more or less self-contained and supplied by the photosynthesis of their algae and water plants. New techniques, using the stable isotopes of carbon that are incorporated into organic matter during photosynthesis, have now cast doubt on this. Land plants take their carbon dioxide from the air and air has a characteristic ratio of the isotope ^{13}carbon to the much commoner isotope ^{12}carbon. Algae and plants in water use both carbon dioxide that has diffused in from the atmosphere, and bicarbonate ions that have been derived from rock weathering. The rocks have a slightly different ratio of ^{13}C to ^{12}C from that of the present air, dependent on the conditions when they were formed, millions of years ago.

The different ratios of ^{13}carbon to ^{12}carbon are recognisable in bacteria and animals that have eaten washed-in detritus or *in situ* plants and algae, and allow us to determine the origins of their diets. The surprising finding has been that bacteria in lakes are heavily dependent on dissolved organic matter washed in from the land, that the invertebrates in the bottom sediments feed on bacteria grown from fine particles of organic matter also washed in from the land, and that even the animals of the plankton, surrounded by a photosynthetic community of algae, take substantial amounts of this imported material.[11] Loch Ness, for example, is so poor in photosynthetic plankton that its animals can only persist because of the imports.[12]

This dependence on organic matter imported from the land is particularly important in pristine lakes, where a naturally low supply of nutrients like nitrogen and phosphorus limits growth of plants and algae within the lake. It is also crucial in brown-stained peaty waters, such as are found where there is much bog vegetation, in parts of northern Scotland, the Southern Uplands, Ireland and the Pennines, where so much light is absorbed by the dissolved organic matter that light becomes limiting to algae and plants.[13] Many lakes worldwide, and most in Britain and Ireland, as Chapters 8 and 9 will show, have now been polluted by nitrates and phosphates from agricultural fertilisers, manures or the effluents of human activity. These have boosted algal growth within them and changed the balance of use of imported and self-produced organic matter towards the latter. Nonetheless, the yardstick for assessing such damage is what happens in undisturbed systems and this is where the third item of importance of the catchment area comes in: the supply of the key limiting nutrients, primarily nitrogen and phosphorus, but sometimes also silicate, iron and manganese.

KEY LIMITING NUTRIENTS

To what extent the nature of life on Earth is dependent on the presumably random amounts of elements that made up the gas and particle cloud that condensed to form our planet is an interesting question. Some of the essential elements, like carbon, hydrogen and oxygen and most of the needed metals, are available in amounts at the Earth's surface that are large in relation to the needs of organisms for them. Others, however, are scarce in relation to need and have particular importance. Phosphorus and nitrogen are among these and their relative scarcity is particularly reflected in lakes and seas. Ultimately they limit the amount of biomass that can be built up and are called key limiting nutrients. Land organisms need the same suite of elements as aquatic ones and have developed many mechanisms to conserve and recycle supplies of the critical nitrogen and phosphorus for continual use so that supplies to the rivers and lakes are even scarcer. Before leaves fall from trees in autumn, or herbs die back

TABLE 3. Concentrations (mean and range) of total phosphorus and total nitrogen in near pristine catchments in the USA (Smith *et al.*, 2003). Because of atmospheric pollution, truly pristine sites exist nowhere but a correction can be made based on what enters from atmospheric pollution.

Region of USA	Equivalent in Britain & Ireland	Total nitrogen (mg N/L)	Total nitrogen corrected for atmospheric pollution (mg N/L)	Total phosphorus (mg P/L)
Western forested mountains	Upland Scotland, western Ireland, English Lake District, Snowdonia, southwest peninsula	0.15 (0.08-0.21)	0.14 (0.06-0.19)	0.019 (0.012–0.025)
Glaciated upper mid-west and northeast	Pennines, poorer soils of the lowlands of Scotland and Ireland, Midlands, South Wales	0.2 (0.14-0.24)	0.15 (0.1-0.2)	0.013 (0.001–0.017)
Cultivated great plains	East Anglia, South East England and richer soils of the lowlands	0.4 (0.12-0.6)	0.07 (0.02-0.13)	0.040 (0.02–0.08)

at the end of the growth season, their mineral nutrients are moved back to the branches and trunk or to the overwintering rhizomes and bulbs, or to the seeds. Soluble ions in soils are quickly scavenged by fungi, the mycorrhizae, associated with the finer roots; earthworms recycle nutrient-rich soil back to the surface before it can be leached into the deep ground. The success of these mechanisms can be shown in experiments where the trees are felled and the effects compared with intact forest. There is a major loss of mineral ions when rainwater leaches the soils and debris, and percolates through to the streams and lakes.[14] The concentrations of key nutrients are thus vanishingly small in pristine waters with intact catchments (Table 3). Phosphorus in all its various compounds (collectively called total phosphorus, TP) is rarely above 0.015 mg/L and total nitrogen is below 0.15 mg/L.

Where the land is disturbed for agriculture, the natural conservation mechanisms are lost and nutrients are released to fertilise the streams and lakes. That is why agriculture can only be continued if fertiliser is repeatedly used, whereas large biomasses of natural forest can be maintained indefinitely without any such management. The concentrations of phosphorus in British and Irish freshwaters are almost always high compared with pristine lakes, and are often up to 0.2 mg/L and even higher (Table 4). Nitrogen is found in concentrations tens or hundreds of times higher than in the pristine state. The least enriched waters are in the mountains, where cultivation is minimal, though stock is grazed, and there are no large settlements. Lakes there have only slightly increased phosphorus concentrations. In the lowlands, phosphorus concentrations are always hugely high. Nitrogen levels can be relatively high even in the mountains. This is because nitrogen compounds can enter from the atmosphere as well as from the catchment. In the lowlands, nitrate levels may be over 50 mg/L in the drainage from arable fields and in some groundwaters.

TABLE 4. Concentrations (mg/L) of nitrogen and phosphorus compounds in British and Irish waters. Means and ranges are given where available.

Region	Nitrate (N)	Total N	Orthophosphate (P)	Total P	Reference
Upland Scottish streams and rivers		0.58 (0.058–3.35)	0.080		Chapman et al., 2001
Pennine reservoirs	0.71 (0.24–1.26)				Evans & Jenkins, 2000
Northern Irish lakes	0.08 (0.01–0.38)	0.56 (0.12–1.28)	0.016 (0.001–0.1)	0.035 (0.008–0.14)	Gibson et al.,1995
Snowdonia lakes	0.14 (0.04–0.23)		0.027 (0.01–0.05)	0.006 (0.005–0.01)	Duigan et al., 1998
River Thames	8.0		0.6		Neal et al., 2006
British streams	4 (0.1–13.8)		0.4 (0.02–3.5)		Davies & Neal, 2007
Thames tributaries	7.5 (2.5–17.4)				Neal et al., 2006
Warwickshire Avon tributaries				0.84 (0.09–4.6)	Bowes et al., 2005
Northwest Midland meres	0.24 (0.02–0.63)		0.34 (0.92–1.7)		Reynolds, 1979
Northwest Midland deep meres	0.68 (0.1–1.76)		0.24 (0.003–1.26)	0.29 (0.05–1.46)	Moss et al., 1994
Northwest Midland shallow meres	1.65 (0.27–5.28)		0.39 (0.05–1.54)	0.59 (0.26–1.7)	Moss et al., 1994
Lakes around London	5.5 (0–66.7)				Bennion et al., 1997
Upland English waters on igneous & metamorphic rocks	0.2				Sutcliffe, 1998
Ditto sedimentary rocks	6.7				Sutcliffe, 1998
Norfolk Broads	3.06 (0–15.5)			0.18 (0.03–0.84)	Moss, 1983

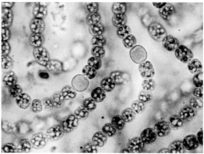

FIG 35. Cyanobacteria, which may accumulate in dense surface blooms in lakes (left), sometimes have specialist cells, called heterocysts, in which oxygen production is minimised and where nitrogen fixation can take place (right). These are the large clear cells.

It might sound odd that nitrogen is considered a key limiting nutrient since there is an enormous supply, amounting to trillions of tonnes, as nitrogen gas in the atmosphere. Most organisms, however, cannot use nitrogen gas; only certain bacteria, including some of the cyanobacteria, once known as the blue-green algae (Chapter 3), can fix it into compounds that they, and the organisms that feed on their live or decaying cells, can use. Initially they fix it into amino acids, which are the components of proteins, but on decay ammonium ions are formed, which other bacteria can convert to nitrate. Ammonium and nitrate are available to other organisms. Nitrogen is naturally limiting because fixation is inhibited by oxygen. Fixation may occur in nodules on the roots of plants from a limited number of families, including the legumes and alders, where haemoglobin is produced to mop up any oxygen; it occurs in special cells of some cyanobacteria (Fig. 35) from which oxygen is excluded, and in clumps of soil bacteria, where a phalanx of oxygen-consuming bacteria surround the cells that are fixing nitrogen and create a local anaerobic refuge.

Nitrate and ammonia are very soluble and it is more difficult for land ecosystems to retain them compared with the relatively insoluble phosphates, which are readily bound in soils as calcium and iron compounds or adsorbed to clays. This explains the generally higher concentrations of nitrogen compounds than phosphorus compounds in water draining even pristine systems. Ammonium and nitrate are, however, valuable sources of combined energy for bacteria in both soils and waters, and are readily converted back to nitrogen gas, especially in waterlogged soils, because low oxygen concentrations also favour these processes. The rates of fixation of nitrogen are thus low and the rates of denitrification to nitrogen gas readily remove the fixed nitrogen, so that as an available element, nitrogen naturally remains quite scarce. There is very little nitrogen to be weathered from rocks because it was driven off from hot igneous rocks during their formation and denitrified in the waterlogged sediments that become sedimentary rocks.

Currently about twice as much fixed nitrogen is available in the biosphere as there used to be because of industrial fixation by the Haber-Bosch process, used to produce ammonia and eventually fertiliser, and fertiliser leaching has become a major source of nitrate to freshwaters. Intensive stock rearing, owing to the high demand for meat, produces manures from which ammonia escapes to the atmosphere and oxidises to nitrate, which, in rain, gives a further source, even in the mountains. There are still large amounts coming from vehicle engines, which release nitrogen oxides that also oxidise to nitrate. From a former state where natural processes kept both nitrogen and phosphorus very low in run-off waters, we now have nitrogen and phosphorus levels much higher almost everywhere. Levels may still set an upper limit to the growth of plants and algae in lakes, but the growth is everywhere greater than it would be had we been able to preserve forests, where there is now managed grassland, agriculture, villages and cities.

MAJOR IONS, NUTRIENTS AND THE DEVELOPMENT OF LAKES

When a lake basin first fills with water, the lake ecosystem is much bleaker than it will eventually become. Glaciers have been steadily retreating in the Arctic over the past century or more, and as they have melted back they have left new lake basins, whose ages are known. At first the basins are bare and full of grey milky water from the clay that the glacier had ground from the rock as it moved over it. The catchment has little vegetation at first, and all around is fresh rock debris that presents a wealth of surfaces for weathering to attack. The milky water is thus at first relatively rich in major ions and even phosphate. It is low in organic matter because of the lack of vegetation cover, and low in nitrogen compounds because nitrogen fixers have yet to become common in the lake and its catchment, and build up the supply. The suspended clays inhibit photosynthesis, but eventually they settle out, the water clears and the first algal populations build up their crops. Meanwhile, vegetation colonises the catchment and intercepts and recycles the nutrients, whilst the initial fresh rock debris becomes weathered out and buried in the maturing soils. The water entering the lake becomes more acid, poorer in bases and phosphate, but increasing in nitrogen compounds and organic matter. The shortage of phosphorus leads to reduced algal and plant production and what started as a nutrient-rich lake becomes a

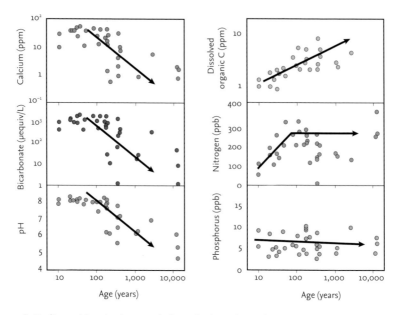

FIG 36. Studies on lakes that have newly formed, where glaciers have retreated over the past few centuries, as in Alaska, can reveal the early processes of chemical change in lakes. Some ions are at first richly present as newly exposed rock debris weathers, but then decline, whilst others, and dissolved organic matter, dependent on the establishment of soils and vegetation, tend to increase.

nutrient-poor one (Fig. 36). For many years it was intuitively believed that the reverse should be the case, that the lake accumulated nutrients and moved from poor to a richer state, but that only happens when agriculture and sewage effluent disposal artificially boost the nutrient levels to values never known in pristine lakes. In Britain and Ireland, we have not had a first-hand opportunity to observe lakes emerging from the melting of glaciers, but we can still see evidence of the process by examining the sediments of lakes that were formed by glacial action ten or more thousands of years ago (Chapter 7).

When new reservoirs are created, a parallel history may be seen. Flooding a valley behind a dam causes death and decomposition of the land vegetation and makes the soils anaerobic. Nutrients are released by both processes and give an early phase of high fertility, and often an anaerobic hypolimnion, before this first pulse of nutrients is washed downstream or is locked anew in the sediments. Within a few years the lake becomes less fertile, sometimes to the chagrin of lake managers, who had been delighted by early productive fisheries, but who are soon sadly disappointed.

CLIMATE AND WATER CHEMISTRY

The final aspect of understanding why lakes differ in their water chemistry, and thence in their ecology, is in the influence of climate. This has minor relevance in Britain and Ireland because climatic differences are not extreme. The east and south are more continental in nature, with warmer, drier summers than the maritime regions of the north and west, but land use and geology have much greater influences. Much of the world, however, is arid and lakes may receive water from their catchments and rain, but lose it not through an outflow, but only by evaporation. Their waters thus become saltier, often to levels greater than that of the ocean. Usually such lakes (Fig. 37) are very shallow (the Dead Sea in Israel is an exception) and their biological communities are restricted to a very few species that can tolerate the high salinity.

There are no such endorheic (internally draining) lakes in these islands now, but there have been in the past, when Britain and Ireland had drifted on continental blocks into tropical latitudes. Underlying parts of Cheshire are the

FIG 37. Salt lakes are no longer part of the British and Irish scene, but almost half of the worlds' land is dry enough for lakes like the Etosha pan in Namibia to be the characteristic kind of water body, with water leaving only by evaporation, so that salt is precipitated at the edges.

Triassic salt deposits from such lakes, which have been mined (Chapter 9) from Roman times. An endorheic lake, of course, surrounds us. The seas and oceans are produced and maintained in the same way as inland endorheic lakes. Water flows into the oceans from the worlds' rivers, but there is no outlet. Water leaves the oceans only by evaporation and thus, in completing the hydrological cycle leaves Britain and Ireland as islands in the world's largest and most ancient endorheic lake.

ECOLOGICAL ZONES AND THE FATES OF LAKE BASINS

I have now sketched out the superstructure of the lake theatre as it is built up from a hole in the ground and have added the internal fittings, the heating and lighting system and the chemistry of the bricks and mortar. Theatres are not all the same; each is unique in its location and details, but there are some common features of design by which we easily recognise them and this extends also to the backdrops and flats, curtains and boards. It now remains to point out the general features of the stage scenery in which the ecological actors will play their parts, and in the end to discuss what happens when the theatre has to close because it can no longer support the freshwater play.

ZONES IN LAKES

The scenery on the stage lies in the broad pattern of communities that form in the physical and chemical settings of the edges and bottom, the mass of the water, the inflows and outflows and the air above. I will refer to zones for convenience (Fig. 38), but they are not isolated; they merge and influence one another. The first is the inflow area where stream or river water meets the mass of lake water, is slowed in its flow and drops much of the load of fine particles it has been carrying, or rolling along its bed. A delta forms that is often colonised by aquatic plants and which slowly spreads into the lake as more silt and sand accumulate. Sometimes the deltas of streams may grow so much that they cut a former lake into two (Table 1, Type 18) or create new small lakes within the delta itself (Type 19) when floods pile up sands and gravels in irregular patterns. Deltas are one way in which a lake is eventually filled with sediment and is converted to dry land, though this is rapid, taking perhaps a few thousand years, only in some very shallow lakes. Other geological upheavals are likely to intervene before it might be completed (in millions of years) in deep ones.

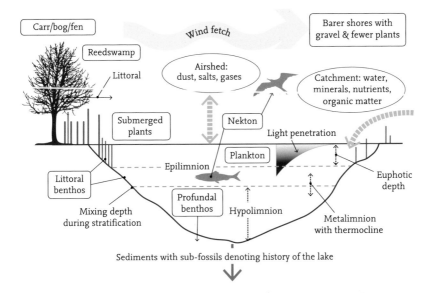

FIG 38. Terms used in describing lake habitats: basically all you should need to know were it not for a tendency among the ambitious to coin new ones.

The second zone is the water mass itself with its mixed or stratified nature, dependent on depth and time of year. It bears the plankton community (Chapter 6), which includes viruses, bacteria, algae and small animals, respectively the virioplankton, bacterioplankton, phytoplankton and zooplankton. It is wrong to say that these organisms float in the water. A very few do (some of the cyanobacteria, for example) but most are denser than the water and rely on wind-generated water currents (the viruses, bacteria and most algae) or swimming (the zooplankton) to remain in suspension and not to fall to the bottom, where they may be trapped and buried, or poisoned by substances like hydrogen sulphide produced by anaerobic bacteria in the hypolimnion.

The plankton is the simplest community, both to understand and upon which to experiment, but simplest does not mean simple. A community of hundreds of species, living in a medium of thousands of different substances, many of them organic, and influenced by the changing seasons and structure of the water mass, is far from straightforward. Among it move fish, fast-swimming vertebrates that, oblivious to any boundaries that we might like to enforce as zones, range throughout the lake. Newly hatched fish stay at the edges but juveniles are voracious predators on zooplankton and their feeding has effects down through the phytoplankton and bacterioplankton even to the water chemistry. Wide-ranging, agile animals are called nekton and include also mammals, though these only occasionally cross the middle of the lake, and birds, including the cormorants, mergansers and ospreys. In tropical lakes the nekton might also include fish-eating bats, turtles, crocodilians, lizards and snakes, but we are not privileged to see these in British and Irish waters, except for the occasional sallies of a grass snake or introduced terrapin. The birds link the lake with the airshed no less than the rain that brings substances from distances far beyond the watershed. Migratory fish, such as Atlantic salmon and sea trout, make links with the ocean or inshore waters, where they fatten and build up body nutrients before migrating back to spawn in the lake and its tributary streams, bringing these nutrient bounties sometimes to support the workings of the lake system.

The richest part of the lake in diversity of life and complexity of chemistry is not the plankton; it is the littoral zone (Chapter 5). The littoral is just at the edge in deeper lakes but may occupy most or all of the area of shallow ones. It is that part of the lake where enough light penetrates to the bottom for growth based on photosynthesis to occur. This is determined by the properties of the overlying water with its plankton, and is defined by the euphotic depth. Algae dominate the littoral zone in rocky basins but both algae and plants are common where sediment accumulates as gravel, sand or mud. Plants grade in from those of the land, in a seamless continuum, through emergent swamps to the submerged communities.

Surfaces underwater rapidly become covered by microoganisms, and a mini-forest, the periphyton, develops on the water plants, from the earliest films of pioneer bacteria and algae to a later community of larger, branched and filamentous algae, protozoa and microfungi. Snails and insects move over the plants and graze the periphyton. Smaller animals, often crustaceans and rotifers, related to the animals in the zooplankton, find refuge from fish in the tangles of plants, whilst their other predators, leeches, dragonfly nymphs, water mites, spiders and larger crustaceans, cruise through or wait in the labyrinths and corridors, nooks and crannies. Fish like pike, and wading birds such as heron and bittern, lurk at the edges for other fish, frogs, ducklings and newts. Plant-eating (herbivorous) birds like coot, moorhen and some ducks abound.

In the sediment under the plants is a community of burrowing animals: bivalve molluscs, fly larvae and worms, and the protozoa and decomposer bacteria on which they feed. Different species of algae from those attached to the plants move over the mud. There is also a plankton among and over the plants, and organisms torn off by wave action or animal disturbance join the truly planktonic organisms. All may eventually fall to the bottom in the stiller water, because currents are damped by the mass of plants. Amphibious snakes, amphibians and otters find refuges or prey in this tangled world and even the water chemistry differs from that of the main mass, for plants are not inert; they take up substances and secrete others, and change items like pH through their activity.

The animals living in the sediments of the littoral have much in common with those that live below the euphotic zone in the last component of the lake scenery, the profundal (Chapter 7). Conditions change as the bottom becomes covered with deeper and deeper water. The light is eventually extinguished, the temperature falls if the lake is stratified in summer, and the oxygen concentrations drop, sometimes to zero. The animals of the profundal sediments are specialists able to cope with this; they feed on the bacteria in the sediment but, if insects, may emerge into the air as flies. Together with insects in the littoral, they make yet another connection with the airshed when birds, bats and spiders feed on the emerging adults. And provided there is some oxygen left in the water, bottom-feeding fish like adult bream will venture into the deepest parts of the lake to take advantage of an abundant, if not particularly diverse community of invertebrates.

THE THEATRE CLOSES

Profundal lake sediment is not just a key part of the habitat; it contains a record of the lake's history. Especially in the deeper parts, sediment is laid down chronologically and is undisturbed after a few years. At first benthic animals will burrow in it, eat it and defaecate it, but this effect occurs only in the top few millimetres. Once sediment is buried under new layers, it is out of contact with the water and rapidly becomes anaerobic and preserves very well the remains of all sorts of lake organisms. There are insect head capsules and mouth parts, beetle wings, parts of the exoskeletons of crustaceans, sponge spicules, resting eggs, cysts and spores of some groups of algae, the walls of diatoms, pieces of cuticle and epidermis, and woody cells, such as sclereids from plants, the oospores of charophytes, and seeds. Moreover, even in the amorphous brown organic matter that is seen on examination under a microscope, and appears featureless, there are chemical fossils: plant and algal pigments, and residues of cell walls, wood and other plant structures that can be characterised by the lengths of their carbon chains. There are techniques for quantifying these remains and relating them to the living lake ecosystems of the past (Chapter 7).

The sediment is also the manifestation of the process of filling-in and is the reason why several metres of sediments will be found even in a lake only

10,000 years old. The rate of sedimentation is usually only a millimetre or less each year, so that a lake 100 m deep is likely to have a lifetime of up to a 100,000 years, but in shallow lakes there is a faster process that starts in the littoral zone, where the reedswamp plants, which are very productive, die back in the winter. Their remains build up on the bottom, because it is too cold in winter for rapid decomposition, and too deoxygenated in the sediment in summer. The plant debris is compressed by new additions each year and gradually a peat, a nearly completely organic soil, is formed.

Eventually the peat builds up to the water surface as the reedswamp advances into the lake, shallowing the water as it goes. To landward, as the peat reaches the water surface, a new group of wetland plants, the fen plants, succeeds the reeds. They too lay down peat and as this rises above the water table, it dries and a wet woodland, a carr, dominated by willows, alders and sometimes birch, starts to colonise and may eventually grow into a dryish woodland. This has been the fate of floodplain lakes in East Anglia, including the Broads.

In the wetter west of these islands, as the peat reaches the water surface and rises above it, the leaching action of rain is enough to acidify it and *Sphagnum*

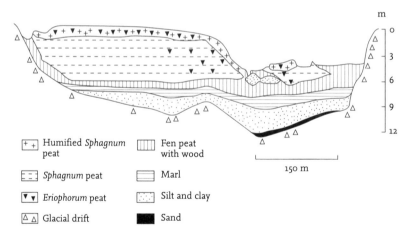

Humified *Sphagnum* peat

Sphagnum peat

Eriophorum peat

Glacial drift

Fen peat with wood

Marl

Silt and clay

Sand

150 m

FIG 39. Small lakes fill in with sediment and peat and succeed through different sorts of wetlands to forest in Britain and Ireland. The process is affected by climate so that bogs and bog forest are found in the north and west and alder and willow carrs in the east. Sometimes the sequence may occur on a floating mat if the lake is deep. The classic sequence can be seen at the edges of Malham Tarn, where part of the former, larger lake has filled in and raised bog has formed.

moss and other acid-tolerant bog plants start to take over. In a small shallow lake, such as many of those formed in kettle holes in the West Midlands and central Ireland, the reedswamp encroaches towards the centre of the lake followed by the fen and bog plants so that eventually the lake succeeds to a raised bog (Fig. 39) that grows fastest in the middle, away from the edges where upwellings of spring water that has passed through mineral soils may inhibit *Sphagnum* growth. In deeper kettle holes, the reed may form a floating mat on which the fen and bog are borne over a lens of water. The lake has become a schwingmoor or quaking bog and sometimes birch trees can colonise, giving an open bog woodland.

In these instances, the lake theatre has closed, but although there are hundreds of thousands of such successions to woodland on former lake basins across the Boreal zone, this is not the fate of all lakes. Some are too deep and, although sediment is always accumulating, they will remain lakes for thousands of years yet. But all lakes are ultimately ephemeral, though the ecological players will still have their stage for some time. So it is now time to visit the casting department and consider where they come from, how they survive and how they combine to form lake ecosystems.

CHAPTER 3

Dramatis Personae: The Small Cast-Members and the Big Roles

LIFE WAS COMPARATIVELY SIMPLE IN 1951, when *Life in Lakes & Rivers* was first published. That is not to say that the intrigues of people and politics were any less complicated than they are today; it is that our understanding of living organisms, particularly the microorganisms, and of their roles in determining conditions at the surface of Earth, was much less than it is now. Macan and Worthington made only token references to fungi and bacteria, the latter mostly in connection with sewage disposal and water supply, though they had a couple of prescient sentences concerning the role of bacteria in food webs, which have been amply fulfilled. There was a greater attention to the microscopic algae, about the same to plants, but the bulk of the book was about animals and, among those, the larger invertebrates and fish had the starring roles.

A glance at a theatre programme, or the list of people that rolls endlessly on the screen at the close of a film, shows that the true cast is much greater than the short list of leading actors, the director and producer. There are scores of scene makers, shifters and painters, wardrobe mistresses and seamstresses, electricians and best boys, the providers of props, the managers of stages, the makers-up and hairdressers, those who wrangle the animals, even the drivers, cooks and caterers. So it is with the cast of the evolutionary play that is staged in the ecological theatres of lakes and every other natural system. The most obvious natural history might come in the leap of the salmon or the breeding of the great crested grebe, the lunge of a heron or even the twilight migrations of a small crustacean, but none of these could happen were it not for armies of microorganisms.

So it is with the entire planet. A litre of ocean water or that of a not particularly productive lake will contain about a million algae and protozoa, 100 million bacteria and up to 100 billion viruses.[1] The biosphere could continue indefinitely without any larger plants and animals, even (especially) ourselves, but a biosphere lacking microorganisms could not exist.[2] A natural history of lakes needs to start with the microbial scene-shifters, before it looks at the names in neon lights. The bonus of doing that comes in an insight into the natural history of most of Earth's story, the nearly 4 billion years before multicellular organisms began to evolve around the Cambrian Period half a billion years ago, in the last 10 per cent of Earth's time.

REVOLUTIONS

The year 1951 was close to the start of a series of revolutions in biology. In 1953, the structure of DNA, deoxyribose nucleic acid, was discovered and that led to a far deeper understanding of life, for DNA makes up the genes of organisms, and the genes determine the potentiality of an organism, what it can do. They are the units of evolutionary change. But this discovery was just the first in a series of advances in techniques and understanding that have completely transformed how we now look at ecosystems and their natural history.

Before 1953 bacteria were mostly seen as the agents of disease. They were studied in cultures on nutrient broths, or plates of agar jelly, and characterised by their reactions with stains, their abilities to ferment different sugars or lyse the proteins in blood. A few thousand (currently about 5,400) bacteria can be grown and identified according to the international rules that assign species and genus names: *Escherichia coli*, for example, for the common bacterium of the human gut, known as *Bacterium coli* in Macan's and Worthington's time, and used as an indicator of faecal pollution of rivers and lakes. Plating out a sample of freshwater onto agar would allow a few forms to grow in whitish, or occasionally coloured colonies; a few would spread across the plates and some would form filaments like flattened tufts of hair.

Viruses, crystallisable particles that contain protein and nucleic acid, were also known, but again largely associated with the diseases of people, farm animals and crops. Fungi were seen mostly as mushrooms and toadstools, rusts and smuts, the yeasts that make bread rise or convert grape juice into wine and barley malt into beer. There was a good understanding of the range of algae, thought of as small photosynthetic plants that colonised lake waters and the rocks of rivers. The plants, invertebrates and animals had been fairly thoroughly described but the scientific world was content to see microorganisms outside medicine as two groups: those studied in botany departments, including the bacteria, algae and fungi, which did not move, and those over which the zoology departments held

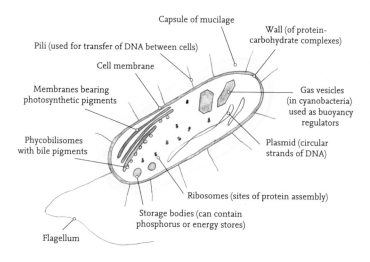

Capsule of mucilage

Wall (of protein-carbohydrate complexes)

Pili (used for transfer of DNA between cells)

Cell membrane

Membranes bearing photosynthetic pigments

Gas vesicles (in cyanobacteria) used as buoyancy regulators

Phycobilisomes with bile pigments

Plasmid (circular strands of DNA)

Ribosomes (sites of protein assembly)

Storage bodies (can contain phosphorus or energy stores)

Flagellum

FIG 40. Structures variously to be found in prokaryotes. This is a composite diagram. Some structures are found in all, others just in some bacteria.

sway: the single-celled protozoa, which did. Some hint that this was not entirely satisfactory came with motile cells like *Euglena* and some dinoflagellates, which both moved and photosynthesised and which both camps claimed.

Most bacteria known by the 1950s were round or capsule-shaped, sometimes with their cells in chains or filaments, but little could be seen under the light microscope. Electron microscopes and other techniques in the 1960s confirmed that the bacteria were much more varied, and different from the other groups. The basic structure included a wall of protein and carbohydrate, an outer cell membrane of protein and fat, internal systems of membranes, bearing enzymes, small bodies – the ribosomes – where proteins are assembled, storage bodies, and DNA present as a series of circular plasmids, distributed freely within the cell (Fig. 40). At the molecular level the cells are complex, with mechanisms for growth, metabolism and reproduction like those of the animals and plants, whose apparently greater complexity comes from their being built of sub-units similar to the bacteria. But bacteria are more versatile than other organisms. They can obtain their energy from breaking down organic molecules, produced by other organisms, or they can take it from inorganic chemical reactions, the oxidation of reduced iron in seeps from rocks, for example, to a rust-coloured iron oxide (Fig. 41). They may oxidise organic matter to methane, convert nitrate

FIG 41. Anaerobic bacteria, dominant on Earth for the first two billion years of its existence, are now confined to the few places where oxygen is scarce. These orange patches, seen in Bankhead National Forest, Alabama, are the result of iron bacteria oxidising grey or green iron salts dissolved in deep groundwater and deriving energy in the process. (Mike Henshaw)

to nitrogen gas or sulphate to hydrogen sulphide, where oxygen is scarce or absent in columns of waterlogged soil or the deep layers of lakes or fjords. Yet other bacteria, purple, pink or green in colour, can fix light energy using hydrogen or some compound of it, like hydrogen sulphide, to convert carbon dioxide into organic matter. Again these bacteria operate under low oxygen conditions, on intertidal muds, or in deep or organically polluted waters, where substances like hydrogen sulphide can persist.

In the late 1960s, there was another major upset to the simple view of the 1950s. One group of algae, the blue-green algae, which is very common in lakes, was shown to have a structure like the bacteria, though it possessed the main green pigment, chlorophyll a, which was associated with the release of oxygen in photosynthesis of green plants and other algae. The name of the blue-green algae was changed to blue-green bacteria, and then to cyanobacteria (Fig. 42). In every respect of structure and function, they are bacteria, but bacteria that 2.5 billion years ago (the evidence is in substances specific to cyanobacteria – 2-alpha methylhopanes for the record – preserved in rocks) started a fundamental change in the biosphere by converting it from one with virtually no free oxygen in the atmosphere to one that became richer and richer in oxygen gas.

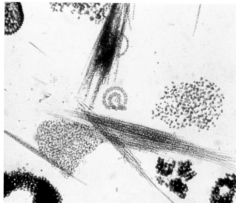

FIG 42. Photosynthetic bacteria include cyanobacteria that use water to provide hydrogen for the reduction of carbon dioxide to organic matter (right) and green and purple sulphur bacteria that use reduced sulphur compounds like hydrogen sulphide (left). The longest filaments (*Aphanizomenon*) of cyanobacteria shown are about 100 μm long and the individual cells of the colonies of *Microcystis* are about 1 μm. A coiled filament of *Anabaena* is also shown. The purple sulphur bacteria occur in patches about 0.5 m across where anaerobic groundwater is seeping upwards in a pond.

TWO SORTS OF CELLS

The revelation of the cell structure of bacteria by the electron microscope was paralleled by a closer look at the cell structure of other organisms. Animals and plants, fungi, algae and protozoa were known to share a common basic structure even before the 1950s. They had a cell membrane, like the bacteria, but sometimes (in animals) no wall, or a wall made up of different polymers like cellulose or chitin, and inside the membrane was a greater internal structure. First there was a nucleus, inside which the DNA, much more of it than in bacteria, was held on chromosomes made of protein (so-called because they stained with coloured dyes).

The chromosomes duplicate before the cell divides, and are organised on a framework of fine fibrils radiating out from poles at either end of the nucleus, each with a complex structure, the centriole, in animals, but not in plants or fungi. The chromosomes are pulled by the fibrils into two matching groups, each of which goes to one of the daughter cells after the nucleus itself has divided, and new cell membranes separate the daughters. The centrioles are cylindrical and

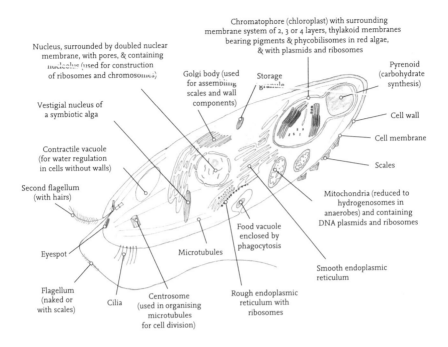

FIG 43. Structures variously to be found in eukaryotes. This is a composite diagram. Some structures are found in all, others just in some groups.

have a structure with eleven fine fibrils running through them, like the lettering in seaside rock, with a ring of nine peripheral ones and two central ones an arrangement that is similar to that of the flagellum (plural, flagella) found on the outsides of some of both animal and plant cells. It is a much more complicated structure than the bacterial flagellum, but has a similar role in cell movement.

These more structured cells (Fig. 43), now called eukaryotic cells (with a nucleus), as opposed to the prokaryotic (before a nucleus) arrangement of bacterial cells, have other membrane-bounded bodies inside them, surrounded by at least two membranes and of two main kinds. The first, possessed by all eukaryotic cells, though sometimes in a simplified and vestigial form, are mitochondria. They have complex infoldings of their inner membrane, contain enzymes responsible for storage and release of energy under aerobic conditions, have some ribosomes of their own, which are smaller than the ribosomes in the rest of the cell, and also have some DNA in a circular plasmid form similar to that of the bacteria. Some animal cells, mostly parasites, or protozoa from anaerobic habitats, have no mitochondria but have mitosomes or hydrogenosomes, now known to be reduced and simplified mitochondria.

The second kind of membrane-bound body is the chloroplast or chromatophore and is absent from animals and fungi, but prominent in plants and algae. Photosynthesis occurs in it, on internal stacks of membranes called thylakoids, on which the pigments are borne. There is a large variety of pigments, in addition to chlorophyll *a*, including sometimes chlorophyll *b* or *c* and orange or yellow pigments, called carotenes and xanthophylls. There are also small ribosomes and plasmids of DNA in the chromatophore, just as in the mitochondria.

THE ORIGINS OF EUKARYOTIC CELLS

The first recognisable organisms on Earth, and solely for at least the first three of the nearly 5 billion years of its existence, were bacteria. Eukaryotic cells came much later, only 1.5 billion years ago. Cells are also either distinctly prokaryotic or distinctly eukaryotic. There are no intermediates. That realisation has resulted in a very large literature speculating about how the eukaryotes evolved from the prokaryotes, a problem that has not yet been fully resolved. No one knows where the nucleus, the chromosomes and the mechanism for precise separation of the chromosomes in cell division came from, but there are clues to the origin of the flagellum and really strong evidence for the origins of mitochondria and chromatophores.

In the 1960s Lynn Margulis revived an old idea of a Russian, Konstantin Mereschkowsky, who in 1905 postulated that the chromatophore came as a lodger or endosymbiont photosynthetic bacterium in a bigger cell, and that the mitochondrion was similarly derived from a symbiotic decomposer bacterium.[3] The new clues were in the plasmids of DNA, organised in the same way as in bacteria, and in ribosomes in the chromatophores and mitochondria that had a size and nature close to those of bacteria. The mitochondria and simpler chromatophores are also surrounded by two membranes, the outer of which is closer in nature to that surrounding the eukaryotic cell, the inner similar to that of bacteria. It was thus reasonable to suppose that an original host cell (whose nature and origin are disputed except that it must have been some sort of prokaryote) had engulfed some free-living bacteria by enfolding them with its outer membrane and that they had then become modified to become the mitochondria and chromatophores.

As techniques of molecular biology developed in the 1990s it became possible to determine inexpensively the sequence of bases in DNA and RNA molecules.

The RNA contained in ribosomes is very useful because it is held in a structure with such a fundamental role that changes in it can only have been quite small without compromising its function. The ribosomal RNA of the mitochondria is closely similar to that of a group of bacteria now called the alpha proteobacteria and the RNA of the chromatophores matches that of the cyanobacteria. Margulis suggested that the flagellum of eukaryote cells had come from a spirochaete bacterium that had attached itself to the outside of the ancestral eukaryote cell, but this idea has never been fully developed. There are spirochaete bacteria that do attach in such a way to protozoa in the guts of termites, and act as propellants, but the flagellum does not contain nucleic acids and spirochaetes do not contain the sorts of proteins (tubulins) that form the strands that run through flagella and typify their structure. Nonetheless the endosymbiont hypothesis for the origin of mitochondria and chromatophores (collectively, the plastids) has stood up well. Many of the genes that entered in the engulfed bacteria were subsequently transferred to the chromosomes, so that the plastids now have a reduced genome, with about 200,000 base pairs (the units of DNA) compared with the 1.5 to 7 million base pairs of their ancestral bacteria.

A NEW GROUP OF PROKARYOTES, THE ARCHAEA

The nature of the host cell of eukaryotes has remained an enigma, but new clues came in the 1970s when Carl Woese compared the ribosomal RNA of different organisms and found three groups: the bacteria, the eukaryotes and a second prokaryote group which became known as the Archaea.[4] The Archaea differed from the bacteria (now called Eubacteria) in the chemistry of their membranes, which had some similarities (in the possession of glycerol ether lipids) to the outer membranes of the eukaryotes, whilst Eubacteria have glycerol ester lipids. The ribosomal RNA sequences of Archaea were also closer to those of eukaryotes than they were to those of Eubacteria. Furthermore, the Archaea then known came only from anaerobic habitats, and only Archaea are able to generate methane from organic matter, a process thought to be important in creating the early atmosphere of the Earth. Archaea are also common in warm and hot places, such as thermal vents in the ocean and hot springs on land. Archaea became hot tips for the host that preceded the eukaryotic cell, but their origin is obscure. There are some indications that they may have evolved from former Eubacteria but evidence also for the reverse.

The evolutionary play is set on an ecological stage and the stage, 1.5 billion years ago, when there is the first fossil evidence of eukaryotic cells, was one in which an anaerobic Earth was being oxygenated by the photosynthesis of the cyanobacteria.

This threatened anaerobic organisms because oxygen is quite damaging, but one solution might have been symbiotic combinations in which cells that could not function in an oxygen-rich world might be able to live deep inside another organism where their enzymes could be protected. It was also a very warm world, so the idea gained credence that an ancient Archaean host entered into symbioses with Eubacteria and Cyanobacteria to produce the basic eukaryote cells.

Alternative work suggests that an archaean might have been engulfed by a eubacterium to produce the nucleus and that this combination then engulfed the bacteria that became plastids. Much more than that cannot yet be said for sure. A recent paper, published in 2011, whimsically entitled '*A new fusion hypothesis for the origin of Eukaryotes: better than previous ones, but probably also wrong*'[5] suggests that the bulk of the evidence favours the engulfment of a thaumarchaeon (one particular group of Archaea) by a bacterium from the Planctomycetes/Verrucomicrobia/Chlamydiae group (see Table 5) followed by invasions of viruses to bring in additional genes. The thaumarchaeon, it is proposed, provided some operational

TABLE 5. Some characteristics of the apparently most abundant phyla of bacteria in freshwater lakes.

Phylum	Characteristics	Ecology
Actinobacteria	High proportion of guanosine and cytosine among the bases of their DNA. Stain with Gram's stain but there are few named organisms. *Planktophila limnetica* and a few others have been maintained in enrichment cultures. *Aquiluna, Flaviluna, Rhodoluna. Actinobacterium.* Formerly called Actinomycetes and Planktophila, *Mycobacterium*, and Acidomicrobiales. Very small isolates (sometimes <0.1 μm), rod, spherical or crescent-shaped, thin walls, red or yellow pigmented. Cultured ones are not the most typical and need to be grown with other bacteria (co-bacteria) for maintenance	Ubiquitous in lakes, often numerically dominant, less common in hypolimnia. Appear cosmopolitan. Suggested to be grazer resistant because of their small size. Ultraviolet resistant (pigmentation and high guanosine content). Can produce spores but conflicting studies in all respects and studies are mostly from soil representatives. Seem to be easily dispersed but not yet detected in aerial samples. May prefer low nutrients. Slow growth. Some have rhodopsin pigments and may be photosynthetic
Bacteroidetes (also known as Cytophaga-Flavobacteria-Bacteroides)	Do not form spores, often anaerobic, rod-shaped. Common ancestry with Fibrobacteria and Chlorobi	Great variation in appearance and physiology. Some are symbionts, others use inorganic reactions to oxidise organic matter, some are photosynthetic. Can be parasites but many associated with detritus particles and decay of organic polymers. Sometimes abundant following cyanobacteria blooms. Filamentous forms resist grazing

Cyanobacteria	Well-established group, photosynthetic using water as a source of hydrogen and releasing oxygen. Large size range from around 1 μm to several cm (in gelatinous colonies). Easily culturable with different sorts of cells	Extremely common in lakes and the ocean. Some propensity for high temperatures but can be found even in polar lakes. See Chapter 6 for detailed treatment
Alpha-proteobacteria	Well studied, stain with Gram's stain and include many of the well-known industrial, agricultural and medical bacteria. Groups alpha, beta, delta, gamma, epsilon and zeta can be differentiated among proteobacteria. The alpha group is the origin of mitochondria. Large variation in genome size	Alpha group often symbiotic or parasitic, N fixers in plants, ubiquitous. Resistant to grazing, can form filaments or stalks. May favour low nutrients, capable of degrading complex organics
Beta proteobacteria	The Beta proteobacteria are by far the most studied and often the most abundant bacteria inhabiting the upper waters of lakes. They do not stain with Gram's stain, and are rods or cocci	Beta group often numerically dominant in lakes, low in oceans, amenable to culturing. Grow quickly in response to pulsed nutrients, readily grazed. Depth, pH, carbon substrate preferences and seasonal factors are all known to differentiate closely related organisms. Opportunistic competitors. Include nitrifying bacteria that oxidise ammonia and nitrogen fixers, as well as pathogens causing gonorrhoea and meningitis
Gamma proteobacteria	Many named genera, *Pseudomonas, Serratia, Escherichia, Salmonella* and *Vibrio* that are disease causing, but also includes photosynthetic bacteria (*Chromatium*) that use hydrogen sulphide	Include gut bacteria (Enterobacteriales), transients from pollution. More common in seawater. Grow well in rich media
Verrumicrobia	The name comes from a warty appearance of the surface of the cells. Minor in lakes but this may reflect methods as some probes suggest abundance. Dominant in soils	Ecto and endosymbionts, but some methane oxidisers, oxidisers of ammonia under anaerobic conditions and users of Fe and Mn reactions

proteins (actins, proteins used for transport), including some essential proteins absent from other archaeal phyla, whereas the bacterium provided phospholipids, tubulin and the proteins needed for the formation of the nucleus.

Even this scheme does not explain all the evidence. In the quest for an explanation of the eukaryotic cell; however, huge amounts of data have become available on the genomes, the sequences of bases in RNA and DNA, of a great variety of organisms and the data have revealed not only a great deal more diversity in bacteria and in eukaryotes than was ever before realised, but have changed our views of how organisms are related to one another, and illuminated the problem of explaining the ecological roles of the microorganisms in lakes. All this has happened in the last 20 years and whole areas of biology are now in an unprecedented state of flux as a result. The simple certainties of 1951 begin to look now like children's story books in the face of electronic multi-volumed encyclopaedias, updated almost on a daily basis.

THE VARIETY OF BACTERIA

It is now possible to take a sample of lake water, concentrate the community of organisms, extract their DNA or RNA, and increase the amounts by a process called the polymerase chain reaction so that the base sequences can be readily determined. The base sequences (usually particular sections of the ribosomal RNA are used) can then be compared with libraries of such sequences in organisms that have been previously recorded. Large numbers (currently about 12,000, but fast rising) of new sequences have been determined, the vast majority of which do not correspond with cells that can be cultured and named by the classic methods of bacteriology. Different sequences can be related to one another and grouped as clades (a name given to organisms that form an evolutionary sequence) and groups along the clades can be distinguished. It is even possible to say something about what the groups do, by picking out particular genes associated, for example, with nitrogen fixation or a particular step in a biochemical pathway; but in almost every case we do not know what the bacterium looks like. It is no longer possible to be sure exactly what we mean by a bacterial species either.

Different RNA sequences can be said to be from different species using conventions such that they differ by at least 3 per cent, or that when their DNA is melted by heating and the single strands that result are mixed from two sequences, less than 70 per cent of the strands from the two sequences will join up on cooling, or alternatively that the temperatures at which the two sequences melt differ by more than 5°C. But these are all arbitrary criteria. For animals, fungi and plants, indeed all eukaryotes, we have satisfactory ideas about what constitutes a species. They are groups of individuals that broadly look alike (they are morphospecies) and will usually sexually reproduce together to give offspring that are fertile and can similarly reproduce. There are some problems with those that do not reproduce sexually, but these are not serious, and a great deal of natural history is made orderly by the maintenance of readily recognised and named species.

With the prokaryotes, both Archaea and Eubacteria, there is complete chaos in understanding what a 'species' means. There is no concept of a morphospecies, for most look very similar, yet in terms of their biochemistry and abilities to transform substances in the great mineral cycles on which the biosphere depends, they are vastly more diverse than the relatively uniform eukaryotes. There is a plethora of definitions, perhaps as many as 20, mostly fuzzy: *a genomically coherent cluster of individual organisms that show a high degree of overall similarity in many independent characteristics*, for example.[6] Terms like 'ecotype', 'operational taxonomc unit' and evolutionary significant unit' abound and reflect the confusion.

Bacteria can easily transfer the plasmids that bear their genes, as they jostle together, simply by injecting them through another's cell wall through projections called pili. There are billions of virus particles mixed in the communities that infect the cells and these can also transfer genes from bacterium to bacterium. Genes for particular processes, like nitrogen fixation or denitrification, have been spread around numerous groups. It may be that a bacterial 'species' has no more permanence than a single generation, that it may be impossible to create orderly 'trees' describing bacterial evolution and that all that can be deduced is the history, reflected in changes in their base sequence, of specific genes.

Even then very small differences can result in hugely different ecology. *Yersinia pestis*, the cause of plague, is very similar to *Yersinia pseudotuberculosis*, a gastrointestinal pathogen that is transmitted through contamination of food by faeces. *Y. pestis* became capable of flea-borne transmission between rodents owing to the acquisition of two plasmids probably about 12,000 years ago. Strains of *Y. pestis* are almost indistinguishable in their base sequence from *Y. pseudotuberculosis*, and would not form a distinct species by the criteria that are normally used to differentiate species. Yet *Y. pestis* has a totally distinct ecology and mechanism of transmission. Moreover, the differences found among RNA sequences that are used to try to classify groups may give different results dependent on the sections of nucleic acid that are compared, or the different computer programs that are used to make the comparisons.

Nonetheless, the total number of bacterial 'species', assuming that these are broadly recognisable over many generations, is likely to be of the order of a million to 10 million or more, compared with the existing list of described species of a mere 5,400. Almost every lake has its own recognisable (as of now, at least) array of thousands of different sorts of bacteria; there is variability over time as genes are transferred around but some groups show a rough correspondence to different environmental conditions. Some bacteria appear to be confined to lakes, a position that changes the view of around 1980 that there were no specifically freshwater bacteria, just a group shared among soils and waters. There is also a view that microorganisms are so easily dispersed that the groups are everywhere much the same, with local details determined subsequently by natural selection acting on millions of small gene transfers, tempering the performance of the individuals to local conditions. There is thus likely to be huge diversity in the details of bacterial communities on the one hand, but a great uniformity in the ranges of major groups and in the functions that the bacteria have in processing elements and substances within lakes in different geographical regions, on the other hand.

Between 1 and 10 per cent of nucleic acid sequences found in lakes are Archaea, mostly in the phylum Crenarchaea, of which we have no species in culture, so can say nothing of their ecological role; the rest are Eubacteria. Table 5 summarises current knowledge of the eubacterial groups (among which most of the named medical bacteria are found in the Proteobacteria) most common in lakes. For some of the groups, which are designated only on the basis of their nucleic acid sequences, we have no idea what they look like, but an inspection of a water sample under a high-powered microscope will reveal spheres (cocci), elongate capsules (rods), star-shaped cells with protrusions, helices, cells with stalks, flat sheets of cells arranged in square order, globular or irregular colonies and filaments. Some may have thick layers of mucilage beyond their walls, others flagella; some may form spores with thick walls.

Overall the diversity of form is small (Fig. 44); it is the diversity of biochemistry that is astounding. Archaea and Eubacteria *inter alia* can take advantage of almost any organic chemical to retrieve energy; they can use inorganic reactions to oxidise those substances, or to fix carbon dioxide to form them; they can exist in conditions without oxygen or with high oxygen concentrations; they can transform nitrogen gas to ammonia, nitrate or amino acids and use the reverse sequence to denitrify proteins to nitrogen gas. They can manipulate the compounds of sulphur and iron and manganese; they can photosynthesise in aerobic or anaerobic conditions provided there is light. There is nowhere on Earth where liquid water exists that one bacterium or another cannot prosper. They can even colonise crystals of salt in the driest deserts, taking the water they need from the hygroscopic water that the crystal extracts from the atmosphere.[7]

New techniques may help to relate the taxonomy of bacteria, reflected in the base sequences, to the roles that bacteria play in lakes. Metagenomics, metatranscriptomics, metaproteomics and metametabolomics aim at complete descriptions of microbial communities. Metagenomics describes what bacteria are present, but these may be normal residents, with significant functions, 'vagabonds' that have a very wide distribution in soils and waters and are

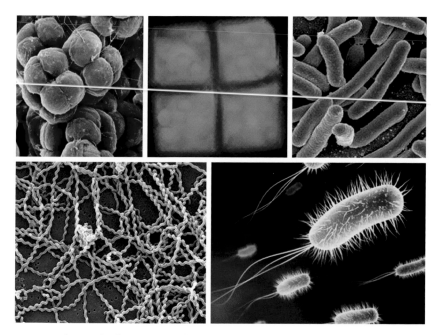

FIG 44. Archaea and Eubacteria. Upper left and centre are two examples of Archaea, the first from very hot water, the second from very salty water, but Archaea are known to be abundant in less extreme habitats also. Eubacteria include rod-shaped cells, upper right (the cells are about 1 μm long) and a spirochete bacterium (lower left), with cells 20 μm long but only 0.5 μm thick. More sophisticated techniques reveal more details as in the common gut bacterium, *Escherichia coli*, which swims with fine hairs, or flagella (lower right).

easily washed in, or 'tourists', cells drifting in on the wind or floods but not persisting. The techniques for isolating and amplifying DNA are so sensitive that these groups cannot be distinguished. Metatranscriptomics, on the other hand, isolates the genes that are actually active at a time. Metaproteomics and metametabolomics demonstrate what proteins are present and what key biochemicals are being produced and processed and together these approaches may tell us more about what the bacterial community is doing. They are technologies that are expensive and complex but may still fall short of even describing what is happening in lake communities.[8] They generate enormous amounts of data and are starting to emphasise processes in a situation where a taxonomic approach is overwhelmingly confusing, but so far they have produced no new ecological insights and may be overly ambitious in seeking to describe activities in lakes of bacterial communities that are fast moving, and occur in adjacent but different patches of water each only millimetres across. The new understanding gained in the past 20 years, however, should warn us to expect further revolution.

VIRUSES

Macan and Worthington made but a single reference to viruses and that only in terms of virus diseases spread through water. We know little about their detailed roles but there are many viruses present in freshwaters, and that can only mean that they are major players in determining the population fluctuations of all other organisms. Viruses are everywhere; they comprise a portion of RNA or DNA in a simple protein structure and cannot reproduce themselves; they must infect a specific host, when they take over the host's systems for reproducing DNA and protein so that more viruses are made then released to infect other hosts. They are very advanced parasites.

They infect all organisms, but most emphasis has been placed on the viruses of heterotrophic bacteria, with about ten viruses per bacterium in the water. Some 5–25 per cent of bacteria are infected at any one time, and burst sizes (the number of viruses produced per host cell) are perhaps 10–40 for bacteria, ten times as many for algal cells, and there is probably a complete turnover of both bacterial and virus populations every day or two. In Lake Erie, it has been estimated that the stock of carbon contained in viruses and bacteria is about the same as that in fish (8 ± 4, 41 ± 14 and 12–64 thousand tonnes, respectively), though 10 or a 100 times lower than those of zooplankton and phytoplankton. The genetic diversity of aquatic viruses, as measured by DNA sequences, is lower than expected and viruses may be less important in freshwaters than in the ocean, but every new study adds to the apparent complexity and variability of virus behaviour in freshwaters, and it is too early to be certain of anything. The same is almost true of the single-celled eukaryotic microorganisms. Many of the certainties of 1951 have disappeared for them too.

THE DIVERSITY OF MICROBIAL EUKARYOTES

In 1969, Robert Whittaker took the first steps in changing perceptions of the kingdoms of organisms that had sufficed in the 1950s.[9] He recognised five kingdoms, the Monera (the prokaryotes), the Protista, the Plants, the Fungi and the Animals, a major elaboration on the two (Plants, including bacteria and fungi, and Animals) that was the working model for Macan and Worthington. The only thing that had placed the fungi with the plants had been that they had cell walls, did not move and were traditionally studied in botany departments. Beyond that they were clearly not plants; they were not photosynthetic, they did not have cellulose walls and they had very different structures, often with several nuciei in long strands of hyphae, not separated by cell walls. Whittaker's separation of them was easily accepted. The Protista and Plants were different matters.

The Protista were all unicellular and the kingdom included algae (other than the large green, red and brown seaweeds, which he placed in the plant kingdom, together with the mosses and ferns, conifers and flowering plants), the protozoa, single-celled animals previously, and some of the fungi that were small, aquatic and often infected algae as parasites or lived on submerged organic matter. The insight that Whittaker had, however, was more than just to put together the single-celled eukaryotes in a group. He had designated the animals as a kingdom whose members ate solid food (phagotrophy), the fungi as one that secreted enzymes that dissolved solid organic matter so that it could be absorbed as soluble compounds (saprotrophy) and the plants as confined to photosynthesis (phototrophy). He pointed out that many Protista, on the other hand, combined more than one of these modes of feeding (mixotrophy) and, though some had specialised on only one, the structural similarities with those that were mixed feeders clearly placed them together. Many of the unicellular algae, though primarily photosynthetic, required external supplies of organic compounds in soluble form, particularly vitamins; others engulfed small particles whilst also being photosynthetic. There were former protozoon groups that had both saprotrophy and phagotrophy and some that had sister genera, one absorbing soluble matter, the other photosynthesising, in otherwise structurally very similar cells that could also engulf food particles. There were even some that used all of organic absorption, phagotrophy and photosynthesis, including one, *Ochromonas malhamensis*, isolated from a pond close to Malham Tarn Field Centre in Yorkshire. The microfungi placed in the group all absorbed soluble matter, but most also had flagellated cells, like some of the algae and protozoa and unlike the mushrooms and toadstools, rusts, smuts, mould and yeasts that were placed in the fungal kingdom.

Whittaker's concept was of a kingdom, the Protista, which linked the prokaryotes with the specialist 'higher' kingdoms: a kingdom from which the specialists had evolved. And central to that concept was the evidence that endosymbiosis had had a major role in the development of eukaryotic cells. Some of the protists had acquired chromatophores, others had not, or had done so then lost them. Treatment of some photosynthetic *Euglena* species with antibiotics, for example, could turn them into colourless protozoa, placed in the genus *Astasia* and dependent on soluble organic matter.

ALGAE

Whittaker's concept was extremely useful; it made a lot of sense and gave a framework to the courses I used to teach on the algae in the 1970s and 1980s. The electron microscope had by then added a great deal of knowledge about eukaryotic cells. At first there was the idea of 'typical' animal and plant cells, the latter with a cellulose wall, a chromatophore with chlorophylls a and b, and storage of starch. That concept worked for some of the green algae, except that many also had flagella. Some of the flagella, usually occurring in pairs on the cells, had smooth surfaces, but others were found covered in tiny scales, and the cell walls of these were also scaled, and not a continuous cellulose cover. The chromatophores were the standard chloroplasts of the higher plants though, until it was shown that those of the euglenoids, previously considered to be green algae, had three surrounding membranes, not two, that they stored a different carbohydrate, paramylon and that their cells were covered by strips of protein, often in a helical pattern. Gradually, more and more differences were found in the algal groups that distinguished them greatly from the typical green algae and the land plants.

Algal groups (Fig. 45), including well-known ones like the diatoms, golden algae, cryptomonads, red and brown seaweeds and dinoflagellates, and several obscurer ones, had long been distinguished, but all had been traditionally put together with the green algae (and also the cyanobacteria, when they were known as the blue-green algae) as 'Algae' to distinguish them from the land plants. The groups had traditionally been recognised as different from one another because they had different photosynthetic pigments (other than the chlorophyll *a* that they all shared), and a few other characteristics. The red algae were distinguished by lacking flagella, but having the red and blue bile pigments also associated with the cyanobacteria. These pigments were contained in small bodies, the phycobilisomes, that had the same characteristics as in the cyanobacteria. The red algae were identified as being close to the line that had first gained a cyanobacterium as an endosymbiont. Chlorophyll *b* occurs mainly in the green algae and land plants. It is not greatly different from chlorophyll *a* and had been identified also in one group of cyanobacteria and so the green algae could be placed also close to the original line of descent.

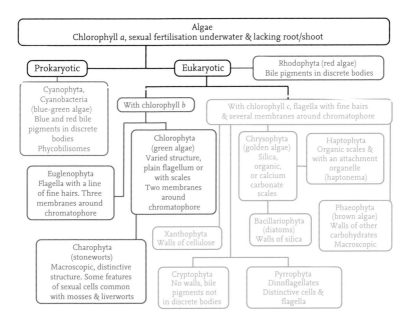

FIG 45. A traditional, late twentieth-century view of the groups of algae. The letter colouring indicates the appearance of the groups, dependent on the prominence of particular pigments: blue-green phycobilins or red phycoerythrins (bile pigments) for the blue-green and red algae respectively, green for the groups with both chlorophyll *a* and *b* and brown-yellow for those where carotenes and xanthophylls tend to mask the chlorophylls. Pigmentation was thought to be the chief distinguishing factor but cell structure was already usurping this. A current view, which uses predominantly nucleic acid sequences and cell structure, and depends less on pigmentation, is shown in Figure 46.

The big problem came with the many groups of algae that did not have chlorophyll *b*, but had chlorophyll *c*, usually with a set of distinctive carotenoid pigments that gave a yellowish or brown appearance to the cell, masking the colour of the green chlorophylls, which were nonetheless present and essential for photosynthesis. This group was quite varied in appearance, ranging from tiny cells, many of which were mixed feeders, to large seaweeds, including the kelps, sometimes many metres long. The group included also the diatoms, with cell walls of silica, the yellow or golden algae, whose cells were covered in organic, silica or calcareous scales, and the cryptophytes, which had also phycobilin pigments, though these were not in phycobilisomes but contained within the space between the membranes that bore the chlorophylls and carotenoids. Then there were the dinoflagellates, very distinctive in appearance with one flagellum trailing downwards, the other in a groove encircling the cell, but with a variety of pigments, with or without chlorophyll c and sometimes with chlorophyll b or even phycobilins. There were some structural features in common, however. When these algae produced cells with flagella, either as the normal cell or as gametes for reproduction, the flagella were very distinctive, with complex fine hairs emerging as a fringe along their lengths, and four membranes surrounded the chromatophores. Moreover, some of the dinoflagellates and the cryptomonads had a second nucleus, a nucleosome, reduced in size and contained within the outer chromatophore membranes.

The explanation for this confusing complexity came from an analysis of the structure of the cells. All these eukaryotic organisms had swallowed a second eukaryote cell, which sequencing of the RNA in the symbiont showed to have been a single-celled red alga. Their cells, either formerly with a Cyanobacterial chromatophore that had been lost, or perhaps never having had one, but always having endosymbiont mitochondria, had captured an entire red algal cell, features of which, like the nucleus, had been preserved in some, but not in others. The four membranes around the chromatophore represented the two membranes covering the chromatophore in the original red alga, the outer cell membrane of the red alga and then the membrane of the host cell that had engulfed the red alga. In some of the dinoflagellates, the red algal symbiont had been almost completely lost, but they had acquired a third symbiont, a green alga, or in one case a diatom. Things became really complicated when it was shown that several protozoon groups, including the malaria parasite, *Plasmodium*, had also formerly captured a red algal endosymbiont, but had lost the pigments and most of its structure, retaining just a few distinctive genes from this source. What could be more bizarre than to find that a major blood parasite and the huge kelps of the ocean littoral had come from the same source through the engulfing of a unicellular red alga?

POST-WHITTAKER

The first decade of the twenty-first century finally overturned the convenient classification of Robert Whittaker. It had been useful, focussing on feeding modes as well as the split between prokaryotes and eukaryotes, but the creation of the Protista and the specialist kingdoms of the Plants, Fungi and Animals had been wrong. The mounting number of genomes that are being sequenced are showing that the links among the kingdoms are very different from traditional views. Figure 46 shows the current understanding, though aspects of this are still controversial and every month brings new information, so the scheme cannot be regarded as final. Moreover, the evidence from gene sequencing sometimes accords with, and sometimes gives very different relationships from that of structure.

We also now realise that sideways gene transfer can occur in unicellular eukaryotes as well as in prokaryotes, so that possession of a gene might not reflect some fundamental link, just a transfer of a gene that long ago was unique to one group but has been passed through numerous lineages ever since. Many of the genes that came with the endosymbiont mitochondria and chromatophores, and gave them their former independence have been transferred by this means to the nuclear chromosomes, and genes can apparently be transferred from food. We also know that the genome does not by itself represent a blueprint for construction of an organism. The same genes, activated in different ways, have different outcomes. We share most of our genes with chimpanzees and there are obvious similarities between us, but also great differences. The genome is thus only one tool in tracing the links among organisms. It is a very fundamental one and is the prime way by which evolutionary links are now traced, but only sometimes can specific genes be linked with particular structural or biochemical features.

KINGDOMS OF EUKARYOTES

Six kingdoms of eukaryotes are now recognised (Fig. 46), though for the time being the uncertainties are acknowledged by calling them supergroups of phyla.[10] It is not known yet which came first. All have mitochondria, or simplifications of them, so there are no clues there, but those phyla (though not necessarily the entire supergroup) containing just primary endosymbionts (the plastids) must have arisen earlier than those with additional eukaryote symbionts. The evolutionary history of the chromatophore has to be seen as separate from that of the host cell. All the supergroups have representatives in lakes, sometimes free-living, sometimes as parasites in free-living organisms.

Two supergroups are well established: the Archaeplantae and the Opisthokonta. The Archaeplantae includes eukaryotes with just one level of endosymbionts (originally Cyanobacteria) forming the chromatophores. The group includes the Glaucophyta, whose chromatophores are still so close to free-living Cyanobacteria that the immediate ancestors can be identified, the red algae, the green algae, the charophytes and the higher plants. The red algae are mostly marine, but in freshwaters there are some unicellular and small filamentous species. The green

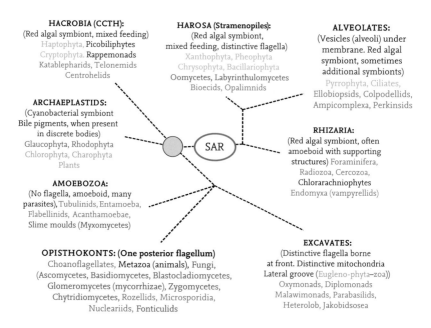

HACROBIA (CCTH):
(Red algal symbiont, mixed feeding)
Haptophyta, Picobiliphytes
Cryptophyta. Rappemonads
Katablepharids, Telonemids
Centrohelids

HAROSA (Stramenopiles):
(Red algal symbiont,
mixed feeding, distinctive flagella)
Xanthophyta, Pheophyta
Chrysophyta, Bacillariophyta
Oomycetes, Labyrinthulomycetes
Bioecids, Opalimnids

ALVEOLATES:
(Vesicles (alveoli) under
membrane. Red algal
symbiont, sometimes
additional symbionts)
Pyrrophyta, Ciliates,
Ellobiopsids, Colpodellids,
Ampicomplexa, Perkinsids

ARCHAEPLASTIDS:
(Cyanobacterial symbiont
Bile pigments, when present
in discrete bodies)
Glaucophyta, Rhodophyta
Chlorophyta, Charophyta
Plants

SAR

RHIZARIA:
(Red algal symbiont, often
amoeboid with supporting
structures) Foraminifera,
Radiozoa, Cercozoa,
Chlorarachniophytes
Endomyxa (vampyrellids)

AMOEBOZOA:
(No flagella, amoeboid, many
parasites), Tubulinids, Entamoeba,
Flabellinids, Acanthamoebae,
Slime moulds (Myxomycetes)

OPISTHOKONTS: (One posterior flagellum)
Choanoflagellates, Metazoa (animals), Fungi,
(Ascomycetes, Basidiomycetes, Blastocladiomycetes,
Glomeromycetes (mycorrhizae), Zygomycetes,
Chytridiomycetes, Rozellids, Microsporidia,
Nucleariids, Fonticulids

EXCAVATES:
(Distinctive flagella borne
at front. Distinctive mitochondria
Lateral groove (Eugleno-phyta–zoa))
Oxymonads, Diplomonads
Malawimonads, Parabasilids,
Heterolob, Jakobidsosea

FIG 46. A current view of the arrangement of eukaryote organisms in kingdoms (capital letters). The SAR (Stramenopile-Alveolate-Rhizarian) group is currently thought to comprise three distinct kingdoms, not one. Colour of lettering indicates former groups of some of the organisms. Grey: protozoa; purple: Fungi; green: green algae and plants; blue, a group with intact and largely unmodified cyanobacterial symbionts; red: red algae; orange: groups of algae with chlorophyll *a* and *c* but a preponderance of orange and yellow pigments. These groups can be located in Figure 45.

algae (Fig. 47) comprise two clades, one of which is well represented in the ocean, and to a lesser extent in lakes, by small flagellates, the prasinophytes, with usually single scaly flagella and walls. The prasinophytes evolved to the many chlorophyte green algae both of the sea and freshwaters, with two smooth flagella (sometimes only in reproductive cells) and cellulose walls, on the one hand, and a line which gave rise to the desmids, charophytes and plants, on the other.

The latter split occurred between 700 and 1,500 million years ago and is distinguished by the ways in which walls form when the cells divide.[11] The desmid/charophyte/plant line, when it has retained them (in the gametes of charophytes, mosses and ferns) has scaly flagella. The desmids have lost their

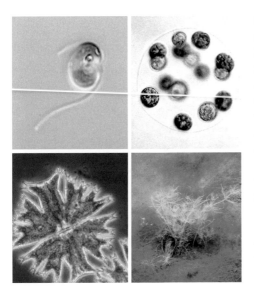

FIG 47. Green algae, now included as members of the Archaeplastida. Upper left is *Nephroselmis* (about 8 μm long) in the Prasinophyceae, thought to be ancestral to the other green algae and much more common in the ocean than in freshwaters. Upper right is *Eudorina*, a mainline green alga, about 40 μm in diameter, with a colony of 16 cells, each with two flagella that are not visible in this photograph. Lower left is a desmid, *Micrasterias*, nearly 80 μm across, and lower right is *Chara*, which is macroscopic (up to 50 cm high) with a distinctive structure of whorled branches emerging along a main 'stem' of a few, very long, single cells.

flagella but have a distinct cell structure typically with two halves separated by a constriction and are particularly associated, in their greatest diversity, with waters of low alkalinity. They were great favourites of the West family of early limnologists (Chapter 1).

The charophytes are visible to the eye, with a distinctive structure of a main axis composed of single, very large cells separated at nodes with plates of cells from which a whorl of similarly structured branches arises. Many are called stoneworts for they deposit lime (marl) on their surfaces, which gives a rough feel. Stoneworts have become increasingly rare in Britain and Ireland because they require very clear water, which is becoming scarce, as well as a large supply of calcium, which is associated with areas that are heavily cultivated and hence subject to eutrophication.

Plants dominate the land, of course, but there is a huge array of water plants, mostly in freshwaters. They are not primitive plants that evolved in water and never emerged, but are secondarily evolved from land plants that recolonised water, and retain many features of their land ancestry. These include vestigial stomata in their epidermis, and aerial flowers, pollinated by wind and insects. Our current water flora is very recent, dating back at most 100 million years and in many cases much less, reflecting the ephemerality of freshwater basins (Chapter 4). Their natural disruptiveness has meant that there has been continual extinction and new evolution of freshwater organisms, so there is a marked contrast between

FIG 48. Chytrids, microscopic fungi that infect other eukaryotes by extending hyphae into the cells and later produce round bodies in which spores are produced for dispersal and reproduction. This species is infecting *Eudorina*, a healthy colony of which is shown in Figure 47.

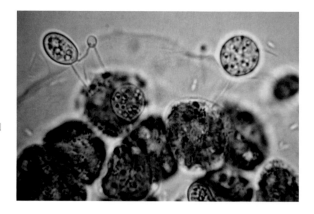

the freshwater microorganisms, which really are for the most part 'ancient' and the larger eukaryotes, the plants and animals, which are very modern indeed.

The Opisthokonta also holds together well as a group, based on the similarities of its genomes. Its common structural feature is that the flagella, where present, are held at the rear of the cells, not at the front as in other supergroups; the name is derived from the Greek for 'rear' and 'pole'; you might have seen films of moving spermatozoa which illustrate this well. The big surprise is that this supergroup includes the animals and the fungi, as well as the choanoflagellates or collared flagellates that are thought to be ancestral to the animals, and a number of parasites of uncertain origin. Animals will be dealt with in some detail in the next chapter. The organisms that traditionally comprised the fungi included many organisms (such as some of the moulds like potato

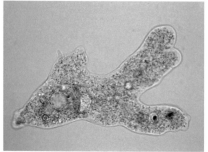
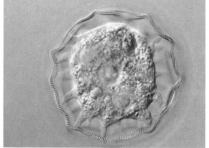

FIG 49. Amoebozoa. A free-living *Amoeba* (left), around 80 μm long. A testate species (right), which secretes a shell of silica or organic matter that can be seen surrounding it in this view from underneath.

blight that infect plants) that are now placed in other supergroups than the Opisthokonta, which retains the mushrooms and toadstools, the bread moulds and the yeasts. These are not particularly important in freshwaters, though some fungi colonise wood that has fallen in, or may grow as yeasts on the surfaces of animals, or as parasites. One microscopic group, the chytrids (Fig. 48), however, remains with the fungi and its members are important parasites of algae and of amphibians, one of them being currently responsible for a current major plague among frog species.

Two of the Opisthokont phyla used to be classified as slime moulds and are amoeboid, meaning that their cells are able to flow around and engulf particles, but the bulk of the amoeboid eukaryotes now falls into a completely separate supergroup, the Amoebozoa, some of the members of which also have flagella, though attached at the front rather than the rear. There are many phyla of Amoebozoa (Fig. 49), both free-living (the Thecamoebae and Acanthamoebae, for example) and as parasites (for example, the Flabellinida, some of which infect salmon) and they are common in lakes. Many are able to survive in anaerobic muds and it is thought (by some, but not all) that the Amoebozoa may be closely allied to the Opisthokonts.

The fourth supergroup, the Excavatae (Fig. 50), again defined by its genomes, has cells usually with a longitudinal groove (an excavation) along the side of the cell. The cells have a particular twisted flagellum with a single line of fine hairs emerging along its length, and many species grow, with reduced mitochondria, in anaerobic places. One group, the Euglenoids, is common in freshwaters,

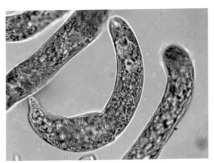

FIG 50. *Euglena* (left), with its helical organisation, red eyespot and gullet, from which two flagella (not visible) emerge, is perhaps the best-known free-living genus of the Excavatae. This cell is about 50 μm long and comes from the scum shown (right) in a farmyard puddle polluted with cattle urine and faeces. Euglenoids can only absorb ammonium as a nitrogen source, and not nitrate. Ammonium is particularly rich in such puddles.

particularly smelly, organically polluted and deoxygenated ones, like farm ditches, with some members having a secondary green algal chloroplast as an endosymbiont. Others are gut parasites (parasites must often survive in low-oxygen conditions) including the well-known *Giardia* (well known, that is, to those who have drunk faecally contaminated freshwaters and suffered the unpleasant diarrhoeic and other consequences). The trypanosomes, which cause various diseases, including African sleeping sickness, are also placed in this supergroup.

The final two supergroups are those in which there has been a secondary endosymbiosis with an entire red algal cell. In many cases the red photosynthetic pigments have been lost but various membrane structures and many red algal genes remain. It is even possible that there had been an earlier symbiosis with a green alga also because there are remnants of green algal genes in the nuclear DNA. Quite recently these supergroups were seen as just one, the Chromalveolates, but opinion is now that there are two, the CCTH (standing for Cryptomonads–Centrohelids–Telonemids–Haptophytes) or Hacrobia, and the SAR (Stramenopiles–Alveolates–Rhizaria) or Harosa. The flux in opinions reflects the considerable confusion that our abilities to sequence genes have wrought when combining this information with structural characteristics.

Both supergroups have some organisms in which the original red algal endosymbiont is manifest by the continued possession of red pigments, and a completely new phylum, the Picobiliphytes, with tiny cells in freshwater plankton, has just been discovered through its gene sequences. Within the CCTH (Fig. 51) are the former algal groups of the cryptophytes, with fine ejectile hairs of

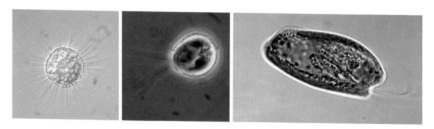

FIG 51. Hacrobia include organisms superficially very different but with enough fundamental common features to group them together, at least for the present. Shown here are a centrohelid, *Acanthocystis* (left), which has sticky, spiny organelles used to catch bacteria; a haptophytan (centre), the coccolithophorid, *Hymenomonas*, covered with calcareous scales; and the photosynthetic *Cryptomonas* (right), which bears structures along a groove that can release sticky threads – their function might be defence or the catching of bacteria. (Society for Microbiology/ Y. Tsuki/Japanese National Institute for Environmental Science)

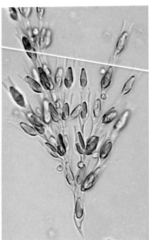

FIG 52. The SAR supergroup includes diatoms (*Asterionella* (top left) with silica-walled cells, 80 µm long), chrysophytes (right, *Dinobryon*, an organism whose cells, each 10 µm long), live in thin silica vases and engulf bacteria as well as photosynthesising, and water moulds, formerly classed as fungi. *Saprolegnia* is here shown (bottom, left) heavily colonising a dead fish.

unknown function on their surfaces, and the haptophytes. These have an unusual organelle, the haptonema, by which some adhere to surfaces, and scaly coverings, sometimes of calcium carbonate (in the coccolithophorids), and abilities in some genera to produce powerful fish toxins.

The SAR group has three main lines. The first is the stramenopiles (Fig. 52), which are the former algae that contain chlorophyll *c*, or rather a modification called chlorophyllide *c* (diatoms, chrysophytes, xanthophytes – the latter two previously informally called the golden or yellow algae – and the brown seaweeds) and structural evidence of a red algal symbiont, but now no red pigments. The stramenopiles also include non-pigmented organisms formerly thought of as fungi or protozoa, including the Oomycetes, Bisoecids and Labyrinthulids, many of which are parasites. Members of the second line, the rhizarians, were formerly included in the protozoa and include amoeboid forms, not least the Radiozoa, with their silica skeleton and fine pseudopodia, and the Foraminiferids, which are extremely important in the ocean and form calcareous tests, or outer frameworks beyond their cell membranes. There is also one group, the Chloroarachniophytes, whose members have recently acquired a tertiary green algal symbiont on top of the former red algal one, and another, the Endomyxa or vampyrellids, that are sucking parasites on other unicellular organisms. Finally, the Alveolates (Fig. 53), distinguished by vesicles or alveoli just under the cell membrane, are otherwise a complete enigma for they include the dinoflagellates, with a variety of tertiary endosymbionts and three rather than four membranes around the chromatophore, the Apicomplexa, which include *Plasmodium*, the malaria parasite,

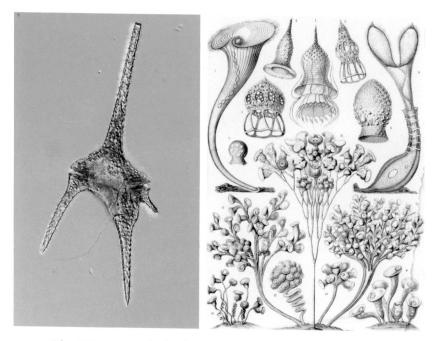

FIG 53. Other SAR groups are the dinoflagellates and the ciliates. *Ceratium* (left) is a large (250 µm) photosynthetic dinoflagellate. The characteristic groove, in which one of the two flagella moves, can be seen, with the second flagellum trailing downwards. Photograph by Holier Adellman. On the right is a page from Ernst Haeckel's' classic *Kunstformen der Natur*, published in 1904, showing a variety of ciliates. Top left is the very large *Stentor*, just visible to the naked eye, and top right a *Folliculina* species. Between them are tintinnid ciliates that produce shells. Centre and bottom are colonial ciliates, including *Epistylis*, *Vorticella*, *Carchesium* and *Zoothamnium*, in which movement of the many cilia brings a current of fine particles to the cell surface and directs them into a feeding groove.

and, not least, the huge group of ciliates, with their many short cilia whose structure is the same as the longer flagella of other eukaryotes. The ciliates used, with the amoebas and colourless flagellates, to be central groups in the Protozoa and are very common and diverse in freshwaters as well as the ocean.

Matters have become complicated, but reflect the fact that understanding of the evolutionary pathways of living organisms that developed early in the Earth's history is still very incomplete. We do not really know how these supergroups are related to one another through common ancestors, or even whether the still limited genetic information is misleading us into setting up largely fictional systems. The sequencing of more and more genomes, a popular occupation now in research laboratories, may well clarify the situation, or make it even more enigmatic. We are a long way from the naivety of the 1950s, but still far from a final solution to the problems of how eukaryotic cells evolved, the pathways taken, and, especially, the reasons why. In truth we may never be able to reconstruct the evolution of microorganisms to the same extent that we can of multicellular organisms, for the latter have left abundant fossils and their genomes are more recent and less altered.

What we can do, however, is to take a general view, and place the enormous diversity of both prokaryotic and eukaryotic microorganisms into some sort of story that explains how the evolutionary drama has been played out. In the remainder of this chapter, I will suggest how the first 4 billion years of Earth's history, when microorganisms solely dominated, is reflected in existing lakes through the communities and activities of their microorganisms. Only in the past half a billion years have multicellular organisms, really just minor components of the Archaeplantae, and Opisthokontae, come into starring roles in the evolutionary play, whilst the operation of the ecological theatre has been and continues to be largely in the hands of the backstage microorganisms.

LAKES AND A MICROBIAL HISTORY OF THE WORLD: THE EARLY ANAEROBIC DAYS

About 3.3 billion of Earth's 4.5-billion-year history had a biosphere solely of microorganisms. For most of the first 0.7 billion years, the Hadean, the planet was too hot for much water to have condensed and for life in its present complex form to have existed at all. During the latter part, however, we believe that simple chemical blobs were becoming more complex and able to reproduce themselves in similar forms using some simple genetic system. Natural selection filtered the most efficient of these and gradually the first Eubacteria and Archaea became recognisable, though it is unlikely that we will ever know exactly what preceded these.

It was a world at first free of molecular oxygen. The ocean waters were hot and less salty than at present, for it took time for salts to accumulate from the land and so the earliest ocean was a huge freshwater lake. Archaeans occur everywhere now but it is likely that the earliest were organisms of extreme habitats, capable of tolerating hot, deoxygenated water. Such organisms must use chemical reactions to obtain energy and to construct carbon compounds. Some can break

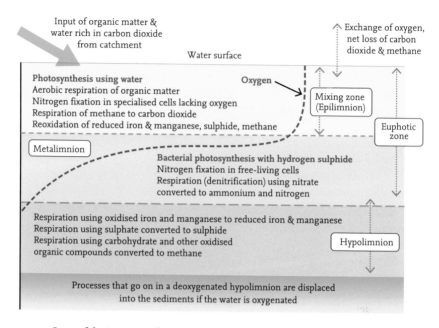

FIG 54. Some of the important chemical processes carried out by microorganisms in different parts of a lake.

down organic matter, but the supply was at first scarce and likely generated by the action of ultraviolet radiation or lightning sparks on a chemically very reactive wet atmosphere. Eubacteria have similar capabilities so that in a largely inorganic, deoxygenated world, with just a modicum of organic matter formed by physical processes, it was possible for living organisms to persist, beginning the development of a great diversity in the processes of obtaining energy.

The descendents of these early cells still maintain this diversity in the sediments of lakes and in the waters of deoxygenated hypolimnia (Fig. 54). Sediments are deoxygenated below the surface, simply because aerobic bacteria consume the available oxygen when they decompose organic matter that has fallen into the sediment, and even if there is dissolved oxygen in the overlying water, it cannot diffuse into the sediments rapidly enough to keep the supply replenished. Chains of different species ferment complex organic compounds to simpler end products like the fatty acids, lactate, propionate, succinate and acetate, or sometimes alcohol; others achieve a more complete oxidation using nitrate, oxidised iron and manganese or sulphate to do the job, reducing the iron and manganese, producing nitrite, ammonia and nitrogen gas or sulphide in the process. Methane is produced in the sediments by Archaea that reduce organic compounds for their energy content, and are very abundant and major food sources of some of the animals that live in the sediment surfaces. Such animals would not have been present 2.5 to 3.8 billion years ago, when these processes dominated the biosphere, but otherwise such deoxygenated habitats directly reflect that early phase.

BACTERIAL PHOTOSYNTHESIS

The supply of organic matter created by physical processes was not great on the early Earth and a major step was taken by those bacteria, apparently all of them Eubacteria, that were able to harness light energy (which was very abundant) from the sun and create the earliest photosynthesis. Photosynthesis does not only need

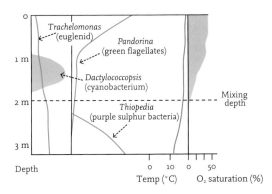

FIG 55. Abbots Pool in Somerset is sheltered by trees that reduce wind mixing enough to allow stratification in summer. In turn this results in a layering of photosynthetic organisms in the water column. *Thiopedia* is a purple sulphur bacterium occupying the deoxygenated layers. *Pandorina* is a green alga attracted to the greater light intensities towards the surface; *Dactylococcopsis* is a cyanobacterium that uses gas vesicles to maintain itself in the middle of the water column and *Trachelomonas* is a photosynthetic euglenid that migrates up and down, obtaining, from the deoxygenated water, ammonium and dissolved iron, which it needs to form its iron-rich theca, an external wall that envelops the cells. (Photo – Heather Cowper; data from Moss, 1969)

light; it requires also a source of hydrogen to reduce carbon dioxide to organic matter and thus store the light energy as chemical energy. The first hydrogen sources to have been used were hydrogen itself, which is released from volcanoes, and hydrogen sulphide, also directly belched out or formed from sulphate by bacteria using it to oxidise organic matter.

There are still photosynthetic bacteria that use hydrogen sulphide and other reduced sulphur compounds such as thiosulphate (Fig. 54). They are found in lakes where there is a simultaneous occurrence of low oxygen conditions and some light, which means usually layers of water towards the top of the hypolimnion. I discovered one such instance in a pond near Bristol (Fig. 55). The pond was very shallow, so that light penetrated nearly to the bottom, but also stratified because it was surrounded by dense woodland and so wind mixing was not vigorous. The bottom layers of water became deoxygenated and the water was coloured purple by a photosynthetic sulphur bacterium, *Thiopedia* sp., which uses reduced sulphur compounds. There were probably more small lakes like this, with deep bacterial photosynthetic layers, until eutrophication increased algal growths in the surface water and reduced the light available at depth. But where they persist, these deep photosynthetic bacteria are the descendents of communities that dominated the oceans around 3 billion years ago.

CYANOBACTERIAL REVOLUTION AND THE RELEASE OF OXYGEN

Three billion years ago, hydrogen and hydrogen sulphide remained relatively scarce because their supply depended on volcanic eruption, so that when bacteria evolved the ability to use the superabundant water as a reductant for photosynthesis, a very significant step was taken. Enormous amounts more energy could be brought into the living systems and the total mass of living organisms must have burgeoned. This was around 2.5 billion years ago and the descendants of the Cyanobacteria (Fig. 42), for it is they who developed this ability, are still very abundant. They can be found in every lake and river, from the poles to the Equator, at least in small numbers, and sometimes to the near exclusion of other photosynthesisers. Their pigments differ from the pigments of the anaerobic photosynthesisers, though some are related.

Among the bacteria, Cyanobacteria are unusual in the range of size and form of their cells and colonies. One distinctive group has two sorts of cells in its filaments; the heterocysts, being larger and rounder than the other cells, look like buckles in a belt (Fig. 35). Heterocysts (in which nitrogen gas can be fixed to combined forms ultimately in amino acids) are unique to Cyanobacteria, so the finding of fossils of such filaments in ancient rocks suggests that the Cyanobacteria have changed little in form in over 2 billion years. In British and Irish lakes you will find Cyanobacteria in the plankton and littoral, as single cells, filaments, colonies visible to the eye, like flecks of paint in the water, and as gelatinous lumps on the bottom. Some of the planktonic forms have inclusions called gas vesicles, which are made of protein, contain air and give positive buoyancy, sometimes to bring the cells or colonies that have them to the surface as scum-like water blooms. Some blooms are notorious for their occasional high toxicity to animals drinking the water (and humans too, were they foolish enough to imbibe). The northwest Midland meres have a long tradition of Cyanobacterial blooms, but recent eutrophication of lakes everywhere has made them very much more widespread.[12]

Evolution of water-using photosynthesis did more than bring an abundance of energy. It also produced free molecular oxygen as a by-product of the removal of hydrogen for the reduction of carbon dioxide. Oxygen, and in particular some of its molecular states created by irradiation by ultraviolet light, is very toxic. As a powerful oxidising agent, it can destroy the proteins that form cells and catalyse reactions within them, especially those that had evolved under a billion years of a deoxygenated early Earth. The Cyanobacteria can also use hydrogen sulphide in photosynthesis (they must have evolved from photosynthetic bacteria that depended on this) and were favoured by a situation in which the small amounts of oxygen that they at first produced were mopped up by chemical reactions. But over several hundred million years the oxygen concentrations in the waters and atmosphere built up to levels, perhaps only around 1 per cent of current concentrations (Fig. 56), where they posed threats to their fellow anaerobic Archaea and bacteria.

DEATH AND DELIVERANCE FROM OXYGEN

By various means, some of these anaerobes evolved devices to aborb small amounts of oxygen, but many could only persist in habitats that, for one reason or another, remained anaerobic. Such are the seeps of springs, lake sediments, deoxygenated hypolimnia and the saline layers that sometimes underlie inland seas and are isolated from the atmosphere, where we still find them. For others there was perhaps a new means of escape, through the endosymbioses that gave rise to mitochondria, where the more sensitive proteins could be protected deep inside the host cells. The eukaryote cell began to emerge as oxygen concentrations, around 1.5 billion years ago, following a billion years of Cyanobacterial world dominance, became persistent and substantial.

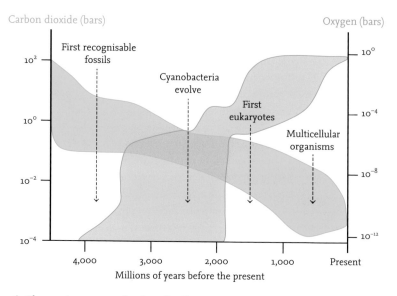

FIG 56. Changes in oxygen and carbon dioxide concentrations in the Earth's atmosphere from its origin to the present. The envelopes indicate the variation calculated from different geological models, but the trends are clear. Major events in evolution are also shown. A bar is the unit of atmospheric pressure. Current total pressure is close to 1 (or 10^0 on the logarithmic scale used) bar. Based on Mojzsis, 2001.

Mitochondria contain the particularly sensitive enzymes responsible for releasing energy from organic matter like sugars. They use oxygen but in a controlled way that might not be possible if they were exposed to the large concentrations building up in the water. The incorporation of Eubacteria as mitochondria may have developed as a response to progressive oxygenation. There are some anaerobic eukaryotes, but they are not primitive descendents from an anaerobic age. They are the highly and recently evolved specialists that have become parasites, or live in animal guts and they all contain structures that are reduced mitochondria and retain mitochondrial genes.

All eukaryotes have fundamentally similar mitochondria, suggesting that this was an early common feature that developed only once, and this is inconsistent with the idea of a disordered and 'panic' response to increasing oxygenation. It is possible therefore that the mitochondrion originated from a bacterium that had already evolved oxygen tolerance, in which case the advantage of the eukaryote cell might lie more in its ability, through the chromosomes in their protective nucleus, to store much more genetic information. However, the vast range of forms, and the mixed feeding modes of many single-celled eukaryotes do suggest a period of experimental response to the rise of poisonous oxygen, in which, once the endosymbiont had been incorporated, a variety of hosts adopted this new institution. There were many ports in the storm. But we still have little inkling as to why so many structures have persisted; each must have particular advantages in particular places, or natural selection would have whittled the range down, and the slightly later acquisition of a cyanobacterium as a chromatophore for photosynthesis added more scope.

The possibilities of endosymbioses must have been greatest where prokaryotic cells accumulated, through gravity, on surfaces like rocks and sediments, and the range of eukaryotic microorganisms is still greater there than in the more rarefied waters that support the plankton. There was a greater food supply, in the form of bacteria, for those that engulfed other cells by phagocytosis, and greater concentrations of substances released by decomposition that supplied the absorbers. Mud is a rich medium but even the surfaces of rocks acquire a film of bacteria, and mucus secreted by them, which is colonised by other organisms that then form an active layer. The primeval soup in which life is said to have begun, the open water, was very thin. The important events much more likely took place on the sediments at the bottom: not a soup but a primeval Sandwich Spread.

There was a problem, though, for the photosynthesisers if they originated on the bottom. The deeper you go in a body of water, the less light there is and bottoms, even if lit, are murky with a light quality that is greenish or yellowish (Chapter 2), and not the red or blue that is most efficiently absorbed by chlorophyll. One solution to this problem is to develop a range of pigments that can absorb light at different wavelengths; another is to develop ways of becoming suspended towards the surface in better-illuminated conditions. To some extent the Cyanobacteria, which evolved from photosynthetic bacteria with green and purple pigments, might have exploited these strategies early in their existence. They have bile pigments that are red and blue, as well as orange and yellow carotenoids and green chlorophyll and it seems most unlikely that, over a billion years, they would not have managed to become planktonic as well as bottom-living. It may just be that the new eukaryote photosynthesisers adopted ways piloted by the Cyanobacteria.

THE VARIETY OF ALGAE

The microscopic Archaeplantae, the glaucophytes, red (Fig. 57) and green algae (Fig. 47) inherited this set of Cyanobacterial pigments. The green algae lost the bile pigments, possibly losing some efficiency in absorption of yellowish light, but acquired chlorophyll *b* from a modification of chlorophyll *a*. Perhaps it was this

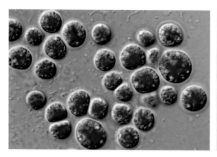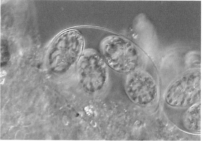

FIG 57. Early Archaeplantae: unicellular freshwater red alga, *Porphyridium* (left); a glaucophyte (right), *Glaucocystis*, in which the chromatophores are essentially intact cyanobacteria (photo by Ishikawa Kanazawa). Cells of both are about 20 μm across. Red algae were probably among the earliest archaeplantids because their chromatophores are among the least altered from cyanobacteria, with, for example, red and blue bile pigments contained in phycobilisomes that are almost indistinguishable from those of cyanobacteria.

modification that left the red algae to proliferate on the sea bed at the margins of the oceans, and stimulated the green algae to exploit the open water as the earliest eukaryote plankton, in the form of a group, the prasinophytes, that is still abundant in the oceans, but not so much in freshwaters. Green algal groups derived from prasinophytes have come to occupy both bottom and planktonic niches in freshwaters. Glaucophytes, with chloroplasts closest to their cyanobacterial forebears, are relatively uncommon and mostly associated with the bottom. What is then interesting is that the remaining prominent algal groups, the stramenopiles, including the dinoflagellates, diatoms, haptophytes and yellow algae did not evolve (judging from the fossil evidence) until 260–190 million years ago, long after the appearance of the first green and red algae at least a billion years ago.

A LONG WAIT FOR THE REST OF THE ALGAE

These stramenopile groups are all secondary endosymbionts, with a former eukaryotic cell having engulfed an entire red algal cell, at least. Oddly there are no planktonic red algae, but diatoms, dinoflagellates and haptophytes, all with red algal endosymbionts, are the most prominent planktonic groups of the oceans and major players also in freshwaters.[13] There are few clues but much speculation as to why these groups evolved at all. They must have some advantages over the green algae, though not such strong ones as to have displaced the latter completely. Many of them have walls that are not of organic compounds (though the brown seaweeds, which are closely related, do have organic walls); they have scales, solid walls or frameworks of silica or calcite (calcium carbonate) and, unlike many (though not all) of the Archaeplantae, some can only use molecular carbon dioxide for photosynthesis as opposed to the alternative of bicarbonate ions. Some are extremely efficient at taking up carbon dioxide from very low concentrations. Obtaining enough carbon might thus be a problem for them, but one whose solution they have found.

The Permian to Jurassic periods, when the stramenopile fossils start to appear in the sedimentary rocks, was one of relatively low carbon dioxide concentrations in the atmosphere. There had been a drop since the Precambrian and the Cambrian periods (Fig. 56), apparently as carbon dioxide was sucked from the atmosphere by rock weathering following the invasion of the land, at first by lichens and then by the development of mosses and liverworts, lycopods and ferns. The forests of the previous Carboniferous and Permian had stored a great deal of the carbon as peat and lignite, deposits that eventually were compressed to coal. Oxygen levels had in turn also risen and there is evidence of great forest fires associated with the major extinctions that took place at the end of the Permian.

It is understandable (just) that the new endosymbioses could have had advantages under such conditions; the silica and calcium carbonate walls of the diatoms and coccolithophorids might give some advantages under carbon scarcity, though carbon dioxide concentrations were at least as high as at present and rose five times higher by the time the diatoms completed their evolution. The stramenopiles are at least as varied on the illuminated bottoms of lakes as they are in the plankton and so the abundance of the carotenoid pigments they acquired, in addition to a second chlorophyll, chlorophyllide c, and residual red pigments in some groups, may not have given them any particular advantage over the pigment systems of the Archaeplantae. Their yellow, orange and brown, even golden colours, are however very prominent and this must mean something. They also have a distinctive flagellum, with the basic structure of other eukaryotes, but with complex hairs emerging along the length. What advantages this might convey are as obscure as the reasons for the emergence of the group at all. Natural selection is ruthless in eliminating the less fit, but tolerates the equally fit among newcomers. The stramenopiles may simply be equally fit as the Archaeplantae.

As a result, any lake examined at present will have representatives of most of the photosynthetic eukaryotes, with cyanobacteria, green algae, cryptophytes diatoms, chrysophytes and dinoflagellates the major players, and glaucophytes, haptophytes, unicellular red algae and the secondarily endosymbiont euglenoids in lesser roles. Additionally there will be a great diversity within each group, with at least a thousand, perhaps many more, identifiable 'algae' in a habitat that might seem, at first sight, a relatively unstructured one.

THE PROTOZOA AND FUNGI

What of the non-photosynthetic, microbial eukaryotes, the former protozoa, split now among almost every supergroup (but still, like algae, a useful word) and the aquatic fungi placed in the present opisthokonts? They too are varied, though their lack of a rigid wall has precluded much fossilisation and therefore added more mystery to the details of their evolution. The protozoa had options to feed on dissolved organic substances or to engulf organic particles (and to mix these modes). They could acquire symbiont algae, which provide an energy source, just as the stramenopiles did, though usually, among the former protozoa, the symbionts are green algal cells that have not become fully integrated by transfer of genes to the nucleus of the host. Or they could become parasites on the larger animals we will review in the next chapter.

There are many small saprotrophic fungi (Fig. 58) in freshwaters; one entire group, the hyphomycetes, commonest in streams, colonises dead leaves and twigs that have fallen in, and eventually forms the major food supply of stream invertebrates that shred the leaves and wood to seek out the protein-rich fungal mycelia; other fungi are parasites even on microalgae.

The life forms of the flagellates, amoebas and ciliates, the former three groups of the protozoa, are still convenient for looking at their natural history. The flagellates tend to be small and are often now referred to as the heterotrophic nanoflagellates. They hang around lumps of organic debris, feeding on dissolved organic matter and engulfing bacteria. Amoebas, with their flowing plasma that engulfs food particles, move slowly and sometimes have thecae, mineral coverings into which they can retreat, whilst ciliates are often highly motile and covered

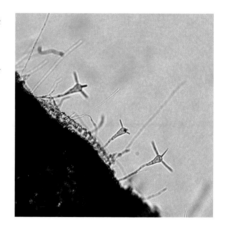

FIG 58. Fungi (in the modern classification) other than chytrids are of minor importance in freshwaters, except for the hyphomycetes, which colonise dead wood, and leaves that have fallen into the water. Hyphomycetes permeate this material with hyphae then produce spores such as these of *Clavariopsis* (photo by Kaisotyo) that are hooked or anchor-like and well adapted for latching onto new leaf material in moving water. The spores are less than 10 μm long.

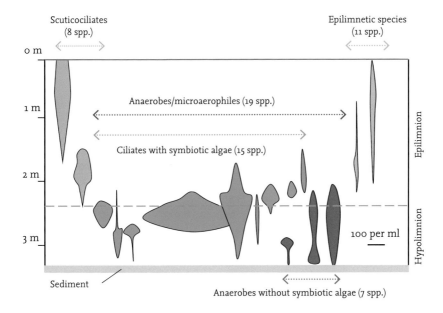

FIG 59. Ciliates are very diverse in Priest Pot. Location in the water column and relative abundance are shown here for a selection of species in relation to the position of the thermocline and deoxygenated hypolimnion on one day in August 1995. Many of the species that tolerate deoxygenation have oxygen-producing symbiotic algae, or chloroplasts extruded from their prey. The scuticociliates are free-living species. Better-known scuticociliates are parasites of fish.

with fine cilia, sometimes aggregated into cirri, like small rigid legs that lever the cells along even faster. Ciliates have a highly organised feeding groove and may sometimes attach by their base or a stalk to surfaces underwater and wait for their bacterial or algal prey.

Few habitats have been thoroughly investigated for their protozoons. One exception is Priest Pot in the English Lake District, where a yet incomplete list has revealed 644 microscopic eukaryotes among 82 viruses, 94 prokaryotes and only 59 multicellular species of plants and animals.[14] The distribution of the protozoa is not random (Fig. 59) but how so many species find individual niches is still obscure. Some of the protozoons are aerobic and live in the surface waters; others are to varying degrees tolerant of lower oxygen concentrations and are layered in the water column. They feed on photosynthetic bacteria around the metalimnion or on chemosynthetic bacteria below it. Some are sediment dwellers and again must tolerate anaerobic conditions, using fermentation as their only means of digesting the bacteria that they have eaten. Many ciliates in Priest Pot have acquired green algal symbionts and the oxygen these release within the cell allows occupation of otherwise oxygen-depleted layers.

The detailed natural history of protozoons is largely unexplored. There are long thin ciliates, clearly fitted to slipping through the narrow channels of interstitial water among the particles of sediments, and the thecae-bearing amoebae are often associated with habitats like bog pools that might dry up, prompting the cell to withdraw into its theca to avoid desiccation. Ciliates may avoid competition by feeding on different sized food particles. *Cyclidium*, for example, has a row of closely spaced (0.25 μm) cilia along its feeding groove that will remove the smallest bacteria, around 0.3 μm, whilst the hypotrich ciliates have cilia bunched into membranelles that will only trap large bacteria, 1–2 μm in size. *Euplotes* specialises on small eukaryotes 4–5 μm in width through more widely spaced membranelles. Some ciliates have endosymbiotic Archaea, and mitochondria with few cristae, called hydrogenosomes, which produce hydrogen from organic matter. They ultimately produce methane from anaerobic feeding on bacteria. Living in anaerobic conditions has its disadvantages but also advantages in avoiding being eaten by multicellular animals that are excluded from such conditions. Symbiotic bacteria in some *Paramecium* species are highly toxic and also may deter predators. Reconstructions of microbial communities reveal as much complexity as is visible to the naked eye in land ecosystems (Fig. 60).

FIG 60. On sediments is a complex community of bacteria (the small white bodies), cyanobacteria (the long filaments) and diatoms (the boat-shaped and S-shaped cells), with ciliates (top left and centre) and nematode worms (one is emerging from among the sand particles at the bottom right). (Drawing by Tom Fenchel)

300 μ

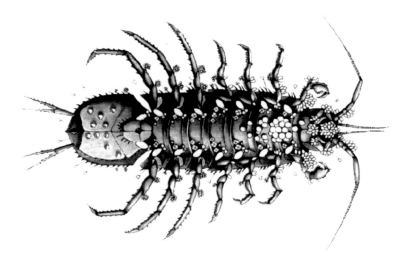

FIG 61. *Asellus aquaticus*, the water hog louse (about 1 cm long), like most animals, bears a community of microorganisms and small invertebrates on its body. They include ciliates and rotifers of at least 22 species. Additionally there are bacteria, which are not are not shown on this drawing of the underside of *Asellus* by Jane Cook. See Cook *et al.* (1998) for more details.

The microorganisms so far recorded in Priest Pot are largely free living but yet unidentified are the protozoon and bacterial parasites of the free-living organisms. These may be very diverse. It is a mistake to think of parasites as a small group that is curious and unimportant. Every free-living organism has at least one parasite, often many, and sometimes there are parasites of parasites. Overall there must be many more parasites than free-living organisms; they influence the host's performance, its population density, its competitiveness for food and space. Examine an invertebrate in freshwater and you will see that it is studded with colonies of bacteria and yeasts, ciliates and amoebae (Fig. 61). And inside its body is a variety of bacteria and single-celled eukaryote parasites.

BIOGEOGRAPHY OF MICROORGANISMS

There are some interesting questions that come from even a listing of the eukaryotic microorganisms in a lake like Priest Pot. If you plot the number of species of particular groups within the lake as a proportion of the total number

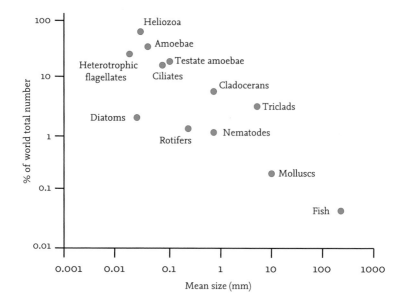

FIG 62. Microorganisms are easily dispersed, multicellular ones less readily. This graph shows the percentage of the total number of known species of various groups that have been recorded from a single lake, Priest Pot in Cumbria. There is an inverse relationship between this percentage and the mean size of organisms in the group. Both scales are logarithmic. Based on Fenchel & Finlay (2004).

of that group in the world, against the mean size of the organisms in each group, a graph like Figure 62 is obtained. For the microorganisms, the lake contains a majority of the total species known, but for bigger organisms the proportion represented within the lake becomes much smaller. Some time ago it was suggested, because microorganisms are so small and there are so many individuals, that they are readily distributed by wind, river flow and floods, droplets of spray, and on the surfaces or in the guts of animals.[15] Thus the distribution of microorganisms is not geographically constrained. Everything is potentially everywhere and local conditions then favour what will grow and survive, but generally speaking a high proportion of such groups will do so. Larger organisms are not so easily moved around. Think of the constraints on a fish, for example. So evolution has produced very different assemblages of the larger organisms in different places, with species often endemic or highly restricted to particular localities. Figure 62 suggests that, as far as the microorganisms are concerned, one lake will be much the same in its microbial community as the next, but lakes in different regions may have quite different assemblages of plants, invertebrates or vertebrates.

However, the microbial species are, like the bigger ones, described from their structures, which, for microbial prokaryotes, are similar wherever you look. They seem to have a less spectacular diversity than trees or dragonflies, birds or mammals. They are now referred to as morphospecies. But all organisms have characteristics that are hidden from simple view. They have different genetic potentialities that govern survival or growth rate, reproductive potential, movement, or production of chemical defences against predators. It is often easy to demonstrate differences in physiology in different cultures of the same morphospecies and usual to demonstrate genetic differences. An opposed school of thought maintains that everything is not everywhere; it only appears so if you simply take its appearance into account. Passions run high on both sides, but the travel costs of twitching for microbiologists are yet much lower than for birdwatchers.

In passing upwards in a lake from the bottom sediments and lowermost hypolimnion, with their anaerobic bacteria and single-celled eukaryotes, through the middle water layers receiving some light and bearing photosynthetic bacteria, to the epilimnion with its oxygen-producing photosynthesisers and aerobic bacteria and protozoons, one is, in a sense, repeating in the water column an evolutionary journey of the first 3.3 billion years of life. Only during the last 500 or so million years has there been enough oxygen to support larger organisms and it took time for the microorganisms to build up the necessary oxygen levels (at least 1 per cent of current values) for these animals, plants and fungi to evolve. In general, the larger organisms are in the better-oxygenated layers towards the surface and these more prominent, but not necessarily more important *dramatis personae* in the ecological theatres of lakes are the subjects of the next chapter.

CHAPTER 4

Animals: The Names in Bright Lights

I T IS ONE THING TO set up the theatre with its staff of microorganisms and keep it working (Chapter 3). It is another to put on the play that is the outward evidence of the theatre's activity. The showier actors must first be recruited and this process started around 540 million years ago with the evolution of multicellular animals and plants. I will leave the plants to the next chapter; the multicellular plants help structure the stage and keep the show running and lend themselves best to an account of the communities in lakes that will follow. In this chapter I will introduce the invertebrates and vertebrates, the opisthokonts, because they are most popular for many people interested in our lakes.

BECOMING A FRESHWATER ANIMAL

The rising oxygen levels stimulated a huge increase in biodiversity at the start of the Cambrian Era, and this activity began in the ocean. There are about 40 major groups, or phyla, of animals. All are represented in the ocean, over 20 are entirely marine, and none is entirely terrestrial. All originated over a short period, once oxygen levels became high enough, but then there was a progressive elaboration over several hundred million years. Among the backboned animals, the Chordates, for example, the ancestral tunicates, look rather like spongy worms, but have a larva with a characteristic long structure of nerves along the length of their bodies. This became supported by cartilage and eventually bone, to develop into the first vertebrates, the fishes, around 400 million years ago. Fish invaded the land, as amphibians, only 20 million years later and then reptiles, birds and mammals evolved as the land was colonised.

The invertebrates came first and have persisted, with levels of organisation broadly as at present, throughout this period, with a major innovation when the spiders and the insects surged in diversity around 300 and 200 million years ago, again on land. The theatre companies of the ocean and the land, however, though decimated from time to time by major extinctions caused by fire and deoxygenation, meteorite impact and perhaps other causes, had a steady history in theatres that were never unchanging, but which had an element of predictability about them.

It was not quite so for the freshwater companies. The vulnerability of freshwater bodies to freezing and drought, through natural climate changes, has meant that the analogy is not so much with the National Theatre or the Royal Opera House, but with a travelling repertory company, performing where it could, in village halls and sometimes in temporary tents, sometimes disappearing entirely then re-forming. Recruitment to such companies required special talents of flexibility and adaptability; recruitment was more or less continual and drawn from the companies of the ocean and the land. In geological time, the freshwater companies were often lost and had to re-evolve.

TABLE 6. Comparative biodiversity of animal species in freshwaters compared with overall diversity on Earth.

	Freshwater	Freshwater as % of total	Total described in biosphere
Total animals	126,000	9.7	1,302,000 (Marine 349,000) (Land 827,000)
Insects	75,874	8.4	900,000
Arachnids	6,150	6.0	102,250
Molluscs	4,998	5.9	85,000
Crustaceans	11,990	16	75,000
Other invertebrates	8,753	10	87,750
Fish	12,740	40.7	31,300
Amphibia	4,294	66.7	6,433
Reptiles	510	5.6	9,084
Birds	567	5.7	9,998
Mammals	124	2.3	5,490

Some of the freshwater animals evolved directly from marine ancestors, others indirectly from land animals, and most came from a limited number of mostly the more abundant phyla. The Porifera (sponges), Cnidaria (hydras and jelly fish), Platyhelminthes (flatworms), Nemertea, Nematomorpha, Nematoda (all unsegmented worms), Gastrotricha (gastrotrichs), Rotifera (rotifers), Ectoprocta (bryozoans), Mollusca (snails and bivalves), Annelida (roundworms), Tardigrada (water bears) and Crustacea largely took the marine route, invading the rivers and lakes through the estuaries. The Chelicerata (spiders and mites), Myriapoda (centipedes) and Hexapoda (insects and collembolans) mostly came later, from land ancestors. The freshwater Chordata came both from the ocean (the fishes) and the land (amphibians, reptiles, birds and mammals). These origins can all be traced in their current physiologies, ecologies and life histories but first some numbers might be interesting.

About 10 per cent of the hitherto described animals occur in freshwaters (Table 6), a remarkably high proportion because there is nearly 50,000 times more ocean water than surface freshwater on the planet.[1] There is a particularly high representation in freshwaters of fish and amphibia and to a lesser extent of crustaceans. Fish have very similar body plans in both the oceans and freshwaters and some (particularly the salmon family and some eels) regularly migrate between the two, whilst close parallels in the Crustacea (crayfish and lobsters) and Mollusca (mussels and oysters) suggest a recent evolution of the freshwater representatives and an easy movement from salt to freshwaters.

SALT AND WATER REGULATION HAVE TO BE COPED WITH…

Colonising the environmentally capricious freshwaters was a problem for both the land and marine ancestors.[2] The ocean is quite salty, permanent and well oxygenated because of the deep ocean circulation, though ocean water holds a little less oxygen (because of its salt content) than freshwater. The large volume of the ocean steadies its temperature and rapid changes are rare; its salt concentration is not far from the concentrations inside the cells of animals. The land environment is more variable in temperature and availability of water, but very well oxygenated. Land animals have developed covers and skins that reduce water loss and help maintain salt concentrations within the body within narrow limits.

Freshwater animals, however, are bathed in a medium that is far less salty than their own cells, and live in habitats that may disappear quite rapidly through freezing or drying, and which may become quickly deoxygenated

FIG 63. In general freshwater animals are less gaudily coloured and simpler in outline form than equivalent marine animals. Shown here on the left are a freshwater hydroid (*Hydra fusca*, photograph by Jalap Costa Budde) and snail (*Bithynia tentaculata*, photograph by Michael Manas), and on the right a marine coral (photograph by Neil Sutcliffe) and the marine jewelled top snail (photograph by Rosario Beach Marine Lab).

through the bacterial decomposition of organic matter. The gaudily coloured, ecologically pampered, fussy species of the coral reefs and rain forest, which can afford to invest energy in breeding colours or warning pigments to discourage predators, have no truck here (Fig. 63). Freshwater animals survive by being tough and tolerant, and allocate their energy to survival of difficult conditions, and to camouflage. Where related animals occur in the ocean and freshwaters, the freshwater forms tend to be smaller, reflecting rapid reproduction of more, small individuals in an unpredictable environment where death rates are high, compared with fewer, larger ones with greater longevity in the ocean. Because of the flexibility and tolerance of freshwater animals, it is much easier to keep animals alive in a freshwater aquarium than in a marine one.

The initial problem to be solved by freshwater animals is maintenance of their salt content, and where salts are regulated, so also must be the water in the

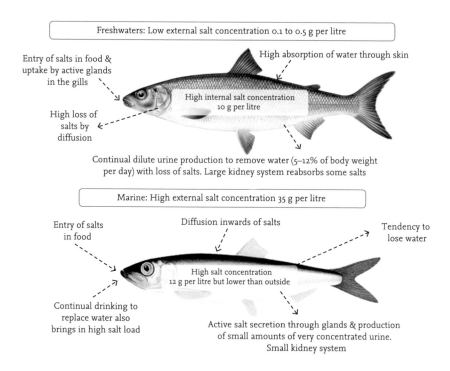

Freshwaters: Low external salt concentration 0.1 to 0.5 g per litre

Entry of salts in food & uptake by active glands in the gills

High absorption of water through skin

High internal salt concentration 10 g per litre

High loss of salts by diffusion

Continual dilute urine production to remove water (5–12% of body weight per day) with loss of salts. Large kidney system reabsorbs some salts

Marine: High external salt concentration 35 g per litre

Entry of salts in food

Diffusion inwards of salts

Tendency to lose water

High salt concentration 12 g per litre but lower than outside

Continual drinking to replace water also brings in high salt load

Active salt secretion through glands & production of small amounts of very concentrated urine. Small kidney system

FIG 64. The problems faced by freshwater and marine animals in regulating their water and salt contents are different, but have been effectively overcome.

cells. The interiors of all cells are basically salty. All of the reactions that keep cells living are carried out in a solution that has to be just right to maintain the shapes of the electrically charged proteins that catalyse these reactions. But cell membranes have to be permeable to small molecules like oxygen and carbon dioxide, which means that they are also open to other small molecules like water and salts. If there is a higher concentration to one side of a cell membrane compared with the other, there will be a tendency for movement to even up the concentrations on both sides. Salts tend therefore to diffuse out from freshwater animals and there have to be mechanisms to compensate for this (Fig. 64).

Because their cell fluids are much more concentrated than the water outside, freshwater animals also tend to absorb a great deal of water and must urinate continually to get rid of it. In turn they inevitably lose salts in the urine as well as by diffusion through the skin, and they must replace these through their food and sometimes using special salt-absorbing glands. A great deal of energy is required to pump in the salts against the concentration gradient between their interior and the outside medium. Nonetheless these problems have been relatively easily overcome, and fish like the migratory salmonids have mechanisms that both eliminate salts when they are at sea, and acquire them when they are in freshwaters.

...THEN GETTING ENOUGH OXYGEN...

The second condition for recruitment of animals to freshwaters, particularly from land ancestors, has been an ability to tolerate low oxygen concentrations. Dissolved oxygen is about 30 times scarcer in water than in the atmosphere. Diffusion is also slow in water, so freshwater (and marine) animals bigger than a few millimetres have had to evolve large surfaces where the blood

FIG 65. Gaining enough oxygen is a general problem for freshwater invertebrates. Some, like *Cloeon dipterum*, a mayfly nymph, use fluttering gills borne on their abdomens (top left). Others, like the great diving beetle, *Dytiscus marginalis* (lower left, photograph by Lucas Koneckny), maintain an air bubble at the tip of their bodies but must replenish it at the surface from time to time. Bugs like *Aphelocheirus* (right) have a felt of hairs on their undersides that supports an air bubble for much longer periods.

vessels are close to the surface to be able to obtain enough. Small animals, like single-celled organisms, can rely on diffusion over their whole body surfaces, so hydras, gastrotrichs, flatworms, mites and nematodes have no particular respiratory organs.

Bigger ones like insects, the larger crustaceans, molluscs and fish have gills over which water is moved either by forced pumping, as with the mouth movements of fish, or by vibrating the gills, as in mayfly and stonefly nymphs. The gills are either connected with a system of air tubes (tracheae) that allow diffusion into the body fluids or with a blood circulation system. Really large animals in freshwaters need so much oxygen that they must be air breathers with lungs; gills cannot absorb enough to support a really large body and the biggest animals with gills, the sharks, must move almost continually to bring a high flow of water over the gills. The Loch Ness monster (Chapter 9) was ever a fiction – to be big enough to be a monster it would have had to be air breathing and air breathers must surface repeatedly to replenish their lungs.

Insects in freshwaters may have aquatic larvae or nymphs, with gills, and aerial adults with many small holes, the spiracles, and trachaeae through which to absorb oxygen (for example, mayflies, stoneflies, dragonflies and damselflies, caddis flies and two-winged flies). Alternatively, both juvenile stages and adults may be aquatic (beetles and bugs). In these, accommodating the adult form, which lacks gills, to underwater life has posed problems except in very small species. The larger ones, like diving beetles, have to return to the surface to breathe, sometimes exserting their rear ends with spiracles through the surface tension film of the water, or holding a bubble of air under their wing covers, or on a mat of hairs on their underside, as a sort of aqualung that has to be periodically replenished at the surface (Fig. 65).

...COPING WITH DROUGHT AND FREEZING...

The third barrier to colonisation of freshwaters has been the risk of their drying up. For marine animals stranded in dried rock pools, that always means death, but in freshwaters a declining water level often leads to production of thick-walled spores or resting stages that can almost indefinitely remain quiescent until water levels rise again (Fig. 66). The same is true where freezing is usual in winter. Such resting stages are also valuable for dispersal and it is common to find new pools rapidly colonised through such bodies brought in attached to flying insects or birds. Retention of adult flying stages in many freshwater insects in itself is an effective escape from drying or freezing.

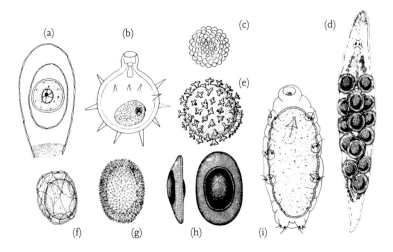

FIG 66. Resting stages are common in freshwater invertebrates and have evolved as a response to the unpredictability of the habitat: (a) and (b) are protozoon cysts; (c) and (e) are resting eggs; and (i), a resting cyst of tardigrades (water bears). Resting eggs of rotifers are shown as (f) and (g); (h) is a bryozoon statoblast; and (d) is a turbellarian carrying thick-walled resting eggs.

...AND VISCOSITY...

A fourth particular difficulty for all aquatic animals is the viscosity (stickiness) of the medium. When an organism moves through the water, it is subject to pressure forces as it pushes away the water in front of it, and drag forces that act like friction over its surface. The relative importance of these forces depends on the size of the animal. A small animal has a large surface area in relation to its size. Think of a sphere; its surface area ($4\pi r^2$) is proportional to the square of its radius but its volume ($4/3\pi r^3$) is proportional to the cube of its radius. The larger the surface area in relation to the volume, the greater proportionately are the drag forces; the bigger the organism, the less the drag but the more water has to be pushed out of the way. Swimming must become more powerful as an organism gets bigger and would become uneconomic were it not for the device of streamlining so that water flows smoothly over the surfaces. Streamlined animals have their maximum width about one third back from their noses, with a body that then tapers steadily towards their tail.

A small organism in water experiences a medium that would seem as thick as treacle because of the drag forces. This means that a great deal of energy is needed for the movement of limbs to overcome this friction, whilst a large organism is restricted in its shape by the pressure forces because they are proportional to density × length × velocity. The ratio of pressure to drag forces is known as the Reynolds number. For microscopic organisms it will be less than 0.1, for the larger invertebrates and small fish it will be between 0.1 and 10, and for very large animals, such as large fish, it might be greater than 10. The same phenomenon occurs in flying; a tiny insect finds the going much harder than a larger one, for even air has viscosity; large insects, like dragonflies, and birds must overcome the pressure forces by streamlining and powerful wing beats. Beyond reducing pressure forces by streamlining, there is little that an animal can do to avoid them; they are simply part of the compromise that living in a fluid medium, either air or water, involves.

...AND GETTING THERE

The cast of the play has repeatedly changed over quite short periods, following local and more widespread extinctions, but even in geologically more quiescent times there have been problems, especially for freshwater animals on islands like ours: those of getting to the theatre. Freshwaters are discontinuous, unlike the ocean with its waters circulating in a single huge basin around the drifting islands of the continents. There are barriers of temperature, even there, that preclude global distributions and make the tropical, temperate and polar marine faunas quite distinct. The barriers among freshwaters are much greater and include the saline ocean as well as the relative aridity of the surrounding land. For islands like Britain, the ice that melted only a few thousand years ago left the stages frozen and near empty, most of the actors dead or driven away. When the ice melted and the rivers and lakes held liquid water again, freshwater animals reinvaded them, but the process of getting back was not necessarily easy, nor is it yet complete.

EFFECTS OF THE GLACIATION

The glaciers removed a great deal of water from the ocean. When they extended to southern England, sea levels were about 60 metres lower than at present. Britain and Ireland were part of mainland Europe and, when melting led to their rivers flowing again, they were then tributaries of bigger European rivers, like the Rhine. There was always some land free of ice in southern England (Fig. 17) and much more was uncovered in the warmer periods between the successive waves of glaciation. The former view of a few major periods of advance of the ice and intervening warmer periods of retreat still has some truth in it, but a simple graph of four or five main cold and warm periods has been replaced by a much spikier one in which the changes are referred to as Marine Isotope Stages (MIS). These are deduced from temperature measurements obtained by correlation with changes in oxygen isotopes incorporated into marine molluscs.[3] MIS 6 marks the start of the last major glaciation, the Devensian (formerly called the Weichselian), with successive advances (MIS 4 and 2) within it, and a maximum advance of the ice that left much of eastern and southern England and the Midlands uncovered. In all of the previous warmer periods (the interglacials), lakes must have re-established and organisms moved back, but we have little information. Deposits of peat formed in wetlands, and give some insights, with plants like the water chestnut and animals like turtles having been present, but most such deposits were eroded away by subsequent advances of the ice.[4]

The final Devensian glaciation, however, would have driven out many of the animals that had entered in the previous interglacial, for the unglaciated land in southern England would still have been very cold, with any lakes frozen over for most or all of the year in a landscape of tundra, and perhaps stunted woodland in places. Convention has it that the freshwater fauna crept back along the tributary rivers of the Rhine, but that is too simple. Molecular studies of DNA of fish like the bullhead, which is now widespread in Europe, show distinctive races of great antiquity, including a British one that must have hung on through at least the Devensian glaciation.[5] If it had recently moved in through the continental rivers it would share the DNA characteristics of the northern mainland European race, but it does not.

If fish can have persisted at the edge of the ice, so can some invertebrates. There was likely a passageway at the feet of the glaciers where large meltwater lakes and smaller pools may have allowed survival of the more cold-tolerant species, like the Arctic char and the whitefish (Coregonidae) throughout the advances of the ice.[6] Lakes at the feet of the present polar glaciers are not devoid of freshwater communities.[7] Reinvasion through the rivers, nonetheless, must have allowed the less cold-tolerant species back, and for fish like the salmonids, eels, mullets and sturgeon, which can tolerate, indeed sometimes require, both marine and freshwater conditions, uncovering of land bordering the seas provided another pathway when the westward rivers again flowed into the ocean.

Re-colonisation was quite fast for some organisms and is still going on for others. Those with wings, and vigorous swimmers, could make rapid progress.

Smaller animals that creep along the
bottom may yet not have reached all of
their potential range. One such group
was examined by T. B. Reynoldson and
his students, particularly J. O. Young,
in the 1960s and 1970s.[8] The triclads,
once called planarians, are small (up
to 3 or 4 centimetres) flatworms that
mostly creep along the bottoms of
lakes (and in two cases in Britain,
only rivers and springs) using large
numbers of cilia on their undersides.
They attack other invertebrates,
usually damaged ones to which they
are attracted by diffusion of leaking
body fluids (Fig. 67), by wrapping their

FIG 67. Two triclad species, *Dugesia polychroa*
(right) and the introduced American *Dugesia*
tigrina (left) move in to attack a wounded snail.

bodies around the prey and inserting the front end of their gut into the wound,
injecting digestive enzymes and sucking out the contents. There are nine native
species in the British Islands (and three further recent introductions) with the
dark-coloured *Polycelis nigra* and *P. tenuis*, the variably coloured *Dugesia polychroa*
and the white *Dendrocoelum lacteum* the commonest.

A pattern of distribution was shown when triclads were sampled in a standard
way from a large number of lakes. The higher the calcium concentration, the
more triclads were found and *D. polychroa* and *D. lacteum* were confined to lakes
with more than 5 mg Ca per litre. *Polycelis tenuis* was found down to 1 mg Ca
per litre, but *P. nigra* could be found in lakes with even lower concentrations.
It was thus tempting to conclude that the occurrence of the triclads was linked
with fertility of the lakes, with the most infertile, in northern Scotland, lacking
triclads at all, but this was not the reason, despite the strong correlation. Triclads
were placed in cages in the most northerly and infertile lakes and given slices
of earthworms as food. All four species thrived and completed their life cycles.
Other observations suggested that predation (leeches, dragonfly nymphs, fish and
newts will all eat flatworms) was not responsible for the shortage of flatworms
in northern infertile lakes, nor the lower temperatures. It seems that flatworms
are still working their way slowly northwards following their reappearance in the
British Islands some time after the ice retreated.

Around 7,000 years ago recolonisation of British freshwaters was severely
interrupted as the melting glaciers raised the sea levels, isolating the mainland of
Britain from the continent, as Ireland had been isolated some time before. The

native fish fauna of Ireland is consequently much poorer than that of England, Scotland and Wales, which in turn is much less species-rich than northern Europe at equivalent latitudes. The same is also true of most invertebrate groups. We are still a pioneer land, in the earliest stages of a set of biological processes that maximise diversity through colonisation (as in the flatworms) and subsequent speciation through evolutionary mechanisms. Many people think of evolutionary change and the process of producing new species as very slow. It is not. It can be extremely rapid, with organisms of markedly different properties being produced over just a few generations, especially in microorganisms and small animals.

The process can be seen even in the fish of Britain and Ireland. The brown trout exists in a large number of coloured forms and indeed has been given as many as 50 different names, implying 50 different species, since Linnaeus gave the first name in 1755. The criterion for separation of different species is that they will not interbreed to produce fertile offspring and this is certainly not true of the 50 purported trout species. But species do not differentiate instantly; there is an intermediate stage when the emerging forms not only look different but begin also to occupy different places in the same lake or to breed at slightly different times of year. Placed together in an aquarium, they might still breed and produce fertile offspring, but what is happening in the lake is the process by which eventually the fish will diverge enough for breeding no longer to be possible even in aquaria, and from the original brown trout several new species will have separated. Some scientists designate new species at this intermediate stage and one current view is that around 25 'brown trout' species exist in Europe with six of them in Ireland alone.[9]

The 22 km² Lough Melvin (Fig. 68) in Northern Ireland has three very distinct forms of brown trout that represent speciation in progress over just a few

FIG 68. Lough Melvin in Northern Ireland.

FIG 69. Brown trout are rarely brown. Different forms occur in different lakes and sometimes several forms in the same lake. A brownish-green form with red spots is widespread (centre). Sonaghen (sonachen) are often bluish (left) and gillaroo (right, headed downwards) have prominent brown spotting. The eventually piscivorous, large, ferox trout are reddish and the males often retain a prominent hooked jaw.

thousand years.[10] The three populations (Fig. 69) are genetically distinct and do not interbreed in the lake. The gillaroo, with its strongly marbled flanks, spawns on the lake shores and outflow river, and feeds on invertebrates living on the bottom. The second form, the sonaghen (or sonachen) feeds on zooplankton in the water column and spawns in the smaller inflow streams. Its back is bluish and its marbling is less pronounced than that of the gillaroo. Thirdly, the ferox trout feeds on bottom invertebrates at first, then on other fish after its third year. It lives longest, and in males often retains, for all the year, the hooked jaw of its spawning period. It is redder and spawns in the deeper waters of the main inflow to Lough Melvin. The main inflow is also used by the sonaghen, but further upstream and later in the autumn. This developing speciation may not be unusual, but is certainly helped in trout by its habit, as with many salmonid fish, of returning to spawn on the same grounds where it was born. Ferox trout are thought to have arisen elsewhere and colonised separately and the sonaghen and gillaroo have close genetic links with similar forms in mainland Europe, but also enough genetic peculiarities to suggest that they have continued to separate since they reached Lough Melvin.

THE FRESHWATER FAUNA: BRITAIN AND IRELAND VERSUS THE WORLD

The cold temperate regions, irrespective of whether they are islands, have much lower biodiversity than warmer latitudes, for several possible reasons.

Not least is the time that has been available, uninterrupted by freezing, in the last few millions of years for species to evolve, and the effects of a cold climate in lengthening growth seasons and thus reducing the number of generations available for speciation. The variability of the weather also means that niches in cold regions must be broader to accommodate setbacks in the availability of particular foods that can be relied on in warmer regions and broader niches mean that fewer can be fitted in to the available conditions. The greater productivity of at least the wetter, warmer regions provides a greater variety of foods and thus they can support a greater variety of feeders. The largely cold-temperate landmass of Europe and Asia, the Palaearctic, though it includes the richer regions of the Mediterranean and North Africa, is thus less species-rich than the realms of South America, sub-Saharan Africa and tropical Asia and Australia, but forms a yardstick against which the extent of the British and Irish freshwater fauna can be compared (Table 7).

Table 7 is divided into three sections, showing the number of known species of major groups of freshwater animals for the world, the Palaearctic realm and Britain and Ireland. The percentages of the world total are given for the fauna

TABLE 7. Freshwater animals on Earth, in the Palaearctic Realm, and in Britain and Ireland. A few groups, e.g. Tabanidae, are not included because of lack of adequate information and most parasites are not included.

	World	Palaearctic realm			Britain and Ireland		
Area	190 million km²	54 million km² (28% of world landmass)			0.3 million km² (0.6% of Palaearctic landmass)		
Group	Total species	Total species	Species (% of world)	Species per genus	Total species	Species (% of Palaearctic)	Species per genus
Annelids	6,109	3,675	60.2	6.4	139	3.8	1.99
Molluscs	4,998	1,848	37.0	4.6	78	4.2	1.90
Crustaceans	11,990	4,499	37.5	7.1	339	7.5	2.33
Arachnids	6,149	1,203	19.6	7.9	327	27.2	4.25
Collembola	414	338	81.6	4.8	22	6.5	1.69
Insects	75,874	15,190	20.0	11.1	2,494	16.4	3.71
Other invertebrates	6,109	3,675	60.2	6.4	717	19.5	3.57
Vertebrates	18,235	2,193	12.0	4.4	146	6.7	1.49
Total	125,530	30,316	24.2	8.4	3,614	11.9	2.74

TABLE 8. Freshwater invertebrate fauna of Britain and Ireland.

Group	Common name	Genera	Species	Notes
Porifera	Sponges	4	5	Animals that have different sorts of cells but which are not organised into distinctive tissues. They pump water into an inner cavity and filter particles from it
Cnidaria	Hydras, corals and jellyfishes	4	7	Rather like sponges except that they have organised tissues and catch prey by stinging it with special cells. Some forms have a polyp (attached to a surface) stage and a medusa (jellyfish) stage. Most British species have only the polyp stage but there is one (introduced species) where the jellyfish predominates
Platyhelminthes	Flatworms: microturbellarians and triclads	33	67	As well as the microturbellarians and triclads, which are free-living predators, there are many more parasitic tapeworms (cestodes) and flukes (trematodes), which infect vertebrates, often with a mollusc as an intermediate host. These are not listed here. The triclads are larger than the microturbellarians, which are tiny (1–2 mm) flatworms that attack other small animals. Triclads attack larger invertebrates by inserting the fore part of their gut into them and dissolving and sucking out the contents. All flatworms have a simple gut, open at only one end. Two of the 11 British triclads are essentially stream dwellers, but occasionally are found in cold northern lakes. Only one of 56 microturbellarians appears to be confined to streams
Nemertea (Rhynchocoela)	Ribbon or proboscis worms	1	2	There is a long proboscis hidden in a cavity when not used for feeding. Slow moving worms, rather little known. Mostly marine
Nematomorpha	Gordian worms	3	4	Parasites of arthropods (of land and freshwater) with free-living adults that live in freshwaters. The adult worm is quite stiff and inflexible, sometimes with a hard 'plastic' feel. Little is known about their ecology
Nematoda	Hair worms	31	70	Very abundant and probably under-recorded. Some are free-living, many are parasitic
Gastrotricha	Gastrotrichs or hairy backs	11	?50	Very small (<1 mm), covered in minute bristles. Probably detritus feeders on fine material. Under-recorded and often overlooked
Rotifera	Rotifers	102	466	Small animals (<1 mm) but very diverse and widespread both the in plankton and on underwater surfaces. All have a ring of cilia around their mouths, which, in many, swirls a water current with suspended particles into the gut. Now includes the parasitic Acanthocephala (thorny headed worms). Some are capable of grasping larger prey
Ectoprocta (Bryozoa)	Bryozoans, moss animalcules	7	11	Small colonial animals that attach to underwater surfaces and filter small particles from the water. Probably commoner in rivers than in lakes

Mollusca [Gastropoda]	Snails, freshwater limpets	31	46	In freshwaters all have calcareous shells and feed by scraping material from surfaces. Some have cavities lined with blood vessels that allows them to breathe air and makes them amphibious
Mollusca [Bivalvia]	Clams and mussels (swan, pea, pearl, zebra)	10	32	Some are attached to surfaces underwater by threads and filter plankton from water pumped into them through a siphon. Others (generally bigger) are free-living in sediment and pump in a suspension of mud on which to feed. The Unionidae have larval stages that attach to fish as parasites. The freshwater pearl mussel is confined to rivers.
Annelida [Oligochaeta]	Segmented worms, oligochaetes, aelosomatids	58	123	The freshwater equivalent of earthworms, though usually much smaller and finer. Sediment feeders, often pinkish in colour because of the haemoglobin many contain
Annelida [Hirudinea]	Leeches	12	16	Only two are bloodsucking parasites (on fish or mammals). The remainder feed on invertebrates
Tardigrada	Water bears	4	42	Very small (1-3mm) fleshy animals that look like miniature bears and are common on wet mats of vegetation, particularly of *Sphagnum* at the edges of bog lakes
Arachnida [Hydracarina]	Water mites	73	322	Tiny (1–3 mm), often brightly coloured animals with the characteristic eight legs of arachnids but no differentiation of the body, as in spiders. The nymphs are parasitic on insects, the adults are predators of other small invertebrates
Arachnida [Araneae]	Spiders	1	1	Just one species is truly aquatic, though many live on wet vegetation mats. The pond spider lives in a 'diving bell' of silk, full of air, and attached to water plants, where it awaits its prey
Arachnida [Oribatei]	Oribatid mites	3	4	Most common in bogs on *Sphagnum* mats
Crustacea [Anostraca]	Fairy shrimps	2	2	Live in temporary pools. Up to 35 mm, with a carapace, and eyes on short stalks. Delicate-looking because of the feathery gills born along both sides of the body
Crustacea [Notostraca]	Tadpole shrimp; Triops	1	1	A rare animal of great antiquity in evolutionary terms and living in temporary pools. It has a rigid carapace but its eyes are not on stalks
Crustacea [Cladocera]	Water fleas	40	90	Four distinct orders that are not closely related, but the term 'Cladocera' has a long pedigree among freshwater ecologists. The common characteristic is a cloak or carapace that surrounds the animal and gives it a smooth outline. Planktonic or associated with vegetation and mostly filter-feeders or nibblers on periphyton, though some are predators. Commonly parthenogenetic, producing females without the help of males, which appear only rarely
Crustacea [Ostracoda]	Ostracods	29	89	Surrounded by a calcareous carapace of two halves joined at a hinge so that they look a little like swimming bivalves (though jointed legs protrude). Usually small (<3 mm) and filter-feeding

Crustacea [Copepoda]	Harpacticoid, Calanoid and Cyclopoid copepods	51	118	Small- to moderate-sized animals (up to 5 mm) with a streamlined body and no carapace, a pair of antennae used for rapid swimming (cf. the slow movement of most Cladocera). Filter-feeding, or predatory using grasping limbs. The females of some species are parasites on fish
Crustacea [Branchiura]	Fish lice	1	3	External parasites on fish, to which they attach by suckers that allow detachment and free-swimming
Crustacea [Bathynellacea]	No common name, but ancient crustaceans	1	1	Interstitial in groundwater
Crustacea [Decapoda]	Crabs, shrimps, crayfish	6	7	Only one species is native, the white-clawed crayfish. The Chinese mitten crab only penetrates to lowland rivers and does not breed in freshwaters. The remaining five species are all crayfish introduced from mainland Europe and North America
Crustacea [Mysidacea]	Mysids, opossum shrimps	3	3	*Mysis salemaai* (formerly *M. relicta*) is a plankton predator, supposed to be a glacial relict and was found in Ennerdale Water (though not recently seen) and occurs in several Irish lakes. A second species, *Neomysis integer* is native to brackish waters, including some of the Norfolk Broads. A third species, the bloody-red shrimp, is introduced
Crustacea [Isopoda]	Water hoglouse	3	4	The equivalents of woodlice on land and flattened top to bottom
Crustacea [Amphipoda]	Freshwater shrimps	8	21	Body flattened from side to side. Several introduced from Europe or North America and three species are dwellers in caves and groundwater, leaving four *Gammarus* species as native to lakes
Myriapoda	Centipedes	1	1	Doubtfully a lake organism but may occur on marginal vegetation mats
Hexapoda [Collembola]	Springtails	13	22	So called because of a forked appendage at the rear, which allows them to jump vigorously. Mostly semi-aquatic on the surface tension film or on vegetation mats, small (<5 mm)
Hexapoda [Insecta] (Ephemeroptera)	Mayflies	20	50	About 18 in lakes, but none are confined to standing waters. Adults are aerial, nymphs are aquatic, with three fine 'tails' at the end of the abdomen. Gills are born on the abdominal segments. Some live on or under stones, scraping the films of organisms that grow there. Some burrow in sediments. None are predators
Hexapoda [Insecta] (Plecoptera)	Stoneflies	17	41	About 7 in lakes, on stony shores, but none are confined to standing waters. More characteristic of streams
Hexapoda [Insecta] (Odonata)	Damselflies and dragonflies	20	44	About 33 breed in lakes, with fewer than five requiring flowing waters. Damselflies (Zygoptera) are more slender than dragonflies (Anisoptera) both as larvae (aquatic) and adults (aerial). The abdomen of damselflies ends in three flattened gills, that of dragonflies in shorter, sharper spikes. Dragonfly adults hold their wings out at rest whilst damselfly adults fold them over the body. There are a further 14 vagrant species that do not normally breed

Hexapoda [Insecta] (Hemiptera)	Bugs	24	67	Mouth parts are modified into beaks or rostra for piercing and sucking out the prey. Juveniles resemble the adults. Some retain the ability to fly. Most (55) can be found in standing waters. The group includes water measurers, corixids, water boatmen, pond skaters, water striders, and water scorpion
Hexapoda [Insecta] (Hymenoptera)	Wasps, ichneumon flies	32	41	Mostly parasitic wasps that lay their eggs in the eggs or bodies of aquatic insects, but which are not truly aquatic themselves
Hexapoda [Insecta] (Coleoptera)	Beetles	111	415	Both adults and larvae are aquatic, with the larvae looking very different from the adults, which retain their wings, protected by hardened wing covers, or elytra. The mouth parts are adapted for grasping, biting and tearing. A few have aquatic larvae and aerial adults, a few others vice versa
Hexapoda [Insecta] (Megaloptera)	Alderflies	1	3	Predators with appendages of unknown function protruding from the abdominal segments in the larvae. Adults are aerial
Hexapoda [Insecta] (Neuroptera)	Spongeflies, lacewings	3	4	Spongeflies feed as larvae on freshwater sponges. Lacewings are detritus feeders as larvae. Adults of all are aerial
Hexapoda [Insecta] (Trichoptera)	Caddis flies	78	203	The adults are aerial, the nymphs aquatic, and characterised by two clawed prolegs at the tip of the abdomen. About 162 in lakes. Larvae may form cases of small stones, sand grains, twigs or segments of leaves, or even the shells of small snails and are then usually scrapers of films from rocks, or may be caseless (47 species) and either predators or spinners of nets to catch fine particles in streams
Hexapoda [Insecta] (Lepidoptera)	China mark moths	5	5	The caterpillars are aquatic and make cases from leaf fragments. The adults are aerial
Hexapoda [Insecta] (Diptera)	Two-winged flies	357	1,610	More probably occur in lakes than in rivers, but the group is surprisingly little investigated. Mostly the adults are aerial and the larvae aquatic and bearing little resemblance to the adult or even the familiar insect plan of head, thorax, abdomen and six legs. Heads of larvae may be obscure, but there is usually a prominent spiracle for breathing on the final abdominal segment. There may be many yet to be described and some may be commoner in small puddles and water-filled holes than lakes. The group includes mosquitoes, horse flies (tabanids), phantom midges (chaoborids), simuliids, ceratopogonids (biting midges), non-biting midges, chironomids, craneflies, moth flies, owl midges, soldier flies, daddy long legs, hoverflies, rat-tailed maggots and meniscus midges
Total		**1,326**	**4,127**	Approximately 80–90% may be found in standing waters although many of these only on occasion or in very limited areas

of the Palaearctic and the percentages of the Palaearctic fauna for our islands. The Palaearctic is well represented for most groups, especially the collembolans (springtails), once regarded as an early insect group but now given greater status. It is significantly under-represented in the spiders and mites (arachnids), insects and vertebrates. Conventional wisdom has it that the British and Irish fauna is relatively poor compared with the mainland. This is true for absolute numbers, but since we occupy only 0.6 per cent of the Palaearctic, we are surprisingly rich. Perhaps the only real indication that our isolation as islands has really limited our fauna is the relatively low number of species per genus.

Matters are now in flux because we have introduced large numbers of species, particularly fish, molluscs and crustaceans, from elsewhere, and current warming trends are extending the ranges, particularly of insects with vigorous flying stages, like dragonflies, quite rapidly.[11] Table 8 shows the current inventory of the freshwater invertebrate fauna of Britain and Ireland. A few freshwater groups are commoner in fast-flowing streams or confined to the underground waters of cave systems, and these are indicated, but most animals can be found in standing waters and so the table is a reasonable approximation of the fauna of lakes in the British Islands. It is incomplete concerning the parasites of freshwater organisms.

Except for some small groups of crustaceans that live in underground streams, all of the groups that are better represented in running waters are insects, which are derived from land ancestors. Groups that are directly derived from the ocean (molluscs, annelids, crustaceans, rotifers, flatworms, and nematodes, for example) are better represented in standing waters and this is consistent with the lower concentrations of oxygen available to marine organisms compared with terrestrial air breathers. Streams have generally higher oxygen concentrations than lakes and this is reflected in the biased distribution of insects, with the interesting anomaly that odonates (damselflies and dragonflies), which, as a group, is tropical in origin, breed predominantly in standing waters. Water mites (Fig. 70) are also anomalous; they too probably came from the land but they are most common in standing waters. Their

FIG 70. A hydracarinid or water mite. These animals are predators, move rapidly and are only a few mm across.

TABLE 9. Freshwater vertebrates of the Earth, the Palaearctic realm, and Britain and Ireland. In the latter, introductions by man have often biased the numbers significantly. Total numbers are based only on native species but the numbers of introduced species that have established are shown in parentheses with a plus sign.

	World	Palaearctic realm			Britain and Ireland		
Area	190 million km²	54 million km² (28% of world landmass)			0.3 million km² (0.6% of Palaearctic landmass)		
Group	Total species	Total species	Species (% of world)	Species per genus	Total species	Species (% of Palaearctic)	Species per genus
Fish	12,740	1,844	14.5	4.85	43 (+14)	2.3	1.34
Amphibians	4,294	160	3.7	6.15	7 (+5)	4.4	1.17
Reptiles	510	17	3.3	1.3	0	0	0
Birds	567	154	27.2	2.26	89	57.8	1.89
Mammals	124	18	14.5	2.25	4 (+1)	22.2	1.0
Total vertebrates	18,235	2,193	12.0	4.43	143	6.5	1.61

small size, a few millimetres, however, means that they are able to obtain enough oxygen even at low concentrations. Lake invertebrate faunas thus reflect their evolutionary origins and this is true also of the vertebrates.

Table 9 shows the numbers of species of vertebrates associated with freshwaters, again on the bases of the world, the Palaearctic region and Britain and Ireland. Compared with the invertebrates, many groups are under-represented in the Palaearctic and only birds hold their own when the area is considered. Absolute numbers are again low for Britain and Ireland, but representation is high on the basis of area of the Palaearctic occupied, except for freshwater reptiles, of which we have none. Grass snakes will swim but are hardly dependent on freshwaters beyond the need to drink. In the cases of fish and amphibians (of which a few introduced frogs and one newt have formed breeding populations), human whim has been almost as effective as natural colonisation. Birds and mammals are especially well represented perhaps because of the ease by which they flew or walked in after the ice retreated.

Table 10 details the vertebrate populations of lakes in Britain and Ireland. Included are species habitually found associated with lakes for significant parts of their time, but some of these are not major players. Despite their siren-like attraction to conservation organisations and the promoters of Biodiversity Action Plans, the bittern, the natterjack toad, the glaucous and Iceland gulls, the

TABLE 10. Freshwater and freshwater-associated vertebrates of lakes in Britain and Ireland. Bird lists include only species frequently seen and do not include vagrants or very rare species seen only in some years. Waders that are predominantly marine but may occasionally be seen on lake shores, for example in stormy weather, are also not included. There are no lake-associated reptiles and the native and introduced fish are shown separately. Among native species, many have been redistributed to Scotland and Ireland from England by people. In the lists of fishes those species with very restricted distributions are indicated by (R). Otherwise the lists indicate those species that are likely to have a significant effect on the functioning of lake communities. Scientific names are given in the index for those species mentioned in the main text.

Group	No. Genera	No. Species	Notes
Fish	**39**	**44**	
Native	25	29	River lamprey, Eel, Silver bream, Common bream, Bleak, Gudgeon, Chub, Dace, Minnow, Roach, Rudd, Tench, Spined loach (R), Stone loach, Pike, Vendace (R), Pollan (R), Powan (R), Atlantic salmon, Brown trout, Arctic char, Grayling, Thick-lipped grey mullet (R), Three-spined stickleback, Nine-spined stickleback, Bullhead, Ruffe, Perch, Flounder
Introduced	14	15	Goldfish, Crucian carp, Common carp, Orfe, False harlequin (R), Bitterling (R), Black bullhead (R), Wels, Rainbow trout, Brook charr, Rock bass (R), Pumpkinseed (R), Pikeperch
Amphibians	**4**	**5**	The tadpole stage of amphibians is very vulnerable to fish predation. Amphibians thus tend to breed in small ponds devoid of fish rather than lakes and so, although they might sometimes be found, are not consistent members of the lake fauna. However, from time to time, the common frog, pool frog, common toad, smooth and palmate newts might lay eggs along shallow lake shores. The Great crested newt is less likely to and the Natterjack toad only lays in small, shallow pools, bare of vegetation
Birds	**47**	**89**	
Swans, geese and ducks	11	29	Swans: Mute, Whooper and Bewick's; Geese: Canada, Brent, Barnacle, Greylag, White-fronted, Bean, Pink-footed; Surface-feeding ducks: Mallard, Gadwall, Pintail, Wigeon, Teal, Garganey, Shoveller, Shelduck, Egyptian goose; Diving ducks: Scaup, Tufted, Pochard, Goldeneye, Long-tailed, Velvet scoter, Common scoter; Sawbills: Red-breasted merganser, Goosander, Smew
Divers	1	2	Black-throated, Red-throated
Cormorants	1	1	Common
Herons	3	3	Bittern, Little egret, Grey heron
Plovers	3	4	Oystercatcher, Lapwing, Ringed plover, Little ringed plover

Gulls	1	9	Great black-backed, Lesser black-backed, Herring, Common, Black-headed, Little, Mediterranean, Glaucous, Iceland
Avocets	1	1	Avocet
Waders	4	10	Dunlin, Little stint, Temmincks stint, Snipe, Common sandpiper, Marsh sandpiper, Wood sandpiper, Greenshank, Redshank, Spotted redshank
Kingfisher	1	1	Kingfisher
Harriers	1	1	Marsh
Terns	1	3	Common, Little, Arctic
Rails	4	4	Water rail, Spotted crake, Moorhen, Coot
Dipper	1	1	Dipper
Buntings	1	1	Reed
Swallows	1	1	Sand martin
Wagtails	1	2	Grey, Pied
Tits	1	1	Bearded
Warblers	3	4	Cetti's, Savi's, Sedge, Reed
Osprey	1	1	Osprey
Grebes	2	5	Great crested, Red-necked, Slavonian, Black-necked, Little
Mammals	**5**	**5**	Bank vole, Water shrew, Otter, Mink (introduced), European beaver (reintroduced)

avocet, most waders, the bearded tit, the osprey and marsh harrier, and half of the complements of rails and grebes, are probably decoration, guest appearances, compared with working might, when it comes to the functioning of lakes. It is the geese and ducks, the mute swan, the commoner gulls, the heron, cormorant, moorhen, coot and great crested grebe (Fig. 71) that have the major roles.

The picture we have is thus of a world freshwater fauna (Table 6) that is absolutely small in terms of world diversity, because of the high rates of extinction that follow from the instability of the freshwater habitat, but proportionately rich on the basis of water volume, suggesting that although extinction may be a high risk, evolution has been very effective in compensating for it. The Palaearctic freshwater fauna (Tables 7 and 9) is about as rich as we might expect on the basis of its area, perhaps because the effects of the very recent prolonged glaciation have been balanced by a rich Mediterranean fauna that was not so affected by the ice. Some groups are over-represented, others under. The British and Irish

FIG 71. Moorhen searching for food (photo: J. M. Garg) and a great crested grebe (photo: Snowman Radio) feeding its chick.

fauna (Tables 8 and 10) is richer than might be expected and this is perhaps a tribute to the abilities of freshwater animals to disperse, traits selected for by the risks of disturbance to their habitats. Totals of over 4,000 species of invertebrates (with perhaps around 100 recent introductions) and 143 vertebrates (plus around 20 introductions) leaves a complexity of communities that we understand only in general and rarely in detail and a richness of individual natural history that provides scientists and amateur naturalists with plenty to investigate, as will be seen in the next three chapters.

THE VERTEBRATES: ACTORS RESTING

There is one unfortunate disconnection, however. Although a former separation of research in fisheries and the rest of freshwaters has been overcome, understanding of the ecology of birds, amphibians and mammals has remained separate, apparently supernumerary to working out how lake ecosystems function. Fish and fisheries were formerly topics for an applied science of management for increasing fish production. We now understand fish to be affected not only by the production of algae and plants (often called bottom-up – through the food webs – effects) but also to have top-down effects through their intense predation on invertebrates, particularly the grazers of phytoplankton and periphyton. Fish can completely change the physiognomy of lake communities, switching clear-water, plant-dominated lakes to ones turbid with algae or suspended mud and devoid of submerged plants. The old, but wrong, fisheries-orientated views that the more and bigger fish the better, and that many big fish meant a healthy lake ecosystem, have been revised.

Where birds, mammals, amphibians and reptiles are concerned, research has been strongly species-orientated, both in understanding their biology and in conserving them. Observations of feeding and mating behaviour, seen merely as curious by earlier naturalists, have been steadily given evolutionary explanations that are intellectually very perceptive and contribute hugely to concepts like that of the selfish gene: appearance and behaviour are driven by a competition among genes for maximal representation in the next generation.[12] But for many behavioural ecologists and conservationists, the rest of the ecosystem has been relegated to a stage supporting the starring roles of charismatic species. Arctic tundra exists to support geese and reindeer; forests, tragopans and tigers; bamboo thickets, snow leopards and pandas; reedbeds, bearded tits and bitterns; and lakes, otters and ospreys. Yet these animals, whose numbers are eternally fussed over (and rightly so where human activities have decimated them) may have important reciprocal effects, which have been largely ignored, on the ecosystems of which they are a part. When I see huge numbers of geese and ducks, artificially fed, on lakes at wetland nature reserves, I am impressed ... by the amount of bird sewage they are producing for export to rivers downstream and the muddiness and deoxygenation in the water.

Like fish, other vertebrates have top-down effects. That abundant cormorants may decimate fish populations is a popular view among anglers but the ravaged populations may often be of species like rainbow trout introduced at artificially high levels for sport fishing.[13] A dislike by bailiffs of otters in rivers (like raptors on grouse moorlands) has yet to be fully revised. But we have no idea of how cormorants and otters influence river and lake functioning, and only a little of how these predators affect their prey – or of other relationships. Fish and ducks may compete for food; pike may take ducklings,[14] and geese and gulls may fertilise lakes with their droppings (a process called guanotrophication) and sometimes promote algal species that are toxic to fish[15] and cause major kills.

What we need to know are the roles of normal populations of the commoner mammals and birds, reptiles and amphibians in lake ecosystems. Are they just the icing on the cake, the court flunkeys of the pantomime, or are they key to the plot of the play? Elsewhere there is evidence for the latter. For example, when Pacific salmon species migrate back from the ocean to their spawning grounds in the rivers and lakes of northwestern North America, they bring nutrients in their bodies to habitats that are naturally very scarce in nitrogen and phosphorus. Adult salmon swim thousands of kilometres to reach the grounds. Many die on the way, and most of those eventually spawning die afterwards. The rivers are littered with nutrient-rich carcases – or at least were before the stocks were overfished at sea and the rivers blocked by dams. Bears, mink and raccoons

FIG 72. Bears and other mammals scavenge carcasses and catch live fish, like this sockeye salmon during the migrations of Pacific salmon to their spawning grounds. (Phil Sanfillipo)

take the carcasses (Fig. 72), and, excreting in the surrounding forest, fertilise the trees to the extent that as much as 25 per cent of their nitrogen may come from the ocean via salmon and scavengers. In turn, the woody debris of trees that fall into the spawning grounds holds back carcasses that might be swept back to the sea. Nutrients decomposed from the dead fish support the fungi that break down leaf litter, and algae on the rocks, that feed the invertebrates on which the young salmon depend once they have exhausted the yolk sacs with which they were born.[16]

Wolves are important influences on stream ecosystems. In Yellowstone National Park, wolves were shot out early in the twentieth century because of a misguided view that they were vermin. Wolves killed deer and deer were prized because people wanted to shoot them so that State legislatures benefited from the sale of hunting licences. The elk population in Yellowstone (where hunting was banned) steadily grew, until a ludicrous situation was reached in which the elk had to be fed imported hay in winter.

An essentially production-orientated management had ignored the greater system and focussed too narrowly on particular species. Wolves were reintroduced to parts of Yellowstone in the 1990s. The result has been a transformation of the rivers (Fig. 73). Elk had previously overgrazed the willowy vegetation around the river channels, simplifying its structure and also altering processes of channel erosion and gravel deposition, which are important for invertebrate communities. Bird diversity and beaver populations had been reduced. Wolves altered the behaviour of the elk because they are easily trapped by a wolf pack in river bottomlands. Elk wisely began to forgo the willow leaves of the streams and to stay in the denser surrounding forests.

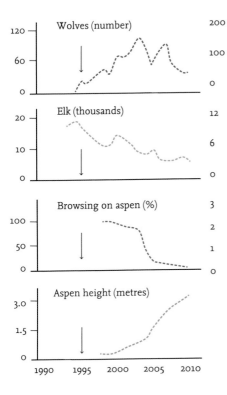

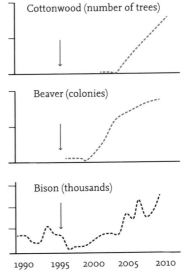

FIG 73. Reintroduction (arrows) of wolves into Yellowstone National Park, after 70 years absence, has brought many advantages to other wildlife, and to functioning of the ecosystem, including better growth of riverine willow, aspen and cottonwood trees, and return of beavers. Through changes in elk distribution and grazing effects on surrounding grasslands, it has also attracted more bison into the area. Modified from Ripple & Beschta (2011).

These are not the only examples.[17] Sea otters can determine, by their presence or absence, the nature of Pacific shores through their feeding on sea urchins. There are rich, kelp-dominated rocks where they control the urchins, and bare shores with low invertebrate, fish, bird and seal diversity, where otters have been hunted out. Moose transfer nitrogen back to the forests, from which it has leached into lakes, by their feeding on aquatic plants and subsequent movement back to land where their dung and carcasses balance the nutrient budget. Hippopotami bulldoze channels through papyrus swamps that increase water circulation, decrease local deoxygenation and favour the fish populations as well as the access of the fishermen that catch them. The fish yields in the flooded forests of the Amazon depend on the release of nutrients through the hunting of the fish by caimans and river dolphins, which follow their spawning movements at high water.

We have sorely incomplete systems in Britain and Ireland. Extinction of bear and wolf, aurochs and boar may have had unforeseen consequences, of which we have no clue, on freshwaters. Near complete deforestation of the landscape has made it difficult to reconstruct what our ecosystems were like, or could be like. We study a deformed and disabled system, and have little insight as to how the commoner remaining vertebrates, the geese and ducks, gulls, heron, coot, grebe and kingfisher fit in. Poring over lists of storm-tossed vagrants and rare birds is doubtless interesting but contributes little to maintaining and managing ecosystems that provide services beyond appeasing curiosity. However, the general adaptiveness of freshwater animals to disturbance means that restoration of diverse communities to lakes that have been damaged is, in theory at least, not as difficult as it might be for terrestrial communities. The freshwater repertory company, recruited to the evolutionary play, is versatile, flexible and less fazed by vicissitude, perhaps, than the showy stars of the West End shows of the rain forests and coral reefs. But an occasional celebrity adds glamour!

CHAPTER 5

On the Edge of the Land: The Littoral Zone

W E SEE THE EDGE FIRST. The natural place for the limnological play to start, indeed the richest part of the lake, is at the margin, in the littoral zone. The kind of bottom (rock, gravel, sand, silt, peat or clay), the slope of the shore and therefore the extent of shallow water, and the properties of the water in absorbing light, dictate what the littoral is like and the sorts of algae and plants that are at its heart.

FIG 74. The rocky littoral of Llyn Idwal, Snowdonia. (Tom Hecht)

FIG 75. The reed-lined, muddy littoral of Martham North Broad, Norfolk.

In a mountain lake, it might be narrow and wave-beaten, a mosaic of rock, sparse clinging algae and patches of gravel with occasional small rushes (Fig. 74), but, as the water deepens, and the waves lessen, it becomes sandier with denser swards of small plants in the brownish water of a peaty catchment. In the lowlands, it is more likely to be wide and muddy (Fig. 75), with sheltered shallow bays, backed by fens and beds of reed, and fronted by swards of lilies and pondweeds. There will be every gradation of appearance and community between these, and indeed several versions even in the same lake, depending on wave fetch, or closeness to inflow streams that bring in sediment, but there will always be some sort of littoral zone in a natural lake. In a reservoir, with its water level changing rapidly according to the whims of water or electricity demand, it might be severely damaged, almost sterile, but I will leave the consequences of such disability to a later chapter.

EVOLUTION OF AQUATIC PLANTS

Where nature has taken its course, the littoral merges seamlessly with the surrounding landscape, for there is no permanent line where the water begins and dry land ends. There is a steady change from dry to damp to waterlogged soils, and then to standing water over submerged sediment. The plants along this gradient reflect the evolutionary pathway that has brought the water plants to their current state. Although the microalgae, the filamentous algae, visible to the naked eye, and the even larger stoneworts (charophytes) have ancestors that entered freshwaters directly from the ocean, the familiar water plants, the mosses and liverworts, ferns and flowering plants, have come from the land.

They are refugees that sneaked back to the water on numerous occasions over the past 100 million years.[1] Colonisation of the continents by plants began only 470 million years ago, when some of the algae gained a landfall, and, especially if they joined with fungi as lichens, spread from a toehold on the rocks. Some grew aerial shoots and water-absorbing buried rhizoids that could keep them supplied in the drier areas. They branched out to the earliest mosses and liverworts, then lycopods and fern allies, which developed internal tissues, the vascular systems, which could conduct water efficiently through a larger plant.

The land was a prize, for in air both carbon dioxide and oxygen diffused more rapidly into the tissues, whilst the risks of drying out were minimised by the evolution of waxy cuticles to cover the stems and leaves. The land plants probably came from one particular group of green algae, now represented by a collection of small filamentous algae, the Klebsormidiales, the similarities in whose details of cell division and DNA make the connection. The mosses and liverworts and psilophytes (the whisk ferns, a group of tropical plants with branches simply bifurcating, rather than emerging from buds with more complex branching patterns) have levels of organisation that are representative of those that typified the early land plants.

They have life histories that involve a vulnerable stage, the moss or liverwort plant, or, in the psilophytes, a small filamentous structure, much like an alga (but growing underground in association with fungi) on which the sexual organs are borne, from which spermatozoids swim through a water film to fertilise the eggs. From the fertilised egg a different sort of plant is born. In the mosses and liverworts it is a stalk surmounted by a round or cylindrical capsule in which spores are made, to be dispersed by wind (in most mosses) or water splashes (in the liverworts). In the psilophytes, it is a much larger green structure, with a waterproof covering and specialised structures at the tips of the branches producing the spores, but the pattern of the life history is the same. There is an essentially aquatic phase, which bears the sex cells, called the gametophyte, and a stage more tolerant of dryness, the sporophyte, which bears the spores that result from fertilisation, and which are used to disperse the plant.

An important step in the colonisation of the land was to evolve a life history in which the gametophyte stage became progressively less important and was then dispensed with, whilst the sporophyte became more important. Thus the modern ferns, lycopods and horsetails, and undoubtedly their much more prominent forebears, which dominated the forests and swamps of the Carboniferous and Permian periods, all had, or have, a tiny, wet, alga-like gametophyte stage to complete their life histories, no matter how big their sporophytes. Only in the eventual development of the conifers and flowering plants was this vulnerability overcome when the gametophyte had become

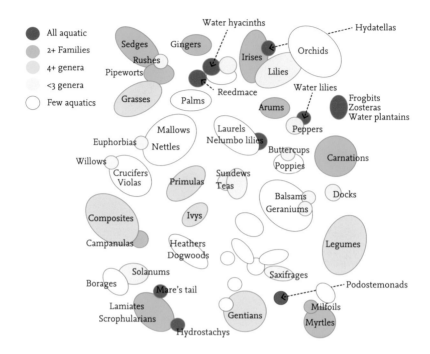

FIG 76. Aquatic species have evolved from many plant orders. Ovals and circles show the plant orders, with the main ones named in terms familiar to naturalists and gardeners, and the size of the symbol is broadly representative of the size of the Order. The colouring indicates the frequency with which aquatic species occur within the Order. Based on Cook, 1999.

reduced to just a few cells, mostly the gametes themselves, which were held deep in the security of structures on the sporophyte, the cones and flowers. Nonetheless even for sporophytes, water is always an issue and water availability is the key factor that determines where land plants persist and how well they grow. Living upright in air is also demanding: supporting tissues, like wood, are expensive to produce and maintain.

There was an opportunity for an apparently easier life in freshwaters, which provide an unlimited supply of the most crucial resource for plants on land, as well as the physical support of a denser medium, and it was an opportunity rather frequently taken up. Few entire flowering plant families are completely aquatic, but a few species and genera, sometimes only one, of many families have gone back to the water. Such a move has been taken nearly 300 times among the land plant groups, more commonly in those that have more recent evolutionary

TABLE 11. Freshwater plants of the Earth, the Palaearctic realm, and Britain and Ireland. In the latter, introductions by man have often biased the numbers significantly. Total numbers are based only on native species but the numbers of introduced species that have established are shown in parentheses with a plus sign. There are about 400 stoneworts, 18,000 mosses and liverworts, 1,000 fern allies and 13,200 flowering plants overall known on Earth.

	World	Palaearctic realm			Britain and Ireland		
Area	190 million km²	54 million km² (28% of world landmass)			0.3 million km² (0.6% of Palaearctic landmass)		
Group	Total species	Total species	Species (% of world)	Species per genus	Total species	Species (% of Palaearctic)	Species per genus
Charophytes	400	?	?	?	23(+2)	?	4.6
Mosses & liverworts	150	?	?	?	6	?	1.2
Fern allies	171	27	15.8	3.4	11(+1)	37	1.67
Flowering plants	2,443	470	19.2	3.2	257(+27)	54.9	2.17
Total	3,164	?	?	?	297(+30)	?	2.2

origins (Fig. 76). Of some 14,000 flowering plants, gymnosperms, and fern relatives, over 2,600 species (17 per cent) are aquatic.[2] None of the gymnosperms and few (about 150, <1 per cent) of the 18,000 mosses and liverworts are aquatic. Almost all of the gymnosperms are trees, and trees, even among the flowering plants, do not take well to sloppy waterlogged soils. Mosses and liverworts are plants of wet places with their gametophyte phase most prominent anyway, because they have no cuticles and need to be covered by at least a film of water to grow and reproduce, so there has been no extra advantage to colonising rivers and lakes. Of the flowering plants, about one in four is aquatic, whilst the total area of freshwater is about 5 million km² (2.6 per cent), compared with a land area of 190 million km².

The picture (Table 11) is a little like that for the freshwater animals: absolutely there is a minority of freshwater genera and species on a world scale, but a great richness when relative areas are allowed for. Nonetheless, the very few families that are exclusively aquatic, notably the pondweeds (Potamogetonaceae) and water lilies (Nymphaeaceae), are not large; most of the aquatic genera and species are minorities within their families. Becoming a freshwater plant, to extend the metaphor of the environmental theatre and the evolutionary play, was a little like running off to the circus! It was sporadic, almost casual, and this too is consistent with the ephemerality of freshwater bodies in geological terms.

BOGS, FENS, CARRS AND SWAMPS

There were difficulties, of course. Waterlogged habitats, the stepping-stones to a completely aquatic existence, offer plenty of water, but problematic conditions for roots. Waterlogged soils quickly become anaerobic below the surface and roots require plenty of oxygen for their growth and nutrient uptake from the soil. But mutation and natural selection provided a variety of solutions, which we can see in the wetland plants that form communities bridging the open water and the land (Chapter 2).[3]

In a sequence from dry land, where the water table is well below the surface of the soil, to open water, the outer aquatic communities are bog forests and carrs, dominated by trees, particularly alder (*Alnus*) and willow (*Salix*), with perhaps some birch (*Betula*). Carr is derived from the old Norse word *kjarr*, then meaning a swamp. The water table, on average during the year, is at the soil surface, but falls in summer, whilst there may be standing water in winter. The ground is bumpy, with tussocks of sedges and woody debris from fallen trees often providing places where plants of drier ground can germinate. The pools between the tussocks and trees can be full of mud and crossing a carr (Fig. 77) can be exciting; getting muddy to the waist, or higher, is normal.

FIG 77. Dense alder carr lines the sides of many of the Norfolk Broads.

FIG 78. *Sphagnum* (left) has many species and comes in a range of reds, browns and greens, but has a distinctive cell structure with large open cells that retain water, and smaller photosynthetic ones. The walls of the larger cells adsorb bases and exchange them for hydrogen ions, which maintains acidity in the habitat and creates conditions in which distinctive bog plants, like the insectivorous round-leaved sundew (right), can thrive.

Carrs develop where the water is relatively base-rich. Where it is much more acid, the community is different; birch predominates over alder and willow, and the ground is covered not so much by large sedges and grasses but by bog mosses (*Sphagnum*) (Fig. 78), smaller sedges and perhaps some heathery shrubs. 'Bog' comes from a Gaelic Irish word meaning soft or moist. The waterlogging, and consequent lack of oxygen in both carr and bog forest soils will result in preservation of woody peat, more rapidly in the pickling conditions of the bog than in the carr.

Further in towards the lake, where the water table is at the surface in summer and above it in winter, trees fail to find an easy foothold and herbaceous vegetation dominates, either fen in more base-rich conditions or bog in more acid. The word 'fen' comes from a variety of parallel sources including old English *fenn* and Dutch *veen* meaning dirt, mire, marsh or moor. Many of the species of the ground flora will be shared with carr or bog forest, but there will be others that thrive better in wetter and less shaded habitats. Fens will have a variety of sedges, grasses and herbs, like ragged robin (Fig. 79), meadowsweet, mint and skullcap. If nutrients are relatively abundant, taller grasses, the reeds, and sedges will predominate, but if scarcer, or the area is heavily grazed, small herbs will fare better. Bog communities have *Sphagnum*, cotton grasses, small sedges, heathers and insectivorous plants like the sundews, bladderworts and butterwort.

There is a gradation in conditions between the most acid bog and the most nutrient-rich fen and modern terminology talks not of fens and bogs as two distinct habitats, but of a continuum of *mires* that are more or less minerotrophic (fed by groundwater and sometimes quite base-poor if the local rocks are poorly weathered) or ombrotrophic, with soil surfaces of peat built up into mounds and fed entirely by rainwater. In wet regions like the north and west of Britain and Ireland, ombrotrophic bog communities may build up on top of fens as peat accumulates, but in the drier conditions of the south and east, the rain is insufficient to leach away bases in the peat and sufficient acidity does not develop to support typical bog. Fen then remains.

As water depths increase, both bogs and fens begin to sport the tall grasses, sedges, horsetails and bulrushes that characterise reedswamp communities. Water stands above the soil surface, sometimes to a metre or so, for most of

FIG 79. Fens have a rich flora of herbs, grasses, sedges and mosses. Ragged robin is common.

FIG 80. In Britain and Ireland, reedswamps and fens are often dominated by common reed. To increase the diversity on conservation sites, grazing by ponies or cattle is often used, as here at How Hill in the Norfolk Broadland.

the year. Reedswamp plants (Fig. 80), archetypally in Britain and Ireland the common reed, are bulky and highly competitive, with vigorous rhizomes. They have abundant water, and since they emerge into the air they benefit from high diffusion rates of carbon dioxide and abundant light. Even at the high latitudes of Britain and Ireland, reedswamps are among the most productive of the world's vegetation; tropical reedswamps far surpass even tropical forest in their productivity.

THE FULLY AQUATIC

Among the reeds and sedges, there develop floating and floating-leaved plants, and fully submerged ones (Fig. 81). Water lilies are rooted in the bottom and include the familiar white and yellow species, but among them may be plants like the frogbit and the water soldier, whose roots make only slight contact with the bottom. There may also be floating duckweeds, benefiting from having their surfaces exposed to the atmosphere, but their roots (and in *Wolffia*, no roots at

FIG 81. Submerged plants characteristically have thin and often finely divided leaves that minimise diffusion pathways for uptake of carbon dioxide and nutrients from the water: (left) *Potamogeton, Ceratophyllum, Naias* and *Elodea.* Floating, and floating-leaved plants, like the frogbit (right) have access to gases in the air and retain the waxy cuticles and stomata of the land plants from which they recently evolved.

all but just the green tissue) absorbing nutrients direct from the water. Small floating plants are easily dislodged by wind and hence persist only where other vegetation harbours them, though they may completely cover sheltered ponds. Finally in the sequence, the submerged species, the milfoils and pondweeds, marestail, water violet, hornworts and starworts, the fern-like quillworts, the stoneworts and a few mosses, occupy the bottom down to whatever level the light allows them to grow. This might be only a few centimetres to a metre or so in turbid lakes, but can be tens of metres in the clearest. Most submerged plants are rooted or, in charophytes and mosses, have simple equivalents, called rhizoids, but they may also absorb nutrients through their leaves. Table 12 (overleaf) lists the aquatic flora of Britain and Ireland, with some notes about growth form and habitat type.

PROBLEMS IN THE WATER

The change in flora from carr and bog forest to submergence reflects the evolutionary colonisation of the lakes, during which the plants have solved the physiological problems presented by increasing waterlogging, and eventual submergence, and taken the advantages that made colonisation of the water worthwhile. The first step was to cope with being rooted in waterlogged and anaerobic soil.[4] If there is a water flow through the soil, as in sandy or gravelly streams, or even wave-washed shores, then anaerobiosis may not develop and plenty of otherwise terrestrial species will survive, even grow, under temporary flooding as stream waters overtop their usual banks. Prolonged waterlogging is a different matter. The first steps in coping were simply shown as a tolerance to the products, notably ethyl alcohol, of limited respiration, called fermentation, which is possible without oxygen. Alcohol is eventually toxic, but can be tolerated by some plants for a time, before it is oxidised through new access to oxygen (a drop in water table, for example), or by diffusion from the roots, as occurs in the bunches of new roots that drape out from the stems of willow trees into streams. Many plants in waterlogged places also produce many roots near the surface of the soil so as to take advantage even of small fluctuations in water table.

AERENCHYMA

An alternative was to convert the alcohol into a different, less toxic, storage product, like malic acid, but other steps can be taken. One has been to channel oxygen internally from the huge supply in the air, or the oxygen produced in the green tissues, down to the roots. All gases diffuse slowly in plant tissues, but by evolving aerenchyma, tissues with pipeways (lacunae) (Fig. 82), the passage could be helped, especially when the pipes were continuous. Sometimes they are interrupted by plates of tissue. Cut across the stem of a rush or reed and you will find it full of such air spaces, which extend into the roots.

In plants with aerial leaves and rhizomes, like the water lilies, where the air-space system is continuous throughout the plant, a means of pumping the air down to the rhizome, and hence the roots, has developed. Warming by the

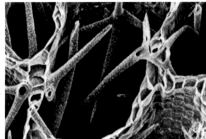

FIG 82. Many aquatic plants, including the yellow and white water lilies (left), have air space systems (right) through which air can diffuse down to their roots. The system in lilies is lined with spiky and woody sclereid cells that are often preserved in sediments.

TABLE 12. Water plants of lakes in Britain and Ireland. Only plants and photosynthetic algae visible to the naked eye (macrophytes) are listed. There are many more microscopic algae. Plus signs indicate introduced species. A liberal view is taken of what constitutes 'aquatic'.

Group or family	Genera and species	Total spp.	Notes
Filamentous and thalloid algae	Green algae: *Cladophora, Aegagropila, Ulothrix, Bulbochaete, Bumilleria, Ulva, Enteromorpha, Draparnaldia, Gongrosira, Stigeoclonium, Hydrodictyon, Chaetophora, Coleochaete, Zygnema, Mougeotia, Debarya, Mougeotopsis, Spirogyra, Zygnemopsis, Vaucheria*. Xanthophyte algae: *Tribonema*. Red algae: *Batrachospermum*. Cyanobacteria: *Nostoc*	?100	There is much difference of opinion as to the number of species in the filamentous and thalloid algae, but there are probably of the order of 100 in Britain and Ireland
Charales (Stoneworts)	*Chara* (16+2 spp.), *Lamprothamnium, Nitella, Nitellopsis, Tolypella*	23+2	Some prefer brackish to fresh water
Liverworts	*Ricciocarpus natans, Riccia fluitans*	2	Both are floating species
Mosses	*Sphagnum cuspidatum, S. auriculatum var auriculatum, Fontinalis antipyretica Cinclidotus fontinaloides*	4	There are many fen and bog species of *Sphagnum* that demand a very wet habitat, but are not usually totally submerged so are not listed
Isoetaceae (Quillworts)	*Isoetes lacustris, I. echinospora*	2	
Equisetales (Horsetails)	*E. × trachyodon, E. variegatum, E. fluviatile, E. × dicei, E. × litorale, E. palustre*	6	
Osmundaceae (Royal fern)	*Osmunda regalis*	1	
Marsileaceae (Pillwort)	*Pilularia globulifera*	1	
Thelypteridaceae (Marsh fern)	*Thelypteris palustris*	1	
Azollaceae	*Azolla filiculoides*	1	An introduced floating fern
Nymphaeaceae (Water lilies)	*Nuphar lutea, N. × spenneriana, N. pumila, N. advena* (intr.), *Nymphaea alba*	4+1	
Ceratophyllacaeae (Hornwort)	*Ceratophyllum demersum, C. submersum*	2	
Ranunculaceaeae (Water buttercups)	*Caltha palustris, Ranunculus lingua. R. flammula, R. × levenensis, R. reptans, R. aquatilis, R. ophioglossifolius, R. hederaceus, R. omiophyllus, R. × novae-forestiae, R. tripartitus, R. baudotii, R. trichophyllus, R. peltatus, R. circinatus*	15	There are six more species and varieties of *Ranunculus* which are confined to flowing waters
Myricaceae (Bog myrtle, sweet gale)	*Myrica gale*	1	
Cabombaceae	*Cabomba carolineana*	+1	Submerged plant, introduced but very localised, mostly in canals
Betulaceae (Alder)	*Alnus glutinosa*	1	One of the few aquatic trees in Britain and Ireland
Polygonaceae (Bistorts & docks)	*Persicaria amphibia, Rumex hydrolapathum, R. palustris, R. aquaticus*	4	

Elatinaceae (Waterworts)	*Elatine hexandra, E. hydropiper*	2	
Clusiaceae (St John's worts)	*Hypericum tetrapterum, H. elodes*	2	
Sarraceniaceae (Pitcher plants)	*Sarracenia purpurea*	1	Insectivorous bog plant – introduced
Droseraceae (Sundews)	*Drosera rotundifolia, D. intermedia, D.longifolia*	3	Insectivorous bog plants
Salicaceae (Poplars & Willows)	*Populus nigra* ssp. *betulifolia, Salix pentandra, S. alba, S. repens*	4	There are many more species and hybrids all of wet places but not truly lake species
Brassicaceae (Cabbage family)	*Rorippa nasturtium-aquaticum, R. × sterilis, R. microphylla, R. × erythrocaulis, R. × anceps, R. amphibia, Cardamine pratensis, Subularia aquatica*	8	
Ericaceae (Heathers)	*Andromeda polifolia, Erica tetralix, E. mackaiana*	3	
Primulaceae (Primroses)	*Hottonia palustris, Lysimachia vulgaris, L. terrestris, L. thyrsifolia*	4	
Crassulaceae (Pigmy weeds)	*Crassula aquatica, C. helmsii*	1+1	*C. helmsii* is a noxious introduced weed originating from the water garden trade
Saxifragaceae (Saxifrages)	*Chrysosplenium oppositifolium, Parnassia palustris*	2	
Rosaceae (Meadowsweet, cinquefoils)	*Filipendula ulmaria, Potentilla fruticosa, P. palustris*	3	
Fabaceae (Legumes)	*Lotus pedunculatus, Lathyrus palustris*	2	
Haloragaceae (Milfoils)	*Myriophyllum verticillatum, M. spicatum, M. alterniflorum, M. aquaticum* (intr.)	3+1	
Lythraceae	*Lythrum salicaria, L. portula*	2	
Onagracaeae (Willowherbs)	*Epilobium hirsutum, E. parviflorum, E. palustre, Ludwigia palustris*	4	
Balsaminaceae (Balsams)	*Impatiens noli-tangere, I. capensis,*(intr.) *I. glandulifera* (intr.)	1 + 2	
Apiaceae (Umbellifers, dropworts)	*Hydrocotyle vulgaris, H. ranunculoides* (intr.), *Sium latifolium, Berula erecta, Oenanthe fistulosa, O. crocata, O. fluviatilis,* (mostly in flowing waters) *O. aquatica, Apium nodiflorum, A. inundatum, Peucedanum palustre*	11	
Solanaceae (nightshades)	*Solanum dulcamara*	1	
Menyanthaceae (bog bean)	*Menyanthes trifoliata, Nymphoides peltata*	2	
Lamiaceae (skullcaps, mints)	*Scutellaria galericulata, Mentha aquatica*	2	
Boraginaceae (Forget-me –nots)	*Myosotis scorpioides*		
Hippuridaceae (Marestail)	*Hippuris vulgaris*	1	

TABLE 12. (Cont.)

Callitrichaceae (Starworts)	Callitriche hermaphroditica, C. truncata, C. stagnalis, C. platycarpa, C. obtusangula, C. brutia, C. hamulata	7	
Plantaginaceae (Shoreweed)	Littorella uniflora	1	
Scrophulariaceae (Speedwells & others)	Mimulus (Monkey flowers, 6 spp. all intr.), Limosella aquatica, L. australis, Veronica scutellata, V. beccabunga, V. anagallis-aquatica, V. catenata, V. × lackschewitzii, Pedicularis palustris	7 +6	
Lentibulariaceae (Bladderworts & butterworts)	Pinguicula vulgaris, P. grandiflora, Utricularia vulgaris, U. australis, U. intermedia, U. minor, U. stygia, U. ochroleuca	8	Insectivorous plants of wet bogs and bog pools
Campanulaceae (Water lobelia)	Lobelia dortmanna	1	
Rubiaceae (Bedstraws)	Galium uliginosum, G. palustre	2	
Valerianaceae (Valerians)	Valeriana dioica	1	
Asteraceae (Thistles, fleabanes, sow thistles, hemp-agrimony)	Cirsium palustre , Sonchus palustris, Pulicaria dysenterica, Senecio aquaticus, Petasites hybridus, Bidens cernua, B. tripartita, Eupatorium cannabinum	8	
Butomaceae (Flowering rush)	Butomus umbellatus	1	
Alismataceae (Arrowheads, water-plantains, starfruit)	Sagittaria sagittifolia S. latifolia (intr.) S. rigida (intr.) S. subulata (intr.) Baldellia ranunculoides, Luronium natans, Alisma plantago-aquatica, A. lanceolatum, A. gramineum, Damasonium alisma	7 (+3)	Damasonium is rare and found only in small ponds
Hydrocharitaceae	Hydrocharis morsus-ranae, Stratiotes aloides, Egeria densa, Elodea canadensis, E. nutttallii, E. callitrichoides, Hydrilla verticillata, Lagarosiphon major, Vallisneria spiralis	2 (+ 7)	All but Hydrocharis and Stratiotes are introduced and except for E. canadensis, E. nuttallii and Lagarosiphon, of very limited distribution
Aponogetaceae (Cape pondweed)	Aponogeton distachyos (intr.)	+1	
Scheuzeriaceae	Scheuchzeria palustris	1	Very rare
Juncaginaceae	Triglochin palustre	1	
Potamogetonaceae (Pondweeds)	Potamogeton natans, P. lucens, P. polygonifolius, P. coloratus, P. nodosus, P. × zizii, P. × salicifolius, P. gramineus, P × nitens, P. alpinus, P. praelongus, P. perfoliatus, P. × cooperi, P. epihydrus, P. friesii, P. × lintonii, P. rutilus, P. pusillus, P. obtusifolius, P. berchtoldii, P. trichoides, P. compressus, P. crispus, P. filiformis, P. × suecicus, P. pectinatus, Groenlandia densa	26	A very few additional species are confined to rivers or ditches
Ruppiaceae (Tasselweeds)	Ruppia maritima, R, cirrhosa	2	Mostly in brackish waters close to the sea
Najadaceae (Naiads)	Naias flexilis, N. marina	2	

Zannichelliaceae (Horned pondweed)	*Zannichellia palustris*	1	
Araceae (Arums)	*Acorus calamus, Lysichiton americanus* (intr.), *Calla palustris* (intr.)	1 (+2)	
Lemnaceae (Duckweeds)	*Spirodela polyrhiza, Lemna gibba, L. minor, L. trisulca, L. minuta* (intr.), *Wolffia arrhiza*	5 + 1	Free-floating plants
Eriocaulaceae (Pipewort)	*Eriocaulon aquaticum*	1	
Juncaceae (Rushes and spike rushes)	*Juncus bulbosus, J. compressus, J. foliosus, J. bufonius, J. subnodulosus, J. articulatus, J. acutiflorus, J. filiformis, J. inflexus, J. effusus, J. conglomeratus*	11	
Cyperaceae (Sedges, cotton grasses, spike rushes, sea club rush, club rushes, bog rushes, saw sedge)	*Eriophorum vaginatum, E. angustifolium, E. latifolium, Eleocharis palustris, E. acicularis, E. multicaulis, E. quinqueflora, E. acicularis, Bolboschoenus maritimus, Schoenoplectus lacustris, S. tabernaemontani, S. triqueter, Isolepis setacea, I. cernua, Eleogiton fluitans, Schoenus nigricans, S. ferrugineus, Rhynchospora alba, R. fusca, Cladium mariscus, Carex paniculata, C. appropinquata, C. disticha, C. chordorrhiza, C. echinata,C. dioica C. lasiocarpa, C. acutiformis, C. riparia, C. pseudocyperus, C. rostrata, C. capillaris, C. hostiana, C. flava, C. buxbaumii, C. nigra, C. pulicaris, C. vesicaria, C. limosa, C. recta, C. aquatilis, C. acuta, C. elata*	44	Most of this family favour wet habitats and other than those listed might be found sometimes at the edges of lakes or pools. There are also numerous hybrids of *Carex*.
Poaceae (Grasses and reeds)	*Catabrosa aquatica, Leersia oryzoides, Glyceria maxima, G. fluitans, G. × pedicellata, G. declinata, G. notata, Deschampsia cespitosa, Phalaris arundinacea, Agrostis stolonifera, Calamagrostis spp., Molinia caerulea, Phragmites australis*	14	
Sparganiaceae (Bur reeds)	*Sparganium erectum, S. emersum, S. angustifolium, S. natans*	4	
Typhaceae (Bulrush, reedmace)	*Typha latifolia, T. angustifolia*	2	
Pontederiaceae	*Pontederia cordata* (intr.)	+1	
Liliaceae (Bog asphodel)	*Narthecium ossifragum*	1	
Iridaceae (Yellow flag)	*Iris pseudacorus*	1	
Orchidaceae (Orchids)	*Liparis loeselii, Hammarbya paludosa, Dactylorhiza fuchsii, incarnata, praetermissa, purpurella, Epipactis palustris*	7	
Total stoneworts		**23 + 2**	
Total mosses & liverworts		**6**	
Total non-flowering vascular plants		**11 + 1**	
Total flowering		**257 +27**	

sun increases the gas pressure inside young aerial leaves. The pressure cannot be easily relieved because the stomatal pores through which gases diffuse into the leaf are small and often closed on warm days. Older leaves on the same rhizome differ; they are often holed by insect damage or fungal decay and pressure cannot easily build up. As the high pressure develops in the younger leaves, it is relieved by air movement down the air spaces to the rhizome and up and out of the older leaves: an internal wind. Air reaching the roots can also diffuse out into the sediment and water in contact with the roots. There it can locally oxidise substances like sulphide, ammonia, nitrite and reduced iron and manganese, which are produced by bacteria under low oxygen conditions and which are toxic to young roots. Root systems can then be extended and continue to function in an otherwise hostile environment. Dig up some rushes in a waterlogged pasture and you may see brown channels of oxidised iron within the otherwise grey soil.

PHOTOSYNTHESIS UNDERWATER

Underwater there are new conditions that the reedswamp, fen and bog plants, with their leaves above the water, do not face. The first issue is in obtaining carbon dioxide. Although carbon dioxide is potentially much more soluble in water than oxygen, and may be supersaturated because of respiration of incoming organic matter, its concentration is governed by other ions like carbonate, bicarbonate and hydrogen with which it enters into reactions that may remove it in its free form. Moreover, the amount that dissolves is governed by equilibrium with the relatively low percentage of carbon dioxide (currently about 0.04 per cent) in the atmosphere so that a natural lake water will typically have less than 1 milli-atmosphere of free carbon dioxide per litre, or about 0.4 mg L^{-1}, but much more in combined form as bicarbonate, and up to about 200 mg per litre in the most bicarbonate-rich marl lakes in limestone regions.

The atmosphere currently has about 400 parts per million by weight of carbon dioxide, or about 0.5 mg carbon dioxide per litre of air. Plants photosynthesising underwater have access to about as much free carbon dioxide as land plants, but potentially much more if they can break down bicarbonate ions, but the diffusion rates of molecules in water are much lower than in the atmosphere. The store may be adequate, but the rate of supply quite low. The supply of carbon may thus sometimes temporarily limit photosynthesis, particularly towards the end of the afternoon, following heavy demands during the day; stocks are regenerated during the night.[5]

Plants must make concessions to cope with low diffusion rates. Submerged leaves have to be very thin, just as animal gills are thin to overcome the parallel difficulty in uptake of oxygen. It helps that submersion means that there are no problems of water loss, so the leaves have only a very thin cuticle that offers little barrier to gas diffusion. Land plants, with a thick waxy cuticle, have pores (stomata) that can be closed in hot dry periods to minimise water loss and in turn this also restricts entry of carbon dioxide. The thin cuticle on submerged leaves, and some remnants of stomata that now have no function, are evidence of the land origin of water plants. But there are still difficulties in getting enough carbon. One set of solutions is called the isoetid strategy and depends on making the most of the available free carbon dioxide supply in lakes with low bicarbonate concentrations. The other is to use both bicarbonate and free carbon dioxide, and to cope with the chemical consequences that this entails.

THE ISOETID STRATEGY

The isoetid strategy is named after the quillworts, species of *Isoetes*, in which it was discovered.[6] In Britain and Ireland, the strategy is shared by two *Isoetes* species and just a few flowering plants including water lobelia, shoreweed and pipewort (Fig. 83). They have short spiky leaves emerging usually from sandy sediments that characterise lakes in catchments with poorly weathered rocks. The leaves are stiff and waxy and the root systems are very well developed, in contrast to most other submerged plants, whose roots are sparse. The functions of roots for anchorage, and acquiring water and nutrients, in land plants, are

FIG 83. The water lobelia (left) and the pipewort (right) are 'isoetid' plants with features that favour uptake of carbon dioxide from the rich supplies in the sediments of base-poor, relatively infertile lakes. One characteristic, seen in the tray of plants at a water garden centre, is a well-developed root system.

less important underwater where currents are less strong than winds and both water and nutrients can be absorbed through the leaves. The abundant roots of the isoetids have a different function: that of absorbing carbon dioxide from the sediment interstices, where bacterial activity produces a rather richer supply than is present in the overlying water. The carbon dioxide can be absorbed even at night and held in the plant by chemical mechanisms that temporarily convert it to organic acids, and then regenerated by day when it can be used for photosynthesis.

This mechanism is similar to that used by succulent land plants where carbon dioxide may be scarce simply because their dry habitat means that the stomata are closed by day and open only at night. Like such succulents, isoetids have also retained a thick waxy cuticle, minimising the loss, not of water in their case, but of carbon dioxide that might otherwise diffuse out into the water. The isoetids nonetheless are small, slow-growing plants, producing only a low biomass,

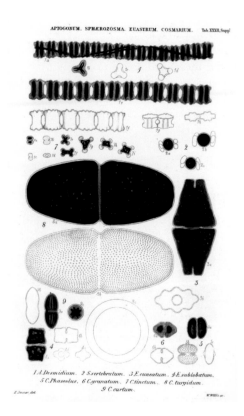

FIG 84. Desmids from acid waters, illustrated in a plate from a classic work by West & West (1904–22).

though this is as much a function of shortage of nitrogen and phosphorus in the waters that they inhabit as of carbon dioxide lack. There is more, however. The isoetids create and maintain conditions in the sediments that preserve their advantages. Oxygen leaks readily from their roots and helps maintain a high degree of oxidation in the adjacent sediments that causes oxidised iron to fix phosphorus into a form unavailable to most plants and stimulates bacteria to convert ammonium in the sediments to nitrate. Most plants prefer to take up ammonium. Creating these conditions makes nutrient uptake more difficult for the isoetids, but even more tricky for potential competitors. The isoetids have acquired mycorrhizal fungi that are efficient in nutrient uptake in association with their roots. Mycorrhizae are much less usual in their competitors. All in all, the isoetids have adapted to an already difficult habitat that they then defend against competitors.

There are also two groups of algae in which many species cannot use bicarbonate and which, like the isoetids, are thus able to use only free carbon dioxide. They include many golden algae, the chrysophytes and some of the desmids and related filamentous species like *Zygnema* and *Spirogyra*, which are most common in acid waters with low bicarbonate (Fig. 84).[7] In more alkaline waters these algae cannot compete with species that have the advantage of using bicarbonate, though they have traits that give them the edge in acid waters, like a genetically controlled low growth rate that is well adapted to a low supply of both carbon dioxide and other nutrients.

THE BICARBONATE STRATEGY

The isoetid strategy works well only in acid waters where there is little bicarbonate. Where there is competition from plants that can use bicarbonate, the greater carbon sources that bicarbonate users can command mean that they grow bigger and more quickly and can readily overshadow the isoetids. But using bicarbonate, which has required the evolution of an enzyme, carbonic anhydrase, which breaks down bicarbonate ions to carbon dioxide, causes quite complex chemical changes in the water. These make bicarbonate progressively much scarcer and force the pH to rise, which causes more and more of the carbon to be present as carbonate, which cannot be used for photosynthesis.[8] One sign that bicarbonate is being used is that carbonate may be deposited as a whitish deposit, called marl, particularly in the most calcium bicarbonate-rich waters, found in chalk and limestone regions. Marl is a precipitate of calcium and magnesium carbonates, which may also bind phosphate. It gives a milky appearance to the

FIG 85. Marl lakes, like Malham Tarn, set in limestone landscapes, have creamy sediments and rocks covered with dried marl. (Rachel Bates)

water and a deposit on the plants (Fig. 85). Stoneworts, with their coverage of marl, are the epitomes of bicarbonate users. Evolving in the ocean, where there are substantial bicarbonate concentrations and relatively high pH, most of the algae early evolved production of carbonic anhydrase, and in moving directly to freshwaters were already equipped to cope.

DIVING IN

We do not know if there had to be a long period for plants gradually to evolve aquatic adaptations, or whether there had only to be minor changes in the genes that regulate plant structure, so that there was a dive into the water rather than a tentative and progressive paddling. The limited amount of information suggests a dive. Big changes can occur through mutations in just a few genes that regulate how other genes are switched on. The modifications needed were quite small and once the problems of living in waterlogged soils had been overcome, the next stage could have been a hedging of bets: production of some normal aerial leaves that had functioning stomata and a thick cuticle and could take advantage of the air, and some that were thinner and able to function underwater. The yellow water lily is a good example, with large, thin leaves emerging from the rhizome in the late winter and the familiar thick lily pads emerging onto the water surface in spring.

It may even, at first, not have required any genetic change to produce the thin leaves; it could simply have been a physiological response to the lower light intensities underwater, just as trees produce thin shade leaves deep in their summer canopies and thick sun leaves on the outside, though the genetic potential to do so must be present.[9] A large rhizome, full of stored energy, would also help subsidise leaves that were just beginning to cope underwater, the stores being replenished by the aerial leaves later in the season. The strategies of the reedswamp plants, the lilies and other heterophyllic (different-leaved) species would seem to be ideal, with access to nutrients in the soils or sediments, unlimited water, as much light as the latitude could receive and carbon dioxide able to diffuse in rapidly from the air.

Why bother then, to move completely underwater, where there were problems of decreasing light availability and lower diffusion rates? The answer is that evolution does not have a director making such decisions; new habitats are exploited where new and random mutations allow it. But there are trade-offs in a submerged existence. The water provides a support, through its density, for plant structures, so that there need be little investment in expensive support tissues to maintain the plant upright, nor in waxy cuticles to minimise water loss from the aerial leaves. On hot days even reeds and lilies may not be able to keep their upper parts supplied rapidly enough with water to cope with the water loss without such help. On balance, however, the disadvantages of a completely submerged existence, though they look greater than the advantages, cannot be so, for submerged plants persist and in great variety. Adaptation, nonetheless, has rarely yet had time to become complete. Most submerged plants still produce flowers that are above the water and are pollinated by insects or wind. Only a few (for example, the water naiad) flower underwater and are pollinated by water currents. The charophytes, aquatic mosses and liverworts, ferns and fern allies continue to produce gametes that are water-borne and it is curious that they are not more widespread. The versatile flowering plants dominate the submerged plant world.

BUILDING THE LITTORAL

Everywhere, the edges of lakes are their most productive parts and in the more mineral-rich waters, the greater stocks of carbon, nitrogen and phosphorus lead often to dense stands of stoneworts, pondweeds and hornwort, mixed

with filamentous algae, lilies, patches of reeds and sedges, and floating
duckweeds, in littoral zones that form the most complex and intricate parts
of the lake stage. The macrophytes (an unnecessary word for a large plant, but
unfortunately one that is now used routinely) are always covered by a film of
microorganisms, the periphyton, a mixture of algae, bacteria and protozoa that
is very active chemically. The plant beds are floored by sediments that teem with
microorganisms, photosynthesising where light gets through to patches among
the plants, or processing dead organic matter sloughing from the plants or
brought in by the streams. In turn there is a rich invertebrate fauna among the
plants, an abundance of fish and a rich variety of birds in the littoral zone.

The plants and their periphyton and the conditions they create at the sediment
surfaces are both scenery and players in the littoral zone. Although we tend to
note particularly the movements and behaviour of the animals, the plants are
far from inert. Their structures and activities provide, for the animal players, a
complex underwater labyrinth, which we will now visit, of water spaces, corridors,
passageways, dark alleys and sloughs, waving with skeins of filaments, rich in
sometimes poisonous chemicals, and descending from sunlit water surfaces to
black cellars around the sediment, in which oxygen is scarce or predators lurk.

A TOURIST TRIP TO THE LITTORAL THEATRES

Were we to make ourselves much smaller, so that as we swim through the
littoral zone, with our SCUBA apparatus, we are scaled down to the size of, say,
a copepod, a couple of millimetres long, we might gain a better view of what
happens there. It would be more detailed than we can see at our human size,
peering down from a boat, and more realistic than when we employ our usual
sampling methods. We use some sort of net swept through the water to capture
animals, or a grab that cuts through the vegetation into the sediment, and like
a mechanical digger on a building site, heaves a jumbled mass of rubble into a
pile to one side.[10] We can sort through the mass and separate out plant remains
and invertebrates, and count or weigh them, but we have lost the structure of the
community. It is like reconstructing the workings of a city from a demolition
site. Moreover, the faster-moving animals may escape. A net swept through the
water catches some, but does not sample the sedentary or slower-moving animals
on the bottom or those deep in the vegetation.

An alternative is to place plastic plants, such as are sold to decorate fish tanks,
plastic brushes (lavatory brushes have indeed been used) or strands of plastic
rope or nylon mesh in the water for several weeks to simulate plant structures.

Careful recovery of such artificial substrata, by lifting them in nets, can standardise the sampling and give some insight into possible differences among, say, long thin leaves versus bushy plants or flat plate-like leaves, as habitats, but plastic is inert.[11] Real leaves are not and by and large the insights obtained will be crude. Careful experiments in laboratory aquaria or, in the field, detailed observations of large invertebrates, such as dragonflies, as they lay their eggs, can help, and increasingly, at least in marine studies, sophisticated cameras, deployed on submersibles, can record the workings of bottom communities without disturbing them. The smaller scale, generally murkier water and shortage of funds for freshwater scientists has precluded use of these so far. Nonetheless we can reconstruct a picture to inform our swim through the littoral zone, in the guise of a small copepod.

LLYN IDWAL

There is no typical littoral zone, so like tourists with limited funds we must choose from the huge range available, and being adventurous, we will choose the extremes. We start in Cwm Idwal, a great ice-carved bowl in Snowdonia, with steep cliffs from which rock climbers dangle, and dripping ledges on which a collection of unusual plants has managed to hang on since the retreat of the glaciers. As the slopes of the bowl lessen, they are covered with an acid grassland of mat grass, bent and fescue. Towards the southern end of Llyn Idwal, a lake of 14 ha (Fig. 74) in the bottom of the cwm, they merge into slightly acidic heath and boggy mire communities.[12] Cwm Idwal has mostly siliceous rocks of rhyolite but also some more base-rich basalts, which temper the acidity of the water. It is nonetheless a distinctly soft water, very low in conductivity and nutrients, that flows into the lake.

Our trip from the grassland into the mires, as a 2-mm homunculus, is not easy: a combination of swimming and scrambling. The vegetation is waterlogged and the terrain hummocky. The plants tower above us, like forest trees, but the forest is open and we can move around the clumps. Underfoot however, the *Sphagnum* provides a rolling terrain, its mounds covered by only a thin film of water, alternating with waterlogged pools a centimetre or two deep. These waters teem with life. There are numerous strands of fungi crossing the surface like trip wires, linking the cells of *Sphagnum* with small colonies of cyanobacteria, associating as simple lichens.[13] *Sphagnum* has a particular structure in which small active green cells lie among much larger, now empty, cells, which hold water and keep the plant moist in dry periods. These cells also adsorb metal ions from the water and exchange them with hydrogen ions, thus keeping the water acidic, a medium in which *Sphagnum* can grow well and compete with other mosses that need more base-rich conditions. Nonetheless there are plenty of other moss species slumped in the water films and impeding our progress. The roles of the fungi and cyanobacteria have yet to be fully revealed. The linkages are not casual; they are intimate and a huge variety of fungi is present. Many are probably mycorrhizal, their huge collective surfaces scavenging sparse phosphates and metals, and exchanging them for nitrogen fixed by the cyanobacteria, and energy, in the form of sugars, from the photosynthesising *Sphagnum*.

At our feet are many algae. Prominent are the slowly creeping desmids (Fig. 84), and small flagellates of green and golden algae that flit about. The desmids are very beautiful, with intricate outlines, mirrored between the two halves of the cell, and separated by a narrow waist or isthmus. This overall structure gives them their name, which means 'twofold'. Some are long and thin and covered with knobbly projections, others have long spines; some are star-shaped, or moon-like or fashioned like cottage loaves. Some desmid genera have a wide distribution in all manner of waters, but many are confined to acid ones. It was once thought that they simply did not tolerate much calcium, but we were misled by a correlation of their occurrence with low-calcium waters.[14] The real reason is that they are confined to using free carbon dioxide. Squeeze out the water from a handful of *Sphagnum* and look at it under a microscope and you will usually be amazed at the desmid diversity.

Picking our way among the shallow pools, tripping over fungi, and stumbling over the bigger desmids, nearly half our size, are not our only problems. There is a bit of a smell and there are some quite large animals about. The smell is sulphurous, with a whiff of hydrogen sulphide. It reminds us that below the living tops of the *Sphagnum*, the rootless plants quickly tail off into dead stems, and the peat that these become as the mat compresses them. Low oxygen levels below the surface limit decomposition by fungi and bacteria, and the sulphurous gases are products of the partial decomposition of proteins and the use of sulphate as an oxidising agent by the bacteria. Reduced iron is also present and in some ancient bogs that had succeeded to bog forest, this iron penetrated into fallen timber, converting it to hard and black ancient bog oak that was buried as the peat continued to accumulate. There is also methane in the air that we are breathing, though we cannot smell it. Methane is yet another final product of anaerobic decomposition and the bogs of the northern hemisphere are major sources of it to the atmosphere.

We see little of this soil activity as we trek over the surface, nor do we see most of the small invertebrates, or ciliates and amoebae that live in the water among the plants and below the surface. Testate amoebae, of some dozens of species,

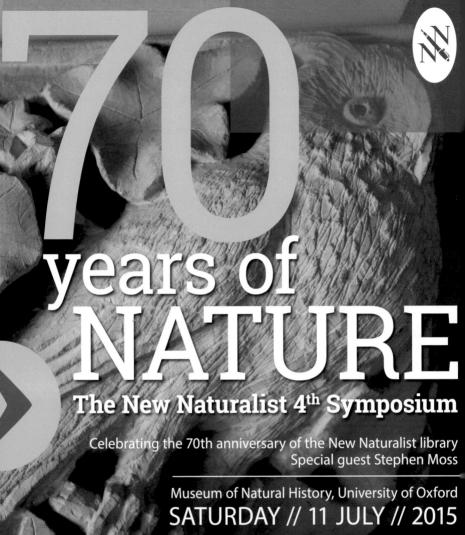

70
years of
NATURE
The New Naturalist 4th Symposium

Celebrating the 70th anniversary of the New Naturalist library
Special guest Stephen Moss

Museum of Natural History, University of Oxford
SATURDAY // 11 JULY // 2015

SPEAKERS INCLUDE

John Altringham // *Bats* • Robert Cameron // *Slugs and Snails*
David Goode // *Nature in Towns and Cities* • John Lee // *Yorkshire Dales*
Brian Moss // *Lakes, Loughs and Lochs* • Clive Stace // *Alien Plants* • Jeremy Thomas // *Butterflies*

WITH

Robert Gillmor // Peter Marren // Ian Newton // Christopher Perrins // David Streeter

TO BOOK TICKETS tbernhard@btinternet.com // 01794 830937

The New Naturalist 4th Symposium

Museum of Natural History, University of Oxford
Saturday 11th July 2015, 9.00am-5.00pm
Booking Form

This special event will mark the 70th anniversary of the New Naturalist library and we are very fortunate to have the opportunity to hold this symposium at the prestigious Museum of Natural History in Oxford. As well as a great selection of lectures by New Naturalist authors there will be an opportunity for limited numbers of guests to enjoy tours of the entomology department and the swifts, made famous by the book *Swifts in a Tower* by David Lack. Tickets will include teas, coffees and biscuits on arrival, mid-morning and mid-afternoon, a buffet lunch, plus a souvenir 12-page colour brochure. Limited edition mugs can be pre-ordered and will be available for collection on the day. There will be a good selection of second-hand natural history book dealers and wildlife artists exhibiting plus book signing sessions in the main lecture theatre. We hope you will be able to join us on what will be a very special day.

Name	
Address	
Email*	
Telephone	

Tickets @ £70 each	number		£
Special limited edition mug @ £8 each	number		£
		Total	£

Please indicate (tick the box below) if you would be interested in the tours which will take place during the extended lunch break. As the swift tour involves a number of steep steps within a very narrow staircase, please only select this option if you are able to undertake these conditions. As there is likely to be a high demand for places on these tours, names will be pulled out of a hat by our special guest Stephen Moss during the morning.

Tour of the entomology department	
Tour of the swifts in the tower	

Please make cheques payable to 'The New Naturalist Collectors Club' and post to:
30 Botley Road, Romsey, Hampshire SO51 5AP

*By supplying your email you consent to be added to the New Naturalist newsletter list, where you will be the first to hear of our upcoming publications, features and discounts on our books. You can also sign up on our site, www.newnaturalists.com.

each with the 'house' it carries, of protein, silica or organic debris, are abundant, like small dogs in the water and we wonder quite how and why so many species coexist.[15] They feed on organic fragments, broken off from the plants by other grazers, or the debris of fungal decomposition, or algae and protozoa small enough for their fluid cell membranes to engulf. Different species occur at different levels on and in the mat. The same is true of the ciliates and undoubtedly of bigger animals like the tardigrades, earthworms, rotifers, slugs and nematodes, some of them as big as we are, or somewhat larger, like cows and ponies, in the mire.

This is a teeming community, but one which tends to be ignored. Where the condition of mires has to be assessed, to appease the bureaucratic needs of conservation, it is usually done just on the plants, or sometimes on the larger insects, but then with emphasis on scarce species rather than on the functioning of the community as a whole. Nonetheless, there are rove and ground beetles, craneflies and other groups of flies (Brachycera, Dolichopodidae, Syrphidae, Scatophagidae), moths, ants and other insects that run over the surface and in some cases embed their larvae among the *Sphagnum*. The latter here include two dragonflies, the common hawker and black darter. There are also wolf spiders and money spiders.

A DIVERSION INTO STABLE ISOTOPE METHODS

We need to pick our way carefully towards the open water, using the cover of sedges and other plants, because many of these insects, and the spiders, are carnivores and much bigger than we are. The dragonflies overhead are unlikely to trouble us, for they are intent on flying prey, but their nymphs lurk in the pools among the vegetation for prey to pass, when they flick from under their heads a hinged mask with teeth that stab into soft bodies. We do not wish to become part of this food web! It is better to study it from a safer viewpoint. The idea of food webs is well known, but recent work using stable isotopes has shown that they are much more complicated than previously realised.

The methods depend on taking single animals, or pieces of plant, or small samples of detritus or sediment, and burning them to vaporise their carbon and nitrogen. The carbon and nitrogen oxides are then passed through a mass spectrometer, which can measure the amounts of different isotopes of carbon and nitrogen. Carbon most commonly occurs as ^{12}C, but there is a small amount of ^{13}C in circulation. Plants using carbon dioxide from the air tend to be low in ^{13}C because it is heavier than ^{12}C and diffuses into the plants less rapidly. However, plants taking up bicarbonate, or carbon dioxide generated underwater from it, tend to have a little more ^{13}C, because rocks from which the bicarbonate is derived are richer in ¹³C. The ¹³C is most conveniently measured relative to a standard and the results expressed as a deviation (∂¹³C) from the standard (a rock fossil known as Pee Dee Belemnite), first used for the technique. Thus material with a very negative ∂¹³C, perhaps –30 parts per thousand or so, tends to have come from plants using air as a source of carbon dioxide, whilst those using bicarbonate have a deviation, perhaps –25, that is much smaller. The carbon isotope can thus give us an idea of the source of organic matter on which an animal has fed, and in freshwaters can tell us whether it has been derived from material produced in the water, or derived from washed-in land vegetation or the emergent reed vegetation, which derive their carbon from the air. As yet we cannot distinguish between reedswamp and truly land vegetation with this technique.

The nitrogen isotopes give us different information. At each step in the food chain, ¹⁵N, a scarce isotope compared with the more usual ¹⁴N, becomes enriched in a relatively steady way by three to four times at each step. The difference in ¹⁵N

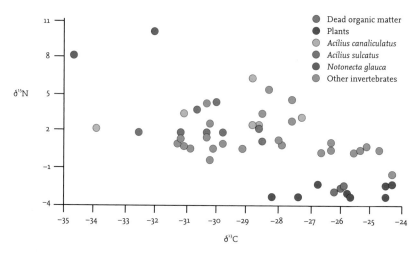

FIG 86. Stable isotopes of nitrogen and carbon give new insights to the nature of food webs. In this diagram from a raised bog lake in the Netherlands (Van Duinen *et al.*, 2006) some of the advantages and problems can be seen. The increase in ¹⁵N content from the base of the food web can be seen. *Notonecta* is a predator, the two beetles (*Acilius*) are omnivores taking many small invertebrates, and the remaining invertebrates are omnivores with a broader diet. However, the points track towards the left, suggesting that there is a dependence on carbon compounds imported into the bog that were not sampled and therefore do not appear. These might include aerial insects falling in, or dissolved organic matter brought in by streams and taken up by bacteria.

is also expressed as a change, $\partial^{15}N$, relative to the ^{15}N content of the atmosphere. By graphing the $\partial^{13}C$, as the horizontal (x) axis, and $\partial^{15}N$, as the vertical (y) axis, for each sample, a useful picture is obtained (Fig. 86). Carnivores will have high enrichments of ^{15}N, and lie high on the y axis, detritus feeders and plant grazers much lower ones, towards the bottom of the axis, and plants and algae lowest of all. Water plants will lie to the right of the x axis, land plants and detritus derived from them towards the left. Animals feeding on water plants will be to the right, those feeding on imported detritus to the left. Many animals will have mixed diets and lie intermediately, but mathematical techniques can be used to calculate the relative amounts of each component that they take, given the isotope contents of the original foods. The picture obtained is that most animals in waters and mires are omnivores with some degree of preference for one food source or another. Some caddis fly larvae, for example, living on underwater rocks, spin bags of silk, in which they live but also use to catch smaller prey animals that wander or drift in. But not only do they create a home and larder in their bags, they also incidentally cultivate algae that grow on the bag, fertilised by their oozing excretions. They eat the algal-infested bag material at one end and make new bag material at the other: a sort of mobile home and garden.[16]

INTO LLYN IDWAL

We have crossed the mire now, between the legs of a sandpiper (a monster wading bird from our miniature view) picking insects from the *Sphagnum* surface, and we have experienced a new perspective that is not so obvious to us at our normal size. It has been a hazardous journey; being two millimetres in size makes us very vulnerable and now we have to pick our way through an underwater forest. A heron's eye view will show that this is not random, but not very regular either. Where the main inflow streams come in at the southern end of Llyn Idwal, a delta of sand, gravel and eroded peat forms deeper sediments than elsewhere in the lake and bears a greater variety of plants. The shores are otherwise stony and gravelly (Fig. 74.), but, as the water deepens, the sediments become finer as the waves sift the fine material washed in and redeposit it at greater depths. There is enough light for plants and algae to grow down to about 5.5 m of the maximum depth of 13 m. The mean depth is about 3.4 m so the littoral zone covers more than half of the bottom.

There is very little reedswamp and no water lilies; the terrain and the lack of sediment preclude those. On the main stream delta there are a few areas of water horsetail, bottle sedge, narrow-leaf bur reed and even of common reed, and there is one patch of floating pondweed, but the colonies are all scant. In deeper

TABLE 13. Invertebrates in Llyn Idwal and Martham Broad, based on sampling in summer. P, Predator; D, Detritus feeder; S, Scraper (of the surfaces of rocks or plants); G, Grazer on plants or algae; F, Filter-feeder.

	Feeding guild	Lyn Idwal	Martham Broad North
		1 min kick sample (converted to per m²)	Grab samples, converted to per m²
Water chemistry			
pH		6.6–6.8	7.85–8.6
Conductivity (microsiemens per cm)		27–28	963–1,311
Total nitrogen (mg/L)		<0.2	<0.7
Total phosphorus (mg/L)		0.004–0.008	0.02–0.06
Bicarbonate (mg/L)		3.0–5.6	175–238
Calcium (mg/L)		1.8- 2.3	180–320
Sodium (mg/L)		2.3–2.8	440–620
Chloride (mg/L)		3.5–4.4	845–1,295
Platyhelminths (Triclads)			
Dendrocoelum lacteum	P		10–100
Annelids (Oligochaetes)			
Limnodrilus hoffmeisteri	D		100–1,000
Annelids (Leeches)			
Erpobdella octoculata	P	0.2	
Molluscs			
Lymnaea peregra	S/D	1.4	10–100
Potamopyrgus jenkinsi	S/D		10–100
Bithynia tentaculata	S/D		10–100
Planorbis planorbis	S/D		10–100
Acroloxus lacustris	S	0.8	
Pisidium sp.	D	99	
Crustacea			
Ostracods	F		100–1,000
Asellus aquaticus	G/S		100–1,000
Asellus meridianus	G/S		100–1,000
Sphaeroma hookeri	G/S		<10
Gammarus duebeni	G/D		1,000–10,000
Gammarus lacustris	G/D	0.5	
Neomysis integer	P/G		10–100

		Insects	
		Damselflies	
Platycnemis pennipes	P		10–100
		Mayflies	
Siphlonura lacustris	S	5.2	
Baetis sp.	S	1.4	
Heptagenia lateralis	S	0.4	
Leptophlebia sp.	D	7.8	
Caenis horaria	S/D	20	10–100
Cloeon dipterum			10–100
		Stoneflies	
Diura bicaudata	P	1	
Bugs			
Immature corixids	D	130	
Corixa punctata	D/G		10–100
Sigara falleni	D/G		10–100
		Beetles	
Oulimnius troglodytes	D	64	
Diving beetles (Dytiscidae)	P		10–100
		Caddis flies	
Polycentropus flavomaculatus	FD	0.7	
Limnephilus sp.	G/D		10–100
Holocentropus dubius	FD	0.6	
Cyrnus trimaculatus	FD	0.6	
Cyrnus flavidus	FD		10–100
Hydroptila sp.	D/G	7	
Oxyethira sp.	D/G	1	
Mystacides longicornis	D/G	2	
		Diptera	
Crane flies	D	3.4	
Chironomids	D/G	173	10–100
Dixa amphibia	SD		10–100
		Mites	
Hydracarinids	P		10–100
Total predators (per m²)		1.2	Up to 450
Total grazers & detritus feeders (per m²)		277	Up to 14,350
TOTAL (per m²)		**278**	**Up to 14,800**

water around most of the lake, is a band of *Nitella* sp., a stonewort that does not deposit calcium carbonate, mixed with lake quillwort, shoreweed and water lobelia, alternate-leaved milfoil, intermediate water starwort, fire moss and bog pondweed. It is a sparse community, with most of the plants short and scattered, but nonetheless it supports a distinctive community of littoral animals.

We enter through the delta and, although this is the richest area for animals, there are very few at first sight. This is an unproductive waterscape; nutrients are scarce. The bigger stones and rocks are only slightly slimy with films of bacteria and diatoms. The gravels are bare, for wave movement jostles them together, scouring off anything that has colonised. The submerged plants form copses and more extensive forests, the flowering stems of some emerging above the water surface, but there is much bare stone among them, especially at the very edge where the waves break. The forest becomes denser with the flimsy plants of *Nitella* as we go to greater depths, and the sediments become sandier, their surfaces more flocculent with dark brown peat eroded from the mires at the edge. The light is yellowish from the dissolved organic matter, but the water is clear and it is not visibility that makes this seem a nearly deserted land.

There are, on average, about 300 animals per metre squared (Table 13), so about one animal per two inch square, in a terrain that has, from our 2 mm point of view, huge boulders. We can see ahead enough to pick out a single animal, or a small flock, here and there, but mostly we are manoeuvring around large obstacles, be they rocks or plants, and most animals are hidden from view. Our first encounter is a large dark-brown snail (*Lymnaea peregra*), a couple of centimetres from its foot to the top of its shell, much bigger than we are, but no threat as it slowly rasps its way, with its toothed and abrasive radula, a sort of tongue, over the film of algae and bacteria on a rock. As it swings its head from side to side it not only scrapes algae but also wears the rock, and every minute or so squeezes out a faecal pellet that rolls into a dip where debris has collected. There we come across a small herd of chironomid larvae, the long, thin young of midges, whose head and fleshy front legs emerge from tubes within the sediment. Rarely leaving their protective tubes, they edge around in a circle to bite and swallow pieces of algae or dead leaf, or lumps of sediment. Continually they churn out faeces from which they have digested the bacteria and fungi, leaving the roughage of raw organic matter and particles of clay for recolonisation by microorganisms. We have read somewhere that chironomids are called bloodworms from the haemoglobin that they contain and which is thought to be an oxygen-store in rich sediments, but these are not red. They are brownish and greenish, and high up in the canopy of plant leaves are some more, equally well camouflaged. This lake is high in oxygen, even in the hypolimnion in late summer, another sign that its catchment is infertile, and there is not much rich organic matter for the bacteria to decompose; the peaty material is too raw. Everywhere, that spartanness is reflected in the animals we see.

A small shoal of young corixids (water bugs) buzzes through the valley where we mingled with the chironomids. They are about our size, and, despite their mouth parts, formed into a beak, which in other bugs is sharp and pierces prey, these use it to gather-in organic detritus; there are also some equally small riffle beetles (*Oulimnius troglodytes*) clinging with their strongly clawed legs to an overhang of rock, biting at strands of algal filaments wafting from it. Both the corixids and the beetles are air breathers, and carry a bubble of air under their wing covers, a little like the aqualung on which we ourselves depend. They absorb oxygen from it, which is replaced by oxygen diffusing in from the water, so that the tiny beetles never have to return to the surface. The bubble is smaller under the reduced wing covers of the corixids and tends to collapse so that every hour or two they must return to the surface and replenish the bubble from the atmosphere. The beetles crawl and cannot swim and this lessens their oxygen demand, but the corixids swim fast using the hairs on their back legs to thrust against the water; the faster the movement, the more oxygen is needed.

Chironomids, beetles and corixids are the commonest animals (Fig. 87). They are the grazing herds of this waterscape and they depend very much on inwashed organic matter. There is richer food of fresh algae on the exposed rocks and boulders, but these are exposed and dangerous places for small animals. There are predators – not many, but lethal if you meet them. In the distance we have spotted a large, anaconda-like leech, *Erpobdella octoculata*, undulating its body to encourage a flow of oxygen-rich water over it, as it anchors itself to a rock. It

FIG 87. Among the most common animals in the waterscape of Llyn Idwal are beetles (*Oulimnius troglodytes*, left), corixids (right, upper) and chironomid larvae (right, lower). These animals are between 2 and 10 mm in length.

was difficult to see, for its body is camouflaged with a mottled pattern of yellow and brown against a brown background, in water that has a yellowish tinge. Its swaying movement gave it away. We had thought that leeches were bloodsuckers of mammals, and so some are, but not most of them in Britain and Ireland. This one seeks out small animals that it can easily catch, like the chironomids, or even the tiny bivalve pea mussels, *Pisidium*, that we are now beginning to notice, half buried in the sediment and sucking in a muddy soup from the looser sediment surfaces. For an animal needing calcium carbonate for its shell, they are more abundant than we might have expected (though like the *Lymnaea* and a small limpet (*Acroloxus lacustris*) that also scrapes over the rocks, they are much scarcer than in the dense mollusc populations of lowland lakes). Llyn Idwal is not quite so acid and calcium-poor as other lakes of Snowdonia because of the outcrop of base-rich basalts that by chance occurs in its catchment.

After a long swim that takes us several metres parallel to the shoreline, we catch sight of another large predator, a stonefly nymph, *Diura bicaudata*, ten times longer than we are, but crawling quite slowly in search of chironomids to eat. We can move too fast for it, but its mandibles, the biting mouth parts with which its seizes soft prey, are fearsome enough for us to decide to swim up into the plant canopy and take a loftier view. There are small animals swimming around us, like birds in the air, and some skimming over the plants, grazing on the diatoms and other algae growing on the leaves and stems. As on the rocks, the film is relatively sparse, because of shortage of nutrients, but there are diatoms growing on stalks, others attached by mucilage pads at their bases, and yet others glued or slowly gliding over the surface on a lubricant of slime pumped out from a slit in their silica walls.[17] There are also filaments of green algae, some of which have epiphytes of their own.

The small animals are largely cladocerans, water fleas, with a chitinous cloak or carapace that gives them a smooth outline despite the numerous feeding limbs borne on the front of the body. Some (for example, *Eurycercus lamellatus*) are bigger than we are, others are tiny, and the most common of these, *Chydorus sphaericus*, attaches itself to algal filaments and collects whatever fine debris comes its way. Like several other species of water flea, it can also swim to the bottom and browse among the sedimentary organic matter, and algae that move over the sediments or are attached to the rocks. None of these grazers and browsers is a threat to us and indeed the predators are scarce, as is normal in ecosystems. Prey is difficult to catch; it swims away rapidly or burrows in sediment, or, like the large mayfly nymph (*Heptagenia lateralis*) whose flattened head we can just see on the under edge of a rock, crawls into narrow crevices where it hides by day and emerges to scrape the rocks by night, when the most agile predators, trout and minnows, cannot see it.

Other mayflies take refuge in their small size and brown camouflage. We can see two more mayfly species grazing on the rocks (*Baetis* sp. and *Siphlonura lacustris*). Like the *Heptagenia*, they are found more often in fast-flowing streams but are surviving in the well-mixed, well-oxygenated water at the edge of this lake. All the mayflies have gills along the sides of their bodies, which they flicker to keep water flowing over them, especially where the bulk of the water otherwise moves smoothly over the worn surfaces of the stones. Two more mayfly nymphs forage in the sediments: the slow-moving *Leptophlebia* and *Caenis horaria*, the most common of the mayflies in the lake, its body often covered with organic debris, which might offer it some camouflage. The mayfly nymphs emerge (as adult flies, known to fishermen as duns) at some time during the summer or autumn for a few hours, maybe a day or so, of mating flight and egg-laying, before depositing on the water surface a raft of eggs which eventually sink, then hatch to produce a new generation. We might see one or two young nymphs on each large stone, but the early instars are very small and become evident only when they move.

As we scan the bottom over the next couple of hours, a few more players pass by. A shrimp, *Gammarus lacustris*, swimming partly on its side, scuds around a rock and then under it. Like many of the browsers and grazers, it takes a broad diet of algae and dead organic matter and bites at the small flocs of filamentous algae that lie, like wads of green cotton wool, in the shallows, or grow from the stones. *G. lacustris* differs only slightly from the more common *G. pulex*, but is quite distinct and has a distribution that is centred on lakes in north and western Britain and Ireland; it begs questions of how the two species differ ecologically and why a few lakes have *G. lacustris* but many others, even in this same region of Wales, have *G. pulex*.

A slight movement in a sandy patch reveals an insect that pokes its head and legs from a conical tube of sand grains. It is the larva of a caddis fly, *Mystacides longicornis*, and it too is grazing over the organic debris and algae among the sediment. This collection of grazers has its parallels in the impala, wildebeest, buffalo, giraffe, elephant, hippo and rhinoceros that we are familiar with in African savannahs, and the list is not yet complete. There are two more caddis species with cases, *Hydroptila* and *Oxyethira*, the first with a sand grain case, the other with a case of just chitin, looking like a tiny bottle, and three more caddis that have no cases at all. *Polycentropus flavomaculatus* spins nets of silk across gaps in rocks or between plant leaves and catches fine material. It eats both net and catch and must weave several nets in a day. *Holocentropus dubius* and *Cyrnus trimaculatus* make tubular bags in which they live, and which trap very small animals or water-born detritus drifting into them.

That exhausts our list of what we have seen in a few hours, but not the complete list of organisms that are present. The films on the rocks and the epiphytes on the plants will include hundreds of species of algae, fungi, protozoa and bacteria. There are rotifers and nematodes deep among the sediments or leaves, and probably as many more large invertebrate species as we have noted, but patchily distributed elsewhere in the lake, or scarce at the time of our visit. Any sampling is selective and incomplete.

We can readily gain a general picture, but not easily a detailed one, and there are always questions. Are these species some unique grouping that reflects the precise conditions of this habitat, or is there an element of chance such that a different group, had it arrived and established first, might survive equally well? Probably. How is the apparently uniform brown peaty debris able to support so many browsers? Are there unique combinations of components of the debris and different species of algae that allow coexistence of many species? Probably not. Or is the community always a transitory, unstable one, continually disrupted by weather and other changes that allow, for a time, species that are ill-suited and declining to coexist with new and up-and-coming ones? Quite likely. But the details will be so fleeting that they will change before we can even investigate them. If we examine another sort of littoral zone, there are general differences that make sense, even with our superficial knowledge.

MARTHAM NORTH BROAD

The contrast might be with Martham North Broad (Fig. 75) in Norfolk.[18] It is not a natural lake, but it has existed for over 700 years, so has had plenty of time to acquire the characteristics of one. Its basin was dug by mediaeval people in the floodplain deposits of a river then flowing out to sea close by. They dug it mostly for the fuel that dried peat provides, but also for clay for building. The Broad is set in fens and reedswamps, and held in by walls of earth, beyond which the former marshland has been drained for agriculture. This drainage has caused the land to sink a couple of metres below mean sea level, so water is pumped up, over the wall and into the Broad and the river which supplies it. Norfolk is covered in soils derived from glacial drift and the underlying geology is of soft rocks that weather easily. Martham Broad is rich in bases (Table 13), with plentiful calcium and nutrients, has deep sediments and even a dose of sea salt sucked in by the pumping.

The swamps and fens around the Broad are dominated by common reed, harvested for roofing thatch, and the yearly adjustments of water levels that are made to make this easier have tended to reduce the number of other species in the drier parts. Nonetheless, some places are kept wet and there are saw sedge, marsh thistle, bottle and carnation sedges and fen rush. An occasional alder seedling or willow bush indicates what the land would eventually become, were cutting to cease. In such habitats, with both a wet, even submerged floor and a dense and productive sward of plants, the invertebrate fauna, particularly the insects, is very rich (though that might reflect a greater interest in them than in other invertebrates by amateur naturalists). Milk parsley grows in the fens and provides food for the caterpillars of the spectacular swallowtail butterfly. In an early New Naturalist on the Broads, a well-known naturalist, Ted Ellis, gave an appendix of nearly 70 pages, mostly in list form, of the insects of the fens, reedswamps and alder carrs.

The reed rather abruptly gives way to the submerged plants in Martham Broad. This is partly because the sides of the basin, created by peat cutting, are near vertical, partly because former floating mats of reed have eroded away. Raised nitrate (from the local agriculture) encouraged shoot growth at the expense of root and rhizome growth, and made the mats top-heavy and vulnerable to wind. The Broad is very shallow, less than 1 m deep, so its entire bottom is littoral. Small patches of yellow water lilies lie among a varied submerged community, dominated by stoneworts. The rough and the bristly are the most abundant, but there are six others, mostly *Chara* spp. but also the starry stonewort. Clumps of pondweeds (blunt-leaved, fennel-leaved, small and perfoliate) are interspersed with water crowfoot, hornwort, ivy-leaved duckweed, Nutall's pondweed, spiked water milfoil, mare's tail, common starwort and the curious holly-leaved naiad, which is confined in Britain and Ireland to Broadland. Filamentous algae, such as *Cladophora* and *Ulothrix*, drape around the plants in cloud-like masses in late summer.

This is a community very different from the isoetid and nitellid one of Llyn Idwal. It contains mostly bicarbonate users, of vigorous growth and high biomass and covered with diatoms in spring. The water is difficult to row through in summer without dragging a mass of waterweed. Though the water is transparent, rather little light reaches the bottom through the mass of plants, and the sediment is rich with debris and marl. The pH and conductivity of the water are high (Table 13) and this very different regime is reflected in the invertebrates. There are many snails and crustaceans (which require much calcium for their shells and exoskeletons), indeed there are many more animals, and although predators are scarcer than the feeders on detritus and algae, the system, in its much greater productivity, supports a higher ratio of predators to prey than in Llyn Idwal.

A 2-mm homunculus, journeying through, would risk death from one or other of the 200 or so predators occupying every square metre, though there is much cover to dodge behind. You would never be less than 20 cm from a

FIG 88. *Gammarus duebeni* (left), which in Britain favours brackish waters, including Martham Broad, is also the only native *Gammarus* in Irish freshwaters. *Gammarus lacustris* (right) is present in Llyn Idwal, though *G. pulex* is otherwise most common in the region. *G. duebeni* has a strongly kidney-shaped eye. Adult shrimps are about 1 cm long.

predator. Two animals, both crustaceans, hint at the increased salinity. *Neomysis integer*, an opossum shrimp that holds its eggs in a pouch until hatching, and the water-louse *Sphaeroma baltica* are also found in estuaries. The most abundant large invertebrates are pond shrimps, *Gammarus duebeni* (Fig. 88), this species again reflecting the slight salinity, and oligochaete worms, living in the surface sediment layers, head down and bottom up, taking in a stream of mud, digesting the bacteria and releasing a continuous ribbon of faeces.

MEASURING THE CHEMISTRY

Inflow water chemistry tells us much about what to expect in the communities of different lakes, but a dense plant community, with its rich periphyton, can modify the water chemistry through photosynthesis and nutrient uptake. Measuring these chemical effects is difficult but, in dense littoral vegetation, a water sample taken even half a metre away from the plants will not accurately reflect the nature of the water among them and even less the chemistry at their surfaces. Iwan Jones showed this by using very small electrodes positioned close to Nuttall's pondweed, growing at different nutrient concentrations.[19] He recorded the pH, measured by the electrodes, at each step as he steadily moved the electrodes closer to the plant surface through the film of periphyton. When the periphyton layer was dense, the pH rose from 8.2 to 9.4 over only 2 mm as the plant surface was approached. This represents a very big change in conditions, brought about by the photosynthesis of the plant and the algae growing on it.

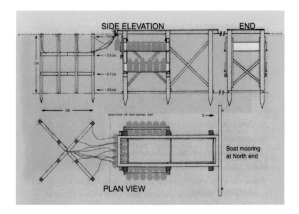

FIG 89. Apparatus used to sample 36 points in one-metre cubed of water. Design by Tom Barker.

Uptake of carbon becomes more and more difficult as pH rises because the proportion of the unusable carbonate increases, and total carbon concentrations fall. Although the chemistry of the water a few centimetres away from the plant would suggest no problems, a severe carbon shortage was setting in at the plant surface. In a windy lake, water movements might destroy this gradient, but conditions in a dense bed are relatively still, and this rise in pH starts to be seen even in the water among the plants by late afternoon on a summer's day. All sorts of other gradients may be set up too. Tom Barker and Haseeb Irfanullah fashioned structures in a bed of water lilies and in the open water of a small lake, Little Mere, in Cheshire, to sample these.[20]

The structures were frameworks of wood, arranged so that around 30 points in a single cubic metre of water could be sampled simultaneously and quickly (Fig. 89). At each sampling point was the outlet of a plastic tube connected to two sample bottles and then through a manifold to a much larger bottle. The air in the system was sucked out before sampling and replaced with nitrogen, so as not to destroy, through contact with air, features of the sampled water chemistry that had been caused by oxygen depletion. The large bottle had a tube that could be opened to the atmosphere above water level but which was closed with a clip at the start. At the moment of sampling, the large bottle was submerged and the clip was opened, causing water to flood through the tubes and fill the sample bottles, displacing the nitrogen from the system as it did so, and venting it to the atmosphere. Each sample bottle could then be sealed and taken for analysis.

The sampling was repeated at dawn and dusk and strong gradients developed from the bottom upwards, as oxygen was depleted during the night and phosphate and ammonium were released from the sediments. Horizontal gradients also developed among the algae suspended in the water and among

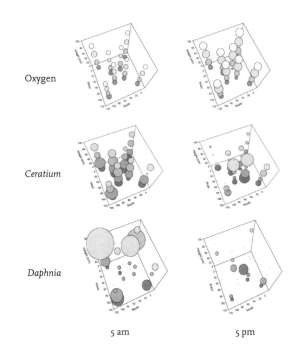

FIG 90. Three items, one chemical, one a motile alga, *Ceratium*, and one a small cladoceran, that varied greatly within the water column and over 12 hours between 5 am and 5 pm in Little Mere, Cheshire. In each diagram you are looking down onto the water. Size of circles is proportional to concentration of oxygen or numbers of algae and animals per litre. Darker shades are for samples at the bottom with the shade lightening towards the surface. Modified from Barker *et al.* (2010).

Oxygen

Ceratium

Daphnia

5 am   5 pm

the cladocera and other small motile animals. Although the reasons for many of these gradients were not easily explained, they illustrated just how complex the structure of the community in the littoral zone could be (Fig. 90). There was a movement from the plant cover into the open water at night of animals that were part of the zooplankton (and feed on phytoplankton in the open water), but habitually associate themselves with the edges of the plant beds during daytime. There they find some refuge against fish predation because fish need to see their prey in order to attack it, and the darkness in the beds acts as a refuge.[21] The refuge is not entirely secure, however, for small fish may also find shelter there from their own predators, like pike, which lurk near the edges of the beds.

FISH PREDATION AND THE SMELL OF WATER

The small water fleas that live among the shadows of the vegetation are less vulnerable to being eaten by fish than those in the open water. If they are filter-feeders, small size brings the disadvantage that they feed less efficiently than the

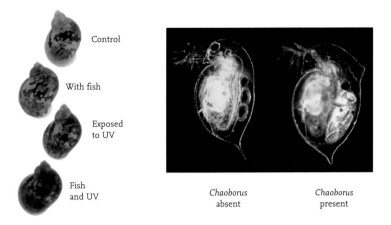

Control

With fish

Exposed
to UV

Fish
and UV

Chaoborus
absent

Chaoborus
present

FIG 91. Many factors may alter the appearance of littoral animals. Pigmentation in a snail, *Radix balthica*, is influenced by exposure to ultraviolet light and also by the presence of fish predators. Brown pigments in the shell shield the body from damaging UV and also provide camouflage against fish predators (from Ahlgren *et al.*, 2013). On the right are individuals of *Daphnia pulex* grown in the absence and presence of one of its predators, the larvae of a fly genus, *Chaoborus*. Handling by the predator is hampered by production of a bulge at the back of the head.

larger species, often from the plankton, which filter the water more rapidly. But the larger animals are more easily seen and attacked in the open water by fish. The larger invertebrates, the snails and mayflies crawling on the vegetation, are also potentially vulnerable to fish but if they keep to the inner sancta, where it is dark and cluttered, there is little space for a fish to launch an attack and little light for the attack to be successful.

There are risks though from the invertebrate predators, the leeches, dragonfly and damselfly larvae, and even some larger water fleas and copepods, which are contact predators. They must detect their prey at very close quarters and then manoeuvre it into a position where they can bite it or swallow it. This gives the prey some leeway to wriggle out, and some prey, in response to substances emitted by the predators, are able, in the next generation, to make themselves thinner, or smaller and less visible, or to change their shape. This confounds the usual way that invertebrate predators employ to handle them (Fig. 91). The prey may also release chemical signals, which alert other prey to the presence of a predator and change their behaviour accordingly.[22] There is a subtle chemistry present, a smell of the water, for which we have yet few details.

PLANTS AND ALGAE COMPETE

Such chemical signalling extends even to the plants. Charophytes have a very distinctive garlicky smell. They, and spiked water milfoil, for example, secrete substances that inhibit algal growth and influence the competition between plants and overlying algae. Especially where nutrients are plentiful, planktonic algae have advantages over plants in the competition for light as it becomes scarcer and scarcer below the water surface. Algae grow faster and earlier in the year and their chromatophores are not shaded by layers of overlying cells as they are in the bulkier plants (another reason why water plants tend to have thin submerged leaves). Algae (either in the plankton, as skeins of filaments, or as periphyton growing on the plant surfaces) could readily take over and shade them out had the plants no measures to restrict algal growth.

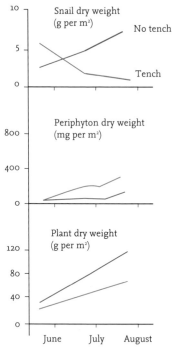

Harbouring grazers of algae, through the refuges provided in the plant beds, is one device; the secretion of inhibitory substances is another; and the creation of still conditions among the plants so that suspended algae readily settle to the bottom, is a third. As nutrients increase, periphyton growth may nonetheless increase and plant growth is lessened, but that can be prevented if snails are available to graze the periphyton (Fig. 92). Fish like tench will eat snails, and if they are present, the periphyton grows better and the plant not so well. Taking the fish away favours the snails at the expense of the periphyton, and benefits the plants. The balance of fish and grazer numbers thus affects the plants' fate.[23]

FIG 92. Aquatic plant growth is influenced by snail grazing on the periphyton, which shades the plants. In turn this is affected by tench predation on the snails. With tench present there are fewer snails, the periphyton is more abundant and the plant does not grow so well.

The chemical conditions the plants incidentally create in their beds may also help in this competition with algae. The

FIG 93. Submerged plants are vulnerable to suppression by periphyton and overlying phytoplankton, but have a variety of devices to minimise the competition.

deoxygenated conditions close to the sediment promote bacterial denitrification in the water, which may make nitrogen compounds very scarce. The plants can obtain nitrogen (before its compounds are fully denitrified) from the sediment through their roots, but the competing algae have no roots and are entirely dependent on what they can get from the water. A well-developed littoral zone thus has devices to maintain its own stability that mutually create a complex structure. There is no suggestion of design or overt purpose in this. A structure assembles as organisms take advantage of resources, like space and sediment, water and nutrients, and as the structure assembles, other organisms take advantage until eventually a community arises that has mutual self-preservation built in (Fig. 93).

WHAT WE DON'T KNOW

There are many unanswered questions about how littoral zones function. One is why detritus is such a prominent food source. Stable isotope studies suggest that direct grazing on green material in north-temperate regions is often less important than feeding on washed-in detritus, but fresh green matter has more nutrients and should be a better food source. The submerged plants themselves are sometimes readily grazed and so is their periphyton, but much of the material of reedswamp plants, a major source of detritus, has to wait until after death before it is eaten.

One reason may be the versatility of microorganisms in breaking down the cell walls of dead plants that would otherwise be inedible to invertebrates. Animals that eat bulky plant material, like ruminants and termites, need bacteria and protozoa in their guts to help them. Land plants often produce toxins to discourage grazers, and taste bitter. Microorganisms break down such poisons in the detritus. Is the littoral zone acting as a very large external rumen for its collection of invertebrates? If matter from tough or woody forest or reedswamp plants is a main energy source, this would make sense. Submerged plants and

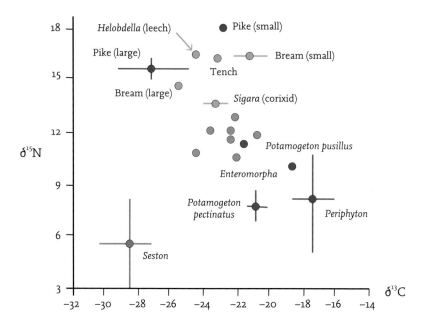

FIG 94. Stable isotope distribution in a littoral community from Stradsett Hall Lake in Norfolk. Red symbols are for piscivorous pike, orange symbols for invertebrate feeders, brown for organic matter suspended in the water (seston), and green for water plants The bunched group shown by blue symbols indicates omnivorous invertebrates feeding on small particles. Included are two cladocerans, *Eurycercus* and *Daphnia*, a caddis, *Mystacides*, ostracods, a mayfly, *Cloeon dipterum*, a snail *Lymnaea pereger* and chironomids (Orthocladiinae). Based on Jones & Waldron, 2003.

algae might be more nutritious food and less poisonous (I can attest, from curious munching, that submerged plants, generally have little taste) but the bulk of the plants, at least, is low, for they have high air and water contents and light limits their productivity.

The importance of detritus, and the general omnivory of many littoral species, evident from dissections and examination of gut contents, has been confirmed by stable isotope studies (Fig. 94) that allow calculation of the proportions of different foods taken. But detritus looks to be much more uniform than fresh green material from different species, and it is worth asking how such a food can support so many species. Perhaps it is not as uniform as it looks and it may have a variety of microorganism communities. Different combinations of several components may allow many species to coexist on what looks like the same diet, or they may avoid competition by eating it in different places or at different times. It may simply be superabundant and not competed for at all.

Coexistence means an avoidance of competition and may be between closely related species, like, for example, the two *Asellus* species in Martham Broad. A similar observation on mutually occurring species of corixids in Italian ponds by G. E. Hutchinson opened up this as a general question in ecology.[24] Hutchinson's answer was that they have slightly different niches, defined by their location, timing of their life histories, susceptibility to parasites, different predators and different food supplies. It may also be that the diversity of species is kept high because changing and unpredictable environmental conditions favour one of the group at one time, the other at another, and that conditions change so rapidly that neither is finally eliminated. We humans are not easily aware of the nature of changes that are important to a small animal; we are much too big and insensitive.

Diversity as such is an important issue. Why are there so many detritus feeders, scrapers on plants, or predators, living together, as opposed to how they achieve it, discussed above. Ten or more of each would not be unusual in a few metres squared. Diversity might be an insurance policy that allows ecosystems to continue functioning despite continual change. At any one time most of the action may be due to just a handful of main players, but there are understudies waiting in the wings. The sorts of changes that might bring the understudies into the play may happen over periods that are much longer than even a prolonged scientific study, and so suggestions that most biodiversity is redundant, and can be lost without serious consequences, could be wrong. Natural selection is so powerful that if an organism persists, however scarcely, there is meaning to its presence.

From the plant's point of view, the species diversity of invertebrates provides an insurance policy that one or other grazer will always be controlling its burden of periphyton, but so far we have little evidence that the plant is able to influence this. Could plants manipulate the nature of their periphyton so as to encourage grazers to feed on it; do they attempt to alter its species composition with secreted substances? Experiments with live plants and plastic surrogates, in laboratory systems with snails showed that the plastic provided just as good a habitat for the snails as the living plants. It was nutrients that largely determined the periphyton growth when the snail population was kept constant, rather than any chemical effect of the living plants.[25] However, in lakes with very low nutrient concentrations, there does seem to be a specificity between plant and epiphytes that breaks down where nutrients are abundant.[26] We have rich communities in the littoral for which the rules of assemblage (if there are any) are not fully understood. In tropical forests and coral reefs there are tight dependencies between particular species, but these are steady, predictable habitats compared with the uncertainties of living in freshwaters. The ephemerality of lakes, the accidents of their colonisation, the recent evolution of their denizens and the flexibility of their food webs mutually frustrate a detailed explanation of the natural history of their littoral zones.

WHAT OF THE BIRDS?

There is something else: the birds and mammals. Littoral zones attract the most birds, because food supplies, whether plants, invertebrates or fish, are richer there than in the open, deeper waters. Herons and cormorants feed on the trout and minnows in Llyn Idwal. There are occasional coot and mallard, goosanders, black-headed gulls and great crested grebes. Whooper swans, pochard and goldeneye visit the lake in winter, but the bird life is not plentiful.

Martham Broad is very different. Nearly 1,000 widgeon and teal may be seen in an average winter month. Many of the plants are perennials that do not die back entirely in winter, and provide steady plant food. Pochard are common, and, among other herbivores, gadwall, whooper swan and pink-footed geese visit in winter. The invertebrates, with their penchant for detritus, are able to continue their lives in winter and provide food for mallard, shoveller, tufted duck and goldeneye. The reedswamps have seed in winter and aphids in summer for bearded tits, summer insects for cetti's, reed and sedge warblers, and cover for the rare bittern in its feeding on fish, frogs and sometimes invertebrates. Heron feed on the perch and roach, pike, bream, tench and eel. Otter and mink (an introduced mammal in the UK), water voles, muntjac and Chinese water deer are present around the Broad. In summer, swallows and martins, and at least four species of bat, will be flying over the water taking the adults of the gnats that have hatched from the chironomids and other insects that have developed in the water. But we have little more understanding than lists and some counts for the mammals and birds.

The interesting questions are not so much what is there, but what would happen were they not there. If the ducks disappeared, would it matter? Are these animals simply bit-part players, of no real consequence to the main plot? That used to be the view where fish were concerned. We now know that fish have major roles (see Chapter 6) and determine the structures of the invertebrate populations and thence of the survival and performance of the plants. By

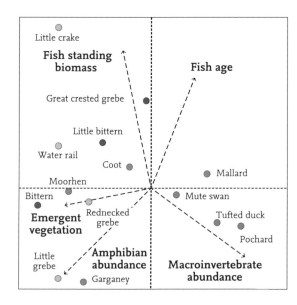

FIG 95. Statistical techniques can be used to sort out patterns in complicated situations. Here canonical correspondence analysis has been used to study links between fish (largely common carp), development of emergent vegetation, amphibian and macroinvertebrate abundance and water birds in a set of 50 small Polish lakes used for fish culture. Relationships among the data are calculated then flattened onto two axes. The abundance of the bird species is related to the environmental factors (in purple lettering) shown as arrows. Arrows in opposing directions reflect inverse relationships. For example, fish abundance is associated with low macroinvertebrate abundance, because the fish eat the invertebrates. Omnivorous birds, shown in green, are thus adversely affected by fish. Fish also eat amphibian tadpoles and thus disfavour birds that feed on amphibians, like bittern, but favour some piscivores (shown in red) like great crested grebe. Such analyses show that there is rarely a single factor that determines a bird's (or any other animal's) abundance, but a variety of influences. The closer the bird is positioned to an arrow, the more important is likely to be the factor represented by the arrow, but most species are influenced by several factors, or, like the little crake, are influenced largely by factors not included in the study. Based on Kloskowski *et al.*, 2010.

introducing a fish like the common carp, it is possible to eliminate plants from a lake, through its feeding, its rummaging around the roots for invertebrates and because it mobilises nutrients from the sediments which encourage algal competitors. But what of the birds?

We know that their populations can be influenced by fish, for they compete for invertebrate food[27] (Fig. 95), and ducklings are often prey to pike, but our understanding of their roles in the system is negligible.[28] So far it seems that fish have the upper hand. Removing fish results in greater numbers of ducks, but when fish are few what effects do the birds have on the rest of the littoral zone? Experiments show that coot graze much of the plant biomass when they are confined to the lake during moult, and feral geese can devastate parts of reedbeds, but otherwise there is much to find out if we are to understand the littoral as well as the plankton to which we turn in Chapter 6.[29]

CHAPTER 6

The Plankton: Hazard and Survival

I T'S HARD TO TAKE AN inspiring photograph of a lake, or at least what
is thought of as a lake: the mass of water. If the picture is interesting,
the focus is usually plants in the foreground, or mountains at the back
(Fig. 96). Where the open water is captured, it is most often for birds flying over
it. In aerial or satellite photographs, the water appears as a grey blob and we look
mostly at the surroundings. To our eyes, the water is usually no more interesting

FIG 96. Ennerdale Water, Cumbria.

than the boredom of an ocean crossing. The osprey, flying over it, might note that the water is clear, or in summer acquires more colour, and takes interest if it sees a fish close to the surface, but by and large, to us, it's just water. So what!

It is all a matter of scale. Osprey and human see only gross features. A 2-mm planktonic copepod faces a very different, viscous world of great intricacy and peril; a perch bridges these experiences. A perch spends its early life in and around the littoral, feeding on zooplankton and then on the bigger invertebrates of the plant beds. If it grows large enough, it may become a fish-eater, and may move offshore where it might have to dodge the talons of the osprey to catch its food in the more open habitat. When all three views, osprey, copepod and perch, are combined, the open water, the world of the plankton, takes on a detail invisible to the landscape artist or photographer. It is a shifting habitat, of great danger for the highly adapted phytoplankton and zooplankton that have evolved ways to survive in it.

HOW MUCH PLANKTON?

The open water is a soup, with particles floating and many things dissolved in it, but it is not a rich broth, not even remotely as rich as the thin consommés that pass for soup in posh restaurants. An exceptionally dense zooplankton community might have a fresh biomass of one gram per litre, and occupy perhaps a tenth of one per cent of the water volume, but more typically is only a tenth or a hundredth of this. In a dense community there might be 1,000 rotifers and 50 crustaceans per litre. Animals will be spread out such that were they humans on the street, the nearest person would be at least 36 metres away and, among crustaceans, more than 100 metres away. Typically they could be several kilometres distant from each other on this comparison and although the phytoplankters and bacteria will be closer, they are still distant and certainly not jostling. I will look at the bacterioplankton and phytoplankton first and then the zooplankton.

The open water is not an easy place for algae or bacteria to grow. Its nutrient supply, inorganic or organic, is naturally dilute, for the land vegetation has conserved the stocks for itself and some of what ran in has been intercepted in the littoral. Light is plentiful at the surface but is readily absorbed with depth. Most of the cells are denser than water and, even if they are so small that the drag forces acting on their surfaces (Chapter 4) slow their fall, they continually sink and may become trapped on the bottom. And continually sweeping through the water are filter- and suspension-feeders against which the smaller phytoplankters and bacteria are virtually defenceless.

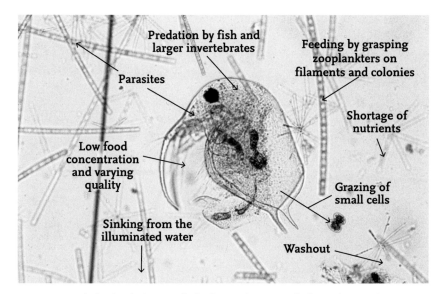

FIG 97. Hazards for the plankton. In the background are a zooplankter, *Bosmina*, about 0.4 mm long, the star shaped colonies of *Asterionella* and the filaments of *Aulacoseira*, both of which are diatoms, and one small cell of a green alga, *Cosmarium* sp., which is the only species here that *Bosmina* can eat. (Fisheries and Oceans Administration, Canada)

The bigger algae may be able to avoid being eaten, but there is a trade-off. The bigger you are, the faster you sink and the smaller the surface area you have, in relation to your bulk, for the uptake of nutrients. Then there is the possibility of being washed out of the lake faster than you can grow, especially when the inflow is high in relation to the lake volume. But natural selection has produced a wonderful set of counters to these hazards of low nutrients, sinking, low light availability, grazing and washout (Fig. 97). The secret of survival is to grow, on average, at least as fast as these hazards allow or can remove you.

NUTRIENTS

The life histories of most planktonic algae are very simple. Most persist by simple cell division, in contrast to many littoral algae, where sexual stages are common. The imperative, in the open water, is to reproduce quickly and the genetic advantages of sex do not usually override this. The dispersion and

FIG 98. As the volume of a sphere increases, its surface area proportionately decreases (left). Small cells thus have advantages in nutrient uptake and gas exchange. As cell size increases (right) it will sink faster (proportionately to the square of the radius), but in doing so will more readily slough off layers of nutrient depleted water in contact with its surface.

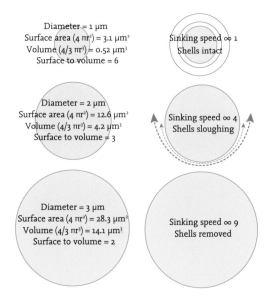

Diameter = 1 μm
Surface area (4 πr²) = 3.1 μm²
Volume (4/3 πr³) = 0.52 μm³
Surface to volume = 6

Sinking speed ∞ 1
Shells intact

Diameter = 2 μm
Surface area (4 πr²) = 12.6 μm²
Volume (4/3 πr³) = 4.2 μm³
Surface to volume = 3

Sinking speed ∞ 4
Shells sloughing

Diameter = 3 μm
Surface area (4 πr²) = 28.3 μm²
Volume (4/3 πr³) = 14.1 μm³
Surface to volume = 2

Sinking speed ∞ 9
Shells removed

continuous random movement of the cells also mean that the contacts that sexual fertilisation requires are few. On the human scale, courtship is not easy if you are kept some metres from your mate. That does not mean that all individuals of a species are genetically similar.[1] There is horizontal gene transfer (among the bacteria at least, but probably also in some eukaryotes), the consequences of mutation and, perhaps more importantly, the bringing in, from time to time, of different clones from other lakes on the feet and feathers of water birds.

The smaller the cell, the faster it divides, so it is common in the plankton to find rapid increases in numbers of tiny cells, a large population establishing in a few days and disappearing equally quickly. Small cells have large surface areas in relation to their volumes (Fig. 98) and on area depends the ability of the cell to take up the nutrients necessary to sustain its bulk. Small cells clearly have advantages in this.

The nutrient content of the water (or strictly the available nutrient content, because much of the total nitrogen and phosphorus may be already bound up in biomass, or in compounds unavailable to algae unless bacteria decompose them first) is low except in winter and early spring. The rising inflows have then brought available concentrations to their maxima for the year, but they become very low by midsummer. Nutrients are then replenished patchily by the excretion of animals. A passing fish or zooplankter emits a cloud of excreted ammonia and phosphate, and phytoplankton cells fortunate enough to be bathed in it, for the few seconds before it dsperses, can take up the nutrients very rapidly.[2] Other ways of gaining nutrients during periods of scarcity include ingestion of bacteria or of organic compounds and a surprising number of phytoplankters have proved to be mixed feeders. Many of the Cyanobacteria and green algae, and a few of the diatoms, can thrive solely on inorganic nutrients and photosynthesis, but the rest of the algae, like the bacteria, animals and fungi, need at least one preformed organic nutrient, often a vitamin, to grow, and the complex, if dilute (Chapter 2) chemical melange of the open water must provide it.

SINKING

The next problem for planktonic algae is that of staying in the upper layers of water long enough to obtain enough light to acquire the energy to grow, when the cell is denser than water and naturally tends to sink. Wind generated eddy currents are relied on to catch the cell and return it towards the surface before it sinks through the thermocline or to the bottom. But some days are windless. You might wonder why the cell has not evolved neutral buoyancy or even the ability to float upwards, as indeed have some cyanobacteria that have gas vesicles. Neutral buoyancy would be disadvantageous. It would mean that the cell remained stationary relative to the water and that the layers of water in contact with its surface would be stagnant. These layers, a fraction of a millimetre thick, stick by molecular attraction. The cell quickly absorbs their stock of nutrients, but the stock can only be slowly replenished by diffusion from the low concentrations in the rest of the water mass, so the cell would be perpetually starved. When a cell sinks, it sloughs away these shells of depleted water, bringing 'new' water into contact with its surface, and the faster it sinks, the more rapidly it renews its nutrient supply (Fig. 98).

Movement upwards (buoyancy) is just as effective at sloughing, but has some snags. Production of gas-filled bags costs energy and buoyancy needs a counteraction for moving downwards, or the cells would become concentrated and trapped at the surface. Wind-generated eddy currents can provide this just as they bring back cells, sinking under gravity, from the depths. There is a danger though, of being trapped at the surface on calm days. There, ultraviolet radiation can be lethal. The problem is acute in high mountain lakes, where both algae and zooplankters may need to have protective orange pigments to shield them from high levels of UV. An alternative to passive sinking or buoyancy is to take control, and be actively motile, using flagella. Many species do this, but not all, suggesting that it too may have a disadvantage. Active movement takes a good deal of energy to overcome the drag forces acting on a small organism (Chapter 4).

FIG 99. Although cells may
have intricate shapes, they may
be covered by smooth layers of
mucilage. (Hilda Canter-Lund,
courtesy of Biopress)

In the nineteenth century, George Stokes, a Cambridge mathematician, formulated an equation describing how fast a sphere falls in a fluid. Stoke's Law can be tested amusingly using tall jars full of a saturated solution of sugar, and small balls of plasticine. The speed of sinking is directly proportional to both the size of the object and the difference in densities between the object and the fluid, and is inversely proportional to the viscosity, the stickiness, of the fluid. A living organism cannot do anything about the viscosity of the water – it is determined by temperature and chemistry – but its density and size are under control of natural selection. Having a water-filled vacuole inside the cell is one way of trimming the density, but a vacuole occupies space and makes the cell bigger. Being able to use substances like silica to form the cell wall, as in diatoms, rather greatly increases the density but may have the advantage of taking less energy to construct than carbon-based walls.

The main way of reducing sinking rate is through size. A small cell, a few micrometres in diameter, falls quite slowly so that there is a good chance of eddy currents bringing it back to the surface before it is too late and it slips through the thermocline. A bacterium, only a micrometre or so in diameter, may barely fall at all; an alga, say 30 microns in diameter will fall a few centimetres per day; but a heavy diatom will fall metres per day and can only survive in vigorously mixed water.

Shape can also be important. Stoke's Law can be frustrated if a cell is not perfectly spherical. A long thin needle shape, particularly if the ends are slightly bent, a star shape, a flat disc, or having radiating arms or bristles, will all delay sinking compared with a sphere of similar volume, and such shapes, comparatively few of them, copied from species to species, are common in the phytoplankton. There are still mysteries, however; some of the desmids, with intricately shaped cells bearing long extending arms, are covered with a thick layer of mucilage that makes them much bigger, and smooth in outline (Fig. 99). The mucilage has an advantage. It has a low density and thus reduces the overall difference in density between the organism and the water but it upsets too simple an explanation of why some phytoplankters have intricate shapes.

Algae that sink rapidly, however, may benefit from a better supply of nutrients (through sloughing of the shells of water that stick to the surface) and a greater protection from grazing zooplankters. Being bigger than a few micrometres takes a cell out of the reach of protozoa and rotifers, and 60 micrometres or so, outside the scope of the water fleas and most of the calanoid copepods. Substances emitted by grazers can influence this. Grown in water that has never been occupied by water fleas, some species of the green algal genus *Scenedesmus* (Fig. 100) will grow as single cells that lack or have few spines; grown in water that has been tainted with whatever daphnids secrete, they will form much bigger colonies with cells in a row of four or eight, and with many spines.[3] Nothing is quite out of the size range of some large cladocerans, and cyclopoid copepods, which can bite, but large phytoplankters are generally colonial and will survive the

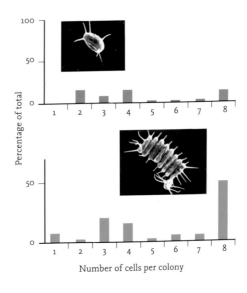

FIG 100. Water in which *Daphnia* has been present (lower) will stimulate the production of larger and more spiny (and hence less edible) colonies of the green alga *Scenedesmus*. Based on Hessen & Van Donk, 1993.

loss of a few chunks; they are often covered with mucilage layers that frustrate the biting, or, should the colony be eaten whole, the digestive enzymes in the animal's gut, so that it is defaecated still alive.

Chemistry can also be brought to bear on both sinking rate and edibility. Most algae store energy as a heavy carbohydrate. A few store oil, reducing their density, notably the diatoms and one genus of green algae, called *Botryococcus*, which is so rich in oil as to have attracted the attentions of geologists, wondering how oil deposits might have been formed, and biotechnologists hopeful to run the world's vehicles on it. Cells with thick walls are relatively richer in carbon, poorer in nitrogen and phosphorus than the more nutritious flagellates, naked but for their outer membranes. Many zooplankters recognise this and may reject food that is high in poorly digestible roughage; the larger cyanobacteria, with complex walls and mucilaginous sheaths, are frequently ejected from the filtering limbs. Diatoms, unless they are very large, are not rejected. They might have completely indigestible silica walls but the walls are riddled with holes that easily expose the inner cells to digestive enzymes.

LIGHT AND PIGMENTS

The photosynthetic pigments are another means of offering alternatives for survival in a shifting, dangerous, dilute medium. Different pigments absorb light most efficiently at different wavelengths. Chlorophylls do best in the red (wavelength around 660 nm (a nanometre is 10^{-9} of a metre)) and the violet (430 nm) parts of the spectrum. Yellow and orange pigments, carotenes and xanthophylls absorb efficiently in the violet, blue (480 nm) and green (530 nm) parts of the spectrum. Some algal groups, the diatoms and chrysophytes, and some dinoflagellates, gain their dominant colour from these pigments, whilst the blue phycobilin pigments of the cyanobacteria, cryptophytes and a few dinoflagellates absorb well in the orange and yellow (540–590 nm).

As sunlight penetrates into water, different wavelengths are selectively absorbed by the medium. Blue and violet light, with the shortest wavelengths, in theory should be the most energetic and penetrative, but they are taken out readily by the generally brown and yellow dissolved organic matter. Red bands (and the infrared that warms the water) are rapidly absorbed by the water itself, for they are not very energetic. What are left to penetrate much below the surface are the bands of yellow, orange and green. In mixed water, phytoplankters will be moved through a range of light climates, experiencing close to white light near the surface, but yellowy-green dankness only few metres below.

Depending on their pigment array, the degree of mixing, and the colour of the water, different algal groups will be temporarily favoured at some times and disfavoured at others, both on a daily basis and as the season progresses. Given their various traits of size, shape, density, chemistry and pigments, it is therefore no great mystery that the cells of some hundreds of species of phytoplankter will occupy the open water stage during the year, briefly speak their lines in the limelight, and then retreat to the wings or dressing rooms to await their next appearance.[4] To mix the metaphor, there are many ways to skin a cat.

ZOOPLANKTON BIOLOGY

The same applies to the zooplankters. Life is just as hazardous for them in the no-man's land of the open water. They are surprisingly varied, and rather strange looking, but they are experts, like the phytoplankters, at survival in a dangerous place. In the lakes of Britain and Ireland, there are some hundreds of species, mostly copepods, cladocerans (water fleas), rotifers and a few ostracods. There are some microturbellarians, flatworms that attack small water fleas, and an introduced jellyfish, *Craspedacusta sowerbyi* crops up, usually unexpectedly, from time to time (Fig. 101). It has a life history with a tiny, difficult-to-find, polyp, like a small sea anemone, attached to underwater twigs or rocks, by which it persists between the years when the medusae suddenly appear, often abundantly, in the plankton, and sting and feed on small zooplankters.

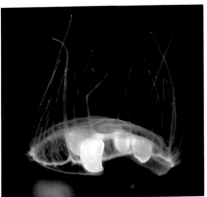 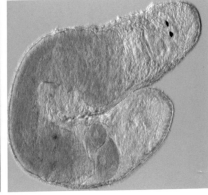

FIG 101. Minority members of the zooplankton in Britain and Ireland are the introduced predatory jellyfish, *Craspedacusta sowerbyi* (left), and a variety of carnivorous flatworms (microturbellaria). The animals are only a few mm across. (Open Cage/Gieystoria)

We tend to forget ciliates, which usually pass through nets conventionally used for sampling, but they are zooplankters too, and indeed dominate the zooplankton in terms of numbers, though not in biomass.[5] Hitherto we have concentrated on the three most obvious groups of the copepods, cladocerans and rotifers. The key things within each group are whether they are large, say more than 0.6 mm, or smaller than this, and whether they are filter-feeders or grasping (raptorial) feeders. Knowing in which of the 12 possible combinations of these a species lies, tells a lot about it.

COPEPODS

There are two sorts of copepods (Fig. 102), calanoid and cyclopoid (well three, but the harpacticoids are tiny littoral dwellers that crawl over plants and sediment and do not figure in the plankton). They are the models for our manikin of Chapter 5. Calanoid copepods are filter-feeders, up to a couple of millimetres long as adults, with long antennae that trail down the lengths of their bodies, a single eye, five pairs of limbs on the undersides of the head and seven on the rest of the body, and a rather distinctive separation of thorax and abdomen. The females bear a single egg sac attached to the abdomen. The spacing of the fine hairs on their filtering limbs, and the sizes of particles that other limbs reject by scraping them away, show that they can eat particles from about 5 micrometres to 50 micrometres. This means that they cannot take bacteria nor the smallest algae, nor large colonial algae, but will take moderate-sized algae.[6] They are most common in the larger and deeper lakes, with five species of *Diaptomus* in Britain and Ireland, and scarcer in shallow lakes, except for slightly saline ones, like some of the Norfolk Broads, where two species of *Eurytemora* are found.

The other group, the cyclopoid copepods, is more diverse, with over 40 species and sub-species of the genus *Cyclops* (now split into several sub-genera) in these islands, though fewer than ten are found in the open water of lakes. The rest grub around in leaves and debris in ditches and temporary ponds, or in plant beds. Cyclopoid copepods are raptorial, tearing pieces from colonies of algae, or manhandling rotifers, small cladocerans or even small insect larvae into their mouths. Their antennae are shorter than those of calanoid copepods, their bodies taper smoothly from thorax to abdomen and they have two egg sacs. Most, like the calanoid copepods, are drab grey or brown in colour but some have bright patches of red, blue or green. Colour matters, for it camouflages, if drab, or exposes, if bright, an animal to predators.

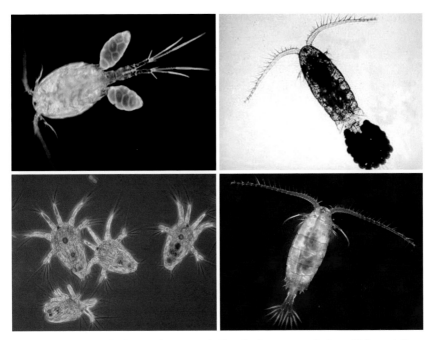

FIG 102. Copepods in freshwaters have juvenile filter-feeding stages called nauplii (lower left), and adults that are either raptorial, *Cyclops* (upper left), or filter-feeding, including *Diaptomus* (lower right) and *Eurytemora* (upper right), which favours slightly brackish waters and can scrape periphyton as well as filter-feed. (EAWAG, Switzerland/University of Florida/Ulrich Hopper)

Copepods move fast. Their antennae, and sometimes other parts of the body, are equipped with sensory hairs that detect vibrations caused in the water by other animals, and their eyes are very sensitive to motion. As a predator moves in to attack, powerful muscles, running the length of the animal from head to abdomen, contract and flick the body out of the way. It is costly in energy, but it is well that copepods have this defence, for in other respects they are less well adapted than the cladocerans and rotifers to the hazards of the open water.

The life history of copepods takes several weeks; after mating and carriage of the eggs until they hatch, there are 12 stages before the next generation of adult, sexually mature, copepods is reached. First are six naupliar stages, where the tiny animals, looking almost like mites, gradually increase in size at each stage, and feed on small algae and particles of detritus, with its associated microorganisms. Then there are five copepodite stages, which, except in small details, look like the final sixth adult stage, but which are smaller. They take a progressively wider range of food particles but copepods tend to be quite selective in what they will eat. Both the amount of food and its quality affect the success of each stage, and the eventual fecundity of the adults, and the early stages are vulnerable to predators, particularly invertebrates, because of their small size and, in the case of nauplii, slow movement. There is a long period of vulnerability before the fast-moving, fish-dodging larger copepodites and adults emerge.

WATER FLEAS

Copepods are more abundant in the oceans than in freshwaters, but the reverse is true of the other main group of crustaceans in the plankton, the cladocerans, or water fleas (Figs 91, 97, 103). They are less sleek and streamlined and have a greater range of shapes than the copepods, have a cloak, or carapace, which folds around their limbed bodies, and usually a large eye that draws attention

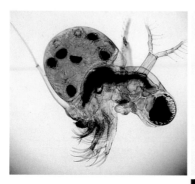
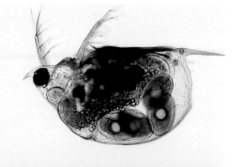
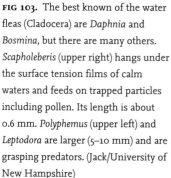

FIG 103. The best known of the water fleas (Cladocera) are *Daphnia* and *Bosmina*, but there are many others. *Scapholeberis* (upper right) hangs under the surface tension films of calm waters and feeds on trapped particles including pollen. Its length is about 0.6 mm. *Polyphemus* (upper left) and *Leptodora* are larger (5–10 mm) and are grasping predators. (Jack/University of New Hampshire)

under a microscope. Most are littoral but there are two main planktonic genera, *Bosmina* and *Daphnia*, with several others (*Scapholeberis, Ceriodaphnia, Chydorus* and *Diaphanosoma*) that are common in the open water, especially in shallow lakes, as well as in the littoral. *Scapholeberis mucronata* hangs under the water surface, attached to the surface tension film, by the parallel edges of its carapace, and feeds on particles like pollen that fall onto the film. The other genera mentioned are filter-feeders. There are also four predatory raptorial cladocerans in Britain and Ireland: *Polyphemus pediculus, Leptodora kindti* (Fig. 103), *Bythotrephes longimanus* and *B. cederstromi*.

The water fleas have a typically crustacean body, with jointed limbs, and the body faces outwards between the sides of the carapace in the fold of which, at the back of the body, is the egg sac. In filter-feeders, the limbs claw through the water to sieve out particles, more or less as the animal holds itself upright and stationary in *Daphnia*, or as it moves horizontally along in *Bosmina*. The filtering apparatus is most effective in *Daphnia*, which can take a wider range of particle sizes and beats more rapidly. *Daphnia* is, however, bigger and more vulnerable to being eaten by fish because it is more easily seen than *Bosmina*. Cladocerans move much more slowly than copepods, making small 'jumps' by a quick downbeat of their antennae, then a pause when they may sink back a little or remain stationary.

The raptors (Fig. 103) are larger than the filter-feeders. *Leptodora* may be a centimetre long but is highly transparent and less visible to fish in the open water than its size would imply; *Polyphemus* is prominent because of its large eye – it is named for a mythical Greek giant with a single prominent eye in the middle of his forehead – and hangs around the edges of plant beds where it may find both prey and refuge. *Bythotrephes* has a long tail, extending two or three times the length of the 2–3 mm body, with sharp backwardly directed hooks in *B. cederstromi*. These spines hamper small fish in swallowing the animal because the gapes of their mouths are not wide enough and they must first bite off the tail, giving the prey a chance to escape as the fish manoeuvres it into position. The raptorial species have much reduced carapaces, giving them more flexibility for capturing and handling their own prey, particularly rotifers, and small cladocerans like *Bosmina* and juvenile *Daphnia*, and sometimes ciliates.

The water fleas (at least the larger ones) are more vulnerable to fish predation than the copepods, but they have an important advantage in that they can compensate by breeding more rapidly because they are parthenogenic. Every few days in spring and summer females produce broods solely of more females, without need of males and mating. A new generation can be produced in a week, compared with three weeks for copepods. Towards the end of the year, when food is scarce, or poor in quality, and the temperature is falling, females may produce some males. These are small, feed little, if at all, but will fertilise young females, who then produce resting eggs in sacs called ephippia, which acquire thick walls. The ephippia ('on a horse', because they are saddle-shaped) sink to the bottom and do not germinate for several months. Indeed they may remain alive in the sediment for several decades.

In the stakes for survival, the copepods hold aces in their sensitive antennae, fast movement and ability to select food, thus wasting less time and energy on less nutritious particles; the cladocerans hold them in their speed of reproduction and their ability to take much smaller food particles, which are likely to be more readily available. Both groups have ways, which I will describe later, of minimising their inevitable vulnerability to predators. But first I need to introduce to you the rotifers.

ROTIFERS

Rotifers (Fig. 104) hold aces in their very small size, around a tenth of that of the crustaceans, and their parthenogenic life cycle, much like that of the water fleas. The dud cards are that they have a very inefficient means of obtaining their food, which is confined, for the filter feeders (or strictly, suspension-feeders) to bacteria and the smallest of algae, and that they move very slowly. Most both feed and move by whirling a vortex of water towards their mouths with a ring of beating cilia, which surrounds the mouth and brings to it the suspension of whatever particles the water contains. They are unable to concentrate it, like filter-feeders. Typical genera in the plankton are *Synchaeta*, *Brachionus*, *Keratella*, *Filinia*,

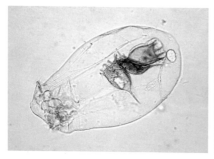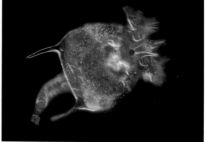

FIG 104. Rotifers are very diverse. Some are raptorial and will grasp and burst other rotifers or swallow them whole, like *Asplanchna* (left), which is about 0.6 mm long and has swallowed three individuals of the smaller *Keratella*. The suspension-feeding *Brachionus* (right), is about 0.1 mm long. (Fred Longing/Frank Fox)

Kellicottia and *Polyarthra*. A few (for example, *Asplanchna*) are slightly bigger and raptorial, and will swallow or squeeze large algal cells or smaller rotifers, bursting their contents in a shower of particles that they can then suck in.

Most rotifers will frequent clumps of detritus, where bacteria, ciliates and tiny flagellates are concentrated. Rotifers are vulnerable to many invertebrate predators but only to the tiniest of fish that have just hatched and used up their yolk sacs and which have mouths too small to engulf even a small crustacean. When just a little larger, the fish find it not worth the effort to expend energy in an attack for such a small meal, and by then their mouths have grown large enough for a small cladoceran to be on the menu.

ZOOPLANKTON COMMUNITIES

To bring all of the above together, two main things explain the composition of zooplankton communities: the amount and quality of the food, which includes size and chemical composition; and the number and nature of the predators. The outcome of these two influences results in a pageant of different zooplankton species that can be seen (Fig. 105) in a lake during the year.[7] The size of the food

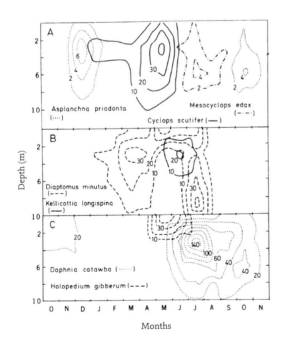

FIG 105. Zooplankters do not occur randomly. They crop out at particular times of year and in particular depth ranges. Shown here are depth–time diagrams for the occurrence of some zooplankters in Mirror Lake, New Hampshire (based on Mackarewicz & Likens, 1975). Numbers are production in micrograms dry weight produced per litre per month. *Asplanchna* and *Kellicottia* are rotifers, *Mesocyclops*, *Cyclops* and *Diaptomus* are copepods and *Daphnia* and *Holopedium* are cladocerans.

TABLE 14. Some major features of crustacean zooplankton genera. Setulae are the fine filtering hairs on the filtering limbs. Based on Barnett *et al.*, 2007.

Genus	Mean body length (mm)	Food size (µm)	Max. clearance rate (ml/individual and hour)	Index of clearance to length	Mesh size of setulae (µm)	Fastest generation time (days)	Max. rate of increase (% per day)	Length of life (days)	Lifetime production per female
Cladocera								40–85	400–700
Bosmina (filter-feeders)	0.38 (0.4–0.6)	3.2 (1.4–5.0)	0.16 (0.013–0.3)	1.83	1.0 (0.4–1.6)	6	27 (24–31)		
Daphnia (filter-feeders)	1.8 (0.88–3.5)	15.5 (0.6–40)	1.28 (0.26–3.6)	2.54 (1.6–3.6)	0.5 (0.24–1.0)	7.4 (5–16)	30 (14–58)		
Copepoda								40–85	250–750
Cyclopoid: Cyclops (raptorial feeders)	0.99 (0.55–1.6)	165 (0.25–900)	1.73 (0.03–7.5)				20.9 (9.7–41.4)		
Calanoid: Diaptomus (filter-feeders)	1.15 (0.89–1.5)	36.7 (2.5–80)	0.91 (0.49–1.67)		10 (1–18)				
Rotifers								5–20	15–25
Filter-2feeding	0.4 (0.2–0.6)	2 (1–5)	0.05 (0.01–0.1)				1.5 (1.25–7)	85 (20–150)	
Raptorial	0.8	20							

available is very important. Table 14 shows the pernicketiness of the zooplankton groups. There is a general relationship with animal size, so that the larger daphnids can take bigger particles than the bosminids. Filter-feeding cladocerans and rotifers take smaller particles than calanoid copepods and this is better reflected in the range than the mean. Most particles in the plankton are edible to one or other species, but the larger colonial green algae, filamentous diatoms and colonial cyanobacteria are rejected by filter-feeders, though tackleable by raptorial feeders like *Cyclops*, *Polyphemus* and *Bythotrephes*, though these may prefer animal prey, such as rotifers, which are more nutritious, not having indigestible cell walls. Some algae may be toxic and avoided, but although the cyanobacteria produce toxins lethal to mammals, and some chrysophytes, for example *Prymnesium parvum*, to fish, it is not quite so clear whether the toxicity really extends to zooplankters, though there are claims that it does.

The concentration of food is important and there are thresholds below which the animals cannot obtain enough to continue growing. These are quite high for rotifers because of the low efficiency of suspension-feeding. Filter-feeders can sweep the water clear and reduce levels to below those on which suspension-feeders can manage. This is why rotifers may often be forced to hang around clumps of detritus where bacteria and small protozoa are concentrated. Rotifers seem to need concentrations of at least 0.1–0.5 mg L⁻¹ as carbon and feed best at around 1–2 mg L⁻¹, whereas daphnids feed best at less than 0.5 mg L⁻¹ and can still feed at 0.04 to 0.12 mg L⁻¹. Calanoid copepods need a broadly similar range, whilst ciliates are the least efficient, needing 0.6 to 4.0 mg L⁻¹. Bigger animals like Cladocera also have greater fat reserves and might survive over a week without food, more than twice as long as a rotifer.

The efficiency of feeding (the clearance rate in Table 14) also increases with size, and more than proportionately. The best data are from Cladocera, where experiments using food labelled with radioactive isotopes, or feeding with tiny plastic balls of precisely known size, has produced a wealth of information. In Table 14, the column labelled 'index of clearance to length' shows the numerical power by which feeding rate increases with length within a species or group. As length increases, the filtering rate increases by around the square of the length, so that big individuals of big species of Cladocera, like *Daphnia magna*, say 3 mm in length, have a filtering efficiency tens to hundreds of times greater than small ones like *Bosmina longirostris*, at around 0.5 mm, only six times smaller. Food quality and amount will vary from day to day as the phytoplankton and bacterial populations change, and depending on the food supply, the number of young zooplankters produced and the times they take to reach maturity are constantly altered. Mathematically elegant, beautifully smooth population growth curves can be produced in cultures of animals fed on ideal food in the laboratory but the week-to-week reality in nature is a jagged graph of numbers, with precipitous swings, created by changes in food supply but also affected by predation.

PREDATION ON THE ZOOPLANKTON

The effects of predators are far from simple. The impact is not one-sided; the zooplankters can shorten the odds. When fish are very small, they take very small prey (diatoms, ciliates and rotifers) but they may detect it more by nuzzling than seeing it, in the same way that invertebrate predators find their meals. Bigger fish need to see their prey. They then decide whether or not to attack, for the burst of speed needed costs energy and if the prey is too small or moves out of the way, the costs will not be repaid. Fish have individual characteristics, indeed personalities, too; some are conservative and others are more likely to take risks.[8] The outcome of a sighting is never precisely predictable. Small size and

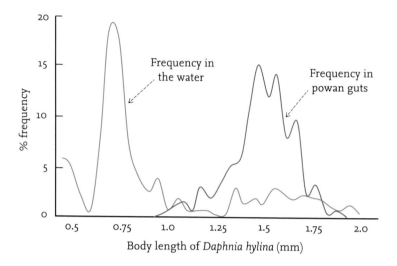

FIG 106. Powan in Loch Lomond select for the larger *Daphnia*, though these are less abundant in the water than the smaller individuals. Based on Pomeroy, 1994.

transparency of body can protect a zooplankter and most rotifers, nauplii and small cladocerans such as *Bosmina* are often safe despite their slow movement. Copepods are more easily visible, but their rapid movement means that they can often escape. Most vulnerable are the larger cladocerans like *Daphnia*. If you examine the guts of plankton-feeding fish like the powan in Loch Lomond (Fig. 106), you will find that large daphnids are commoner in the guts than they are in the water. The fish deliberately target them.

The zooplankton community in spring will have a mixture of rotifers, copepods and cladocerans, and daphnids will be quite common. Their rapid reproduction and efficiency at feeding give them advantages at a time when the food supply, in the form of diatoms and flagellates, is increasing. But once the new generation of young fish has hatched, the days of the large and slow-moving daphnids are numbered. Most young British and Irish lake fish are zooplanktivorous in their first few months and so the pressures on the daphnids are intense. As the summer progresses, the zooplankton community becomes less rich in daphnids, and even some of the medium-sized cladocerans, and more and more dominated by copepods and rotifers.

Daphnids never entirely disappear, however. Once released from the egg pouch on the mother, juvenile daphnids undergo several moults of their exoskeleton as they grow, and at these stages they are able to change their form. They do it under the influence of chemicals inadvertently released into the water by the fish and the result might be an animal that is smaller and thinner, or more translucent, with a smaller eye, and more difficult for the fish to see. It may have a longer spine at the lower end of the carapace that makes it more difficult for the fish to eat, or it may reproduce earlier than its mother did and produce more but smaller eggs that will hatch to smaller, less vulnerable, individuals. *In extremis*, males might be produced and the species might retreat from the field in the form of resting eggs until the next spring.

The animal may also change its behaviour. Where fish are present, both cladocerans and copepods will swim down to deeper, but cooler, waters by day and hide in the dark. At twilight they swim upwards to feed in the warmer surface waters where the algal density is greatest. There are disadvantages to such migration for the lower temperatures, and usually shortage of food at depth, lower the growth and reproduction rates and thus reduce the abilities of the animals to compensate for inevitable losses through predation. There is invertebrate predation (in the dark) also to consider,[9] and the fish are not completely fooled; some will move up under the zooplankters as they migrate to the surface at twilight and are more visible against the sky.

Migration is costly and avoided where it is not needed. The substances, called kairomones, which warn zooplankters about fish, are yet unknown, but exposure to water that has had fish swimming in it will stimulate vertical migration whilst there will be no such migration in water innocent of such exposure, for example in high mountain corrie lakes that lack fish. In 1999 it was announced that trimethylamine, a nitrogenous substance produced by fish decay, was the kairomone for vertical migration, but by 2000 it had been decided that the amounts released into the water were vastly smaller than those needed in the laboratory to stimulate vertical migration and that trimethylamine was an unlikely candidate. Since then it has also been suggested that avoidance of exposure to ultraviolet light in very transparent lakes might also be a reason for vertical migration.[10]

Kairomones are also important in warning zooplankters against attacks by invertebrates. Some insect larvae, like the phantom midges (*Chaoborus*) that live in the sediments and in their later instars move up into the water column at night, are predators. They are nearly transparent (Fig. 107), being themselves vulnerable to fish, and detectable in the water only by their small black eyes and two buoyancy sacs that also look black because of the way they refract the light. Kairomones produced by phantom midges stimulate changes of shape in the prey. One daphnid produces small bumps (Fig. 91), the neck teeth, at the back of the head that apparently frustrate handling by *Chaoborus*. Others produce greatly enlarged heads or pixie-like 'hats' (Fig. 10), sometimes also formed in response

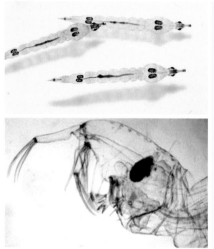
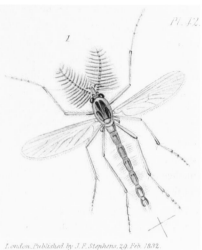

FIG 107. Phantom midge larvae (top left) move up from the bottom sediments to prey in the plankton, grasping small zooplankters with specialised antennae (lower left). They hatch into small flies (right). (Stephen Luk/Field Studies Council)

to fish as part of the defence of becoming smaller. Rotifers defend themselves against *Asplanchna*, a raptorial rotifer, by producing long spines. Of course all these devices cost energy, but insurance policies are never cheap.

FISH AND PRODUCTION

Fish strut the plankton stage. In comparison with the phytoplankters and zooplankters, there are not many of them. Even in the most productive lakes we might expect to find, on average, no more than two or three fish per metre squared and typically less than one. (The production of a lake is best seen on the basis of unit area rather than volume, simply because light enters through the surface and, irrespective of how much water is below, the amount of energy available remains the same.) Fish are most plentiful, though they are very small, just after the eggs hatch in early summer, but there are many fewer, but larger, by autumn when competition for food, parasites and predators have taken their toll.

The overwintering population of fish in a modestly deep, middlingly productive lake of 30-m average depth might be about one fish in every 150 cubic metres of water. Were the lake 100 hectares in area, a typical Scottish loch, there would be 200,000 fish. Despite the ambitions of anglers to catch big fish, on average each fish will weigh only 10–20 g, so the total fish biomass in the loch would be about 3 tonnes.[11] The mass of water, by comparison, would be 30 million tonnes and that of the phytoplankton about 15 tonnes. Three tonnes might seem comparatively large because the conversion of energy through food webs generally conveys only about 10 per cent at each step and there are likely to be two to three steps (algae to zooplankton to zooplanktivorous fish to piscivorous fish) from algae to fish. But when the turnover is considered, the numbers look much more reasonable. Algae will replace their biomass in the face of grazing and other losses about 30 times per year, fish, if their length of life is on average about four years, about 0.25 times per year. The relative productivities will then be 450 tonnes per year for the phytoplankton and 0.75 tonnes per year for fish.

Within this fish production, the ratio of numbers of piscivores like pike, charr, trout and perch to their fish prey may be quite variable because these fish are piscivorous only as they become relatively large. It may be as low as a few per cent, so that the 450 tonnes of algal production might translate to as little as 0.1 tonnes of the piscivorous fish that anglers particularly prize. The angler's dream of lots of large, hungry fish is just that. They may be hungry, but there are few and even fewer that are likely to be large.

OPEN WATER FISH COMMUNITIES IN BRITAIN AND IRELAND

In Britain and Ireland, the fish community of the open water is sparse in species and somewhat peculiar. Elsewhere in the northern hemisphere, in big lakes, the open water fish communities have perhaps five to ten species of specialist, streamlined, plankton-feeding fish. They cruise through the water, often in shoals, sieving zooplankton through their gill rakers, the feathery structures emerging from bones that also support the oxygen-absorbing tissues of the gills. Many of these fish are whitefish, Coregonidae,[12] silvery blue or green, and related to the salmon and trout, though lacking the bright red spots that often decorate the latter. The spacing of the gill rakers determines the size of food that is retained and is generally geared, in specialist planktivores, to at least small water fleas and copepods.

Where several coregonids are present, they will divide the available food, with some taking bottom animals and only large zooplankters, and having few short gill rakers, and others being more planktivorous, with more and longer gill rakers. The most specialist planktivorous species, including the very widespread vendace, have the most and longest rakers and take the greatest range of zooplankton, including the smaller animals. In the tropics are fish that feed on fine detritus and algae in the plankton, but there are none in temperate regions. The algal food supply is too seasonal and never builds up the high enough biomass that is often found in tropical lakes to give a reliable food supply.

Coregonids grow only to modest sizes, perhaps 30–40 cm, and scatter their eggs over rocky parts of the littoral zone in autumn or winter. The hatchlings move out in spring to the open water but even those that live longest have short lives of two to five years. Especially when young, they are very vulnerable to piscivorous fish and birds. Such a planktivorous fish community is functionally the equivalent of the huge shoals of planktivorous herring, anchovy and sprat that are found in the coastal seas. But oddly, in Britain and Ireland, this coregonid community is almost absent.[13]

There are only three species (Fig. 108); one has ever been close to extinction, and the other two are confined to a very few lakes. The vendace, *Coregonus albula*, is limited to Derwentwater in the English Lake District. It formerly lived in Bassenthwaite Lake, which is downstream of Derwentwater, but has not been consistently found there for many years. It also grew in Mill Loch and Castle Loch in Scotland at least until the nineteenth century. The second species, *Coregonus lavaretus*, is known as the powan in the two Scottish lochs, Eck and Lomond, in which it naturally occurs, the gwyniad in the sole Welsh location, Llyn Tegid, and the schelly in its four English Lake District homes, Ullswater, Haweswater, Red Tarn and Brotherswater. The pollan, *Coregonus autumnalis pollan* is the third species and is found only in two loughs in

FIG 108. The three British and Irish coregonid species are the pollan (upper); powan (middle); and vendace (lower). Their sleek, streamlined profiles lend themselves to energy-efficient cruising as they filter the water through their gill rakers.

Northern Ireland, Lough Neagh, where it is common and commercially fished, and the island-strewn Lower Lough Erne, where it is now rare, and in Loughs Ree and Derg on the River Shannon in the Republic of Ireland.

Coregonids come from an order of fish where many species, notably the salmonids, are anadromous: they spawn in freshwaters and then move to the ocean, returning to freshwater only when they are about to breed, and it is presumed that the three coregonid species in Britain and Ireland entered these islands from the sea as the ice retreated. However, our coregonids are not anadromous, although there is a rare estuarine coregonid, the houting, *Coregonus oxyrhyncus*, that used to frequent estuaries in Britain and Ireland. Our three coregonids are species, or races of species, that are widespread across the boreal zone that may have hung on as precarious relict populations in shifting lakes at the feet of the glaciers. Their now very scattered occurrence might be consistent with this as there would have been many opportunities for them to have moved up rivers, especially in Scotland and Ireland, as anadromous fish. As a group, coregonids prefer deep, cold, well-oxygenated waters and British and Irish lakes are puny in size and relatively warm, and that might have disfavoured them, but the abundance of pollan in the very shallow Lough Neagh belies this. There is something of a mystery for Ireland is well outside the range or other instances of this species. Two similar instances are an isolated population of the otherwise estuarine twaite shad, locally known as the goureen, in Lough Leane in Killarney, and of the similarly coastal smelt in Rostherne Mere, south of Manchester, though it is probably now extinct.

Two of our coregonids frequently take bottom-living organisms to some extent, as well as plankton, and only the vendace is a near strict planktivore. Indeed all the other native planktivorous fish in British and Irish lakes are generalists, combining planktivory with bottom-feeding, or with both bottom-feeding and piscivory. The first group includes, silver bream, common bream, bleak, gudgeon, chub, dace, minnow, roach, rudd, grayling, three-spined stickleback, nine-spined stickleback and ruffe. These are also often riverine fish, taking entirely a diet of bottom animals, but in lakes, though spawned in the littoral, they may move to the open water in their first year or so and feed on zooplankton, before returning to the littoral, or sometimes the bottom sediments, as they grow larger and need the larger meals that bottom animals provide. Compared with the coregonids, they are inefficient plankton feeders and take the easy prey of large, slow-moving cladocerans in preference to the less visible smaller water fleas and more agile copepods. They must decide to attack and lunge at their prey, capturing single animals at a time, whereas the coregonids will sweep a large volume of water, clearing it even of small animals.

Coregonids will also follow their prey into dark water by day and may continue feeding, whilst the predominantly littoral fish that enter the open water can hunt only in the light. Nonetheless the littoral species can make substantial inroads on the most efficient grazers, the larger daphnids, and have potential effects on the amount of phytoplankton in the water, particularly in spring; but these fish are only able to exploit the open water in Britain and Ireland because of the lack of competition from specialist planktivores.

In highly seasonal temperate waters, fish need to be able to eat whatever animal prey is big enough to be worthwhile and small enough to get into their mouths. In comparison, in tropical lakes, with year around productivity, there is some extreme specialisation, for example in the African Great Lakes, with specialists on egg eating, fin and scale eating and even attacks on the eyes of other larger fish. The necessary versatility in temperate lakes is also well shown in the second group of native generalist planktivores, with perch, trout, pike and Arctic charr all able to take some plankton (and also bottom invertebrates) when they are small, but moving to piscivory as they grow bigger. There are no solely piscivorous native fish in Britain and Ireland. As illustrated by the Arctic charr, a different strategy works best in the less predictable lakes of the north.

ARCTIC CHARR AND ADAPTABILITY IN TEMPERATE FISH

The charr, a common fish of the boreal and arctic regions (Fig. 109), is at the edge of its preference for cold waters in Britain and Ireland and is now declining as waters are becoming warmer.[14] It persists in about 200 populations in the cooler northern and western lakes. Above 65°N, it is anadromous, but it is solely

FIG 109. Arctic charr in Britain and Ireland are at the southern edge of their range and never grow to the size (98 cm) and magnificence of this mature male fish caught by Nils Rinaldi in Nunavut, Canada.

a freshwater species in Britain and Ireland. Throughout its range it epitomises the flexibility that fish are capable of, modifying its body, behaviour and diet to local circumstances, particularly competition with other species, to form sometimes several distinct races within the same lake, as discussed for trout in Chapter 4. Fish taxonomists in the nineteenth and early twentieth centuries, not least the charismatic curator of fish and later Director of the British Museum (Natural History), Charles Tate Regan (1878–1943), were prone to describe charr as different species in different lakes, often just from single locations. Modern studies on DNA show that these are all the same species, *Salvelinus alpinus*, and that Tate Regan's *S. fimbriatus* from Lough Coomasaharn, with its long, fringed gill rakers, the slim *S. gracillimum* from Loch Girlsta in Shetland, and the 13 or so others, were understandable misnaming. Tate Regan was faithful to his own definition of a species as an animal or community of animals having 'distinctive morphological characters [that], in the opinion of a competent systematist, [are] sufficiently definite to entitle it, or them, to a specific name'. In his time the existence of genes was still controversial and he never espoused them. Only much later did his distinguished successors in British ichthyology, with less self-importance, bring our understanding of fish species to a more sophisticated and infinitely more fascinating level.

Where the lake is shared with trout, charr will move to the open waters, trout more to the littoral. With vendace and grayling, a not uncommon combination in mainland northern Europe, charr will extend to piscivory whilst vendace specialises on plankton, and grayling on the bottom animals. Where the competition is minimal, charr will form separate piscivorous, bottom-feeding and planktivorous groups. In Loch Rannoch, for example, the biggest charr eat other fish, and live longest, up to 17 years; the smallest are short-lived planktivores, lasting up to 7 years, and the intermediate-sized ones are bottom feeders with middling longevity of 11 years. The planktivore is quite brightly coloured, the others more subdued. The three races spawn in different areas and invest differently in the numbers and sizes of eggs they produce, though a full rationale for this is yet not clear.

COPING WITH HAZARDS IS SOMETHING FOR FISH TOO

Adjustments in life history, size, shape and behaviour in response to competition and predation are as common in fish as they are in the zooplankton and phytoplankton. Prey fish will sometimes change their shape in the presence of piscivores, gaining deeper bodies that frustrate the predator's gape, or they may stay small and less attractive as a meal, compensating for the nonetheless still large losses by early maturity and production of many young. The spines of the three-spined stickleback are thought to help frustrate handling of it by predators like perch, and the greater the predation risk (measured as a greater variety of predators), the longer are the spines, though sometimes if calcium is scarce in the water, spines are not produced even if the risks are high. Its reaction to an artificial image of a predator, its fright response, is also greater when it comes from lakes with a high risk.[15]

THE REAL TOP PREDATORS

The specialist top predators of the open water are birds (Fig. 110): primarily the cormorant, goosander and merganser, the much less common osprey and the terns, which take small fish but are unlikely to have very significant effects. It is difficult to be certain how these animals fit in, and views are coloured by the

FIG 110. Cormorants are probably now the most significant fish predators in open waters. (Frank Drebin)

protests of anglers and fish farmers that they are damaging, but the prediction of an ecologist would be that fish communities are unlikely to be seriously depleted by bird predation, simply because any such serious effect would undermine the future of the predator population. Studies in Canada on double crested cormorants, in lakes with undisturbed natural communities, suggest some specialisation on the cisco (a coregonid), yellow perch and nine-spined stickleback, but that another nine species are not taken; studies on Lake Huron suggest some inroads of cormorants only on one particular age-class, three-year-olds, of perch. Reviews in the UK and of the Baltic Sea have found none of the devastating effects that have been feared as cormorants have become more common in freshwaters.[16]

In recent years, Scottish freshwaters overall have had about 7,000 cormorants, 4,000 red-breasted merganser, 5,000 goosander and 9,000 heron, around 25,000 piscivores in all. With 2,400 km² of freshwaters, this gives around one such bird in every 10 ha, compared with upwards of 100,000 fish in the same area. A bird would have to be exceedingly voracious to make much impact, though where fish are concentrated in farms that attract abnormal concentrations of birds, or where alien and poorly adapted species such as rainbow trout have been artificially heavily stocked in reservoirs, there could be noticeable, indeed inevitable, effects. The same appears to be true of the otter. It will take a variety of fish, particularly slow-moving ones like members of the carp family such as roach, and eels, but will eat anything it can catch, irrespective of size or species. Nonetheless, its dependency on air breathing, and a need to return to the surface after a minute or two, means that fish will usually outmanoeuvre it and that severe depredation of the fish population is very unlikely. Piscivory brings rich food and faster growth, but it is not an easy life.

THE PLANKTON'S YEAR

Horizontal variation in types of shore and structure of the community set the picture in the littoral (Chapter 5). Plankton is spatially more uniform because of wind mixing, though there is a great deal of vertical structure, but the big picture that integrates all of the detail already discussed is best seen in the change of seasons.

Typically in Britain and Ireland, winter presents a lake well mixed by the winds. The inflow streams are full; water cascades in, circulates from top to bottom of the water column, and gleans oxygen from the air as the winds froth its surface. The plankton community is sparse and there may be only a few

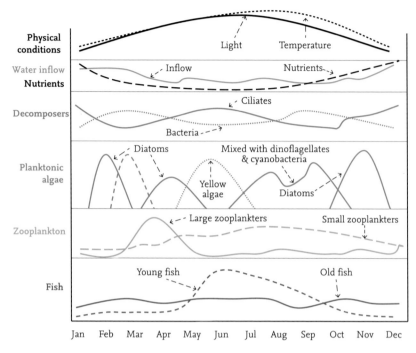

FIG 111. The general pattern of seasonal changes in the plankton system of British and Irish lakes.

thousand phytoplankters and fewer than tens of zooplankters per litre. Bacteria are more common and growing slowly on the dissolved organic matter and detritus in the water. The sun's angle is low and light is scarce. In Shetland, at the winter solstice, there will be only six hours of daylight and the sun will rise to no more than 6 degrees above the horizon. In southern England, there will be only two more hours of daylight and the solar angle will be a mere 16 degrees. Photosynthesis will be limited by light, but some phytoplankters and zooplankters will grow slowly, just ticking over. Fish find little food in winter and will be skulking, conserving their energy, in the littoral or on the bottom, their activity slowed by the cold water. Meanwhile the water pouring in from the catchment builds up the concentrations of the key nutrients, phosphate, ammonium, nitrate and silicate in the water. By late winter these will be at their maxima for the year (Fig. 111).

Spring

As the daylength and the solar angle rise in January and February, algal cells, particularly diatoms, will divide more rapidly. A few will have overwintered; some may be resuspended from where they have sunk to the bottom mud; others may hatch from resting spores. Doubling every few days, the populations will have risen to some millions per litre by March or April (Fig. 112) and the water may have a tinge of brown. The winds remain strong enough to mix the water, keeping the heavy diatom cells, with their glassy walls, in suspension, but their populations cannot continue to grow indefinitely. Four omens portend the fall of the spring diatom peak in late April or May. First, evaporation rates are rising and less water is entering the lake in the streams. That means lower nutrient supply, whilst the growth of the algae is depleting the stocks that had previously built up.

Secondly the winds are dropping and stratification is setting in. The diatoms sink more rapidly than weakening wind eddies can return them to the surface, and they may fall to the sediments, where invertebrates will find them a welcome

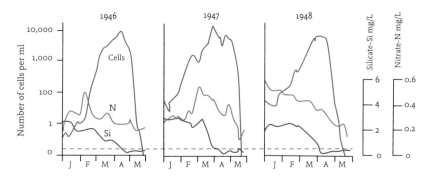

FIG 112. *Asterionella formosa* (shown in Figs 52 and 97) was the subject of classic work done by John Lund in Windermere and other lakes of its catchment. He followed its population changes over many years in relation to changes in physical conditions and water chemistry and was the first to provide reliable data that linked particular aspects of chemistry to the decline of a phytoplankton population. The data here (from Lund, 1950) are from Esthwaite Water and show how the population starts to decline as the silicate–silicon concentration is reduced to about 0.5 mg/L (shown by the hatched line). Nitrate was also taken up but there was no such close correlation. Lund later showed that phosphate was involved and that if phosphate was added, the remaining 0.5mg/L of silicon would be taken up. It was thus phosphorus that ultimately limited growth of the population, but the principle of severe nutrient limitation of planktonic algal growth had been firmly established.

new source of food. The peak populations will also mean that the third influence, internal parasites of the cells – protozoa, chytrid fungi and viruses – will be able to multiply into epidemics, weakening the diatoms, slowing their multiplication and eventually killing them. Lastly, the rising temperatures will have quickened the multiplication of the zooplankters and many of the diatoms are small enough to be taken by the filter-feeders. The combination of nutrient limitation, lower turbulence, parasites and grazing may lead to a week or two of clear water in April or May, with only a few algae remaining, but almost as soon as the diatoms go into serious decline, new populations of flagellates such as the chrysophytes and cryptomonads will prosper. Their lower cell density, modest sinking rates, greater abilities to glean nutrients from low concentrations and speedy growth that can match the filtering abilities of the animals mean that they can succeed the diatoms in the new conditions (Fig. 111).

Early Summer

Early summer brings new players to the scene. Fish have bred in the shallows and the eggs have hatched. The young at first feed on yolk, then on algae, rotifers and protozoa, in the littoral, but eventually these young-of-the year are forced out by the competition of sheer numbers towards the open water. There, the swarms of zooplankters, now at their peak (Fig. 111) from the bounties of the spring algal growth, are vulnerable, and the hungry, indeed voracious, young fish take eager advantage. With reduced loss to grazers, and some regeneration of nutrients from excretion by the zooplankton and fish, the algae get a second wind.

The phytoplankton species that grow now are different. The water is chemically changed and the lake, if it is deep enough, has stratified. Available phosphates, ammonium and nitrate are scarce, but there is an expanding menu of dissolved organic substances that have been produced by the vigorous biological activity during spring. There are excretions and secretions of algae and animals, products of decomposition when cells have been destroyed by parasites and lysed by viruses, and new substances washed from the spring growth on land as litter warms, microorganisms quicken and worms and woodlice become active. pH of the lake water will have risen because of the rise in photosynthesis, and free carbon dioxide will be scarcer. The fast-growing algae that thrived in the rich water of spring are replaced by a more esoteric bunch: those that can glean nutrients from low concentrations and that can benefit from the new chemical brew.

There is a greater diversity: chrysophytes, cryptomonads, euglenoids, desmids, other green algae, dinoflagellates and cyanobacteria, even some small diatom species that sink more slowly than their bigger spring sisters. The flagellated groups may be mixotrophic, taking advantage of the pulse of bacteria that thrived on the death of the spring diatoms. Bacteria are especially abundant just above the thermocline, where the change in density slows the rate of sinking and causes both algal detritus and bacteria to accumulate. The flagellates are able to maintain their position in a water column that is now stiller, with less strong eddies to maintain heavy cells in suspension.

Other new species are larger, perhaps long filaments or mucilaginous colonies. They are too big to be easily filtered out, or they pass through zooplankton guts protected by the mucilage, benefit from the release of nutrients from the digestion of less well-protected species, and emerge bright and green in the faeces to resume their tenure in the water. Some of the summer phytoplankters are simply slow growers that were present but scarce in winter and spring, and have plodded their way to becoming more noticeable by August. Others, in contrast, are small fast growers, vulnerable to grazing by the remaining zooplankters, but able to persist because they multiply faster than they are eaten. And some are the remnants of the boom and bust of spring, luckily surviving on chance eddies despite their weight. There are refugees from every onslaught.

Scarcer now are the large water fleas (cladocerans) that fed on the spring bloom (Fig. 111). They filtered efficiently but their limited movements and large size made them easy targets for the fish. A few persist but the smaller species dominate, together with even tinier rotifers that have thrived on bacteria and organic debris. This is now quite varied: algal cells dead from nutrient deficiency or parasites; zooplankton and fish faeces; the continuing, if reduced, wash-in from the catchment; and the rising supply from dead or damaged plants and algae in the littoral. Copepods are also common with their rapid movements that frustrate attacks by fish, but the open water is always a dangerous place.

By midsummer, there are fewer small fish (Fig. 111). Of the hundreds of thousands hatching from eggs in May and June, some were early eaten in the littoral by the nymphs of dragonflies and the diving beetles, but most now by piscivorous fish and birds. Those agile or cunning enough to dodge this fate have grown bigger and need larger animals than zooplankters for their meals; these are more likely to be found at the edges of the littoral zone, on the plants or in the sediments. It is safer also for the fish to stay in the shade of weed beds than be exposed in the open water, their silhouettes outlined against the sky as a predator approaches from below. There will be sorties of fish into the open water in small lakes, where there can be rapid retreat to the weedbeds, but in a large lake, young fish will spurn the centre unless they are specialist planktivores or piscivores hunting these planktivores.

Late summer

By August, the water is warm; the total algal biomass may have recovered to its previous peak of spring as phosphate has been released from decomposition in the sediments and nitrogen is provided by biological fixation; phytoplankton diversity is at its highest for the year, with actively growing species and the refugees of previous conditions. There will also be casual species of algae that originated in the littoral and have been displaced by wind and waves or flurries of activity by fish and birds. The bacteria and protozoa in turn will be more varied. The simple cycle of growth and decline seen in the spring-growing algae will have been replaced by complex, almost random-seeming peaks and troughs in numbers, the situation changing somewhat by the day and markedly by the week.

There may be one last prominent feature, before overturn of the stratification by autumn gales and washout by the rising winter streams, which resets the stage. The cyanobacteria have been part of the plankton community since spring, but in July and August their multiplication seems particularly favoured (Fig. 111). They grow slowly and their increased numbers may simply be a reflection of this, but higher temperatures and low available nitrogen concentrations favour them; the strongly stratified water column is also greatly to their liking. The cyanobacteria are an ancient group, evolved when the oceans were very warm, hot even, and they have retained genes that respond to warm conditions, but the other reasons for their late-summer peak are less obvious and concern the structure of the water column in late summer.

The summer growth of other algae keeps available nutrients in short supply towards the lake surface. The water column, if the lake is deep enough, is stratified; the surface temperature is at its highest and the winds at their lowest. Decomposition is rife in the hypolimnion, and ammonium is being released from the breakdown of proteins in sinking debris; sediment surfaces are becoming deoxygenated and releasing phosphates as the iron compounds that have bound them are reduced. But these supplies of nutrients are locked into the deep waters by the stratification. Occasionally a summer storm will disturb the water enough to start internal waves that ripple along the top of the hypolimnion and shave a little water up into the epilimnion, but the consequences are minor. For most algae, conditions are now difficult; competition is severe for both nutrients and light. But for some cyanobacteria they are ideal.[17]

These cyanobacteria are species that produce gas vesicles (Fig. 113): small, protein-bound bodies in the cells that contain air and give buoyancy, so that unlike the rest of the algae, which tend to sink, these may float upwards. As the cyanobacteria rise towards the surface, they fix carbon dioxide into sugars

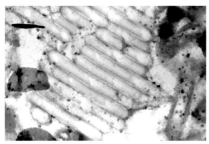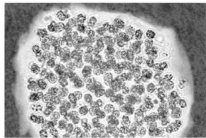

FIG 113. Movement of cyanobacteria up and down a stratified water column depends on air-filled, collapsible gas vesicles (left), which can be seen as dots in the photograph of *Microcystis aeruginosa* (right). The cells are about 1.5 μm and the gas vesicles are about 0.08 μm in diameter.

but lack phosphate and nitrogen compounds to turn these into proteins and cell structures. The sugars absorb water through the cell membranes, and the pressure inside the cells increases, flattening and bursting some of the gas vesicles. The cells, most usually in colonies or filaments, then become denser and start to sink through the thermocline and into the phosphate- and ammonium-rich waters of the hypolimnion. Many of them also are able to fix nitrogen from nitrogen gas dissolved in the water and this process is favoured by low oxygen conditions that are found in the deeper waters.

The sinking cyanobacteria, over a day or two, are thus able to start converting their sugars into new cell material, including new gas vesicles, as they fix nitrogen and gain access to phosphate around the top of the hypolimnion (or at the surfaces of the sediments in a shallow lake that does not stratify). The new vesicles restore buoyancy and the reinvigorated cyanobacteria begin to rise again to the surface, and the cycle repeats itself. Sometimes the mechanism does not cope. There may be so little light that sugar concentrations are not increased enough. Too few gas vesicles then burst to send the colonies downwards, so that they gather at the water surface as a scum that may drift to the edge of the lake and may be very obvious. Some of these scums, or blooms, are of strains of cyanobacteria that produce toxins very poisonous to mammals or birds. Why they should do so is still a mystery, despite much research. The blooms usually, but not always, signal the death of most of the cells. Protozoa, particularly amoebae that have attached to the colonies, may then eat them and viruses will lyse them, but few of the bigger zooplankters can ingest enough to survive on them. Bacteria will rot most of them in the sediments. A few, however, will persist, sometimes as large resting spores that will not hatch until the following year, or sometimes as refugees.

Autumn

The sun dips in autumn; the winds blow more vigorously; evaporation rates fall and the streams start to rise, bringing in cool water and renewing nutrient supplies that have been depleted in summer (Fig. 111). The wind deepens the epilimnion and weakens the thermocline. A surge of diatoms may prosper in the more turbulent water, now also enriched by hypolimnion water that has been mixed upwards. Some of the algae that have held sway in summer may also grow a little more vigorously, but conditions for photosynthesis are worsening and, in a wet autumn, the inflowing water may wash cells out faster than they can reproduce. In a dry one the populations may remain high, not increasing much, if at all, but persisting so that if the winter is also dry and the lake does not freeze, the nature of the following spring growth will be influenced by what has been carried over from the previous autumn.

Cooling lowers the feeding rates of the zooplankters. Some have had a more difficult time in summer than they had in spring; others have taken new opportunities. The small cells that filter-feeders were able to ingest became scarcer as they were consumed and, in summer, larger and often colonial species of algae grasped the nutrients available. Some zooplankters could bite off chunks from the colonies, but the nutritional quality of the food was falling. Nutrients were deficient; mucilage made up more of the food. Parasites of the zooplankters and new predators, like chaoborids, were also taking a toll. By autumn many of the zooplankters shift into survival mode, producing thick-walled eggs that will rest on the bottom until the rising temperatures of spring cue their hatching, though a few will tough out the winter, their prize being an early start on the new food supplies a few months later.

Winter and the next year

Only in northern Scotland will there be a lengthy ice cover, and inverse stratification of the water beneath it. Under the ice, streams still flow and new debris and dissolved organic matter is brought in. Photosynthesis is possible under ice (it is transparent and in the Antarctic, diatoms grow attached to the underside of bergs in summer) and flagellates may be attracted upwards to green the water just below the ice, unless a cover of snow cuts out all of the light. Even then, the work of bacteria and flagellates, ciliates and rotifers, breaking down organic debris, still carries on. So long as there is liquid water, however cold (and in volcanic springs, however hot) there will be biological activity.

The stage will never be entirely cleared and so, the next year, there may be differences in spring depending on conditions in the previous autumn and winter. The more obvious features – spring growth and decline of the diatoms; a burst of zooplankton activity; fish spawning and hatching; a decline in zooplankters a little later; a mixed community of algae and zooplankton in summer; and some rise in cyanobacteria in mid- to late summer – will generally be seen, against a steady background of processing of organic matter by the bacteria, flagellates and ciliates.[18] But the details will differ a great deal from year to year. Temperature, water flow into the lake, windiness, all the elements of weather, will influence the play. Some of the main players will appear year after year, but their time on stage will never be exactly the same and the cast of bit-part players will differ from one year to the next.

AN OVERVIEW

Since the 1950s and the publication of *Life in Lakes & Rivers*, there have been significant changes in our understanding of how the plankton system works. The early view was one of a simple set of food chains, based upon the phytoplankton, a solely photosynthetic community, controlled by the supply of phosphorus, nitrogen and, in the case of diatoms, silicate. Production of the phytoplankton controlled that of zooplankton and in turn of zooplanktivorous fish and then of piscivorous fish and birds. About 10 per cent of the energy processed at each step was transferred and 90 per cent was dissipated through respiration. One unit of algae might then support a thousandth of a unit of piscivore.

The concept of food chains and a relatively small transfer of energy at each step still holds, but the chains are much more interlinked in a web and 10 per cent is seen as a notional value, higher where animals eat animals and lower where zooplankton eat detritus and bacteria. It is now realised that the bases of the food web may include a substantial contribution from detritus washed in from the littoral or the catchment and that the plankton system is often net heterotrophic. This means that the total (or gross) photosynthesis of the phytoplankton is lower than the total respiration of the plankton community (bacteria, algae and animals), the shortfall in energy requirements being met by the incoming organic matter. Photosynthesis can be measured by placing water in clear glass bottles and measuring the release of oxygen over a known time. Respiration is measured in bottles made opaque to light with black tape. If the measures are done by day, photosynthesis often exceeds respiration but when the night hours are accounted for, when respiration continues apace but photosynthesis is not possible, the effect over 24 hours is a high ratio of respiration to photosynthesis, especially in lakes that have not been polluted by nutrients, running in from sewage effluents or agriculture, which stimulate greater algal growth.[19]

Another advance in our understanding of the plankton food webs is that the distinct layers (called trophic levels) of the older concept (primary producer, grazer or herbivore, predator, top predator) have been replaced by overlaps. Algae may be partly phagotrophic on bacteria, zooplankton will take all of bacteria and algae, flagellates and ciliates. The raptorial zooplankters may take large algae and small animals; hatchling fish will take algae and rotifers, then bigger zooplankters, either grazers or predators as they get bigger. Piscivores like pike become carnivorous on their own young when other prey is scarce. Studies with ^{15}N (Chapter 5) never show distinct grouping of values that would indicate firm separation of trophic levels. There is always a continuous series.

The simple food chain idea has also been modified because of the strategies and devices that algae, zooplankton and zooplanktivorous fish use to reduce the risk of being grazed or seized by their predators. The prey is able to evolve defences and in turn the predator develops devices to overcome them, in a continuous 'arms race' that sees vulnerabilities continually and sometimes rapidly changing.[20] The food web concept remains, but in a less orderly and predictable picture. As weather and the amount of water entering the lake

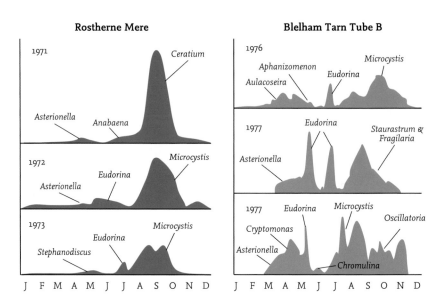

FIG 114. Phytoplankton succession shows some constant features from year to year but there are many differences in detail, ultimately caused by the vagaries of weather reflected in degrees of stratification and mixing, and inputs of water. Data are shown for different years from Rostherne Mere in Cheshire and an experimental Lund Tube installed in Blelham Tarn. The most abundant genera explaining the peaks in biomass are shown but many others were also found. Based on Reynolds, 1980.

continuously vary, different algae become selected to take advantage of the changed and changing conditions, and there are dozens of consequences and adjustments that are made in the planktonic system. Broadly it will look the same from year to year, but in the details of exactly which species grows and to what extent, there will be many largely unpredictable differences (Fig. 114).

Another major change in understanding since the 1950s has been that the plankton web is not entirely controlled by nutrients from the bottom upwards. Parts of it are controlled top-down through predation and grazing, particularly in shallow lakes where the littoral plant beds offer refuges where the zooplankters can maintain large populations. This has been studied in many experiments carried out in plastic enclosures (mesocosms), a few metres cubed in volume (Fig. 115). Fish can be removed from, or added to the mesocosms, plants can be gardened and nutrients can be manipulated. Such experiments usually show that removal of fish leads to increased zooplankton and reduced algal growth, irrespective of nutrients, and that the reverse happens with an increase in the number of fish: reduced zooplankton, more algae. Sometimes the mechanism might also involve increased recycling of nutrients owing to the activity of the fish.[21] It is the story of the overstocked garden goldfish pond, with its bright green water.

FIG 115. Microcosms can be constructed from plastic tubing or bags set in lakes (left), or made from concrete or fibreglass tanks (right). They allow controlled and replicated experiments but are too small to reproduce all the features of a large lake.

When such experiments are done on whole lakes, the principles still apply but in the more complex and larger environment, with its connections with the littoral, the outcomes may be different from what the theory predicts. Experiments in some small lakes, Peter, Paul and Tuesday, in Indiana have illustrated this.[22] Paul Lake was left as a control and showed small differences from year to year but no major changes in the balance of zooplankton and phytoplankton. In Tuesday Lake, as anticipated, addition of the piscivorous large-mouthed bass and removal of a large biomass of several species of zooplanktivorous minnows increased the zooplankton biomass, and shifted the summer community from copepods and rotifers to cladocerans, with a reduction in algal biomass and photosynthesis. But in a third lake, Peter Lake, removal of bass and addition of minnows led to a more complex outcome of decreased zooplanktivory because the minnows fled to the littoral plant beds to escape from some remaining piscivores. Both zooplankton biomass and the dominance of large cladocerans unexpectedly increased, as did (expectedly) algal biomass and primary production because gelatinous colonial green algae, which are not easily grazed, took over the phytoplankton community.

Similar experiments may be carried out inadvertently. Piscivores may be killed on hot, calm summer nights in shallow lakes when respiration reduces

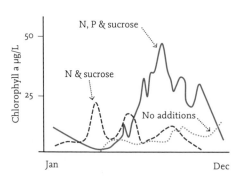

FIG 116. Experiments on whole lakes, especially where the lake can be divided by plastic curtains, as at Lake 227 in the Canadian Experimental Lakes Area in Ontario, offer realism but no replication and therefore pose statistical problems. However, results are often clear-cut as here where the distant half of the lake was treated with various nutrients in different years in contrast to the near half, which was used as a control. The experiments showed that phosphate additions but not those of nitrogen or carbon (as sucrose) stimulated more algal growth and that therefore phosphorus was the limiting nutrient. (David Schindler, on whose data the graphs are based)

oxygen levels. This will result in increased survival of small fish, greater removal of zooplankton and thence increased survival of algae. Sometimes, even more deoxygenated conditions will kill most of the fish, resulting in surges of large zooplankters and water cleared of algae even in midsummer.

There is a view that only by experimenting at the scale of whole lakes, rather than in small mesocosms, can the workings of the ecosystem be accurately revealed.[23] Doing such experiments is, however, very difficult as it is virtually impossible to find two (or preferably four to allow for proper statistical replication) identical lakes to provide a control and an experimentally altered lake. Rarely, a lake can be divided for experiments into two equal halves, using plastic curtains (Fig. 116). A compromise is to use very large mesocosms of tough butyl rubber, heavily anchored against storms. Known as 'Lund Tubes' after their first user, John Lund, in Blelham Tarn, they are expensive and so great replication is not possible. In Blelham Tarn, with their black inflated collars, they were prominently visible and, on amenity grounds, tolerated only for a limited time by the landowners, the National Trust. In Hickling Broad (Fig. 117), similar tubes suffered a number of setbacks, including the polluting effects of hundreds of black-headed gulls favouring their rims for overnight roosting, and a storm which moved them several hundred metres and tangled them, despite half a tonne of metal anchoring weights.[24] Only by experimentation, however difficult, and not much by monitoring and observation, however, can further advances in understanding be made. Nonetheless, the observed patterns of plankton communities in Britain and Ireland suggest how such experiments can be sensibly targeted.

FIG 117. A compromise between whole-lake experiments and mesocosms is to use large butyl rubber reservoirs set in the lake (Lund Tubes), but there are always practical problems to be solved. Black-headed gulls perched on the inflated rims of the tubes in Hickling Broad, greatly increasing the fertility of the water with their droppings, and were undeterred by fluttering plastic strips (left). The problem was solved by enclosing the tubes in large tents of fruit-cage netting (right).

SOME GEOGRAPHY

As related in Chapter 2, the northern and western lakes are larger, deeper and less nutrient rich in their hard-rock and hilly catchments. The southern and eastern lakes and ponds, on sedimentary rocks and rich deposits of glacial drift, are smaller, shallower and more nutrient rich; agriculture and large populations have magnified these differences.[25] The plankton communities reflect all of this.

In the north and west, despite much artificial stocking of pike, the predominant piscivores and planktivores are charr, trout and perch, the littoral zones are relatively smaller and the water clearer. The zooplankton has a deep-water, rather than a littoral refuge and the generalist fish are unable to build up large populations because of the limited littoral zone. Calanoid copepods are more common than in the south, and the algal community, in the cooler and less nutrient-rich waters, will tend to have fewer cyanobacteria, whilst desmids will be more prominent. The shallower lowland lakes have proportionately greater littoral zones, a more abundant plankton with bigger populations of diatoms, green algae and cyanobacteria, communities of cyprinid fish like roach, rudd and bream, and pike and sometimes perch, as the top fish predator.

It is as if the shallow lakes of the south are extensions of the riverine floodplains dominated by plants and the littoral, whilst the deeper northern lakes are too warm or small, or too early isolated, to have acquired the truly open water communities of the really big lakes of the northern hemisphere. Only two of our lakes, Loughs Corrib and Neagh are listed in the 100 largest (by area) lakes of Europe. The diversity of a lake appears to depend on size rather than productivity or fertility so at best our invertebrate and fish communities are puny.[26] The business of recolonisation after the glaciation was suspended early and is unfinished, and the maritime setting of Britain and Ireland brings nuances of weather that disturb these systems much more frequently than those of the more settled climates of the mainland continent. The players on our planktonic stages are fewer than elsewhere, the action changing more from performance to performance than on the mainland, and the centre stage is more dependent on what is happening in the littoral wings.[27] That connection extends also to the areas under the main stage, the bottom muds, where a different but equally interdependent community prevails, and where the archives of the theatre's past are kept in sediments laid down year after year. These shall be the topics for the next chapter.

CHAPTER 7

The Deep, the Old, the Dark and the Cold

BLACK SWARMS HOVER, ON CALM and warmish days in May, over many British and Irish lakes. They are small reflections of the thick clouds of midges that tower over more northerly lakes and over Lake Malawi (Fig. 118), where they choke fishermen, whose nostrils can be blocked by thousands of these small flies, but they have parallel origins. From larvae feeding in the sediments in the deep water, the flies emerge, crowd together for their mating flights, lay a new generation of eggs on the water surface, then die: a brief and dramatic climax to a long development in a seemingly dull environment. Yet the profundal sediments are far from that; as Michael Flanders and Donald Swann had it, in a song celebrating the love life of hippopotami, it is *mud, mud, glorious mud*. Its biodiversity may be relatively low if you look only at the midges, oligochaete worms and pea mussels, but they are astounding creatures; its microbiology has global implications for the carbon dioxide and methane concentrations in the atmosphere; and it contains a detailed, if selective, record

FIG 118. Midge mating swarms over Lake Malawi.

of the history of the lake that is rewarding to reconstruct. There is nothing less interesting in the deep and cold, dark and sometimes smelly layers of mud in a lake than in the littoral or the plankton. They are all essential parts of a whole.

MUD

Mud is not just there; it has to get there, and once it is there, it is not inert. Mud comes from many sources. There is what is washed in from the catchment: eroded sand grains and clay, coarse and fine organic debris. To it is added the debris of the littoral and plankton, working its way down the lake slope, or steadily raining down. The coarsest material falls out in the stream deltas at the edge; the clays and the finer organic matter travel further and this silt will already be colonised by microorganisms. In shallower lakes, some may be resuspended from time to time by the wind or delving fish, but where there is deep water, it becomes the latest of orderly layer upon layer of sediment that has been building up since the lake first formed.

If most of the sediment comes from the catchment, as in mountainous regions with steep, eroding slopes, the sediments will be more inorganic and clayey. They will be more organic where the catchments are rich and fertile and the lake has an extensive littoral with swamps at its fringes. They will be almost entirely organic where the lake is set in peatlands, especially where the bogs have been drained, or burned to maintain grouse moors, and the peats are left exposed to the rain. Within a lake the sediments may be less and less organic with water depth, for those in the deeper parts have had to travel further to get there and thus have had longer for microorganisms to process their organic matter to carbon dioxide. For animals living in the sediments in the deeper parts, the prospects do not look promising, especially when the conditions in the hypolimnion water that overlies the sediments are also considered.

LIFE IN THE HYPOLIMNION

Light is extinguished in many lakes even above the bottom of the eplimnion, and the hypolimnion is entirely dark. With the darkness, as the summer progresses, may come an increasingly dire set of chemical conditions created by the bacterial activities discussed in Chapter 3 and shown in Figure 54. In the extreme, the hypolimnion waters will be acidic, ammoniacal, toxic with hydrogen sulphide and reduced iron and manganese, and saturated with carbon dioxide and methane, as well as dark and cold. This chilly maelstrom may be separated from the sparkling sunlit surface by just a few metres of epilimnion.

When the lake is fully mixed, of course, the water at the bottom is just like that at the surface: well oxygenated and chemically equable. If the hypolimnion is very large, or the lake is very infertile, such amenable conditions may persist throughout the summer. Animals living in the bottom sediments then have little problem respiring, but grow only slowly because the temperatures are low. But if there is severe summer deoxygenation, the bottom animals find favourable conditions only in spring and autumn. During the summer many shut down their activities or tick over, reliant on a limited ability to respire anaerobically. The sediments in deep water are often difficult habitats, and few species can tolerate them.

Even in lakes where the hypolimnion remains oxygenated, the bottom community is less rich than that of the littoral because the quality of organic matter that reaches the community is low. It is dominated by the resistant compounds, like cellulose, and lignin from wood, that other organisms, which encountered the organic matter first, in the littoral or the plankton, found least rewarding to deal with. The sediment nonetheless will still tend to be deoxygenated below its surface, even if the overlying water and its top few millimetres are oxygenated, because there is still a high concentration of bacteria, and oxygen is slow to diffuse in from the water. The temperature at these depths is generally low because hypolimnia may retain the 4°C of the densest winter water, at least in deep lakes in Scotland. Further south, the water will begin to stratify in spring when the water has reached perhaps 8 or 9°C, whilst the epilimnion may warm to above 20°C, so hypolimnion temperatures are still modest.

The sediment habitat has little structure. The muddy plain of the deep water is relatively uniform, amorphous, shifting as more sediment arrives, and flat. It is very different from the miniature forest of the littoral zone. Even the rugged surfaces of the rocks of the underlying basin are smothered by the fine accumulation of years. In all respects it looks an unpromising place for an animal community. But typically, several thousand animals will occupy the top centimetre or so of each square metre of sediment, a density not so high as in a rich littoral, but not sparse either.[1]

PROFUNDAL ANIMALS

The larger invertebrates of these profundal sediments are sampled by grabs of various kinds, manhandled from a boat, or in recent years and shallow enough water, by a scuba diver. Grabs (Fig. 119) are sometimes spring-loaded and released

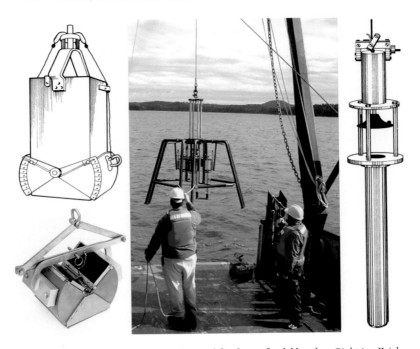

FIG 119. Some of the many samplers designed for the profundal benthos. Right is a Kajak-Brinkhurst sampler, named, as often, for its inventors. It is dropped vertically and takes a core of surface sediment. The stopper is then released using a weighted messenger dropped down the line, and blocks the top of the tube as the sampler is hauled to the surface. Centre shows a multiple corer, a series of such samplers mounted together. Top left is an Ekmann dredge, whose jaws are held apart by springs, which are released by a messenger weight when the sampler is positioned in the sediment. The vigorous snap of the jaws is useful if there is vegetation debris or plants to cut through. Bottom left shows a Ponar grab, in which the jaws are held open by a catch, which falls off when the sampler rests in the sediment. Pulling the sampler up then closes the jaws around the sample.

by a weight sent down the line when the operator feels, through the line, that the grab has reached the bottom, or sometimes, before lowering, are set open by ingenious levers. These are released when the grab reaches the sediments, and the jaws close around a lump of mud as the grab is pulled upwards. Grabs are perfidious things, though, and sometimes the spring or the levers slip on the way down and the grab closes before it reaches the bottom. Or when it reaches the bottom, a buried stone or lump of waterlogged wood jams the jaws open and the

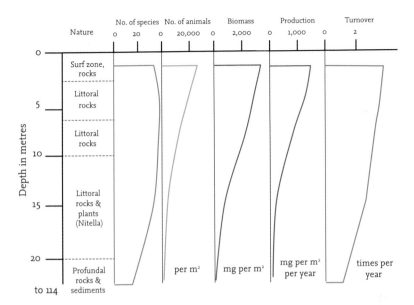

FIG 120. Changes with depth in the benthic invertebrate community of Lake Thingvallavatn in Iceland. Based on data from Lindegaard, 1992.

grab is empty when pulled up. This is of minor consequence in shallow lakes, an irritation in deeper ones and a source of bad language in very deep ones. It can take well over half an hour to send down a grab and wind it steadily up again from a depth of 100 metres.

A successful set of samples will, however, show an interesting change in community with increasing depth. The sediment in the shallow littoral will have the rich community already described in Chapter 5, but as the profundal zone is approached there is a marked fall in diversity, which then continues steadily to decrease into the greatest depths (Fig. 120). If the hypolimnion is well oxygenated, there may be some burrowing mayflies, two-winged flies, including chaoborids and chironomids, copepods and small cladocerans, ostracods, water hoglice and related crustaceans. There may be small bivalve molluscs, particularly pea mussels (for their small size) of the genera *Pisidium* and *Sphaerium*, larger swan mussels and several species of oligochaete worms. There will be a much greater diversity of nematodes and ciliates, probably constituting the bulk of the total biomass, though they have been less well studied compared with the animals that are visible to the naked eye and can be conveniently sorted from the mud.

FIG 121. Common bream, with their downwardly directed mouths, feed in the profundal when oxygen is adequately present.

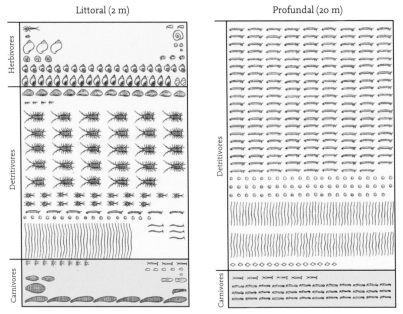

FIG 122. The different invertebrate communities in 200 cm² of sediment from 2 m depth, in the littoral, and 20 m depth, in the profundal, of Lake Esrom in Denmark. (Based on Jonasson, 1972.) Each symbol represents one animal and different symbols represent different species drawn to the same scale. Snails, zebra mussels, water hog lice, mayflies, oligochaetes and leeches dominate the littoral, but the profundal is less diverse with primarily chironomids, pea mussels, oligochaetes and phantom midges. I find these hand-drawn diagrams immensely more charming than the standard figures now produced by computer programs.

Fish will not move into deoxygenated waters, but where there is oxygen, bottom-feeding fish, such as bream (Fig. 121), will visit, though most of the predators in this realm are invertebrates.

In deoxygenated hypolimnia, many of these animals cannot survive and the community is reduced to the more tolerant genera of chironomids and oligochaetes and the immensely resilient nematodes and ciliates. Figure 122 shows some of the features of how the communities change in the moderately deep Lake Esrom in Denmark; British and Irish limnologists have shown interest in the profundal benthos, but not to the comprehensive extent of their continental colleagues.[2]

CHIRONOMIDS, THE GREAT SURVIVORS

Chironomus anthracinus (Fig. 123) is a common inhabitant of the profundal in many lakes and can be our guide to life in the sediments. It has a worm-like larva but, being an insect, has a distinct head, behind which is a pair of fleshy,

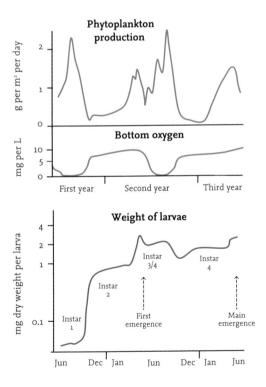

FIG 123. The course of the life history of *Chironomus anthracinus* in Lake Esrom, in relation to the food supply sedimenting from the plankton, and the state of oxygenation of the hypolimnion. The larvae are growing rapidly when the curve has a strong vertical component but are inactive when the curve is horizontal, and are losing weight in winter when the curve dips downwards. Based on Jonasson, 1972.

but not jointed legs. At its rear are two projections which function as gills, each with tracheae for absorbing oxygen. The first instars (growth stages in insects, separated by a shedding of the exoskeleton) are colourless or pink but the later ones become distinctly red with haemoglobin. In Lake Esrom this midge starts life as an egg mass laid in May on the lake surface, between sunset and darkness, in the calm lee of beech woodlands on the western shore.[3] As the mating swarms of flies disperse, the females dip their abdomens into the surface water and lay the egg masses, only a few millimetres in size at first but swelling a hundredfold when wetted. Wind and water currents subsequently distribute the eggs throughout the lake and they sink to the bottom.

By June, the eggs have hatched into instars less than 2 mm long, the first of four stages that precede pupation and the emergence of the adults, up to 23 months later. Growth is rapid, and the third instar is reached by July. There is a ready supply of food falling from the epilimnion where the spring population of planktonic diatoms is now dying (see Chapter 6). The first instar is transparent and moves along beneath the sediment surface, swallowing sediment as it goes; the second has heavier muscles and some haemoglobin, not enough to act as a store of oxygen, but possibly sufficient to improve the rate at which oxygen can be absorbed from low concentrations. This stage builds and lives in a tube of sediment, glued together by salivary secretions. It is open at the surface and tapering at the base, and the larva, head up, pumps a current of water past its mouth by undulations of the body. It may also reach out from the tube to gather sediment encircling it. The third instar larvae also build tubes, which project a little way above the sediment surface. They spread a net of salivary threads over the surrounding mud, to which particles stick, then drag the net down into the tube to eat it.

Lake Esrom is fertile and dissolved oxygen concentrations fall rapidly in its hypolimnion. By July the lower few metres are almost deoxygenated, and at around 1 mg oxygen per litre, growth of the *Chironomus* larvae stops. This may be because only limited respiration is then possible, or because the supply of sedimenting food has changed in quality or amount as the overlying plankton community produces less and processes it first. On the other hand, predation by bottom-feeding fish ceases. They cannot tolerate the deoxygenation and move to shallower waters. The larvae lie quiescent for the rest of the summer.

After mixing and reoxygenation of the water in September, growth of *Chironomus* resumes and the third instar larvae moult and change into fourth instar larvae. These are bigger, over 1.5 cm, heavily muscled and bright red in colour. Their tubes of sediment particles are now 'chimneys' projecting 1–2 cm above the mud surface. The chimneys reach water that is marginally better oxygenated than that immediately in contact with the sediment.

Growth of the fourth instar larvae depends on the supply of phytoplankton and detritus reaching the bottom, but is soon reduced as plankton production falls off in the shortening autumn days. Most larvae are not mature enough to pupate. They must therefore remain as fourth instars to make further growth in the spring and the autumn of their second year. Pupation then follows in the succeeding spring, when, one evening, the pupae emerge from the tubes and float to the water surface. Within about 35 seconds of reaching the surface, the pupal skin splits and the adult emerges, turning from the pupal red to black. The adults (imagos) rest on the surface until sunrise, when the rising warmth quickens their metabolism sufficiently for them to fly, and later in the day to mate and the females to lay eggs on the water. The life of the adult midge is only a few days, compared with the 23 months spent as a larva in the profundal. At lesser water depths, where there is no summer deoxygenation, C. *anthracinus* is able to grow sufficiently in one year to emerge the next. A few of the deep-water population also manage to emerge after only 12 months, in the spring following their birth, but they do not contribute any young to the population. Their eggs are cannibalised, when they reach the sediment, by the large population of remaining fourth instar larvae.

Invertebrate predators in the profundal of Lake Esrom are few (about 10 per cent) compared with the sediment-feeders. The main species is *Chaoborus flavicans* (Fig. 107), which feeds mainly on the plankton and only partly on the sediment animals. Such phantom midges are the main source of the swarms over Lake Malawi. In Lake Esrom, their eggs are laid in late summer and the first instar larvae appear in September. The zooplankters on which *Chaoborus* mainly feeds are reasonably abundant in autumn and the larvae quickly pass into their second and third instars. These spend some time in the plankton, particularly during overcast weather when their visibility to prey is least, and some in the sediment. Fourth instar larvae are generally produced the following spring, and these migrate nightly during the summer from the sediment to the surface water, where zooplankters are again abundant. The following winter, *Chaoborus* spends most of the time in the sediment, possibly feeding on oligochaete worms. Pupation and emergence are in the following July.

Meanwhile the rest of the sediment community has a less eventful existence. The animals are concentrated in the top few millimetres, where at least some oxygen is available for part of the year. Below that, the sediment is permanently deoxygenated and lacks invertebrates other than anaerobic ciliates. Thin, pink oligochaete worms (Fig. 124) insert their heads into the sediment and hold their bodies vertically, spending their lives eating the sediment at a few millimetres depth and defaecating the residues onto the sediment surface. Bivalve molluscs (Fig. 124) suck in a mixture of sediment and

FIG 124. Oligochaete worms (*Tubifex* sp.) together with some ostracods (the bean-like animals). The worms are about 1.5 cm long. Shells of *Pisidium* (right), about 4 mm across. (Matthias Tilly/University of New Hampshire)

water through siphons, filter out the more edible parts and emit the rest. But all this begs the question of exactly what it is that all these sediment animals are eating. Mud is unprepossessing-looking stuff and, as with most processes in lakes, it turns out that it is the bacteria that are the key players. Studies in the invertebrate community of a bog lake, Blaxter Lough, in Northumberland, throw some light on this.[4]

REAL FOOD

Blaxter Lough is a shallow lake set in the peat of an extensive bog. Erosion of the peat by waves at the windward edge provides a ready source of organic matter but the major sediment-feeder, *Chironomus lugubris* (Fig. 125), is conspicuously distributed at the opposite side of the basin. Water movements wash the eroded peat across the lake bottom to the leeward shore and, as it moves, it is broken down into smaller particles. However, although *C. lugubris* has some restrictions

FIG 125. Blaxter Lough, Northumberland, an adult of *Chironomus lugubris* (upper left) and *Chydorus sphaericus*, which feeds on the faeces of *Chironomus* larvae.

on the size of particles it can eat, these do not explain why it does not colonise the area where the peat is freshly eroded. Suitably sized particles sieved from eroding or *in situ* peat will not support its growth.

But if microorganisms are allowed to colonise fresh peat over a few days, it will support growth of *Chironomus*, whether in the laboratory or in chambers placed in any area of the lake. The natural distribution of the chironomids in the lake reflects the distance travelled by suitably fine peat particles in order for them to become colonized by palatable bacteria and fungi. The microorganisms absorb nitrogen compounds from the water and, by the time the peat particles have become palatable, their calorific value per unit weight has increased only 23 per cent, but their protein content has doubled.

Peat eaten by *Chironomus lugubris* contains more bacteria than fungi but the balance changes as the microorganisms pass through its gut. *Chironomus'* faecal pellets are relatively large, coherent and dominated by fungi. They are used by a small cladoceran, *Chydorus sphaericus* (Fig. 125), which can rasp fungal material from them, digesting most of the microorganisms, and ejecting fine faeces of its own. These are small and are recolonised by bacteria, to become nutritious again to *Chironomus*. A reciprocal relationship exists between the two animals, resulting, with the help of microorganisms, in the ultimate breakdown of the peat.

We can now be a little more specific about which are the most important bacteria as food for the bottom-living animals. Studies on the carbon isotope contents of chironomid larvae in lakes suggest that methane-producing or metabolising bacteria might be the major source[5] and, at least in one lake, 34–44 per cent of the organic matter entering the sediment is converted to methane.[6] Biologically produced methane is characteristically very low in

[13]carbon and this signature can be traced through the animal community. Carbon signatures of chironomid larvae in profundal sediments resemble those of methane and up to 60 per cent of the food of chironomids in deep water sediments is methane-derived, whilst 20 per cent of the carbon ingested by fish in these habitats is ultimately methane-based. It is not yet clear whether it is the methane-producing bacteria (methanogens) deep in the anaerobic sediment, the methane-oxidising bacteria (methanotrophs) at the more aerobic sediment surface, or protozoa that have eaten these bacteria, that are the immediate sources for the chironomids. Because activity of the chironomids depends on some oxygen being present, it is most likely that the methanotrophs, and protozoa that have eaten them, are the prime sources.

There remains a problem in explaining how several species of chironomids that are sometimes present in what looks like a uniform environment with a single food source, manage to coexist. Indeed, there might be more than ten plus three or four species of oligochaetes and two or three of pea mussel. There could also be 20 or 30 species of ciliates and as many nematodes. In theory, one should out-compete the others, if the habitat is completely uniform, but that does not happen, which means that ways have been found to divide the available space and food, such that competition is minimised or avoided.

Two particular chironomids, *C. anthracinus* and *C. plumosus*, often occur together, for example in Blelham Tarn, Esthwaite, Rostherne Mere and Lough Neagh. Stable isotope studies suggest that *C. plumosus* takes more methanotrophic bacteria, and *C. anthracinus* a greater proportion of fresher organic matter falling from the epilimnion.[7] Both make tubes but of different shapes. That of *C. plumosus* is U-shaped, allowing movements of the larvae to create a water current that might bring slightly better-oxygenated water into the sediment, thus promoting the activity of the methane-using bacteria, whilst the tube of *C. anthracinus* is J-shaped and usually sealed at the lower end. *C. plumosus* also appears to be able to respire anaerobically to a greater extent than *C. anthracinus* and thus to be able to live deeper in the sediment. Separation of the niches of the smaller animals, like the ciliates, is easier to conceive because their 'world' is so much smaller and they respond to small gradients in chemistry and the quality of the organic matter. The larger species of ciliate seem to prefer the better-oxygenated water, the smaller are more tolerant of anaerobiosis. This is understandable because the surface areas of larger cells are small in relation to their volumes and greater external concentrations of oxygen are needed to maintain an adequate diffusion into the cells over smaller surfaces. Many questions remain, however, concerning the coexistence of the other chironomids, the oligochaetes and the molluscs.

REAL SEDIMENT AND REAL FOOD

Activity in the profundal ultimately depends on the organic matter that reaches the sediment from the catchment, the littoral and the plankton, but the relative importance of each will vary in different lakes and even in different parts of the profundal in the same lake. The possibility that in many lakes, and particularly in pristine ones, organic matter entering from the catchment may be a major source of carbon and energy, resulting in a consequent net heterotrophy of the whole lake system (Chapter 2) or at least the plankton (Chapter 6), has made understanding of carbon processing of great interest.

It is possible to dose whole lakes with sodium bicarbonate labelled with [13]carbon, and follow changes in the [13]carbon concentrations of various components. Calculations can then establish what proportion of the carbon metabolism in the lake comes from photosynthesis within the lake (in which [13]carbon levels are enriched by the addition made) and from external supplies (where the carbon is not artificially enriched). At Crampton Lake in Midwestern USA, damselfly and dragonfly nymphs, sampled at 1.5 m in the littoral zone, derived 75 per cent of their carbon from within the lake, but chironomids from 1.5, 3.5 and 10 m depths took only 43, 39 and 17 per cent respectively from this source.[8] The remainder came from catchment sources or possibly old organic matter from within the lake that had been buried in the sediments. Stable isotope measurements are easy to make and are increasingly used, though a number of assumptions have to be made for the subsequent calculations because few animals have diets of single sources. Moreover, they give only a snapshot of the system but not a profound understanding of the processes going on. To obtain this is more time consuming and the best such study is still one carried out some time ago in the Bay of Quinte, on the northern shore of Lake Ontario in Canada.[9]

THE BAY OF QUINTE

The Bay of Quinte (Fig. 126) is long, narrow and winding. It is shallow (about 5 m deep) at its inner end, where several towns enrich it with sewage effluent, and opens out, over 100 km distant, into the 30 m-deep waters of inshore Lake Ontario, where dilution with the main lake has reduced the fertility of the water. At places along this gradient, the amount of sedimenting material and its fate were followed as the bacteria, invertebrates and fish processed it. The results emphasise both quantity and quality of the sedimenting material as important in determining the productivity

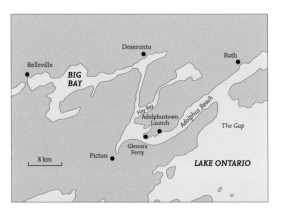

FIG 126. The Bay of Quinte, part of Lake Ontario, Canada.

of the bottom-living animals. They also illustrate how local circumstances can upset the classic sequence described above of an increasingly less diverse and less productive community of bottom animals as depth increases in a lake.

The big contrast was between the landward end, at Big Bay, and the open waters of Lake Ontario with a steady change between these two extremes at other places along the bay. At Big Bay the invertebrate community was dominated by chironomids, and not much else, whilst in Lake Ontario, there was a much more diverse community. Sedimentation rates were measured by catching the falling sediment in traps. Big Bay had a much greater rate of sedimentation of organic matter than in Lake Ontario. Much of it came as waterlogged sawdust from wood processing, and from large growths of cyanobacteria in the polluted water. The respiration rates of the microorganisms and invertebrates, which measure how well they were processing this organic matter, were separately determined by their uptake of oxygen in small sediment cores in the laboratory. By difference, the contribution of the sedimenting material to the permanent sediment at the two places could then be calculated.

The overall community respiration decreased from Big Bay to Lake Ontario, despite the greater sedimentation rate at Big Bay. Much of the Big Bay sediment was too refractory to be used, whilst most of the sediment falling in Lake Ontario was processed and passed into the food web. As a result, the turnover of the animal community, its ratio of annual production to mean biomass, was much higher in Lake Ontario.

Figure 127 shows the flow of energy through the sediment community (microorganisms, invertebrates and fish) at the two stations, and all quantities have been converted to kilocalories per metre squared per day for rates, and to kilocalories per metre squared (in brackets) for the standing biomass of the various components. Community respiration degraded less than a quarter of incoming organic matter, and animal production less than a twentieth at Big Bay, so that much of it was not used. Microorganisms were responsible for most (90 per cent) of the respiration but, despite this investment, much of the organic matter was not used because it was difficult even for bacteria to degrade. The amount of unused organic matter was small in Lake Ontario. The

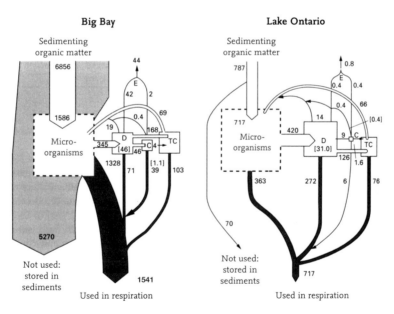

FIG 127. Mean rates of energy flow in the inner Bay of Quinte (Big Bay) and in Lake Ontario. Boxes represent standing crops and stocks (kilocalories per m²) and pipes the rates of flow in kilocalories per m² each day. E: emerging insects; D: detritivores; C: carnivores; TC: top carnivores (fish). Black pipes show respiratory use. (Redrawn from Johnson and Brinkhurst, 1971)

incoming organic matter (largely from the overlying plankton) was of higher quality and needed less microbial effort (73 per cent of the respiration) to degrade it, and more of it, indeed ten times more than at Big Bay, was used in animal production. Mud is less unprepossessing in some places than at others!

SEDIMENT AND THE HISTORIES OF LAKES

The material reaching the bottom that is not used by the invertebrates and microorganisms forms the permanent sediment, to which we now turn. It contains a record of activities in the lake and can be used to reveal the lake's history. The recent history of many lakes, recorded in the sediments, or in contemporary data, is one of considerable change through human use, and the sediments are the books that record the long-term sins and ambitions of the human state. They also contain a record of how a natural lake might be expected to alter in time and, against this background, the human influences can be assessed.

NATURAL LAKE DEVELOPMENT

To the early limnologists it was obvious that lakes must change as they aged. Encroachment of vegetation at the edge and accumulation of sediment in the middle must eventually fill in the basin and convert it to dry land and, as sediment accumulated, so also must nutrients so that a lake should become more fertile with time. There was a process of eutrophication.

In Sweden, in the early twentieth century, Einar Naumann (Fig. 128) had been studying shallow lakes that appeared to be in an advanced stage of the process, with extensive littoral zones, large amounts of phytoplankton, high concentrations of calcium and other ions and small hypolimnia that became completely deoxygenated. In Germany, Auguste Thienemann (Fig. 128) was examining both shallow and deep lakes in the Eifel Maare region, as well as reports from others studying the deep lakes at the foot of the Alps, and noting the contrasting characteristics of the deep lakes: narrow littoral zones, sparse plankton, low calcium content and large and well-oxygenated hypolimnia. He also saw that the chironomid community in the profundal sediments was different in the deep lakes, where the genus *Tanytarsus* was prominent, from that in the shallower ones where *Chironomus* held sway.

It seemed obvious what was happening. As more and more nutrients entered, the productivity increased, more sediment fell to the bottom and the volume

FIG 128. Einar Naumann (top left) and Auguste Thienemann (top right) and one of the Eifel Maar lakes in Germany on which Thienemann worked and which contributed to the formulation of their ideas on lake development.

of the hypolimnion became smaller whilst the amount of decomposable organic matter falling into it increased. The oxygen concentrations in the hypolimnion must therefore decrease, whilst the build up of sediment also shallowed the water, encouraging the extension of the littoral zone and an ever-widening band of plant colonisation. Eventually the plants would cover the entire surface and the sediments would build up to the water table; the lake would have become some sort of wetland and finally the original inflow streams would be flowing through a forest. The deep lakes came to be called oligotrophic, the shallow ones eutrophic and a concept was born that was central to the thinking of the next half-century.[10] It was, alas, despite shards of truth, basically wrong and it was studies on the accumulated sediments that changed it to our current understanding.

What was wrong with it? To start with it spawned the idea of 'types' of lakes: eutrophic and oligotrophic at first, then dystrophic. Naumann and Thienemann added dystrophic to accommodate brown-water lakes, surrounded by bogs, that were very low in calcium and other nutrients (being fed by rainwater) yet had hypolimnia that were severely deoxygenated (because of all the organic matter falling into them from their peaty edges).

Thienemann then went on an expedition to Indonesia and studied some deep lakes in old volcanic craters. Surrounded by dense forest with nutrient-poor soils, the lakes had water low in calcium and nutrients, but the hypolimnia were both deep and deoxygenated, because the lakes were almost permanently stratified. Their surfaces were oligotrophic, their depths eutrophic. Thienemann was having doubts about lake types! Meanwhile W.H. Pearsall (Chapter 1) in England was showing a graded series of characteristics, a continuum not a set of types, from infertile deep lakes to shallower fertile ones in the Cumbrian Lake District. Naumann hung on to the idea of particular lake types, coining new terms, for example for lakes that had a lot of suspended clay (argillotrophic), or iron, in mining regions (siderotrophic). This idea of lake types was not universally accepted. In a published comment, the Danish limnologist, C. Wesenberg-Lund (Fig. 10) wrote in 1926 that:

> *Naumann has tried to press nature into a series of highly artificial schemata which are unquestionably very valuable for all those scientists whose time is just as scanty as his own, whereas from a purely scientific point of view, as far as I can see, they have very little value.*

He was tart but right.

The second error was that nutrients and other ions did not accumulate with time as the early workers, including Pearsall, had thought. When corers were developed that could take a sample of the accumulated sediments, from the latest to the earliest, it was found that the deeper sediments had been laid down in mineral rich, essentially eutrophic conditions. Rain had leached a plentiful supply of calcium, phosphorus and other ions from the freshly exposed rock debris exposed by the melting of the ice, the same process as recounted for new glacial lakes in Chapter 2 (Fig. 36). Thereafter, so long as the catchment was not disturbed by human activity, such as agriculture, conditions had become less and less nutrient rich as vegetation had developed and sealed over the raw soils and conserved to itself much of the remaining supply. Phosphates and nitrates had not accumulated in the water, but had either been washed through to the ocean, denitrified, or fixed in the sediments.

And, thirdly, the process of filling-in with sediment was not quite as speedy in undisturbed lakes as was first thought. Sediment did accumulate, but not rapidly. In mountainous areas, with steep eroding slopes, most of the accumulation was in the stream deltas, but these were quite small in area. The accumulation of fine material on the bottom, especially because plankton production is low in areas of poorly weathered rocks and low nutrient concentrations, was very slow, perhaps a fraction of a millimetre per year,[11] so that a typical upland British or Irish lake, gouged out to say 50 metres by the ice, would have a life of at least 100,000 years, and would not be showing any rapid development in the lives of many generations of limnologists.

For lakes that began as shallow basins in the lowlands, filling in *is* discernable (Fig. 39). Such lakes, perhaps only a few metres deep at their origin among the glacial drift, for example, of the northwest Midlands, would have had much of their area as littoral zone once the climate had warmed enough. Plant colonisation of the edges led to an accumulation of peat that is more rapid than the accumulation of sediment from a plankton community, as in the deeper lakes, though the process occurs over at least hundreds, if not thousands of years. There might be a form of natural eutrophication at this late stage when the lake has become very shallow and is about to expire, but we are not certain.

When the sediment or peat becomes anaerobic at the surface as temperatures increase in summer, insoluble compounds of oxidised (ferric) iron and phosphate are converted to soluble ferrous phosphates, and phosphate is released to the water. Ferric phosphates should then re-form on contact with oxygen but in extreme conditions, where the bacteria have converted sulphate to sulphide, very insoluble, black ferrous sulphide, or iron pyrites forms, and there is a shortage of iron to re-precipitate the phosphate. In deep lakes, if this occurs, the phosphate is locked into the hypolimnion and cannot support more growth in the epilimnion, but in shallow lakes it can easily reach the surface waters and could stimulate growth of more phytoplankton. What is not clear is whether this really would happen because at the same time nitrogen would become much scarcer through denitrification, which is also promoted by summer temperatures, and potentially limiting.

The issues of how undisturbed lakes change in time are now of great interest because we are changing them by our activities, not least in causing eutrophication through pollution with nutrients from agriculture and our wastewaters. Studies on the history contained in lake sediments provide a reference against which we can assess the changes we are making, and the science of palaeolimnology is one in which British and Irish scientists have made leading advances.[12]

THE SEDIMENTS AS HISTORY

Scientists love new instruments that open up new avenues, and the years around the Second World War provided a welter of novel toys. One, developed for the navy, was the echo sounder, in which high-pitched sound signals sent out from just below the water surface are reflected from the bottom, the time taken for the reflection to return being used to calculate water depth. The Admiralty had surveyed Lake Windermere using such a device in 1935. Clifford Mortimer, at the Freshwater Biological Association, then borrowed an echo sounder and, with Barton Worthington, surveyed all the other main lakes of the Cumbrian Lake District in 1937. They noted that several echoes were obtained from the bottom and thought that these indicated the sediment, and major discontinuities in it, lying above the main echo of the rock basin. If so, the sediment depth was greater in the lakes in the south of the Lake District, on sedimentary rocks, than in the north with their igneous and metamorphic rocks. They tried to confirm that the echoes really were recording the sediment structure by direct measurement of the depths of sediment in Low Wray Bay in Windermere by hammering a pipe into them. This compressed the sediment but showed that there was a sequence of two thin clay bands separated by brownish ooze at the bottom, before the sediments became uniformly of ooze towards the surface.

In turn this prompted the invention of a sediment corer by Benjamin Jenkin (an engineer and father of Penelope Jenkin, then a research student at the FBA) that would not compress the sediment. It comprised two concentric tubes, four feet long, capped at each end, with a third of the circumference of the outer one cut away and replaced by a flat metal plate, leaving only a narrow slit between the plate and the remainder of the tube. The inner section was a semi-circular half-tube that could emerge through the slit and enclose a sample of sediment against the flat plate of the outer tube. A set of spring-loaded levers, and a weight sent down on a line to trip them, was used to exsert the inner tube when the corer was in position within the sediment. The corer could be pushed to

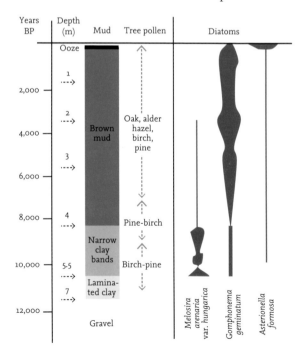

FIG 129. Winifred Pennington's (1943) summary diagram (modified) of her studies on cores from Lake Windermere. BP stands for 'Before Present', conventionally fixed now as 1950.

FIG 130. Water draining from glaciers, here in Greenland, is always turbid and milky in appearance from the clays eroded by the ice from the underlying rock. (US National Science Foundation)

different depths within the sediment by rods and weights but was quite heavy and needed a moored pontoon for its operation. Nonetheless it provided, in the early 1940s, the first complete sequence of the sediments of Windermere (Fig. 129) for a graduate student, Winifred Pennington, who became a very distinguished palaeolimnologist.

Winifred Pennington was thorough and took cores along the axis of the deeper northern basin of Windermere, and also in shallower water to the side.[13] The shallower water produced a more complex sequence of sediments, influenced, for example, by stream deltas, but overall there was a consistent pattern. At the bottom were gravels, the remnants of the retreating ice before the basin was dammed by moraines and began to fill with water. The milky water draining from retreating glaciers (Fig. 130) then laid down a layered clay, the layers perhaps corresponding to the annual differences in summers, when flows of melt water were high and coarser particles were washed in, and winters, when flow was minimal and carried only fine particles.

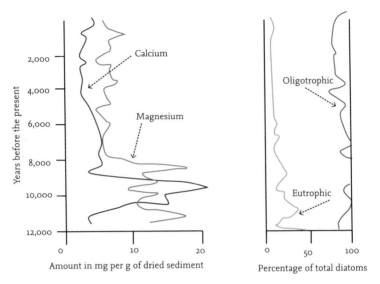

FIG 131. The same processes as shown in Fig. 36 can be detected in the development of older glacial lakes by analysis of their sediments. Immediately post-glacial sediments are rich in ions, but these decline with time. Early diatom communities were richer in species characteristic of fertile (eutrophic) lakes, but these were replaced by those of less fertile (oligotrophic) lakes as the ion concentrations decreased. The chemical data are from Esthwaite Water, the diatom data from Blea Tarn (which has been less influenced by human activity) in the English Lake District, with data matched age for age. Original data from Mackereth (1965, 1966) and Haworth (1969).

There was little evidence of lake organisms in these clays but Pennington could date the core approximately from wind-blown pollen in the sediments, the regional pollen changes having been dated elsewhere by radiocarbon dating of peat. The clay layer, beginning around 7 m below the sediment surface, ended at around 5.5 m, around 10,500 years ago when the landscape was acquiring a thin woodland of birch and pine. From then until about 8,300 years ago there was a zone, nearly a metre and a half thick, of about 1,000 narrow clay bands interleaved with browner sediment that is rich in diatom remains. Most of these layers may be annual varves, a Scandinavian word for such layers, with those more clay-rich laid down in winter, and the browner layers representing summer growth. Some of the diatoms in this part of the core, such as *Melosira arenaria* var *hungarica* are large and more abundant in cores from the edges of the lake. They probably represent a productive littoral growth in nutrient-rich conditions. The landscape was then wooded with birch and this phase ended when the sediments became a uniform brown with more organic matter but without clay layers, for the remaining upper 4 m of sediment. The diatom community changed a little as a warming landscape became covered with oak, alder and hazel, with some birch and pine still persisting, from about 7,000 years ago. Finally, some new diatoms appeared in the upper 20 cm of surface ooze layers, including *Asterionella formosa*, now very common in the lake and reflecting fertilisation from agriculture and sewage effluent disposal.

Pennington's interpretation was that the clay and brown layers between 10,500 and 8,300 years ago represented a transitional period in which clay was still being washed in, but enough light penetrated in summer for growth of algae to have begun. After the final loss of the mountain glaciers just after 8,000 years ago, extensive growth was possible and the lake entered a relatively steady period (there were some fluctuations in diatom species) until recently. This was an interpretation that differed from the ideas of Naumann, Thienemann and Pearsall of a development from nutrient-poor (oligotrophic) to more nutrient-rich conditions. The meaning of the different community of diatoms in the transitional period, with many large species, did not become clear until John Mackereth started to investigate the chemistry of the sediments in the 1950s and Frank Round, also a former graduate student at the FBA, examined cores from Kentmere and Esthwaite, and Elisabeth Haworth, a student of Winifred Pennington, one from Blea Tarn (Fig. 131).[14]

What they collectively found was that the earliest phases of the lakes, as the water cleared of clay, and photosynthesis became possible, were productive and nutrient rich. Mackereth joined the FBA as a chemist, narrowly avoiding a career in industry but possibly having a shorter life as a result. He was inventive and designed a new corer that was much lighter and easier to use than Jenkin's original.[15] It worked by sending a single thin tube, propelled by compressed air, into the sediment. The apparatus (it is still widely used) has a large chamber, a bit like an oil drum, on which is mounted a wide tube and inside that the coring tube (Fig. 132). The corer is lowered to the sediment and air is pumped from the drum to settle it into the sediment and give a firm base for coring. Compressed

FIG 132. A Mackereth corer being towed through a lake in New Zealand. (University of Hamilton)

air is then pumped into the wide tube, forcing the coring tube down into the sediment, the air inside it escaping through a thin central tube so that the sediment is not compressed. As the coring tube, which can be several metres long, reaches its full extent, the compressed air is redirected into the drum, forcing it by buoyancy out of the sediment and allowing the whole apparatus, the wide tube being now full of air as well, to float to the surface. In the earlier models it was so buoyant that it more than floated but whooshed upwards, emerging with some speed. It was this rocketing tube that unfortunately capsized John Mackereth's boat and left him for some time in the freezing winter waters of Windermere, resulting in severe hypothermia that probably contributed to his death some months later in 1972.

By then he had established two important things. First, that the sediments were much deeper in the lakes with sedimentary rock catchments and therefore that the catchment was the main source of sediment, not the organic matter produced within the lake and, secondly, that the early sediments, during the transitional period between the pure glacial clays and the brown, more organic sediments that followed the final melting of the glaciers, were much richer in ions like calcium and magnesium than the later sediments. The raw landscapes following the glaciation had much fresh rock debris that the rains readily leached. The diatom communities during this early period were of types that characterised more nutrient-rich conditions, with genera like *Fragilaria* and *Epithemia*, whilst after about 7,000 to 8,000 years ago, they gradually switched towards more acid-loving species, such as *Eunotia*, *Frustulia*, *Cymbella* and *Gomphonema*, associated with lower nutrient levels (Fig. 133). The change occurred when the climate was also changing from the drier Boreal to the wetter Atlantic phase and this will have diluted water running through the soils.

Thus lakes do not inevitably become steadily eutrophic as they fill in and age; they become less fertile as their catchments mature and their surface rocks are leached out, unless something happens to disrupt the catchment or rejuvenate the rock weathering. This might be a volcanic eruption, a period of very heavy rainfall causing landslides, a long drought followed by rain that erodes bare soils, or a new advance of the glaciers and their retreat. But in the moderate climate, and passive state of the geology, of Britain and Ireland, these are naturally unlikely. A much more pervasive disruptor, however is not: ourselves.

The long period of oligotrophication, the converse of eutrophication, recorded in Windermere, Kentmere and Esthwaite Water was eventually reversed by one or other activity of man in the catchment. A trend towards increasing nutrients began in Esthwaite Water around 5,000 years ago when pollen from agricultural weeds appears in the sediment and that from trees like oak began to decline. The process of removal of the forest had begun with the late Neolithic

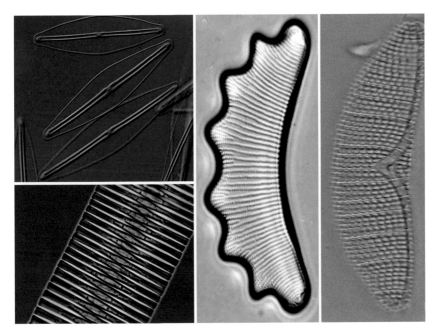

FIG 133. Diatoms characteristic of infertile (top left *Frustulia* and centre, *Eunotia*) and fertile waters (bottom left, *Fragilaria*, and right, *Epithemia*). The *Fragilaria* cells are live, the others have been cleaned by boiling in acid leaving just their silica walls. It is the walls that are preserved in sediments. The cells are variously about 40 to 80 μm long.

and then Bronze Age farmers and has now converted much of the Cumbrian Lake District into bare fells of over-grazed and eroded grassland.[16] *Asterionella* appears towards the top of the Windermere cores (dating to the twentieth century) examined by Pennington, but more finely sectioned cores and use of new techniques have shown that more intense changes began in the early nineteenth century as more of the slopes were farmed, a railway was built and the population of summer tourists began to increase.

These effects of human activity were to herald a major expansion in the work of palaeolimnologists in the late twentieth century, led in particular by Winifred Pennington, Frank Oldfield, and Richard Battarbee at University College, London, with a widening in the range of techniques for dating, and for extracting information from many constituents of the sediments in addition to pollen and diatoms. There has also been a revolution in the use of statistical techniques for reconstructing past conditions that puts numbers, though not always absolute, in place of opinions, however well informed.

NEW DATING

The dating of cores taken from the 1940s to the 1960s depended on recognition of particular pollen zones, reflecting the nature of the vegetation, particularly the trees. These zones (see Chapter 8) had been determined from many studies on the pollen in peat and reflected the warming of the climate after the glaciers retreated. They had been dated using the radiocarbon technique developed in 1949 by Willard Libby, and then somewhat expensive to use. Radioactive ^{14}carbon is generated in the upper atmosphere, at a nearly constant rate, by bombardment of nitrogen atoms by solar particles. The ^{14}carbon becomes incorporated into carbon dioxide and thence into plants, and their remains in peat and sediments. It decays with a half-life of 5,730 years, so that from a knowledge of its initial ratio to the most common isotope, ^{12}carbon, and the ratio in a sample, the age of the sample can be calculated.

Small historical fluctuations in the rate of ^{14}carbon formation are now recognised and can be corrected for by calibration against tree ring dating,

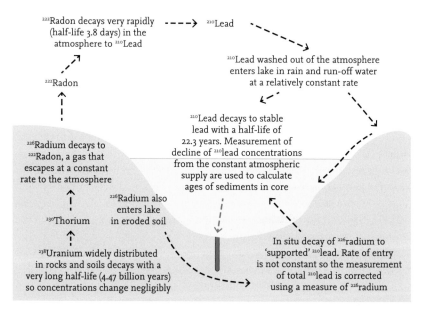

FIG 134. The principles behind the dating of sediments using the 210 lead method. Dates back to about 150 years can be obtained. Beyond this time, there is insufficient isotope left for detection.

whereby a continuous record of changes in the growth rings, laid down year-by-year, has been established from overlapping generations of trees, or rather the wood derived from them in archaeological samples or preserved in bogs, over the past several thousand years. ^{14}Carbon dates can be measured for the past 70,000 years or so until the last two or three centuries, when they become useless. This is because the burning of fossil fuels, largely since the eighteenth century, when coal fuelled the industrial revolution, has upset the previously nearly steady ratio of ^{14}carbon to ^{12}carbon in the atmosphere and therefore the initial ratio in plant material. Fossil fuels, being ancient, have negligible ^{14}carbon contents.

Human activity has been most intense over the very period that carbon dating cannot be used, but fortunately a new dating method (Fig. 134) was developed in the 1960s that overcame this problem. It uses the natural decay of ^{238}uranium. ^{238}Uranium is widely distributed in rocks, though fortunately not abundant. It slowly decays to ^{226}radium, which then decays to a gas, ^{222}Radon. This radioactive gas diffuses into the air and is spread by the winds. It has a short half-life and decays to ^{210}lead, which is washed out of the atmosphere by the rain and into lakes and eventually their sediments, where it decays to ^{210}bismuth and eventually stable lead. The concentration of ^{210}lead is determined at the sediment surface and then at suitable depth intervals down to about a metre. From the rate of decline of ^{210}lead in the sediment, and its half-life of 22.7 years, the age of the sediment at successive levels can be calculated and dates determined back to about 100–150 years.[17] There is a further useful date marker in two isotopes released in nuclear weapons testing: ^{137}caesium and ^{241}americium. The first appearance of these isotopes in the sediment marks the year 1954, when testing began, and the peak of their concentrations, 1963, when testing was at its zenith. Both isotopes have very short half-lives and were fast disappearing until, in 1986, an accident at the Chernobyl reactor in the USSR released a new batch, which will give a useful dating horizon for studies for at least a few more years.

Further techniques of dating use magnetic properties of the sediments. John Mackereth discovered that the Earth's magnetic field, which changes direction from time to time, leaves an imprint on the magnetisation of minerals in the sediments and that a time scale could be reconstructed from this. It proved too coarse, however, for precise dating but led to studies on the magnetic properties of the sediments which have proved useful, for example, in relating levels in different cores from the same lake when only one core could be dated by radiometric methods and in tracing the origins of soil particles in a sediment from mixed sources.[18]

WHAT CAN NOW BE ANALYSED

Taking a core and dating it are the preliminaries to a paleolimnological study. The analysis of sediment particle size, organic and inorganic contents and a variety of elements is the next. Diatoms, with their generally excellent preservation, except under very alkaline conditions when silica dissolves, and pollen, whose waxy cell walls are virtually indestructible, have been respectively used to determine changes within the lake and in the catchment, and often the region. Thereafter the list of potentially useful components of the sediment grows longer almost every year (Fig. 135).[19]

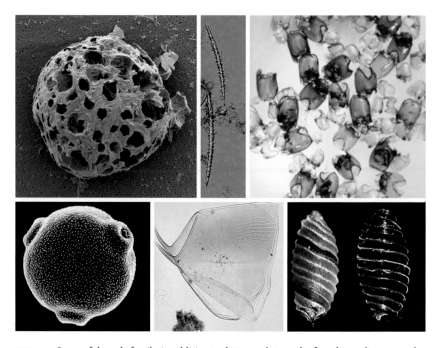

FIG 135. Some of the sub-fossils, in addition to diatoms, that can be found in sediments and used to reconstruct ecological history. Top left is a soot (sphaeroidal carbonaceous) particle from a power station smoke. Top centre are siliceous freshwater sponge spicules and top right are head capsules of chironomids. Bottom left is a pollen grain of birch, centre. the remains of a *Bosmina* carapace and right, oospores of *Chara*. Photographs variously by Yarrow Axford, Anna de Sellas and Amy Myrbo. The *Bosmina* fossil, oospores and chironomid heads are about 0.2 mm long, the remainder are microscopic and about 50 μm in length or diameter.

Stable isotopes can reveal information about sources of nitrogen and carbon, about temperature and about the degree of dissolution of the diatoms and therefore their faithfulness to the original community. Organic matter can be analysed to reveal its origin from plants in the catchment, or algae in the lake. The remains of photosynthetic pigments can show changes in the balance of different groups of algae; and substances produced by the guts of farm stock and humans can reveal contamination by faeces. Sponges leave traces in the silica spicules that stiffened their bodies, and chrysophytes leave siliceous spores. Charophytes leave oospores, the structures produced around their fertilised eggs, and tubes of marl that are precipitated around their cells. Water plants leave seeds, fragments of epidermis and sometimes, as in water lilies, their star-shaped sclereids (Fig. 82).

Zooplankters leave parts of their exoskeletons: claws, carapaces and ephippia; sometimes information about fish predation can be deduced from the species and sizes of these remains. Snails and ostracods leave shells, beetles leave wing covers and chironomids the head capsules shed when they moult their exoskeletons, by which, because of the strong links between chironomid genera and oxidation of the hypolimnion, a great deal can be deduced. Even people leave distinctive remains. Bodies sometimes turn up in peaty lakes and bogs, though they are so rare that sediment cores will miss them, but power stations, burning coal, release soot, and in soot are often distinctively shaped rounded particles, sometimes attributable to particular stations, that are washed out from the atmosphere and into lakes. Occasionally fish scales are preserved but large animals are relatively scarce in lakes and the chances of finding remains are low. Soft-bodied animals leave no structures, but, for these, the possibilities of using traces of DNA have yet to be exploited.

Using historical records, even oral accounts from local people, as well as remains in the sediments, allows a very good picture to be built up, but there are some snags. Preservation of organic remains is selective. Some things preserve much better than others and it is not necessarily the most abundant in life that is the most prominent in death. Chemicals like phosphates may diffuse up or down a core and, of course, as the sediment is forming at the surface, chemical processes, water movements and the activities of bacteria and invertebrates will alter and mix it. What is eventually fixed for examination by a palaeolimnologist can give a misleading picture and interpretation inevitably requires experience, skill and insight. Some numerical approaches have helped, though, stimulated originally by the problem of acidification.

In the 1970s, there developed increasing problems of acidification of surface waters. Though it was widely believed that the cause was sulphur dioxide released from power stations, there was widespread denial of responsibility by the electricity generating industry. Progressive leaching of catchments by rain was blamed, as was the planting of conifer trees in the uplands. The trees were supposed to take up basic ions from the soils and replace them with hydrogen ions, but there was increasing evidence of high sulphur levels in the atmosphere. The uplands were particularly affected because their base-poor soils are poorly buffered and it was realised that lake sediments in these areas might contain a record of changing acidity.

The problem was in reconstructing changes in pH from the evidence in the sediments. A simple measurement of pH in the sediment was not possible because the chemical changes that occur with decomposition and deoxygenation greatly affect pH. A first approach was to use indicator species of diatoms. Diatom species were classified according to their pH preferences and various formulae developed that linked the percentages of acid-loving, indifferent and alkali-preferring species to pH from existing lakes, in a single numerical index. This worked quite well but there was a criticism of subjectivity in that 'acid-loving' and other categories could be based on biased information. This resulted in a much more sophisticated approach.

What was (and is) done is first to carry out a survey of the surface sediments in a large number of lakes to establish their diatom communities (or those of chironomids or aquatic plants, or whatever remains are being used) and to measure the feature of the environment (e.g. pH, salinity, total phosphorus, total nitrogen, temperature) it is wished to determine during the history of the lake. Over the set of lakes (called a training set) the distribution of each species is then examined and generally its abundance will be found to form a hump-backed graph in relation to the range of the environmental measurement. A species will be most abundant at some optimum (the top of the curve) but will become less abundant to either side. This establishes an optimum concentration for each species. The communities in the historic sediments are then examined and the proportions of each species are determined. If, say, the community was of just one species, a value for the feature would then be computed that was the optimum for that species, but many species will be present, so a calculation is made that takes the optimum for each species and weights the calculation by the proportions of each species in the community. An estimate is thus made for the value of the feature at the time the sediment was laid down, and changes in the feature can be tracked over time. The method can be misused, for example if there is not a considerable overlap between the species in the training set and the species in the sediment assemblages, or if there is not a strong and causative link between the ecology of the species and the feature, but, if used conservatively, the results can be relatively precise and can sometimes be checked against real historical records.

The method has allowed very good reconstructions of past pH values and salinities, for these vary over wide ranges (pH is a logarithmic measure of hydrogen

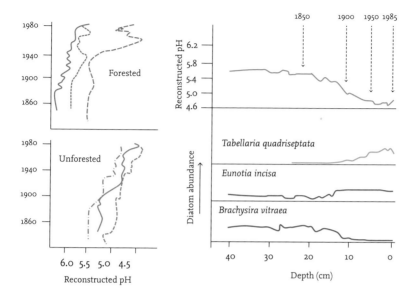

FIG 136. Reconstructions of changing pH in lakes using diatom communities. On the left are shown changes since 1840 in six Galloway lakes, three of them in largely forested catchments, and three unforested. pH has declined irrespective of afforestation. On the right are results from the Round Loch of Glenhead showing how pH has declined and promoted growth of two acid-loving diatoms and reduced growth of one that favours more alkaline conditions. Many other species occurred also in the core. (Diagrams based on Flower et al., 1987, and Jones et al., 1989.)

ion concentration which varies over many orders of magnitude). Reconstructions are less secure for phosphorus and nitrogen, partly because, where diatoms, at least, are concerned, the environment in which most of the diatoms in the communities live, the interstitial water of the sediments, is likely to be much richer in nutrients than the open water where the measurements are made. Where acidification was concerned, an examination of several lochs in the Galloway region of Scotland (Fig. 136) showed that they had all become acidified (from around pH 6 to lower than 4.5), regardless of whether there were conifer plantations in their catchments and that the acidification had begun in the nineteenth century when the burning of fossil fuels, particularly coal, intensified.[20] Faced with such evidence, and the progressive increase also of soot particles in the sediments, the power-generating industry was forced to begin installing scrubbers on its chimneys to remove sulphur dioxide. Direct evidence cannot be denied. That brings us to an overview, in the next chapter, of how humans have used, and often abused, lakes in Britain and Ireland and what can be done about it.

CHAPTER 8

People and Lakes in Britain and Ireland: Damage and Repair

W E LIKE TO PUT THINGS in boxes. Classification is how we cope with the complicatedness of everything. But sometimes boxes impose a view that is artificial, indeed entirely misleading. Thus we talk of the Ages of this or that: Neolithic, Bronze, Iron; or Periods: Roman, Saxon, Viking or Norman. These were lengths of time with some common features, but the implication is of uniformity and then sharp changes, neither of which are ever true. Even more mentally controlling is the idea of revolutions, agricultural or industrial,

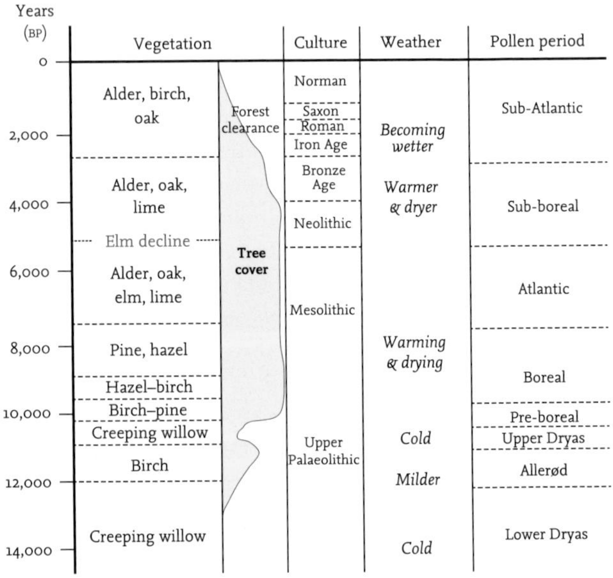

FIG 137. Chart of conventional Periods and Ages since the final retreat of the ice from Britain and Ireland. The Lower and Upper Dryas were periods when the ice briefly advanced. The vegetation is that of England. There are minor variations for northern Scotland and Ireland.

Years (BP)	Vegetation		Culture	Weather	Pollen period
0			Norman		
	Alder, birch, oak	Forest clearance	Saxon	Becoming wetter	Sub-Atlantic
2,000			Roman		
			Iron Age		
			Bronze Age	Warmer & dryer	
4,000	Alder, oak, lime				Sub-boreal
			Neolithic		
	Elm decline	Tree cover			
6,000	Alder, oak, elm, lime				Atlantic
			Mesolithic		
8,000	Pine, hazel			Warming & drying	
	Hazel–birch				Boreal
10,000	Birch–pine				Pre-boreal
	Creeping willow		Upper Palaeolithic	Cold	Upper Dryas
	Birch				Allerød
12,000				Milder	
	Creeping willow				Lower Dryas
14,000				Cold	

with implications not only of instant transition but also of unquestionable bounty. I shall use some conventional categories (Fig. 137) but challenge some common assumptions about them, in considering how lakes and people have rubbed along together in Britain and Ireland over the past few thousand years.

THE EARLIEST LINKS

The earliest evidence comes from the Mesolithic, when bands of hunter-gatherers are supposed to have been moving around following game, prior to the introduction of settled agriculture in the Neolithic. Until they were drained in the nineteenth century, there was a series of lakes, some of them quite large, in the Holderness region between the North York Moors and the Yorkshire Wolds, of which part of only one, Hornsea Mere, remains as open water. Deposits of many more are known, and among them, at Star Carr, are remains from about 11,000 years ago, of a substantial settlement covering 2 hectares (Fig. 138) at the edge of the former Lake Flixton.[1] About 30 m of shoreline were consolidated with brushwood and small birch trees, some of them with the tooth marks of beaver, and it is possible that the human settlers took advantage of a clearing made by beavers. Few remains of fish were found, perhaps because so early after the ice had retreated few species had yet colonised the lake, but the bones of mammals are abundant, including aurochs, the wild cattle of the time, and there is evidence of grebes, divers and mergansers being used as food. Reeds at the edge of the lake were burned, perhaps to flush out game or to give access for boats. There is at least one large hut structure and extensive scatters of worked flint on the surrounding land. Star Carr was occupied, perhaps intermittently, for several hundred years and lay in a huge landscape that extended over the bed of

FIG 138. Star Carr now appears only as featureless fields. The Mesolithic settlement at the edge of the former lake is here reconstructed by Kirsty High.

the present North Sea and allowed people to move freely over northern Europe until, around 7,000 years ago, when the British Islands were finally cut off by the sea, which submerged a Mesolithic landscape now known only from incidental archaeological findings during surveys for oil.

FARMING

Farming did not bring settlement; settlements were already established by the hunter-gatherers, but farming had a much greater impact on the landscape. It was not revolutionary but a gradual development of social slavery over several thousand years. There are two lines of evidence for its early impact on lakes. Around 5,000 years ago, the amount of elm declines in many pollen sequences from peat and lake sediments in northern Europe. No one quite knows why, but one possibility is that elm foliage was cut for feeding stock, implying that enclosures were being cleared. Domestication of cattle and pigs followed that of dogs, there being advantages in keeping your meat close by, instead of having to follow it over hilly terrain through sometimes dense thickets. The impact on lakes was to release nutrients through soil erosion.

The pollen of agricultural weeds, such as plantain, starts to appear in the sediment record at about the same time as diatoms indicating more nutrient-rich conditions begin to replace those of the naturally less fertile state of pristine waters (Chapter 7). The effects were local; the population of Britain and Ireland was probably less than a million and the impacts were probably confined to the warmer parts of the uplands. The Scottish Highlands were wet and boggy and the lowlands still covered by dense forest that was not easily cleared with stone tools. A limnologist at the time would not have been unduly concerned but merely interested in what would seem to be a mild change. In 1961, I was shown the effects of a septic tank draining into a small lake at Brown Moss in Shropshire, and causing a ribbon of growth of a particular plant, marsh St John's wort, to appear in the reedswamps around the lake. It was a curiosity of no great impact at the time. But it was an early warning of an extreme eutrophication to come.

Stone walls began to cross the landscape in the Neolithic, and with them barrows and henges: monuments to a settled existence. Agriculture was supporting a larger community, with a hierarchy of leaders and followers marking the development of personal importance.[2] It took much labour to erect the stone circles and build long barrows in the changing landscape of 4,000–5,000 years ago. Many of these monuments are found in positions that seem to have been chosen for their wide visibility, and this suggests an open landscape with fewer trees.

Ploughing was not then as effective as it would become, because the ploughs were simply cylinders of hardwood or stone and drew a furrow in the soil, rather than turning it over. But 1,500 years on, the mouldboard plough, a curved surface of iron, brought deeper soil to the surface and exposed its rich nutrients to erosion in the rain. Meanwhile, the fashion in barrows became round rather than elongate, the weather a little warmer, the fields more extensive and after bronze had been introduced, regalia and domestic implements became more elaborate. But the impact on British and Irish lakes remained modest and the subtleties have not yet been explored by detailed studies of lake sediments. There would undoubtedly have been some, especially when it was discovered that manuring the fields with animal dung gave better crops. There is evidence from the [15]nitrogen contents of cereal remains and animal bones that this was happening at least from around 5600BC, in the Neolithic in Britain.[3]

A modern technique called nutrient export modelling allows the concentrations of nitrogen and phosphorus in river waters to be calculated from information on land use, fertilisation rates and numbers of domestic stock and people in a catchment area.[4] Calculated values can be within a few per cent of those measured. The overall contrast, shown by these calculations, between natural vegetation and farmed land is much greater than among different sorts of natural vegetation or among different sorts of cultivation. Tying down fine changes in lakes in the past to detailed changes in farming is thus not easy; the conversion of land to farming, however, is the key change. With it came an expansion in settlement sizes and the problem of disposal of human wastes, especially as villages became towns with the infiltration of the Romans, Saxons and Vikings during the first millennium.

The centuries after the Roman armies retreated have been referred to as the Dark Ages but this is a misconception. The Dark Ages are myths fostered by the writings of Gildas (*On the Ruin of Britain*) in the mid-sixth century and Bede (*Ecclesiastical History of the English People*) in AD731, who suggest disorganisation. Perhaps there was in the towns but the archaeological evidence from the landscape gives a different view. Life carried on regardless of who thought they were in charge. A variety of farming patterns developed. In the uplands, farms were small and interspersed with wooded copses. By the end of the Iron Age, some centuries previously, much of the forest cover had been removed, and Britain and Ireland were dominated by artificial grazed or cultivated landscapes. In the lowlands of a belt from Dorset to Humberside, fields were often large and communal, with a rotation of crops decided by local courts. The population had risen from about 2 million to 4–6 million, with the establishment, in the south and east, of Saxon kingdoms. There was a move from cereals towards husbandry with the withdrawal of the over-stretched Roman armies, and a reduced export

FIG 139. The Abbot's Fish House in Meare, Somerset was built between 1322 and 1335 when Adam of Sodbury was the abbot of Glastonbury Abbey. The chief fisherman lived on the upper floor and the ground floor was used for storing nets and the salting and preparing of fish caught in Meare Pool, which was drained after the dissolution of the monasteries.

of cereals to the rest of the Roman Empire. In the north and west, a Gaelic Christianity was rich in culture, the monasteries were expanding their lands into large sheep granges; there was some reforestation. By the eighth century of the Christian era, Saxon towns, wics, were prospering and there was a trading network around the rivers, the old Roman roads, the coasts and beyond.

The custom of not eating meat on Fridays and in Lent, as well as the lack of fresh meat in winter, led to much digging of fishponds, and establishment of fisheries in natural lakes and rivers (Fig. 139). The eleventh-century Domesday Book, despite its incomplete coverage, has numerous references to inland fisheries, particularly for eels, but often for salmon in western districts, and occasionally lampreys.[5] Large areas of wetlands, with many small lakes, covered the lowlands and provided food and building materials, like reed, willow, osiers, and alder poles. Trackways of carefully fashioned wood, the earliest two or three thousand years old, connected villages across the swampy ground and are known from the Fens around the Wash, the Suffolk river valleys and the Somerset Levels. The end of the Bronze Age had been cool and wet and during the subsequent Iron Age, wetter weather and removal of tree cover was reflected in the upland plateaux by extension of blanket bogs. Such areas were acid and not favourable to farming, but the swamps and marshes of the lowland floodplains were more base-rich and when drained could provide fertile soils. The sixteenth century marked a change in the fortunes of these areas when the first serious attempts were made to drain them, the eastern English Fens in particular.

DRAINAGE OF THE FENS

The Fens comprise a huge area around The Wash, with salty clay sediments to seaward, largely in the north in Lincolnshire, and freshwater peats to landward in the south, in Cambridgeshire (Fig. 140). The Romans had built a long bank to reclaim some of the salt marshes from the sea, but the freshwater fens remained wild throughout the mediaeval period. Islands were set in them where chalk outcrops remained between the river valleys of the Welland, Nene and Ouse, and settlements, including monastic houses, were sited on these, drawing much of their wealth from the fisheries, reed and grazing that the fens offered. There were many shallow lakes in the fens, with Whittlesea Mere, then the second largest lake in England, heading a long list that included Ugg Mere, Trundle Mere, Ramsey Mere and Benwick Mere. The Domesday Book records that:

In Witelsmare the abbot of Ramsey has one boat (navis), and the abbot of Peterborough one boat, and the abbot of Thorney two boats ... The fisheries and meres (marae) of the abbot of Ramsey in Huntingdonshire are valued at 10 libris, those of the abbot of Thorney at 60 solidis, those of the abbot of Peterborough at 4 libris.

Celia Fiennes, in a journey made around England in 1702, records her impressions of Whittlesea Mere:[6]

Ffrom Huntingdon we came to Shilton 10 mile, and came in sight of a great water on the right hand about a mile off. Looked like some sea it being so high and of great length; this is in part of the ffenny country and is called Whitlsome Mer, is 3 mile broad and six long. In ye midst is a little island where a great store of wildfowle breeds, there is no coming near it; in a mile or two the ground is all wett and

FIG 140. The fens around The Wash. Only the main drains are shown (in red) and the courses of the former rivers (in blue). The area of peaty soils was laid down under freshwater conditions, that of silt soils under marine, though flood defences have now removed the influence of the sea.

FIG 141. A regatta on Whittlesea Mere in 1842, pictured in H. M. Heathcote's *Reminiscences of Fen and Mere*, published in 1876.

marshy but there are severall little channells runs into it which by boats people go up to this place. When you enter the mouth of ye Mer it lookes fformidable and its often very dangerous by reason of sudden winds that will rise like hurricanes in the Mer, but at other tymes people boate it round the Mer with pleasure. There is abundance of good ffish in it.

For centuries Whittlesea Mere (Fig. 141) provided reed and sedge, and cut peat, for domestic burning and for the production of salt by evaporation, as well as a navigable connection to The Wash, but it was finally drained around 1850 to become land for the growing of cereals and vegetables. It was almost the last part of the freshwater fens, the black fens because of their peaty soil, to be drained in a process that began with some modest attempts in 1530, and the straightening of the River Ouse to become the Old Bedford River in the 1630s. Landowners then brought in a Dutch engineer, Cornelius Van der Muyden, who straightened the river courses even more, so as to take water as rapidly to the sea as possible. He dug, in 1650, the New Bedford channel (after the Duke of Bedford who led the group of landowners intent on this destruction) finally to replace the River Ouse. The fens had long been the refuge for the poor, the offending and the dissident, and no doubt this colossal act of vandalism was viewed by the rich and privileged as socially desirable, though it was opposed by the local people, who depended on the fen for their livelihoods.[7]

FIG 142. The current landscape of the fens is a taste that I have not acquired.

The drainage has produced huge profits, but only because large sums have since been invested by the state in sea and river defences (Fig. 142). When peat is drained it shrinks and wastes so that the land sinks and the water table in the rivers is perched metres above it. The top of an iron post, sunk flush with the peat surface of one of the tiny remnants of fen vegetation at Holme Fen in 1852 by William Wells, stood six feet above the surface ten years after it had been installed and presently stands thirteen feet above the fen, now the lowest point of Britain and Ireland. And from the sediments of the former Whittlesea Mere some curious finds have been made: a silver censer from Thorney Abbey, the skeleton of a killer whale and the bones of a wolf, each of them hinting at unknown details that make up the true interest of history.

DIATOMITE

Another reason for the early drainage of British lakes was to exploit deposits of diatoms in lake sediments, where they have been compressed to a soft rock called diatomite.[8] It has properties of high porosity and permeability, large internal surface area, chemical inertness and low heat conductivity that make it useful as a filter in processing drinks and solvents, as a filler in plastics, explosives and paints, in making insulation bricks, and even as an abrasive in toothpaste

FIG 143. The Kentmere reservoir was inadvertently expanded by the digging of diatomite by dragline, giving the irregular bay to the left. (Di Newton)

and polishes. The richest deposits are marine and of Miocene-Pliocene age at Lompoc in California, but most diatomites are of freshwater origin. The current major producers are the USA, France, Romania and Russia, but there have been smaller scale workings at Loch Cuithir and Loch Valerain, among others, in the Trotternish area of the Isle of Skye, near the village of Dinnet in Aberdeenshire and at Kentmere in the Cumbrian Lake District. The Skye operation, in sediments now covered by littoral peat, was once a major employer and produced some 2,000 tons of diatomite, locally called caile, and used, between 1899 and 1914, in cleaners and polishes for cars. The industry was plagued by a wet site and its isolated location; it was revived briefly in the 1950s though it was still uneconomic as the diatomite had to be dried and ground some distance away and was contaminated with too much organic matter.

A shallow lake in the Kentmere Valley, near Staveley in Cumbria, was drained in the 1840s and again in the 1870s for farming, but the meadows proved too wet and the natural lake had to be replaced by a reservoir to control flooding in the River Kent. In the 1920s, deposits of diatomite were found in the drained sediments to the side of the reservoir and exploited by dragline and then burned at a factory. Around 10,000 tons per year were mined in the 1930s but eventually the span of the dragline was exceeded and a dredger on a floating barge was used, creating an irregular lobe in the side of the reservoir (Fig. 143). The workings were abandoned in the 1980s when the work became uneconomic to maintain. The diatomite was used mainly in producing breathing mask filters for quarry workers.

ACIDIFICATION

The middle of the nineteenth century brought rapid change to the lakes of Britain and Ireland. Drainage had been made easier by the invention of more powerful pumps to raise water from the sinking land into the embanked rivers of the Fens, the Somerset Levels, the Broads and elsewhere. Other machinery came with the industrialisation, begun in the previous century, which was to change agriculture, pollute the rivers and acidify the landscape. Coal, the mining of which was to be aided by the development of pumps to prevent the flooding of the mines, was the fuel that powered much of the machinery and the burning of coal produced ammonia, and sulphur oxides.

Sulphur oxides and smoke particles polluted the air of the cities from the eighteenth century onwards and, by the mid-twentieth century, the incidence of dense smogs and bronchitis was so great that legislation was passed (the Clean Air Acts, 1956, 1968) in Britain to ban the domestic burning of cheap, high-sulphur coals in favour of less-damaging anthracites that produced less sulphur dioxide and smoke. Factory chimneys were built higher so as to take waste gases away from the cities. This did not destroy the sulphur oxides but distributed them more widely. In the atmosphere, the sulphur oxides reacted with oxygen and water vapour to form sulphur trioxide, and then droplets of quite concentrated sulphuric acid.

The acid impinged as fogs directly on trees, killing them, or dissolved in rain that fell onto the catchments and acidified the soils. Acidified water then drained from them into the streams and lakes. Rain that had a natural pH of around 5.5 acquired values as low as 2.0 and despite some neutralisation in the soils, drainage waters typically had pH values of 4.0 in uplands where the rocks were generally igneous or sandstones. The lowland lakes were less affected, for soils derived from finer-grained sedimentary rocks, particularly limestones and chalks, or base-rich glacial drift, coped with the acid. In the acidified regions, there were severe effects.[9] The most obvious was the death of fish, and it was the widespread fish kills in lakes in Norway and Sweden, caused by the drift, in the prevailing winds, of sulphur dioxide from the tall chimneys of British power stations that triggered a diplomatic crisis, a period of denial by the power-generating industry, then finally an admission of responsibility and the start of remedial measures.

The acidic rainfall and the 'dry' deposition of droplets of sulphuric acid on snow, which gave particularly severe episodes of acidification after snow melt in spring, dissolved aluminium ions from soil mineral particles, and increased aluminium concentrations in the waters. In the rivers, stream invertebrates that need to produce calcium carbonate to form shells and exoskeletons, particularly snails, bivalves and crustaceans, did not survive. Other stream invertebrates, particularly insect nymphs, accumulated aluminium that passed into birds, such as dippers, that fed on them, reduced the thickness of the eggshells that they produced, and led to a decline in egg survival and a loss of populations. The low pH directly affected fish in both rivers and lakes. It changed the conditions close to the egg membranes such that the enzymes, which the embryo uses to dissolve its way out of the egg, could not function, and the embryo was trapped. In adult fish, the aluminium ions stimulated production of copious mucus around the gills and led to asphyxiation.

Fishless lakes meant better survival of the more pH-tolerant zooplankton grazers, and thus lower phytoplankton crops, whilst the aluminium ions flocculated particles from the water, leaving it strangely crystal clear and of very low phosphorus content. *Sphagnum* began to replace other water plants at the edges, and flocs of green, cotton-wool-like filamentous algae, from groups that do not compete well for bicarbonate in high pH waters (Chapter 5), proliferated. The causes and effects were slowly pieced together and in the process there were attempts by government and industry to find blame that would have less impact on the economy and the generation of profits. Afforestation with conifers, which were claimed to remove bases from the soil and replace them with hydrogen ions, thus reducing pH, was targeted, but, as shown in Figure 136, catchments both afforested and not showed similar trends of acidification, its roots in the eighteenth century but its flowering, if that is the word, in the twentieth.

Release of sulphur dioxide has now been much reduced, partly by conversion of some power stations to oil burning and mostly by passing the exhaust gases through wet limestone scrubbers that neutralise the sulphuric acid to gypsum. The sulphate concentrations of upland streams and lakes have greatly declined but the biological communities have been slow to recover. Sometimes this is because, deep in the soils, there are still pockets of high acidity that are flushed out in heavy rain, causing brief episodes of acutely damaging conditions that are barely reflected in the long-term average sulphate concentrations. These set back the recovery of animal communities almost as effectively as chronic acidity.

Perhaps more important is that there is still a major source of acidity in the atmosphere: nitric acid produced by further oxidation of nitrogen oxides produced by burning petrol and oil in vehicles, heaters and generators (Fig. 144).

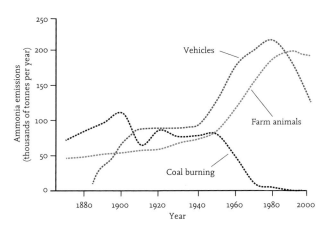

FIG 144. Emissions of ammonia and related reduced nitrogen compounds from coal have now declined, but those from farm manures have increased. Those from vehicles are high but have declined a little owing to the use of catalytic converters.

Ammonia, which volatilises abundantly from farm manures and intensive feeding units, also generates acidity in soils as it is taken up by plant roots and replaced by hydrogen ions. I once landed at Schiphol airport in the Netherlands from a cheap airline that deposited us on the tarmac to take a bus to the terminal. An atmospheric scientist with me took a deep breath and gave a credible estimate of the high ammonia content of the local atmosphere. Although some of this nitrogen loading has been reduced by use of catalytic converters in vehicles, there are still large amounts of nitric acid raining down and exceeding the capacities of the soils of the north and west of Britain and Ireland to neutralise them. Moreover, nitrate is a nutrient and contributes to eutrophication, the next problem that lakes face from human activities.

EUTROPHICATION: NUTRIENT POLLUTION

The modest increases in nutrients that resulted from conversion of forest to grassland for grazing in the later millennia BC were the start of eutrophication, or nutrient pollution. Intense cultivation of land, heavy use of artificial fertiliser and the great expansion in numbers of stock, coupled with the increased discharge of sewage effluent from an expanding human population have now made it the world's foremost problem for lakes.

Farming was dependent on recycling of animal manures back to the land until the start of the nineteenth century. Some nutrients are always leached away by the rain, and there was a steady loss of fertility of the land. Recycling slowed the decline but without artificial fertilisation, or the supply of new nutrients from river-born silts in floodplain farms, agricultural production inevitably declines over time because cultivation removes the inherent nutrient retention of a natural vegetation cover.[10] There were early experiments with fertilisers in the eighteenth and nineteenth centuries with the import of rock nitrate fertilisers and guano from South America. Then John Bennett Lawes in 1842 patented a process of treating phosphate rock with sulphuric acid to produce superphosphate, a product in which the phosphorus content per unit weight was greatly increased.

With these new nitrogen and phosphorus fertilisers, production increased in the nineteenth century, in a period known as Victorian high farming. Large profits were made as the price of grain increased, but these were eroded by the repeal in 1846 of the Corn Laws, which had limited the import of cheaper corn from overseas and led to much unrest among the poor. Farming nonetheless had entered a phase in which new practices, including a resumption of crop rotations on large farms, the use of steam engines to drive machinery and interest in crop and animal breeding made it more intensive. Import of nitrogen fertilisers was expensive, but the Haber-Bosch process for making ammonia from nitrogen and hydrogen, and its availability on an industrial scale by 1913, gave a cheap source.

Farming in Britain expanded after the Second World War, owing to government policies to make Britain as independent as possible of food imports. It now has a major influence on the water running into the rivers and lakes, as well as on the nitrogen being volatilised as ammonia from animal wastes into the atmosphere. Leaching losses from farmland give concentrations around ten to one hundred times greater than run-off from intact natural vegetation, and the problem is particularly acute with nitrate. These losses are referred to as diffuse loading or diffuse pollution and contrast with point source loading, which comes from discrete outlets such as the pipes from factories or wastewater (sewage) treatment works. Diffuse loading comes also from towns and cities because gardens and pets, riding stables and parks, litter and dust can all be sources of nutrients, but the greatest source from cities is the sewage treatment works.

The popular idea that domestic sewage was simply thrown in the streets prior to the nineteenth is probably misleading. It did occur, but was not appreciated by town councils, which passed regulations to minimise it. Particularly good records from York and Coventry in mediaeval times show that local rivers were becoming choked with all sorts of town wastes, including sewage, and arrangements were made to dump rubbish in pits outside the town boundaries.[11] Farmers could collect these valuable deposits from the pits for manure; indeed at Norwich a charge was made. The main issue at the time was not the effects on rivers and lakes of the ammonia and phosphate that the wastes contained, but the deoxygenating effects of the organic matter. In the larger rivers, the biological communities could process some of the organic matter and the local nuisance was tolerated, but by the nineteenth century with the major expansion of towns into cities, that was no longer acceptable. Rivers were also used for water supply, and cholera and typhoid epidemics were becoming common.

Sewage farms, where wastes were spread on land, had been established, but were too small to cope. The principle that waste water filtered through soil improved more rapidly, however, led to the first trickling filters, in which a film of bacteria, coating stones a few centimetres in diameter, removes organic matter by converting it to more bacteria and carbon dioxide. There has to be some prior settling of solids as sludge, which is dried and dumped or used as manure, or the filters would be blocked. Oligochaete worms and fly larvae control build-up of the bacterial film between the stones. These attract birds like wagtails to the filters, and birds also break up the film as they pick among the stones, but flies are regarded as a nuisance by all but sewage works managers. In 1914, a new process, in which the bacteria were contained in flocs (activated sludge) kept in suspension by bubbling air, was invented in Manchester by Edward Arden and William Lockett, supported by the Worshipful Company of Grocers, and first used at the Davyhulme works. It was more efficient and avoided the problems of blocked filters and flies, but required more energy for the running and maintenance of the pumps.

The effluent from these new works was much better than the raw sewage that had previously been discharged to the rivers and, in 1912, a Royal Commission decreed minimum standards of 30 mg per litre for suspended solids and 20 mg per litre over a five-day period for biological oxygen demand in the final effluent. It also made some stipulations for ammonia content, because ammonia can be toxic to fish. A well-functioning works converted organic matter to its inorganic components, carbon dioxide, phosphate, nitrate and ammonium, with minimal levels of the latter. Not until the 1940s was it fully realised that these products caused problems of eutrophication (Fig. 145): increased plant growth with reduced diversity of species in rivers and lakes; more phytoplankton in lakes, often with dominance of cyanobacteria, some of which were poisonous to stock and potentially people; increased costs of filtering the water for the public supply and for removing tastes and odours imparted by different sorts of algae; changes in fish community from whitefish and salmonids to percids and, finally, coarse fish of the carp family; and a general loss of amenity with slimy rocks and algal scums at the lake edge.

The grossly polluted rivers, disease epidemics and shortage of water as populations increased led the Victorians to dam rivers in the uplands to create

FIG 145. Eutrophication has many effects, which intensify the more nutrients that enter.

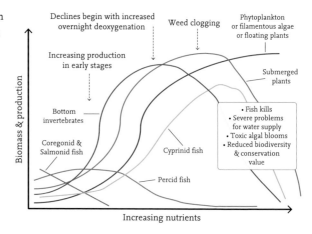

drinking water reservoirs, and to draw water from some large lakes. At first there were few eutrophication problems, but when tourism expanded in areas like the Cumbrian Lake District and around the more accessible Scottish lochs, local waste effluent disposal was noticeably reflected in the algal communities and the costs of filtering the water. Meanwhile, in lowland areas like the Norfolk Broads, the unrealised effects of sewage nutrients were seen in a loss of charophytes and an expansion in growth of other water plants. These were ignored until the ultimate effects of eutrophication, replacement of water plants by dense growths of algae, were seen 100 years later, and it was realised that the dense plant growths of the first half of the twentieth century in the Broads were early warnings of the problem.[12]

Eutrophication was first documented in the scientific literature in 1947 and has now become a global problem. Costs of it are high. Table 15 shows the calculated costs in England and Wales, but the real costs are likely to be much higher because the cost of buying an alternative drinking water supply, in bottles, was not considered. This cost dominated a parallel assessment in the USA, also shown in Table 15, where an estimated $813 million per year was spent on bottled water, usually bought because of taste and odour problems in the local drinking water supply. The irony is that tap water everywhere in the UK is perfectly drinkable but sales of bottled water are huge. The emphases in the US study were also on the loss of property values, because many people in North America own lakeside cottages and do not appreciate excessive weed growth, slippery rocks and rotting algal blooms. Planning laws have restricted lakeside development in the UK, and another major loss of value, in angling, particularly from power boats, is also much less important in the UK but prominent in the USA.

TABLE 15. Estimates of the costs of eutrophication in England and Wales and in the USA (na = not assessed).

	USA – US$ million (2009) per year	England & Wales – £ million (2002) per year
Fisheries	189–589	0.04–0.17
Recreational boating	82–567	13.5–47
Other tourism	na	4.1–16.3
Lakeside property values	4,500	13.8
Biodiversity & conservation (recovery plans)	44	10.3–14.2
Water treatment	813+	54.7
Industrial (abstraction, irrigation, stock, navigation)	na	0.7–1.4
Clean-up costs (e.g. fish kills, weed cutting)	na	0.7–1.4
Gas emissions (nitrogen oxides, ammonium) effects	na	7.17–11.19
Sewage effluent treatment (removal of P)	na	70.4
Treatment of algal blooms	na	0.7
Cost of adoption of new farm practices	na	4.8
Monitoring & investigation of incidents	na	0.9
Cost of policy development to cope	na	0.28
TOTAL	5,728–6,513	183–238

DEALING WITH EUTROPHICATION

The earliest approach to dealing with eutrophication has long been known to water engineers and is to dose the lake or reservoir with chemicals to kill the algae. Copper salts were first used but are toxic, as are most other algicides if they persist in the water. Such treatment of symptoms, however, is only temporary. It is nonetheless cheap, as are other symptom treatments that do not involve dosing with chemicals. One is to use pumps or aerators to mix a stratified water column in summer. This tends to discourage cyanobacteria and favour diatoms, which are less mucilaginous and easier to filter out, but it gives only temporary relief. By alternating a period of mixing with a period when the mixers are turned off, it is possible to 'confuse' the

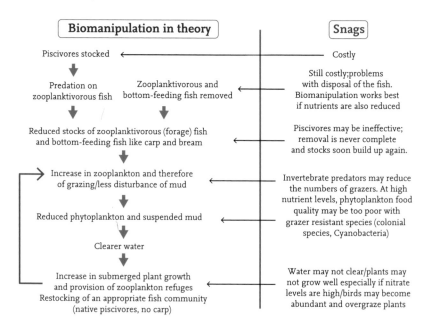

FIG 146. The principles of biomanipulation and some of the many things that can reduce its effectiveness as a symptom treatment.

algal community so that there is never time for large numbers of cyanobacteria or diatoms to develop, but there are often unexpected effects.

It is also possible to reduce algal crops by biomanipulation (Fig. 146), in which planktivorous fish are removed or piscivorous fish are added, though growing up enough predators like pike is expensive, and in the end they cannibalise themselves once they have exhausted the populations of zooplanktivores. In theory either approach reduces the predation on the zooplankton, which then are able to grow in large numbers and eat more algae, thus clearing the water (see Chapter 6). Biomanipulation can work well if the removal of the fish is near complete and has been used to create conditions for aquatic plants to grow again in highly eutrophicated shallow lakes.

The problem is that it is never possible to remove all the fish and eventually the populations re-establish and the algal growths return. The fishing thus has to be done every year or two and, in a big lake, needs a commercial fishery, and therefore a market for the fish. Often this is not available nowadays because zooplanktivorous fish like roach and bream, though they were eaten in the nineteenth century, and in one Finnish lake were tinned for sale to tourists, are no longer delicacies. For small lakes of previous conservation value, biomanipulation is appropriate as a stopgap measure, but has been restricted in the Netherlands, where it was widely used, on grounds of animal cruelty. In the end the eutrophication problem is only resolved by cutting down the supply of the nutrients to the lake and this can be done on two levels.

The first is to reduce the amount in the lake by treating the lake water. This is only one step removed from treatment of symptoms using algicides, mixing or biomanipulation and involves precipitating phosphate using iron ammonium sulphate, calcium carbonate, various industrial waste products containing iron or calcium silicates, or, more recently and more expensively, compounds of lanthanum.[13] Ideally these substances not only precipitate what is in the water but also form a seal at the sediment surface to prevent stocks in the sediment from coming out. This they may do for a time, but eventually new sediment buries the seal and if the external supply from the catchment has not been reduced, the new sediment will act as a phosphorus source. In some American lakes, aluminium compounds have been used to seal sediments, and work well provided the lake is essentially a recreational boating lake and not used as a fishery or cherished for its conservation value. Unfortunately the most effective and long-lasting treatments are either the potentially toxic ones (aluminium and some industrial waste products) or the very expensive ones (lanthanum) and field trials over several years with proper controls for comparison, rather than laboratory studies, have yet to prove the long-term effectiveness of any of them.

A more drastic and expensive approach is to remove significant quantities of sediment by dredging or suction pumping (Fig. 147). The former is slow and used mainly to remodel river banks and beds to cope with flooding

FIG 147. Suction pumping of sediment can be used to increase water depth, but rarely has permanent effects on nutrient content of the water.

problems, and is not really suited to fluid lake sediments. Pumping sucks out a suspension of sediment and water, and deposits it in storage lagoons, constructed on land by heaping up soil to form low walls, where it can drain and dry and eventually be ploughed into the soil. Quite a lot of land, and a willing landowner, are needed and the sediment must not be contaminated by pollutants (such as heavy metals) other than nutrients.

Suction pumping is often used to increase water depth for navigation in shallow lakes, like the Norfolk Broads. A couple of centuries of determined agriculture, and several decades of erosion by boats, have brought in a lot of soil, but pumping is only a palliative for eutrophication problems unless it is coupled with measures to reduce the amounts of nutrient coming in from the catchment. Even then it has to take out a great deal of sediment so that only early sediments laid down prior to the eighteenth century are left. Otherwise, phosphorus can migrate up through the sediment to its new surface and start to emerge again. Sediment removal delays the natural process of filling in, which may have conservation advantages, but removes the historic record contained in the sediments and any archaeological remains. It should be done only after careful consideration of whether there really will be benefits. Often there have been few but there are many pressures from commercial companies eager to keep their expensive dredging, pumping (and chemical dosing) equipment in operation.

CATCHMENT NUTRIENT CONTROL

Ultimately, eutrophication problems can only be solved by reducing the amounts of nutrients entering a lake from the catchment, which means careful control of land use, and treatment of effluents released from industry and wastewater treatment works. Many industrial effluents are now routed through the former sewage treatment works, which in consequence have been rechristened wastewater treatment works. The first step in a control programme is to find out the sources of both phosphorus and nitrogen to a lake, and then to tackle the largest of these first. Sewage effluents are rich in nitrogen compounds but once the effluent is diluted in the rivers they provide much less nitrate (though much more phosphate) than the run-off from agricultural fields, so that overall there is a high correlation between the phosphorus in the water and the human population in the catchment and between the percentage of the catchment in agriculture and the nitrogen concentrations (Fig. 148).

The mixture of sources will differ from lake to lake, and the patterns will be different for phosphorus and nitrogen. The reservoirs serving London, for

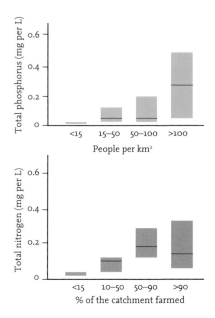

FIG 148. Links between human population in a catchment and total phosphorus, and percentage of the catchment area that is farmed and levels of total nitrogen. The box size shows the range among several hundred catchments in Europe and the black lines are the means.

example, store water from the River Thames and in summer most of this water will be wastewater effluent. Some of the Norfolk Broads have about equal sources of phosphorus from the land and from effluent. Most of the Cumbrian lakes, bar the more popular southerly ones like Coniston, Grasmere, Esthwaite and Windermere, and in the north, Bassenthwaite Lake, which are all close to sizeable towns or villages with wastewater treatment works, are supplied mostly from the land. There are unusual cases too. In the past Hickling Broad was fertilised by flocks of roosting gulls, gleaning food and nutrients from a local waste tip, and Loch Leven has been plagued by the phosphate detergents used in a woollen mill.

Nutrients can easily be removed from the effluent of wastewater treatment works before it is discharged to rivers. The easiest nutrient to remove is phosphorus because phosphate concentrations in effluent are high, perhaps up to 20 mg P/L as opposed to 50 to 100 micrograms in water draining cropland, and the source is easily identifiable. The effluent from traditional wastewater treatment works can be treated with iron or aluminium salts to precipitate much of the phosphate, and the precipitate can be settled and spread (unless aluminium has been used) on the land, or recycled into industrial processes. This is known as phosphate stripping or tertiary treatment. Surprisingly, it has been used with great reluctance in Britain and Ireland and only in limited areas and in very recent decades.

Eutrophication was noted as a problem on Lough Neagh in the 1970s and several wastewater treatment works had phosphorus precipitation installed, and then in the 1980s the same was done for a handful of works in the Norfolk Broads. It was regarded as experimental, though it had been widely used for a couple of decades in Scandinavia, and North America. Only with the passing of the European Union Urban Waste Water Treatment Directive (UWWTD) in 1991 did the practice become more widespread in Europe. The UWWTD is one of a series of European Directives that have forced a more responsible approach to water quality by European governments.[14] First, it made provision to stop the discharge of raw sewage to the sea, which had been common previously, and to treat it to at least secondary (organic matter removal) level.

It then required that phosphorus and nitrogen be removed from effluents where it was considered there was a risk of eutrophication. Some European countries rightly considered that their entire area was at risk, but the British and Irish governments included only areas where there were problems with treatment of water supply, and nutrient removal is still carried out only at a minority of works, mostly affecting river sections where there are drinking water intakes. More lakes than Lough Neagh and the Broads now benefit, including the major Cumbrian Lakes, but the UK is well down the list of member states in its compliance (around 60 per cent) for tertiary treatment and then only for 'sensitive' areas, and Ireland is 23rd out of 27 with a 2 per cent compliance. Denmark, Finland, Greece, Austria, Germany and the Netherlands all have 100 per cent compliance, or close to it, and have designated all of their territories as sensitive to eutrophication.

There have not always been immediate benefits of the UWWTD for three reasons. The first is that lake sediments contain large phosphorus stores resulting from decades of past pollution and it will take some time for these to be released and washed away or satisfactorily buried by new sediment; the second that even after treatment substantial amounts of phosphorus may still be present in the effluent. The effectiveness of the process depends on the enthusiasm of the works manager and up to 1 mg of phosphorus per litre can, in any case, legally remain in the discharged effluent.

The third reason is that effluent is not the only source of phosphorus. Diffuse sources, largely from agriculture, may be nearly as important and have tended to increase. It takes only a small increase in phosphorus over natural background levels for serious algal problems to emerge and much more stringent control is needed than usually thought. It is not a question of every little bit helps. A lot of small removals may bring little improvement; it is almost a case of all or nothing. Moreover, although the UWWTD mandates removal of nitrogen from effluents, this is more expensive and more difficult to do. Algal growths in many lakes are controlled by nitrogen, or both nitrogen and phosphorus, rather than phosphorus alone, and the diffuse supplies of nitrate are far greater than those derived from the wastewater treatment works even before tertiary treatment for nitrogen.

DIFFUSE SOURCES

Diffuse sources of nutrients (and also toxic pollutants like pesticides) are very difficult to stop. The techniques overlap for nitrogen and phosphorus, but nitrate and ammonia are very soluble and cannot easily be controlled; there are countless small sources in a catchment, and voluntary co-operation by landowners and farmers has largely, perhaps naively, been relied on. The UWWTD has plenty of legal loopholes that the water industry and the British and Irish governments have taken advantage of, but there are at least some legal requirements that are unavoidable. New legislation in the form of the Water Framework Directive (see Chapter 12) may eventually help in the case of diffuse pollutants, but there will be few signs for the next couple of decades.

The keys to reducing phosphorus and nitrogen losses from the land are to restrict fertiliser use, minimise cultivation and not leave soil bare to erode. Not ploughing a strip of land close to a river may help, but basically such measures make only a marginal difference once the land is tilled or fertilised at modern rates. Leaving a buffer zone around streams and lakes is supposed to restrict nutrient input, but for phosphorus it needs to be very large, its soils need to be

FIG 149. Hule wetlands in Georgia: constructed wetlands are beds of usually emergent aquatic plants that create conditions for denitrification of nitrate in wastewater effluents. They are not so good at removing phosphorus because the anaerobic soils generally lead to release of phosphate. (American Academy of Engineering and Environmental Sciences)

well aerated, and water needs to percolate across it rather than be short-circuited through small channels. Control of nitrogen using such zones is more effective, especially if the buffer zone is of swamp or marsh, because nitrate becomes denitrified to nitrogen gas, but this is favoured by deoxygenated rather than aerated soils. Buffer zones thus need to include substantial areas with differing conditions to cope with both nutrients and this has rarely, if ever, been achieved. On the other hand, artificially constructed wetlands (Fig. 149) can be effective in finally polishing the effluents of treatment works that have already had tertiary treatment installed. The scale of the problem of creating buffer zones often defeats effective control. If an arable area is leaking water with 10 or 20 mg per litre of nitrate nitrogen, at least the same area is needed to retain the water long enough for denitrification to a desirable value of say 0.5 mg per litre and no landowner would be willing voluntarily to take such an area out of cultivation.

STOCK

The nutrients from stock can be more effectively managed than those from crops. Manures can be used back on the land, but must be ploughed in during dry weather or large quantities of ammonium and phosphate may run off during rain. Schemes exist in the UK to subsidise farmers to provide more manure storage, to roof manure piles, to divert pathways, along which cattle walk to milking, away from streams, and even to relocate gates at the upper ends of fields. Animals disturb soil and cause erosion that is better directed to run into a field than out of it, down the lane and into a stream. Despite an enormous amount of fuss and goodwill, however, it is unlikely that much difference will be made by any of these measures. Evaluations of a voluntary scheme called 'Catchment Sensitive Farming' are notably coy about the extent of nutrient control. Reductions by a few per cent and perhaps up to 36 per cent are predicted, but these are based on modelling rather than measurements.[15] Worse, in some areas of Northern Ireland, at least, the soils have been so heavily fertilised for so long that their capacity to retain phosphate has been exceeded and phosphate is now running off in large quantities so that the effects of tertiary treatment of sewage effluent on Lough Neagh are being superseded.[16]

What reduction in diffuse nutrient pollution there has been in European countries, including the UK, has resulted mostly from the increased cost and therefore more parsimonious use of fertilisers in recent years. There is some legislation in the form of the EU Nitrates Directive, created largely because of problems with high nitrate levels in water supplies for young babies being bottle-fed. Nitrate reacts in their stomachs to form nitrite, which then combines with the methaemoglobin in the blood, preventing it from carrying oxygen, and the baby may asphyxiate (blue-baby syndrome). The problem does not occur after six months of age because a different form of haemoglobin, which is not affected, is produced. The Nitrates Directive stipulates that Nitrate Vulnerable Zones be created where there are problems for either water supply or conservation, but it sets the maximum level of nitrate as 7.5 mg N per litre, which is effective so far as babies are concerned, but around ten times too high to create any conservation improvement, such as restoration of plant biodiversity. The UK at first set only a few Nitrate Vulnerable Zones, and those entirely for water supply. It was taken to the European Court and fined, so later designated many more, but there has been no detectable benefit for conservation and the baby problem could be (and was) easily avoided in critical areas by using blended water specially bottled. The Nitrates Directive was well intentioned but had little point and indeed measures to change farmer behaviour have had virtually no effect on the nitrate concentrations in ground and surface waters.[17] The Directive has been effectively superseded by the Water Framework Directive (Chapter 10).

A CASE STUDY OF WINDERMERE

Many of the human uses of lakes and the problems they cause are linked. A classic case is that of Lake Windermere, where a formerly disparaged area of 'wilderness' and mining, when Celia Fiennes travelled through in the late eighteenth century, was converted to a fashionable tourist destination by the poetry of William Wordsworth, the paintings of J. M. W. Turner, and the building, in 1847, of a railway. Tourism led to an effective quadrupling of the population between 1801 and 1921 and an even greater expansion since (Fig. 150).[18] People need feeding, must be kept occupied and produce sewage.

FIG 150. Windermere is a popular tourist destination.

FIG 151. During the Second World War, perch was caught in Windermere and canned in tomato sauce as 'perchines'.
(E. D. Le Cren)

Sewage was piped directly to the lake in the 1860s and the first treatment works was built in 1886. The increasing amounts of nutrients led to increased algal growth and moderate surface blooms of cyanobacteria in quiet bays. Meanwhile the numbers of stock, particularly sheep, and fertiliser use in the catchment, have increased since the 1950s. In 1991, phosphate removal was installed at the main wastewater treatment works. This reduced the algal crops temporarily but they have increased again perhaps because of the sheep and fertiliser but also because of the influences of climate change (see Chapter 10).

Tourists love boats, and sailing boats, though still common, became superseded by powerboats on Windermere. A penchant for water skiing then created a lot of noise, unappreciated by other users. Speed restrictions to 10 mph, now 10 knots, were introduced in 2005. Boats need moorings and docking but the shoreline has been protected well by the planning regulations and the natural edge has been destroyed only in the towns, though part of the shore was disturbed by the building of mansions by the wealthy merchants of Manchester and Liverpool in the nineteenth century. A fishery for charr persisted until charr numbers declined in the late twentieth century, probably as water temperatures have increased, and during the Second World War there was an attempt to create a fishery for perch to boost national food supplies (Fig. 151). Recreational angling has now replaced commercial fishing in extent and value and brought with it the third most significant problem after acidification and eutrophication for British and Irish lakes, that of introduced species.

INTRODUCED SPECIES

Apart from those that hung on in the lakes at the feet of the glaciers, all the species that we now have are invaders from other places, jostling for niches over several thousands of years of attempts, with a degree of randomness about what came and what survived. But the process has been accelerated by people, especially since trade links were established with the mainland. Where freshwaters are concerned, the best data have been compiled for England and there have been at least 200 freshwater introductions, both accidental and deliberate, mostly since 1800, from a total of 2,400 plant and animal species introduced by people to all habitats of Britain and Ireland. There are probably many more introductions than have been recorded and in particular every new free-living organism is likely to bring with it several new parasites, which are not readily detected. Many exotic species in freshwaters are quite innocuous and hang on in small isolated populations; a very few are considered economic assets but may be environmentally damaging (common carp, goldfish and rainbow trout); and some result in severe problems. In recent decades, Canada goose, mink, coypu and diseases of alder trees and amphibians have had substantial effects. Topmouth gudgeon, feral greylag geese, and four aquatic plants, New Zealand pigmy weed (Fig. 152), *Lemna minuta*, a tiny duckweed, water pennywort and parrot feather, have been increasing their ranges and pose local problems.

FIG 152. New Zealand pigmy weed (with small leaves) is a fast-spreading aquatic plant that easily outcompetes rare native species such as the broader-leaved floating water plantain, here at Brown Moss in Shropshire.

TABLE 16. The more important species of introduced free-living freshwater invertebrates in standing waters Britain and Ireland.

Scientific name	Common name	How introduced?	Native to:	Comments	First 'wild' record	Date of introduction
Corbicula fluminea	Asiatic clam		Asia	C. fluminalis may also be present	Norfolk Broads	1998
Dreissena polymorpha	Zebra mussel	With timber from Baltic	Caspian and Black seas	Recent spread in Ireland	Wisbech	1820
Marstoniopsis scholtzi	Taylor's spire snail	? Roman introduction	N Europe			Early
Menetus dilatatus	Trumpet ram's-horn snail		Eastern USA	Mostly in canals	Pendleton	1869
Musculium transversum	Oblong orb mussel		North America	Found only in canals/canalised rivers	Kensal Green	1856
Physa (alien spp.)	Snail		North America	P. gyrina widespread; P. acuta and P. heterostropha present		1800
Potamopyrgus antipodarum	Jenkins's spire snail	Introduced in drinking water barrels in ships from Australia	New Zealand	Abundant and ubiquitous	Grays; Thames Estuary	1859
Asellus communis	Water hoglouse				Cumbrian Lake District	
Astacus astacus	Noble crayfish	Restaurant trade	Europe	An offence to release this species		1986
Astacus leptodactylus	Turkish crayfish	Restaurant trade	Asia Minor	An offence to release this species		1975

Species	Common name	Introduction/vector	Origin	Notes	Location	Year
Corophium curvispinum	Freshwater shrimp		Ponto-Caspian basin		River Avon, Tewkesbury	1935
Crangonyx pseudogracilis	Freshwater shrimp		North America		London	1930
Echinogamarus berilloni	Freshwater shrimp				Channel Isles	
Dikerogammarus villosus	Killer shrimp		Ponto-Caspian basin		Norfolk Broads, South Wales, Graffham Water	2010
Dikerogammarus haemobaphes	Killer shrimp				Midlands canals and spreading	2012
Gammarus tigrinus	Freshwater shrimp		Atlantic seaboard of N America	Prefers brackish water; Midland canals		
Orconectes limosus	Spinycheek or American river crayfish		North America		Warwickshire	1990
Pacifastacus leniusculus	Signal crayfish		North America	An offence to release this species; crayfish plague vector		1975
Procambarus clarkii	Red swamp crayfish	Probably released by aquarists	SE USA		Hampstead Heath	1991
Craspedacusta sowerbyi	Freshwater jellyfish	With aquatic plant imports	China			1880
Dugesia tigrina	Triclad flatworm	Probably with aquarium trade	North America		Thames reservoirs	1922
Planaria torva	Triclad flatworm	Timber trade	Scandinavia		East Anglia	1930
Stenopelmus rufinasus	Azolla weevil	Introduced for control of *Azolla*	North America	Effectiveness for biocontrol in England has yet to be established		1921
Daphnia ambigua	A water flea				Kew Gardens and Regent's Park, London	

The effects of introduced species are varied but they tend to displace native species because their own predators are not introduced with them and thus there is a limited check on their population growth. The effects may be compounded by eutrophication, which allows the introductions to grow vigorously. Tables 16–18 summarise the more important free-living freshwater introductions to Britain and Ireland. Some of these species may have died out, and some are very local, but the lists have some interesting features.

There are 21 invertebrates (Table 16), undoubtedly an underestimate, because invertebrates are not so easily spotted as vertebrates and plants. Most came in accidentally, associated with commercial imports of water plants and fish, or on wet timber floated down European or American rivers to the docks. One, the Azolla weevil, was deliberately brought in to help control another introduced species, a velvety floating water fern. The zebra mussel has caused some difficulties for water supply companies by blocking pipes, and, of several crayfish escaped from farms supplying the restaurant trade, one has proved devastating to native crayfish by bringing crayfish plague, a chromalveolate (Chapter 3), once classed a fungus, with it. In North America, many freshwater invertebrates have been introduced in the ballast water of ships travelling from the Baltic and Black seas and discharging their ballast when they take on cargoes at ports in the St Lawrence Great Lakes system. Ballast water is potentially a problem also for Britain and Ireland, though most of our ports are on the sea coast where freshwater organisms will not easily survive. There are several brackish water-tolerant shrimps, however, that are steadily spreading through

FIG 153. *Dikerogammarus* of two species, *D. villosus* and *D. haemobaphes*, referred to as killer shrimps by those who have watched too many television crime series, may spread throughout British lakes. They originate from the Ponto-Caspian region, have advanced through mainland Europe, reached Britain after 2010 and are voracious predators on other invertebrates. Water lettuce is sold to water gardeners but usually does not survive the winter in Britain and Ireland. It may do so with warming trends and may become a pest.

TABLE 17. The more important introduced species of vertebrates in standing waters in Britain and Ireland.

Scientific name	Common name	How introduced?	Native to:	Comments	First 'wild' record	Date of introduction
			Amphibians			
Alytes obstetricans	Midwife toad		Western Europe		Bedford	1898
Bombina variegata	Yellow-bellied toad		Europe	Colonies died out in 1960s and 1970s	Devon	1960
Rana catesbeiana	American bullfrog	Pet market	USA		Bexhill	
Rana esculenta	Edible frog	Deliberate introduction	Europe		Norfolk	1837
Rana lessonae	Pool frog	Possibly native	Europe			
Rana ridibunda	Marsh frog	Deliberate release	Europe	Often mistaken for other species of green frog	Surrey	1884
Triturus alpestris	Alpine newt	Accidentally introduced with aquatic plants	Alps		Surrey	
Xenopus laevis	African clawed toad	Deliberate release	Southern Africa	Common laboratory organism; colonies in Wales & Scunthorpe	Isle of Wight	1962
			Fish			
Acipenser baerii	Siberian sturgeon		Siberia	No detailed information		
Acipenser ruthenus	Sterlet	Imported as ornamental fish for garden ponds and aquaria, despite ultimate large body size, which leads to covert release	Central & Eastern Europe			1900
Ambloplites rupestris	Rock bass	Angling?	Central North America		Linkside Lake, Oxford	1990

Scientific name	Common name	Reason	Origin	Notes	Location	Date
Ameiurus melas	Black bullhead	Ornamental?	North America	Not in Ireland	Essex	1800
Aristichthys nobilis	Bighead carp	Ornamental/angling	Asia			1900
Carassius auratus	Goldfish	Ornamental	Asia	Not in Ireland		1600
Carassius carassius	Crucian carp	Ornamental?	Asia	C. gibelo (Prussian carp) also reported. Not in Ireland		
Catostomus commersoni	Common white sucker	Ornamental	Eastern North America		R. Gade (Hemel Hempstead)	1985
Clarias batrachus	Walking catfish	Ornamental	Southeast North America		Church Street Canal, St Helens, Lancashire	1960
Coregonus clupeaformis	Lake whitefish	Stock enhancement	Northern USA & Canada	Very limited information. May be confused with other coregonids		1800
Ctenopharyngodon idellus	Chinese grass carp	Control of aquatic weeds	R. Amur, Russia	Does not breed in Britain	Fens (Cambs)	1960
Cyprinus carpio	Common carp	Originally as food, then for angling	West/Central Asia	Well naturalised	London?	1400 or earlier
Hucho hucho	Huchen (Danube salmon)	Angling?	Danube basin			1900
Hypophthalamichthys molitrix	Bighead carp	Angling?	R. Amur			1990
Ictalurus punctatus	Channel catfish	Ornamental?	East/Central North America		Bucks & Surrey	1900
Lepomis gibbosus	Pumpkinseed (Sun perch, Sun bass)	Ornamental	East of Rocky Mountains, North America	Airport Pond, Sandown, Isle of Wight & occasional specimens in River Tamar (Cornwall/Devon)	Pease Potage (West Sussex) or Tunbridge Wells (East Sussex)	1890
Leucaspius delineatus	Sunbleak, Belica	Ornamental or accidental	Europe & Asia	Not in Ireland	Hampshire	1985

Species	Common name	Ornamental or accidental	Origin	Notes	Location	Date
Leuciscus idus	Ide (Orfe)	Ornamental or accidental	Central & East Europe	In vicinity of thermal effluents, but populations died out when power stations were decommissioned	Woburn Abbey (Beds)	1800
Maylandia (Metriaclima) sp.	Zebrafish species	Ornamental and laboratory	Lake Malawi		River Nene (Cambs)	1900
Micropterus dolomieu	Smallmouth bass	Angling	Eastern USA & Canada	May have died out	Surrey and Dorset	1800
Micropterus salmoides	Largemouth bass (Black bass)	Angling	East/Central North America	May have died out	Oulton Broad (Norfolk)/Wareham (Dorset)	1800
Misgurnus fossilis	European weatherfish (Pond loach)	Ornamental	West & Central Europe		River Roding (Essex)	1900
Misgurnus mizolepis	Chinese weatherfish	Ornamental	China & Korea		Sussex	2002
Oncorhynchus clarki	Cutthroat trout	Angling	Northwest North America			
Oncorhynchus mykiss	Rainbow trout	Angling	W/NW North America	Widely stocked	Delaford Park, Iver (Bucks)	1800
Oncorhynchus gorbuscha	Pink salmon	Vagrant	W/NW North America	No detailed information		1900
Poecilia reticulata	Guppy	Ornamental	S America	In vicinity of thermal effluents, but died out when power stations were decommissioned	Church Street Canal, St. Helens, Lancashire & Lower River Lee, Hackney (Middx)	1960
Pseudorasbora parva	Topmouth gudgeon (False harlequin)	Ornamental	Asia		Outflow stream, Crampmoor fishery (Hampshire)	1985

Rhodeus amarus	Bitterling	Unknown (ornamental?)	West/Central Europe & Western Asia	Introduced range in England linked to presence of unionid mussels, in which eggs are laid	Cheshire & Lancashire (Blackbrook Canal near St Helens?)	1900
Salmo salar sebago	Sebago (landlocked) salmon	Angling	Maine			
Salvelinus fontinalis	Brook trout	Angling	NE North America		Chertsey Bridge (Surrey)/London	1860
Salvelinus malma	Dolly Varden charr	Angling	NW North America	May have died out		
Salvelinus namaycush	American Lake charr	Angling	Canada	Unsuccessful establishment		1900
Sander lucioperca	Pikeperch (Zander)	Angling	Central & Eastern North America	Abberton Reservoir, Essex	Woburn Abbey (Beds)	1800
Silurus glanis	European (Wels) catfish	Angling	Central & Eastern Europe	Not in Ireland	Morton Hall (Norfolk)	1800
Tilapia zillii	Redbelly tilapia	Ornamental?	Tanzania, Uganda	In vicinity of thermal effluents, but believed to have died out when power stations were decommissioned	Church Street Canal, St Helens, Lancashire	1960
Umbra krameri	European mudminnow	Ornamental?	Middle & Lower Danube	Unsuccessful establishment		1900
Birds						
Aix galericulata	Mandarin duck	Escaped/released from waterfowl collections	Eastern Asia	Escapes occurred almost 200 years after its importation to British waterfowl collections	Woburn Abbey (Beds.)	1745
Alopochen aegyptiacus	Egyptian goose	Escaped/released from waterfowl collections	Africa			
Anser caerulescens	Snow goose	Escaped/released from waterfowl collections	N America	Breeding records refer to escaped or released birds but wild vagrants also occur	Thatcham (Berks.)	1700

Anser canagicus	Emperor goose	Escaped/released from waterfowl collections	North America			
Anser indicus	Bar-headed goose	Escaped/released from waterfowl collections	South Asia			
Branta canadensis	Canada goose	Escaped/released from waterfowl collections	North America			1731
Cygnus atratus	Black swan	Escaped/released from waterfowl collections	Australia	Unlikely to form fully self-sustaining populations in future		1791
Netta rufina	Red-crested pochard	Escaped/released from waterfowl collections	Europe, Asia	British breeders derived from captive birds but wild vagrants also occur		
Nycticorax nycticorax	Black-crowned night heron	Escaped from zoo	North America	British breeders derived from captive birds but wild vagrants also occur	Edinburgh	1950
Oxyura jamaicensis	Ruddy duck	Escaped/released from waterfowl collections	North America		Slimbridge, Glos.	1949
Tadorna ferruginea	Ruddy shelduck		Asia, Europe	Wild vagrants have occurred and may still do so but picture clouded by frequent escapes from collections and wanderings by birds reintroduced and escaped on the near continent		
Mammals						
Mustela vison	American mink	First brought to England to stock fur farms in 1929/ escapes regularly occurred thereafter	USA, Canada, N. Mexico		Breeding in wild first proved in 1956 in Devon	1929
Myocastor coypus	Coypu	First brought to England to stock fur farms in 1929/ escapes occurred mainly in the 1930s	Southern half of South America	Probably now removed		1930
Ondatra zibethicus	Muskrat	Escaped from fur farms	Most of N. America			1925

mainland Europe in the navigable river systems, and which might become established, and two species of *Dikerogammarus*, a genus of large and predatory shrimp (Fig. 153), have already established, one in several unconnected locations, the other spreading through the canal system.[19]

Many fish species (Table 17) have been brought in, either for ornamental purposes, especially by the owners of grand estates, or for angling, and 38 species appear on the list, of which at least 30 are still thriving. Some that persisted in canals warmed by factory cooling waters in St Helens and Stockport seem to have disappeared with the decline of manufacturing. Common carp is an introduced species, but brought in probably in the thirteenth century or earlier, and now thought of as naturalised. It is a popular angling fish, having the appealing characteristic to macho anglers that it fights on the line, and has been spread around Britain and Ireland for competitive match angling. It destroys water plants as it forages in the sediment around them for invertebrates, and has converted many shallow lakes from clear water havens of high diversity to turbid pools devoid of plants. It is not a problem in its native range in Eastern Europe and Western Asia, where it has many more competitors, but it is very damaging here.[20] In a lake at Llandrindod Wells, carp caused problems, but the recommended solution was so bungled by the local authority that a paper on the topic was entitled 'A restoration comedy'.[21]

BIRD, MAMMAL AND WATER PLANT INTRODUCTIONS

Wealthy individuals in the past liked to create private collections of exotic animals in their parks and estates, from which species, especially birds, inevitably escaped. Sometimes these birds are of species that are native to Britain and Ireland but the genetic races that were stocked, and escaped, came from elsewhere. An example is that of greylag geese, a normally migratory species but now establishing as a prolifically breeding species. Escapee birds may also be of species that are occasional or rare vagrants, and sometimes, rare vagrants; for example, two species of egret, have started to establish breeding populations because climatic or other changes have favoured them. I have not included these categories in the list of 11 given in Table 17, among which the Canada goose is the only real problem, because of its habit of leaving large quantities of green and slimy droppings on the immaculate lawns of public parks, whose designers were imaginative enough to include a lake.

Of the three aquatic introduced mammals, coypu (Fig. 154), a South American rodent, is believed to have been eliminated. Like the mink and muskrat, it

FIG 154. Coypu (nutria) have been eliminated (it is thought) from Britain since 1989, but caused damage, mostly to sugar beet, but also to reed and the floodbanks of rivers, for several decades after their escape in the 1930s from fur farms. In their native South America, numbers are easily controlled by predators like alligators, garfish, turtles and large snakes; in Britain cold winters were followed by reduced populations. (Petar Milosevic)

escaped from fur farms in the 1930s, when fur was a desirable fashion, and it established in southern England, particularly in East Anglia. The damage it caused was primarily to sugar beet but it burrowed in the floodbanks of engineered rivers thus bringing on its head a concerted but prolonged campaign of control, finally concluded in 1989 with the payment of large bounties to the group of trappers paid to catch and shoot the animals. Mink remain common and are widely believed to compete for fish and crayfish with the native otters, especially as these declined greatly in the twentieth century. However, the competition seems to be minimal and the otter decline much more related to poisoning by pesticides accumulated in fish. Mink have a penchant for chickens and water voles, but so far have evaded attempts to remove them.

Exotic plants (Table 18) are usually escapees from gardens and they entered Britain and Ireland through the horticultural trade. Early introductions such as the Canadian pondweed became prolific in the canal system but, with the genetic

TABLE 18. The more important introduced species of plants found in British and Irish standing waters.

Scientific name	Common name	How introduced?	Native to:	Comments	First 'wild' record	Date of introduction
Chara braunii	Braun's stonewort	One of numerous aliens in the Reddish canal, their origin uncertain	Cosmopolitan distribution, including Europe	Occurred in water warmed by cotton-mill effluent. Last seen in 1955; not present in 1961, 18 months after mills closed	Reddish canal, Stockport	1800
Riccia rhenana	Pond crystalwort	Probably introduced with aquatic plants	Europe	Some populations may be casual	Royal Holloway College, Englefield Green	
Azolla filiculoides	Water fern	Introduced for horticulture	South America		Pinner, Middlesex	
Crassula helmsii	New Zealand pigmy weed	Introduced for horticulture	Australia, New Zealand		Greensted, Essex	1927
Egeria densa	Large-flowered waterweed	Introduced for horticulture	South America			
Elodea canadensis	Canadian pondweed	Original pathway unclear; spread via botanic gardens	North America			Ireland, 1836 Britain, 1842
Elodea nuttallii	Nuttall's waterweed	Introduced for horticulture	North America			1966
Hydrocotyle ranunculoides	Floating pennywort		North America			Britain,1990, Ireland, 2002
Impatiens glandulifera	Indian balsam	Introduced for horticulture	Himalaya		Kew Gardens	1839
Lagarosiphon major	Curly waterweed	Introduced for horticulture	South Africa		Arlesley, Bedfordshire	
Lemna minuta	Least duckweed	Perhaps introduced with aquatic plants?	North America, S America		Cambridge	
Lysichiton americanus	American skunk-cabbage	Introduced for horticulture	Western North America		Wisley	1901
Mimulus guttatus & hybrids with M. cupreus and M. luteus	Monkeyflower	Introduced for horticulture	Western North America			1812

Species	Common name	Introduction	Origin	Status	Location	Date
Mimulus luteus	Blood-drop-emlets	Introduced for horticulture	Chile		Lingfield, Surrey	1826
Myriophyllum aquaticum	Parrot's-feather	Introduced for horticulture	South America			1878
Potamogeton epihydrus	American pondweed		North America, confined in Europe as a native to Scotland	Native in Scotland but not England	Salterhebble Bridge, Yorkshire	1850
Sagittaria latifolia	Duck-potato	Introduced for horticulture	North America, South America		Epsom Common	1818
Salix alba & hybrids	White willow	Introduced as useful tree	Europe, Asia			Early
Salix fragilis	Crack-willow	Introduced as useful tree	Europe, Asia			Early
Salix triandra & hybrids	Almond willow	Introduced as useful tree	Europe, Asia			Early
Salix viminalis	Osier	Introduced as useful tree	Europe, Asia			Early
Salix acutifolia	Siberian violet-willow	Introduced for horticulture	Europe			1798
Salix daphnoides	European violet-willow	Introduced for horticulture	Europe			1829
Salix elaeagnos	Olive willow	Introduced for horticulture	Europe		Ambleside	1820
Salix eriocephala	Heart-leaved willow	Introduced for horticulture	North America			1812
Salix udensis	Sachalin willow	Introduced for horticulture	Eastern Asia			1920
Aponogeton distachyos	Cape-pondweed	Introduced for horticulture	South Africa			1788
Cabomba caroliniana	Carolina water-shield	Introduced for horticulture	Eastern North America			
Calla palustris	Bog arum	Introduced for horticulture	Europe, Asia, North America			1738
Sagittaria rigida	Canadian arrowhead	Introduced for horticulture	Eastern North America		River Exe	1806
Sagittaria subulata	Narrow-leaved arrowhead	Introduced for horticulture	Eastern North America		Shortheath Pond	
Sarracenia purpurea	Pitcher plant		Eastern North America	Well-naturalised in Ireland		1640
Vaccinium macrocarpon	American cranberry		Eastern North America			1760
Vallisneria spiralis	Tapegrass	Introduced for horticulture	Europe, Africa		Northwick, London	1818

changes and selection that are features of all organisms, have settled to be more or less welcome. This may eventually be the case for the four introduced species of water plant listed above and currently feared for their abilities to overcome eutrophicated ponds and over-enriched lowland rivers. A solution to the eutrophication problem would mean that most problems with introduced plants would disappear.

The appearance of a new species, often increasing in numbers locally, so that it becomes noticed, is often greeted with a degree of hysteria by naturalists and government agencies, but it is the more cryptic introductions of disease organisms that are probably most significant. Most introduced free-living species have been assimilated with no lasting damage. They may displace some native species, sometimes ones regarded with affection, and introduction should be discouraged where possible, for its effects are unpredictable. But movement of species, introduction and extinction are all normal processes that cope with changing environments. Hysteria is inappropriate. As our climate continues to warm we will need to contemplate new species to replace native ones that may not survive in the warmer waters. Although there is a general belief that introductions are now more frequent because of increased trade and travel, what matters is not just introduction but also successful establishment. Where we know the dates of introduction (Tables 16–18), 16 species were introduced before 1800, 34 in the nineteenth century and 40 in the twentieth. A prediction based on introductions since 2000 might be for around 30 in the twenty-first century. A general rule of thumb is that about 10 per cent (more for animals, fewer for plants) of invaders become established and only 10 per cent of these become invasive and real problems. It would seem that the situation is not entirely out of control.

Nonetheless it is wise to minimise the risk of new introductions, for the 1 per cent that become invasive may be very damaging. The Wildlife and Countryside Act of 1981 makes it an offence to release non-native animals to the wild without a licence, or to allow their escape from captivity, and specifically prohibits any release of certain organisms. However, these are generally species already present in the wild, though three floating aquatic plant species, water hyacinth, water lettuce and water fern (*Salvinia* spp.) that are commonly stocked in gardens, but die over winter (they are tropical species), might become problems if, with a warming climate, they survive milder winters. The only regulations that cover imports for the pet and garden trade are concerned with disease introduction and 55,000 existing garden plant species testify to the ease with which aliens may be introduced. Animal import regulations are mostly concerned with protecting endangered species by banning their import. The

Salmon and Freshwater Fisheries Act of 1975 makes it an offence to introduce even native fish to outside their normal range within the UK and makes provision for screening for disease of fish to be transferred, but its provisions are widely ignored by anglers. As a result fish used as live bait have appeared in Lake Windermere (roach) and in Loch Lomond, where the escaped ruffe eat the eggs of the rare powan.

Once a species has been introduced it becomes increasingly difficult to remove it. Obliteration is generally possible if it is present in only one or a very few localities but once it spreads more widely the efforts of conservation organisations and government agencies become futile. All organisms have built-in strategies for promulgation of their genes and in general they are cleverer than any of our control strategies. Once an organism has spread it can only be partly controlled and this may be expensive. The current annual costs of controlling invasive freshwater species in Great Britain are estimated as £26.5 million, largely for Canadian pondweed and zebra mussel, but would be doubled if these species were controlled in all their locations.[22] Even so this cost is not high compared with the costs of controlling acidification and eutrophication.

The approach to limiting spread of invertebrates is to minimise transfers on boats and fishing tackle by asking anglers and yachtsmen to disinfect their equipment, but floods and water birds will frustrate these efforts. For amphibians there is no general approach but none of the introduced species cause major problems anyway. For fish, treating a lake with rotenone may work but kills other species at the same time. Netting or electrofishing will always leave survivors to repopulate. Birds can be shot, but are adept at evading guns, or their eggs can be pricked, which works locally to reduce populations of Canada geese, but has not prevented their spread. In the end, as has been the case in our dealings with the Romans, the Saxons, the Vikings and the Normans, we have no choice but to learn to love the invader!

RESERVOIRS

Acidification, eutrophication and invasion are the three most prominent problems that people have caused for lakes, but do not exhaust the possibilities. Creation of lakes and manipulation of existing ones for water storage generally brings opposition, even outrage, and it was the modification of Thirlmere in the Cumbrian Lake District that catalysed the environmental movement in Britain, indeed the world.[23] From the point of view of the Manchester Corporation's Waterworks Committee in the 1870s, the matter was straightforward. Manchester was a booming city, rich from the processing of cotton and other manufactured goods, and expanding its population of factory workers. Its rivers, the Medlock, Irwell and Irk, were in a bad state and Friedrich Engels had described the confluence of the rivers as so polluted with waste dye that it looked like a dye vat itself. Raw sewage poured into them. The private Manchester and Salford Waterworks Company was managing to supply only a quarter of the city with this water, which it had treated only by storage to settle out the grosser solids. It charged high rates, and some people were supplied with rainwater collected in lead cisterns. There was a devastating cholera epidemic in the slums in 1832. Manchester needed clean water and a lot of it.

Other cities were facing similar problems, and the Reform Act of 1832 and the Municipal Corporations Act in 1835 gave the cities greater influence and elected councils, with a mayor and aldermen as well as councillors. With a bumptious, efficient and dictatorial young Town Clerk, Joseph, later Sir Joseph, Heron, Manchester set about getting its water supplies on a better footing. Heron engaged Frederick LaTrobe Bateman as engineer, bought out the water company and set about establishing a series of dams on the River Etherow in Longendale, 12 miles to the east. Bateman calculated that about 20 gallons per person were needed per day and Longendale could provide that. Establishing the reservoirs was not without problems because local mills needed the river water to drive their wheels, and the rock, in which the dams were set proved less strong than envisaged, so it took from 1846 to 1877 to complete the scheme, which had a noticeable influence in Manchester. Buildings could be built taller because the fire brigade could rely on better supplies and, moreover, the water running off the Pennine Moors needed no treatment. But the city was growing, and Bateman warned that the supply would not be enough.

Meanwhile, in 1859, he had established a water supply for Glasgow from Loch Katrine with very little controversy, for no damming was needed and civic confidence in the possibilities of large engineering schemes was growing. A drought in 1868 underlined the urgency of a bigger scheme for Manchester and, in 1876, Alderman John Grave, chairman of the Waterworks Committee, sent out surveyors to explore the possibilities in the Lake District, an area he knew well for he had been born and brought up in Cockermouth. The Committee had it in mind to buy a whole catchment as well as the lake and did not want land prices to be speculatively raised, so the surveying was covert. The small and indented, but deep lake, also called Leathes Water, Brackmere and Wythburn Water, for its basins were nearly separated, in the Thirlmere valley, was ideal (Fig. 155). A narrow gorge at the north end could be easily dammed to raise the water level by 50 feet; the valley was remote, though the road from Windermere to Keswick passed it;

FIG 155. Thirlmere as it was, on a postcard produced before it was dammed, and as it is now.

there were few people living in it; and the terrain was craggy and would produce little sediment to fill the reservoir over time. Possibilities at Ullswater and Haweswater (both later used as supplies by Manchester) were discarded because of the costs of tunnelling to bring the water to Manchester, and a proposal to share the costs and water with Liverpool fell through. (Liverpool was to build a dam to create Lake Vrnwy in mid-Wales in the 1880s.) But it is not possible to snoop secretly around a rural area with instruments and maps; the surveyors' cover was soon blown and the problems began.

Longendale and the Lake District were two very different areas. The grandeur of the latter's landscape was already celebrated. Daniel Defoe's verdict of the area being '*eminent only for being the wildest, most barren and frightful of any I have passed over in England, or even in Wales itself*' was being replaced by a romantic joy in the ruggedness. Grasmere, Wordsworth's home, was only a few miles to the south of Thirlmere and with his sister, wife-to-be and Coleridge, he had carved their initials on a rock by the condemned lake. Opposition to Manchester's plans, once they were made fully public in 1877, was unexpected and came from many sides, not least articulate middle-class aesthetes and intellectuals with formidable reputations.

John Ruskin, the artist and philosopher, Octavia Hill, the social reformer, Robert Hunter, founder, back in 1865, of the Open Spaces Society, the geologist, Thomas Carlyle, James Clifton Ward, a distinguished literary editor, and the cleric, H.D. Rawnsley, later, with Octavia Hill, to be a founder of the National Trust, headed an army of headmasters, bishops, architects and painters, all keen on walking the fells and enjoying landscapes that they believed to be entirely natural. Support came from the quality newspapers, the *Yorkshire Post* and the *Leeds Intelligencer, The Field* and the *Medical Press and Circular* (but not the then *Manchester Guardian*, of course). There were satirical poems in *Punch* magazine and even a play written in defence of keeping the landscape as it was. Ruskin's writings went severely over the top as he talked of Manchester draining the little lake of Thirlmere into its water closets, and plotting to steal the clouds of Helvellyn. The Thirlmere Defence Association was no pushover so the Manchester Corporation, its heavy-booted businessmen pounding the table, ridiculed the opposition at every step, calling it a pantomime, with the cant of aestheticism.

Meanwhile the relatively few landowners, not yet faced with the compulsory purchase orders that the Manchester Corporation Water Bill, due to be read in Parliament in 1878, would allow, were wilily pushing up the prices. The Countess Ossalinsky (originating from a local family called Jackson, who had acquired her title from a short and early marriage with a Polish nobleman), was offered £28,000 for her 714 acres at Armboth, on the west side of Thirlmere, and held out for an eventual £70,000. But buying the land was not the major problem for Manchester; the influence of the Thirlmere Defence Association was. When the Corporation Water Bill was introduced in Parliament in 1878, local Cumbrian MPs strongly opposed it, and opposition came also from towns and villages along the proposed pipeline to Manchester, who feared that Manchester was appropriating water to which they too had a claim. Victorian farming was eutrophicating their local water supplies with its fertilisers.

Parliament set up a special commission to examine the Bill and the arguments were played out in a formal legal setting with the Goliath of Manchester Corporation opposed by the David of the Defence Association (Fig. 156). Goliath argued the crucial need for the water, that the raised level would make the lake more impressive and enhance the view, and that a new road around the lake perimeter would improve access. Pugnacious lawyer Edmund Beckett, for the Corporation, referred to the Defence Association as 'the picturesque people', whose views were 'rather communistic'.

The Commission met for over a month and produced its report a month later. It found for the Manchester Corporation, of course; the city needed the water and alternatives were not so suitable; it believed the valley would not be despoiled. Manchester had to make provision to provide water to towns along the pipeline and to plant trees to improve the landscape. Although the Thirlmere Defence Association lost the battle, it had introduced a novel argument based on a moral and national ownership of landscapes and views, as opposed to the more concrete local ownership of land and property. The former was eventually to be ensconced in the formation of the National Trust, almost a direct descendant of the Thirlmere Defence Association, in 1895, and in the creation of the National Parks, by an Act in 1949. Thirlmere spawned the modern environmental movement.

FIG 156. Personalities in the Thirlmere debate. The supporters of Goliath (upper row, l. to r.):
Edmund Beckett QC, Sir Joseph Heron and Frederick Lake Trobe Bateman, the design engineer.
Supporters of David (lower row, l. to r.), Canon H. D. Rawlinson, Octavia Hill and John Ruskin.

The Thirlmere scheme was not built for several years following passage of
the Bill in 1879 because some years of high rainfall meant that existing supplies
were just sufficient, whilst the cash needed was less plentiful. It was eventually
begun in 1885 and completed in 1893 with civic pomp, a carriage procession from
Windermere railway station to the dam site, and banquets both at Thirlmere
and, the next day, in the monumental Manchester Town Hall. H. D. Rawnsley
had reconciled himself to the scheme and, being a cleric, prayed at the opening
ceremony that '*this river of God flow through the far off city to cleanse and purify*' and
composed four sonnets for the occasion.

The Waterworks Committee was now the landowner of over 11,000 hectares
of the Lake District and proved to be restrictive and dictatorial. It would
not tolerate angling on grounds of maintaining purity of the water and had
removed all sheep from the uplands surrounding the lake. It felled much
existing woodland, especially on the western shore, and replaced it with conifer

plantations of lodgepole pine, sitka spruce and European larch, and attempted to restrict access (illegally) by placing prohibition notices on the shore and elsewhere. The scheme has remained controversial to this day, with complaints about the conifer plantations obstructing the view, about the ugliness of the bare shoreline when the reservoir is drawn down (Fig. 157) and about links between its management and the risks of flooding downstream in Keswick. Its ownership has changed hands since the Water Act of 1973 created the Water Authorities and then the Act of 1979, which privatised them. The North West Water Authority was successfully sued for its forestry policy violating the 1879 Act, which provided that *'all reasonable regard shall be had to the preservation … of the beauty of the scenery'*, but much conifer forest remains.

Thirlmere was the first very large scheme in which water was transported long distances to provide for the cities, but not the last. Manchester promoted the use of Haweswater in 1919, with some, but more muted opposition. There was no road along the lake so it was known mostly to ramblers and was not associated with the lake poets. A village, Mardale Green, was flooded, and an access road was built, seen by the Manchester Corporation as an asset. H. H. Symonds, a local commentator, called it *'a real disaster, an engineer's vulgarism … sheer wickedness, an otiose parade ground for those who sit in cars and wax fat'*. Haweswater did not come on stream until 1941 because of the economic situation during the 1930s depression. In 1961, Manchester wished to take water from Ullswater, but there was severe opposition. Water is now taken from Ullswater, and also from Windermere, but using underground pumps and with no provision for the catchment control granted for Thirlmere. Water treatment works have been built and the Thirlmere water, mixed in the pipelines, is also treated, so that the restrictions around Thirlmere have been relaxed.

Elsewhere, Birmingham dammed the rivers of mid-Wales in the Elan and Claerwyn valleys to form five reservoirs between 1892 and 1952, and Sheffield, the River Derwent and its tributaries, in the Peak District, between 1914 and 1931. There are now over 1,000 substantial artificial reservoirs in Britain and Ireland, some of them, such as those supplying London in the Thames Valley, more or less concrete bowls held behind raised embankments, but most having been created by damming on land formerly cherished by someone or other.

There has always been controversy, for farms, churches, graveyards and villages have been flooded, but the provision of more and more water is always the trumping argument. Much of it is wasted in leaky water mains, oversized lavatory cisterns, power showers and in evaporation from those peculiar British prides in immaculate green lawns and well-washed cars. The 20 gallons per person per day of Bateman's estimate has now about trebled to 66 m³ per year

FIG 157. Reservoir edges are never pretty; the bare zone is caused by unpredictably fluctuating water levels.

and industrial, farming and corporate uses boost this to about 315 m³ per person. When the water use needed for production of food, particularly meat, produced outside the UK but imported for consumption, is added, the figure becomes 1,285 m³ per person per year, just short of the global average of 1,385. Ireland uses slightly more with 1,301 m³ but, compared with the USA's usage of 2,842, the requirements of Britain and Ireland seem only moderately excessive.

It is no wonder that there are serious concerns about future water supplies, with worries that international tensions will be worsened where rivers flow between countries that compete for the water. Water supplies are of course essential and some reservoir building is unavoidable. But when I stand by a reservoir, no matter how amenable the water companies now are to provision of recreation, no matter how well landscaped the dam and how attractive the leaflets explaining the wondrous engineering of the scheme, there is always a completely different feeling from that I experience by a natural lake. Reservoirs are about control, and in a society whose citizens are increasingly managed and scrutinised, even spied upon in the alleged interests of health and security, my feelings are solidly with the Thirlmere Defence Association.

PONDS

Creation of new lakes takes on a more positive aspect if ponds are included. Enormous numbers were dug for a variety of needs over the past few centuries, but there has been a major loss as agriculture has intensified. Mixed farms with small fields, each with its cattle pond, have been converted to entirely arable deserts, with hedges removed and ponds filled in so as not to impede the movements of large machines. Widely distributed rural industries requiring small pond water supplies have been lost or consolidated in industrial estates.

Ponds were made not only to water stock in the fields but on the droveways along which cattle were taken to market; they were formed for the cultivation of watercress, and to hold fish or ducks for the pot. A few were fashioned as decoys where ducks could be caught in long netted corridors, radiating out from the centre, and into which they were lured using small dogs. Some were used for refilling the boilers of steam engines, for dyeing, for providing for the needs of the village blacksmith or for the cooling pipes of alcohol stills. Others were for the retting of flax, for providing ice to be stored in deep ice houses on wealthy estates, for the driving of mill wheels, as moats around fortified houses, for swimming, or as ornaments to gardens. Some ponds are natural, others were deliberately dug. Overall we have only a hazy idea of how many ponds there were and how many remain, for ponds do not always show up even on the largest scale Ordnance Survey maps, but there may formerly have been up to 2 million in Britain and Ireland, at least 80 per cent of which have been lost since the Second World War. Rates of loss may still be a few per cent per year in some areas.[24]

Gravel extraction in the lowland river valleys is creating new ponds as the workings are abandoned and there is a strong movement headed by a charity, Pondlife, eventually to create a million more. The new motivation is not utility but conservation, for ponds collectively have a high diversity of plants and animals and are particularly valuable for amphibians (especially the common frog and the three species of native newt) because they often lack fish, which eat the tadpoles. Of around 4,000 freshwater macroinvertebrates in Britain and Ireland, 60–70 per cent can be found in ponds. Red Data books, a concept created by Peter Scott in 1963 as a way of cataloguing rare and threatened species in different categories of risk, list two thirds of 300 such British and Irish invertebrates as found in ponds, though they may occur in larger lakes and rivers too.[25] Some, especially those that are particularly vulnerable to fish predation and which require a period of drying out to compete with others, such as the tadpole shrimp, are confined to temporary ponds.

Creation of ponds is popular, especially in gardens! There are sensible places to make them (where the water table is close to the surface and where they will fill naturally and maintain their water level) and foolish (at the tops of dry hills or on freely draining soil where artificial liners or membranes are needed). Liners crack and membranes can be punctured and such ponds dry out too frequently for lack of rain. It is sensible to create ponds in groups, providing a variety of depths and sizes, and best to create them in semi-natural terrain, well away from ditches bearing the drainage of farm yards and stock units, streets and motorways. A single pond in the middle of a wheat field, were the agribusinessman to tolerate it, or in a building development, surrounded by manicured and fertilised lawns, has little value or diversity. Wetland or wet pastures around a group of ponds allow movement of amphibians and amphibious insects like water striders.

Conservation groups often meddle with ponds, by cutting surrounding trees, dredging and deepening them, introducing frog spawn (and sometimes diseases of amphibians) and planting irises and other colourful flowers, especially water lilies, which may not even be native. By and large, natural processes can be relied upon to do the jobs of colonisation and establishment of a persistent community far more effectively. A pond, once created, is usually best left well alone. There are also issues about shape and size. Artificial ponds often fail to blend with the landscape because they are either too square or too curvy. They may have banks, cut by a mechanical digger, too precipitous for young ducks or amphibians to negotiate; they may have odd-looking artificial islands that erode in the wind because someone was too keen on creating bird roosting or nesting areas, and they may be over-zealously provided with absolutely every feature that their creator has read of in a manual. As in many things, the best approach is that which fits the local circumstances, melds into the background and celebrates the pond habitat, not the ego of a conservation organisation.

There are many common myths about pond management. These include: *the bigger the better* (very small ponds, however, may harbour the more unusual of crustaceans, able to compete with the more robust ones because they can survive drying out); *ponds should not be shaded by trees* (but trees provide fallen leaves, which are important sources of energy for some invertebrates); *ponds need to be dredged to keep them from being choked by vegetation* (plants provide habitat and 'choking' is a human concept not unlinked with the urge to control things that characterises the more demonic of gardeners); *ponds must have oxygenating plants* (not necessarily; plants produce oxygen by day but consume more or less just as much by night or even on dull days; oxygenation is largely provided by diffusion from the atmosphere, helped by wind); *new ponds need to be planted because natural colonisation is slow* (but it is really quite fast and the advantage of leaving it to

FIG 158. Adder's tongue spearwort growing around a pond at Badgeworth in Gloucestershire, one of its two localities in Britain and Ireland.

natural processes is that what manages to colonise will generally persist; what is planted in may often die); *water level fluctuations should be minimised* (no they shouldn't; changes in level open up niches for small plants in the exposed mud, and water level changes are normal features of lakes, to which organisms are well adapted); *livestock should be denied access* (it depends on how heavy the trampling is; sometimes plants depend on the bare mud created by poaching of the edges for seed germination. One of only two British sites for adder's tongue spearwort (Fig. 158) at Badgeworth in Gloucestershire was almost lost when cattle were excluded, ostensibly to protect the plant); *there should be an inflow to prevent them becoming stagnant* (some ponds are rain fed, others groundwater fed and still water is not necessarily bad; what is usually meant by stagnant is not stillness but extreme pollution from farm yards and silage heaps; having an inflow from these makes the problem worse); *ponds are self-contained islands in a sea of dry land* (but absolutely, like all lakes, they are not!).

All that is not to say that occasional management is not useful. Diversity will be increased by dredging a pond completely silted up, or by tree cutting from a pond so overhung that it is densely shaded. It is to say that continual meddling is to be discouraged and that some specialist organisms need silted up and shaded ponds and that over-zealous management will obliterate these conditions.

The key to having diverse and attractive ponds is not to fuss but to ensure that nutrient pollution from the surrounding land is minimised, that there are other ponds in the vicinity for colonists to arrive from, and that there is variety in the surrounding land (trees, varied topography and as much wet habitat as possible) – basically the same principles for maintenance of any freshwater system of high conservation value. Ironically, the best places for creation of new ponds are on river floodplains, with contact of some ponds through flooding with the river, and isolation of others to keep fish out. Such creation is discouraged or banned by the national environment agencies in Britain and Ireland. Attitudes may be changing with extreme flooding, but hitherto such organisations have preferred control of the river between high banks and a dry agricultural plain beyond the banks. They are also somewhat fussy (and in this case rightly so) about creating dams on streams for pond formation. Dams are dangerous things. They may breach and cause damage as the water runs out and they interfere with fish movements. There is much legislation concerning their establishment, and specific licences are needed. Much easier is the creation of new water space from mineral, particularly gravel workings.

GRAVEL PITS

Government policy is that the construction industry should be allowed an adequate and steady supply of gravel and sand, and there are extensive deposits, as a legacy partly of the glaciation, in the now drained river floodplains of the

FIG 159. A series of lakes was created by the Wildfowl and Wetlands Trust from four redundant concrete reservoirs to form the London Wetland Centre. Cattle are used to prevent bush colonisation and to maintain surrounding grassland for geese and other birds. The fringing flowers are purple loosestrife, native to Britain and Ireland but a much disliked exotic pest in North America. (Mo Hassan)

Midlands, southern and eastern England.[26] Creation of new lakes in worked-out gravel pits represents a benefit though does not entirely reinstate the wetland values that the former floodplains provided. About 100 million tonnes per year of gravel and sand are extracted, and 1,500 ha of worked-out excavations become available each year, 500 ha of which are refloodable. Overall about 60,000 ha of exhausted workings exist, a quarter of them bearing water. Moreover, the Town and Country Planning Act 1971, amended 1990, requires restoration, within five years, of abandoned workings to agriculture, forestry, amenity, or conservation. The costs of restoration, mainly for landscaping, are around only 1–7 per cent of the value of minerals extracted and the reflooded workings have considerable wildlife value. More than 20 per cent of the breeding and wintering populations of several duck species are found on gravel pits.

Another example of restoration of an industrial site to a diverse wetland with small lakes and ditches has been the creation of the London Wetland Centre (Fig. 159) on the site of four redundant concrete reservoirs at Barn Elms in London between 1995 and 1997. The site occupies 40 hectares, is a Site of Special Scientific Interest for its birds, and is remarkable in that the planning permission for the site required that no new material be brought in, nor existing material taken out. It is a site formed on the rewetting of crushed concrete and underlying river deposits and lake sediments.

FISHERIES AND ANGLING

Improved transport has killed most of the market for freshwater lake fish in Britain and Ireland. Roach, bream, pike and perch fed both rich and poor until the nineteenth century, but sea fish taste better and became cheap when they could be quickly brought inland. The rivers and estuaries have dominated commercial fisheries for salmon, and riverside farms those for trout, though usually the introduced rainbow trout rather than the native brown and sea trout. The only real lake fisheries have been for pollan and eels in Lough Neagh, and charr in a few scattered lakes, including Windermere, but apart from Lough Neagh, there are no significant commercial fisheries left.

The Lough Neagh fishery is mainly for eels, though the local co-operative of fishermen, ably organised until his recent death by a local priest, Fr Oliver Kennedy, also has rights to catch pollan, but does not extensively use them. The eel fishery has been declining since the 1970s, as older fishermen retired and were not replaced by younger ones, but mostly because of a general decline in European eels, the main reasons for which are not yet known. The Lough Neagh eel fishery has had to be stocked in some years with fish from the River Severn, but is well run, with about 300 fishermen, closed seasons, restrictions on gear and boat sizes, patrols to enforce the rules, licensed dealers and the statutory 40 per cent of young eels allowed to escape the lake to travel to the Sargasso Sea to breed.

Few of the eels caught, from what is the largest wild fishery in the EU, are eaten in Ireland. Legend has it that when St Patrick allegedly banished snakes from Ireland some took to the waters and became eels and that seems to have put the Irish off. However, the eels are prized elsewhere and there is an export market of some 400 tonnes per year (down from over 1,000 in the 1970s), of fish averaging about 16 years of age. Young eels (silver eels) are distinguished from older ones (yellow eels) and are caught at weirs on the outflow rivers as they move to the sea. Pollan was taken much more in the early years of the last century (up to 400 tonnes per year) but the stock is declining and only a few tonnes per year are taken at present, though the fish is the second most abundant (after roach) in the lake and more abundant than eels, though much smaller in total mass.

Where recreational fishing is concerned, however, the importance of freshwater fish is very different. In England and Wales, of the 44 million people over 12 years old, 20 per cent (8.8 million) had been freshwater fishing in the last 10 years (though not me; I have never taken to it); and 6 per cent (2.6 million) in the last year, according to a 2005 survey.[27] Despite animal welfare concerns about the damage done by hooks and the stress to a fish of being caught, 71 per cent of the population agreed with the statement that 'Angling is an acceptable pastime', though there is concern about the damage anglers may do to banks, and in discarding broken line and tackle, which may injure water birds. 'A Survey of Angling Rod Licence Holders' in 2001 showed that 86 per cent of anglers in England and Wales go coarse fishing for species such as carp, roach, tench, bream and chub, which makes coarse angling the most popular form of fishing.

Coarse anglers prefer to fish on lakes, and carp, and then roach and perch, are caught most often. Bream, chub, barbel, tench and pike are less popular. Coarse-fish anglers can then be divided into people who fish for pleasure, match (competition) anglers, and specialist groups of specimen hunters. Each type of angling has particular requirements from its fishing waters and differing philosophies regarding their management. In contrast, game angling for salmonid fish, particularly trout, but also salmon and grayling, is less popular and more riverine-based. Nonetheless, still water game fishing goes on in upland salmon and trout lochs, there are natural lake fisheries for brown trout and charr, and artificially stocked (put-and-take) fisheries in reservoirs and gravel pits, largely for rainbow and brown trout. Around £3 billion are spent on freshwater angling each year in the UK and 20,000 people are variously employed.

Stocking by angling clubs is common but needs a licence, so that the fish can be checked for disease and appropriateness, but much illegal transfer is thought to go on and there is legislation banning certain fishing methods (guns, spears, explosives) and licensing others (electrical techniques) though the less nefarious anglers generally confine themselves to rods and lines. The Salmon and Freshwater Fisheries Act (1975) allows the passing of byelaws specific to particular areas, which cover mainly statutory close seasons, catch returns for migratory salmonids, closed areas for angling, size limits on fish that can be removed and use of split lead shot (which can be poisonous to birds ingesting it) and other weights.

Stocking is generally pointless except to replace fish that have been killed by a pollution incident. It will only temporarily increase the availability of fish in other circumstances, though sometimes very large carp are stocked for the pleasures of their repeatedly being caught. This is an interesting peculiarity of some anglers and large carp change hands for many thousands of pounds each. As with ponds created by conservation organisations, ponds created for still water fisheries by angling clubs or commercial operators are often managed in undesirable ways. Heavy stocking leads to fish kills often caused by disease.[28] Trees, local shade, woody debris and a variety of aquatic plants will all contribute to better fish growth and variety but are often removed in the interests of tidiness and avoiding snags for tackle.

ECOSYSTEM GOODS AND SERVICES

In 2011, a heavy book, in more ways than one, the UK National Ecosystem Assessment, was published. You can get it free online.[29] It was written by around 200 people and assessed the state of the nation's habitats. By and large it found them in a rather bad and worsening state, though that was not news to professional ecologists. It also tried to assess the remaining value of these habitats to the national economy. The value was high, again not particularly novel to ecologists but possibly so to the rest of the nation. It was the start of 'official' interest in a new way of looking at the links between man and nature by turning ecology into a branch of economics.

Currently all of Britain and Ireland, and about 70 per cent of the world's continents, is covered by anthromes (human-determined landscapes, largely crops or grazed land), leaving only about 30 per cent, most of it tundra and boreal forest, and some tropical forest, as relatively untouched natural biome. In 2005 there was a major study, the Millennium Ecosystem Assessment, of the state of the world's biomes, which developed the concept of ecosystem goods and services, which were

FIGS 160 & 161. Provisioning services (left) provided by lakes include water itself but also an eclectic collection of lake and wetland plants as well as fish. Rushes are used for chair seats, osiers for basketwork and willow for cricket bats. Aspirin originated from willows, medicinal leeches are still used to prevent clotting during microsurgery – for example, to reattach severed fingers – and mint has uses in cooking. Photograph from Purseglove (1988). Cultural services (above) are here represented by the opening of the salmon fishing season on the River Tay in Scotland in 1961. A bottle of whisky was broken over the bow of a boat whilst a piper played a traditional air. (*The Times* archives)

provided to the human community by natural biomes, and by anthromes through their semi-natural components. It recognised regulating services, provisioning services (Fig. 160) and cultural services (Fig. 161). The general idea was that ecosystems contribute to the human economy by providing these services and

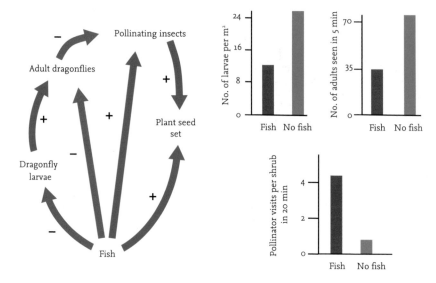

FIG 162. The presence or absence of fish can determine the pollination of lakeside plants through changes in predation on dragonflies, which feed on bees and other pollinating insects. Based on Knight *et al.*, 2005.

that therefore the services could be given cash values and properly taken account of in policy and planning decisions. The ways that the chief economist to the UK treasury sees ecosystems supporting human societies are in making a contribution to good physical and mental health, for example, through access to green spaces, both urban and rural, and genetic resources for medicines; in natural processes, such as climate regulation and crop pollination; through providing raw materials for industry and agriculture or through tourism and recreation; and in giving social, cultural and educational benefits, and wellbeing and inspiration from interaction with nature.[30]

For example, lakes supply economic benefits from swimming, sailing, canoeing, rowing and water skiing, through the infrastructure of sales of equipment, boat buying and hiring, accommodation and catering, that would not exist were it not for the availability of the lake. Then there might be biochemicals contained in lake plants or algae that could be developed as medicines. Carbon uptake and storage in the lake sediments contribute to climate regulation (see Chapter 10) and, somewhat bizarrely, lakes might contribute to the pollination of food crops. A study of ponds with and without fish (Fig. 162) showed that fish

FIG 163. Malham Tarn Field Centre is one of several, situated by lakes, which provide much needed field education in freshwaters, to generations increasingly disconnected from the natural world.

reduced the number of dragonfly larvae, thence of adult dragonflies. The reduced predation of bees by dragonflies then allowed a greater intensity of pollination of flowers by the waterside.[31]

In terms of raw materials, lakes can store and supply water for drinking, for crop irrigation and for industrial processes; and lakes supply fish as food, or for anglers. The very existence of the lake might be regarded as a raw material because a view of it increases mightily the value of land on which houses are built. Tourism and recreational benefits might be reflected in holidays and boat trips and the transport costs to reach the lake, and in the rows of small shops selling the luxury goods tourists are more prone to buy in the relaxed circumstances of a lakeside holiday. The towns of Bowness, Windermere and Keswick in the Cumbrian Lake District testify richly to this.

Pond dipping for 'minibeasts' is a popular educational activity, and school trips to lakes for either their interesting animals or glacially derived scenery bring in money. Several residential or day field centres for ecology and geography courses run by the Field Studies Council and other bodies, are sited by lakes, notably at Blencathra, Malham (Fig. 163) and Slapton. The Royal Geographical Society lists 125 such centres in the UK, and four in Ireland, 22 of them specifically concerned with freshwater. Finally, the social and cultural benefits include the money spent on a quiet walking holiday in a lake district, and the inspiration provided by a lake landscape for writers and painters (and thence the sales of their work).

Many of these benefits can be costed by increasingly arcane methods developed by economists. The values given are not constant, but depend on demand and everything else that determines market prices, which vary greatly from place to place and time to time, so you will find no simple table of prices here. Provisioning services are easiest to cost and must take account of how the good concerned might become pricier if it becomes scarcer. One lakeside building plot might be very valuable; the value of one of 1,000 in a housing estate overlooking a lake will be much less. Water for the domestic supply is virtually worthless, dipped in a bucket at the lakeside, but carried a 100 miles to Manchester in an expensive pipeline, filtered, disinfected and relieved of any tastes and odours caused by its original phytoplankton, it might sell for quite a lot. The value of a lake for sailing or cultural reflection might be quite low if the peace is disturbed by the noise of water skiing and greatly increased if skiing is banned. Alternatively, if a lake is the only one in 100 miles where water skiing is allowed, it will produce very large revenues from this activity. Values can be reduced if water quality declines and vice versa. Table 15 gives a good example of how eutrophication can increase costs and reduce values. Recreational values are more difficult to obtain but one way is to ask people in a questionnaire survey how much they have spent in travelling to a lakeside holiday or to a fishing site and how much extra money they have spent in staying there compared with staying at home.

Cultural benefits are more nebulous to value and there is much more variation in the estimates, compared with those obtainable for provisioning. What is a view over Loch Lomond worth? People can be asked how much tax they would be prepared to pay per year to preserve it, or to guarantee clear water through removal of nutrients from the wastewater treatment works, but the numbers are largely plucked from the air. They will be higher if some threat is perceived, or the closer the lake is to home. They will be influenced if the person asked is feeling angry or tranquil, if they are well-off or have just lost their job, by their political preferences, age and interests. Ideally a questionnaire balances all these things by using a large and randomly chosen sample, but costs mean that a sample large enough to be truly representative is usually not possible. The same group of people asked on one day may give a completely different view if asked a few weeks later, when collectively circumstances have changed, due, for example, to announcement of the latest government propaganda on the state of the economy.

Regulatory services are even more difficult, indeed almost impossible, to value; they are mostly priceless and valuations have been described as underestimates of infinity. Consider the role of ecosystems in regulating the composition of the atmosphere (Chapter 3). To maintain equable conditions in the atmosphere, with low carbon dioxide concentrations associated with an equable climate (Chapter 10), around 13 billion tonnes of organic matter or calcium carbonate are stored every year in soils, peats, wood and the dead shells of marine creatures falling to the ocean floor, but to compensate for current fossil fuel burning this needs to be doubled to about 25 billion tonnes. A great deal more is circulated through photosynthesis and respiration. In comparison, only about 30 million tonnes of organic matter, on a world scale, need to be disposed of by sewage treatment, burning or in landfills. This is about one thousandth of what needs to be stored by ecosystems and already overwhelms our abilities to deal with it.

Had there been no storage of carbon in the past to provide the fossil fuels we now so wantonly burn, few of our current conveniences and comforts could have been provided. It is inconceivable that we could afford machines or processes that could replace this regulatory function for carbon provided by ecosystems. The same is true of pollination of crops, of the storage of water in soils, rivers, floodplains and lakes, and the clarification and improvement in water quality they provide (by removing heavy metals, pesticides and nitrates, for example, and reducing soil erosion), of mitigation of urban flooding by storage in floodplains, and of protection of coastlines by saltmarshes and mangrove swamps against storms.

The original idea of putting values on ecosystem services was good in principle; it offered a way of talking to those who exploit the environment on terms with which they were familiar, and preferred. But it has severe limitations and may only be useful in balancing provisioning services with any proposed ecosystem destruction. Environmental economists will be kept busy for a long time, but this approach is unlikely to stop the present overexploitation of our natural resources because the most important services are priceless. Pricelessness is a concept that economic theory is unable to deal with and so environmental damage will continue largely to be regarded as an externality and not factored into economic decisions. A vastly different approach is needed and will be discussed in Chapter 10 when we consider the future of lakes in their landscape setting.

CHAPTER 9

Moss's Tour: An Itinerary Among the Lakes of Britain and Ireland

TRAVEL HAS ALWAYS APPEALED: the lure of new surroundings, the grass being greener. Its literature is given much shelf-space in bookshops, and serves, for all of us, as some small substitute for where, for various reasons, we cannot go. But where we can go has widened with cheap air travel and an industry of tourism. Often though, travel has become stereotyped with our expectations of comfortable hotels, visitor centres, information boards and audio guides, and our armoury of digital cameras, sunscreen and easily washable trousers. Often we visit much but see little, in parallel with the slow and difficult travel of the past where journals, kept daily, illustrated difficulties of coaches stuck in mud, sundry brigands and the deficiencies of roadside inns, so missing the profounder detail that gives substance to a journey. We will overcome these drawbacks. We will simplify the logistics by using a magic carpet to tour the lakes of Britain and Ireland, or at least a selection of them that, as your guide, I have chosen to be an interesting sample.[1] A magic carpet overcomes the problems of railway and ferry timetables and limited time, but more importantly it allows us to hover and see a lake in its catchment and then float down to its edge, equipped mostly with our eyes.

Our precedent for such a journey is the International Phytogeographical excursion of July and August 1911: a tour, by railway and ferry, of the vegetation of Britain and Ireland that brought together up to 22 ecologists from the USA, mainland Europe, Britain and Ireland on a trip to increase their mutual understanding when plant ecology was just developing. Led by Arthur Tansley, it was recounted in some detail, including the times of some of the trains, in his new journal, the *New Phytologist* in 1912.[2] They began in Cambridge, and moved to the Norfolk Broads (mostly for the fens), but then largely ignored freshwaters

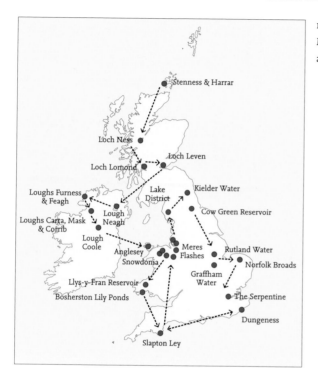

FIG 164. Itinerary for Moss's tour of the British and Irish lakes.

apart from viewing a drained lake bed in Silverdale for the sequence of peats from lake to fen to bog, and the aquatic plants of Cally and Butterstone Lochs, though there they were more preoccupied with the stump of what had been the oldest larch tree in Britain.

There followed a series of international excursions, the next in 1913 in the USA and a sequence following the First World War. Accounts of them invariably relegate the freshwater systems to minor mentions, so, with the decline of country railways, it is time to take to the magic carpet and have a good look at the lakes. We will start in the north with some of the Scottish lochs and end on the epitome of human modification of lakes, the Serpentine, in London's Hyde Park. Figure 164 maps our route.

ORKNEY

Orkney is a good place to start. The geological maps show it to be Devonian in origin, and its rocks are sandstones and flags, giving good soils for the most

FIG 165. Map of the Lochs of
Stenness and Harrar.

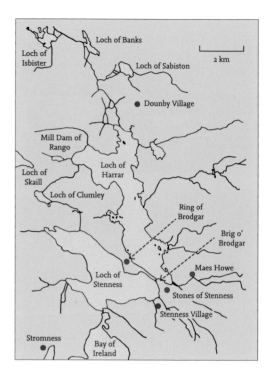

part in the catchments of its glacial lakes. The rocks were once the sediments of
the large Lake Orcadie, set, 370 million years ago, in dunes and deltas where fish
had evolved great diversity, and were about to produce the first land vertebrates.
The weather is grey and wet as we reach the Mainland of Orkney and the sea
foams on the shorelines. The drizzle parts to show the mountains on the island
of Hoy to the southwest and some of the smaller inhabited islands (around 22 of
a total of 72 in the group), where the fields are still small and clung to by crofts.

On Mainland, the largest and most populous island, the towns of Stromness
and Kirkwall stretch 16 miles apart on a road that skirts the south of the joined
lochs of Stenness and Harrar, totalling 1,780 ha in area.[3] The 12,600 ha catchment
of these lochs has large fields of heavily fertilised improved grassland, potatoes,
barley and turnips in a land whose natural wetness has been part-dried by the
straightened streams that run through it. It is a rolling land, with the sea very
close, hills to the northeast and lowlands that formerly bore rough grassland, bog
and moorland where now there is farmland. The Loch of Stenness (Fig. 165) is
connected through a narrow channel to the Bay of Ireland, part of the Scapa Flow,
the sheltered harbour where first the Viking longships landed to give Orkney its

distinctively Scandinavian feel, and where the warships and convoys collected during the World Wars of the twentieth century.

Seawater gets into Stenness on most tides. It is like a miniature Baltic Sea, with a mixture of seaweeds and a few salt-tolerant flowering plants and brackish water charophytes, and a fauna that owes more to the sea than the freshwaters. Seals move in from the Flow. The salinity of Stenness drops to 8 parts per thousand (ppt) in winter and rises to 22 ppt in summer (seawater has 35 ppt). The rare bearded stonewort was recorded in Stenness up to the 1920s but has disappeared since. There are peculiar balls of a filamentous green alga, *Cladophora aegagropila*, that start as a small tangle of filaments and as they grow and are rolled up and down the rocky beaches and eroded into spheres, sometimes several centimetres across (Fig. 166). They are recorded from other suitable rocky lakes, and even revered as religious objects in Japan. They are common both in Harrar and Stenness.

Stenness is like one of a pair of horns, the other being Harrar. They are joined not far from the outflow to the sea, where the Brig o' Brodgar spans the narrow gap between them and carries a road that runs along the peninsula between the horns. Both lochs are large (together the fourth largest in Scotland) and into

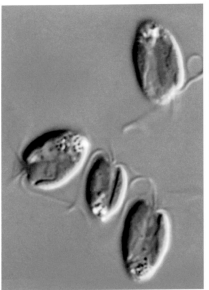

FIG 166. *Prymnesium parvum* (left), about 8 μm long; and balls of *Cladophora* (right), about 3 cm across, found in Loch Harrar.

them come torrents of freshwater, so there is a tension between the effects of land and sea, for Harrar is fresh (salinity 0.2 ppt in winter, 1.2 ppt in summer). The effects of man are everywhere, and date to earlier than the Neolithic. Along the peninsula is a dramatic stone circle, the Ring of Brodgar and a newly discovered temple complex. Near the loch's south shore is Maes Howe, a huge mound with stone-lined chambers where the Vikings left graffiti, in runes, some of which recount sexual dalliances, in words alien to the New Naturalist series, but common enough in modern novels.

The lochs are shallow, five or six metres at most, and rich in submerged plants, though the strong westerly winds and high waves leave most of the edges as rocky beaches not much colonised by reeds and other emergents. The wind has whistled across this treeless plain for a long time, but there are many birds: goldneye, wigeon, pintail, red-throated diver, pochard, tufted duck and scaup.

We are visiting for a particular reason, as always we will on this tour. The two lochs are becoming polluted by nutrients. Some of the plants recorded in the nineteenth century have disappeared; the water in Harrar is said to have become less clear in the last few decades, and the few records of increasing chlorophyll a, a measure of the amount of phytoplankton in the water, seem to support that. In the 1980s Canadian pondweed appeared and has become abundant, as have the mute swans that feed on it. Two sewage treatment works and some septic tanks serve the human population of about 1,000 in the catchments, but about 90 per cent of the phosphorus comes from the land. Overall the eutrophication problem is not so serious as with other shallow lakes in the UK; but the fish have some problems.

Brown and sea trout have long supported good fishing and still do in Harrar, if not in Stennness, where the streams that used to support sea trout breeding have been much damaged by drainage engineering. The fish stocks have not declined overall and may have increased in Harrar, but in the 1960s there were some notable fish kills, with carcasses washed up onto Harrar's shores. The problem was traced to a tiny alga, *Prymnesium parvum* (Fig. 166), which grows in a range of salinities. It is a flagellate, one of the haptophytes (see Chapter 3) that sometimes produce poisons, comprising a string of amino acids, like a very simple protein.[4] The toxin is produced in brackish water but not in the sea, and the alga is normally quite scarce but will increase in numbers if nutrients are increased.

At the time of the fish kills, there was free flow of water between Stenness and Harrar, which naturally would have had salinity gradients capable of stimulating toxin production. These would depend on the height of the tide, and the mixing of the wind. We do not know whether an occasional outbreak of *Prymnesium* was not a natural feature of the loch. There are reports of occasional kills in the past and the loch still reaches salinities (up to 1.2 ppt) that would support *Prymnesium* (greater than 0.4 ppt). Fish kills in undisturbed lakes are not uncommon, even normal, for many reasons, and are not disasters.

With the fish kills of the 1960s, however, consternation set in among the angling clubs and hotels, and consternation breeds management. The entry of seawater from Stenness, coupled with the rising nutrient levels, were diagnosed as the causes of the *Prymnesium* outbreak. Flaps of heavy wood, hinged at the top, were installed across the seaward openings of the Brig o' Brodgar in 1968 so that that less water could pass upstream but freshwater could pass downstream. The average salinity of Harrar has not substantially decreased, but there have been no *Prymnesium* outbreaks since, or at least none have been noticed, whilst the beaked tasselweed, a salt-tolerant plant, has disappeared from Harrar. We shall never know whether the flaps are really necessary but they are now rotting and there is talk of replacing them with steel ones. The option of removing them might be discussed, but the urge to manage is pervasive, so it is difficult to get agreement to go back on earlier decisions. The matter remains undecided, and it is time for us to fly south to the famous Ness.

LOCH NESS

The Highlands of Scotland have been put together in a series of blocks by the sundering and re-forming of continents. Most obvious from our vantage point, indeed from the Moon also, is the straight line of the Great Glen fault that runs from beyond Inverness to Oban. It is 300 million years old, lies among hard, metamorphic and igneous intrusive rocks and Old Red Sandstone, and separates Wester Ross, Kintail and Affric to the north and west, and the Monadhliaths and then the Cairngorms to the south and east.

Down the weakness of the fault, ice was able to gouge a deep channel, which now bears Loch Ness (Fig. 20) and Loch Oich, draining northwards, and Loch Lochy draining southwards, the whole being linked by the Caledonian Canal. The Canal was dug by Thomas Telford in the early nineteenth century, as much to provide work in a depressed time, as for small boats travelling between the North and Irish Seas to by-pass the stormy Cape Wrath at the tip of Scotland. That economic depression has bearing on the lochs. The eighteenth century had seen the Jacobean Rebellion – to replace a catholic king (Bonnie Prince Charlie) on the English throne – defeated at Culloden near Inverness in 1746, resulting in persecution of the highlanders who had supported it. The English landlords pushed them from the land.

The catchment of Loch Ness, once covered by Caledonian forest of birch, pine and rocky fastness, has since remained relatively unpopulated, though grazed by sheep and red deer, and planted with conifers, especially on the slopes bordering the lake. Its catchment spans almost the width of Scotland, with an area of 1,730 km², but only 7.5 of these are urban, with around 1,000 houses, and only 32.6 under arable agriculture, at the north end near the outflow. Mostly the land is rough moorland, bearing some 355 smaller lochs, totalling around 76 km² in area. Loch Ness is simple in shape, parallel sided, with a width of only around 1.5 km but a length of 37 km, and is deep, 230 m at greatest, 123 m on average. The Scots will never tire of telling you that it contains twice the freshwater of all the lakes of England and Wales combined, and one fifth of all British freshwater. But it is interesting beyond that.

The grain of the land is that of the prevailing wind, which blows strongly along the length of the loch, keeping it well mixed. High rainfall and a great ratio, about 31, of catchment area to lake, mean that the water is replaced rapidly, about once every two years, for such a voluminous lake. Ness stratifies in summer, but quite late in the year and fully mixes again relatively early. The thermocline is deep, about 30 m, and stratification is often overturned and re-formed in windy summers. The loch is thus well oxygenated even at its greatest depth, and supports a fauna that is diverse, but sparse on account of the very low productivity of the water. There is almost no phytoplankton.

This low productivity is key to the interest of Loch Ness[5] and has several reasons. First, the low population and lack of cultivation of the catchment leave the water low in nutrients and much of these is intercepted and retained in the sediments of the smaller lochs on the inflowing rivers. Secondly, the water is stained brown with organic compounds from the peaty moorlands. With the vigorous mixing, this means that the phytoplankton is perpetually short of light as well as devoid of nutrients. Its biomass barely reaches 1.5 micrograms per litre of chlorophyll *a* (for comparison Lake Windermere has 20–30). The low numbers of bottom animals mean that the sediments are little disturbed, so few nutrients are recycled from the sediments. Indeed paired varves are found in the upper several metres, probably representing winter (light bands) and summer (dark bands with organic matter). Sedimentation rates until recently were less than 0.5 mm per year, but have increased a little, perhaps reflecting disturbance of soil when the plantations are being felled.

The paucity of light and nutrients, not helped by the cold water (6°C in winter, 13 in summer), means that the bacteria, the benthos, the zooplankton and the fish (sticklebacks, arctic charr and trout) are ultimately more dependent on the organic matter that washes in from the catchment than on the phytoplankton or plants produced within the loch. (The steep sides mean that the littoral zone is negligible.) This is unusual for a large lake where the balance usually lies towards production based on photosynthesis. Ness is little more than a drainage tank for rainwater.

Which takes us, of course, to a consideration of the monster. There isn't one, despite the best attempts of the local tourist industry to conjure it. There was the remotest of possibilities until underwater sonar surveys in the 1980s failed to find anything, but that has not dampened local enthusiasm. One consequence of these surveys may have been the introduction, on the equipment being used, of an American triclad, *Phagocata woodworthi*, which appears to be competing with the native species and possibly steadily displacing them.

The erstwhile monster was given a name by Peter Scott, so that if it existed it might be conserved (bureaucracies cannot cope otherwise). It was *Nessiteras rhombopteryx*, for an alleged rhomboid-shaped flipper, and turned out to be an anagram of 'Monster hoax by Sir Peter S', who vehemently denied such levity, but the coincidence would seem too remarkable to be random. There is a (sort of) serious side too. Models are often used in science to determine possibilities, especially when the future is to be predicted or data are scarce. Two attempts have been made to calculate the potential size and numbers of the monster from models using basic ecological principles.[6]

First it must be big (or otherwise it was not a monster), very long lived (no bodies have ever turned up) and there must be at least one breeding pair. It cannot be a herbivore, owing to the sparseness of the phytoplankton and plants, but can be no heavier than the total fish stock on which it must feed. The fish stock can be predicted from a formula called the morphoedaphic index (total dissolved solids (as a measure of nutrient availability) divided by mean depth (as a measure of spawning habitat and release of nutrients from the sediments)). This relationship can be derived from a series of similar lakes where fish production, water chemistry and depth have been measured. The morphoedaphic index of Loch Ness was determined and from it the fish production. With a turnover in fish communities from about one to five years, the fish stock would be between 0.55 and 2.75 kg per ha. With an area of the loch of 5,700 ha, there must then be between 3,135 and 15,675 kg of fish. Assuming the monster has a minimum size (to be a monster) of 100 kg, there could be between 1 and 156 of them. The best estimate, bearing in mind the lack of bodies washed up, the need for a breeding population and the need for fish as a food supply, might be minimally two monsters each of 4,000 kg, or up to ten between 300 and 1,500 kg. A 1,500 kg monster would be about 8 m long. On our flight southwards towards Loch Lomond, we can muse on the power of modelling techniques in theoretical ecology.

LOCH LOMOND

We will hover briefly around Loch Lomond,[7] a lake that we would never be forgiven for not visiting, because of its status as the largest (in area) of the British (though not British and Irish) lakes, as one of the few still to retain a whitefish, the powan, its importance for the tourist industry as the centre of the Loch Lomond and Trossachs National Park, its provision of water supply to one sixth of the Scottish population and the fame of its bonny banks in the well-known song.

The bonny banks, at least in the south, are under some pressure from the wash of the proliferating tourist boats, and the powan is in decline partly because the ruffe, introduced when anglers brought it in as live bait, eats its eggs. Nonetheless there are major features of interest for a limnologist. First, Loch Lomond lies north–south, across the grain of the country, unlike the other large Scottish lochs that lie parallel to the major faults. A very powerful glacier gouged out the northern part of the lake, the Tarbet basin, to a depth of 190 m in a narrow trough, then spread across the southern rocks and the Highland Boundary fault to give, first, the Luss and Strathcashel basins with a maximum depth of 60 m and, finally, the broad south basin, never deeper than 23 m, with its many islands.

All the basins stratify in summer, but stratification occurs earlier and lasts longer in the north and is easily disturbed in the south, where there is a much smaller difference in temperature (about 2°C compared with 9°C in the north) between surface and bottom. There are two main inflows. The Falloch Water flows from the high Grampians to the north, and brings in water of low conductivity (around 43 microSiemens per cm), pH (6.7) and nutrients (in 1989/91, nitrate 0.25 mg N per litre, phosphate-P, 0.003 mg per litre). The River Endrick, in contrast, comes from the Campsie Fells through agricultural lowlands to the south end of the loch, and delivers water with higher conductivity, pH and nutrients (178, 7.4, 0.72 and 0.09, respectively). Wind mixes these northern and southern waters and there are smaller inflows draining into the middle basin, but the north–south differences in inflow water are reflected in the relative amounts of phytoplankton, though these are not very large. As in Ness, the invertebrates and fish depend also on organic matter coming in from the land. Aquatic plants are scarcer in the north, where the shoreline is steep, and sediments do not accumulate at the edge, though they grow to 10 m depth, but richer in the south, where the transparency is lower, and they grow much more shallowly in the sheltered bays.

Loch Lomond (Fig. 167) shows, in the contrasted basins of one lake, the characteristics that Naumann and Thienemann (Chapter 7) originally used to distinguish eutrophic and oligotrophic lakes and is notable in other respects. It

FIG 167. A view to the northwest of Loch Lomond shows the shallow southern basin, with its islands, and the lake tapering towards the north with its streams coming from the Grampians. (Frogwell)

has an unusually diverse fish community (because of its varied character), with a population of river lampreys that unusually does not migrate to the sea (though the Firth of Clyde is only a few kilometres away along the outflow River Leven). Powan, brown trout, salmon, pike, minnow, eel, perch, roach and stone loach are present as native species. They have been boosted (if that is the word), by the ruffe, in 1982, the dace in 1987, the gudgeon in 1981, the chub in 1987 and the crucian carp in 1991, mostly introduced as live bait for catching pike, a practice now officially banned. Tench, rainbow trout and brook charr have also been brought in, but did not persist. Ruffe is particularly derided. It is quite numerous and shows the thuggish (or admirable: take your pick) characteristics of many invasive species: it is omnivorous, hardy, fecund and versatile.

Because of the threat that ruffe poses to the powan population, transfers of powan have been made to other lakes in the catchment, including Loch Sloy, which lies in the hills to the west of Loch Lomond. Loch Sloy has its own fame. It was deepened by damming between 1945 and 1950, and its catchment was increased by diverting streams through tunnels and aqueducts to boost its water supply, which was then used to provide a head of water for generation of electricity at a power station (still the largest hydroelectric station in Britain) on the northwestern shore of Loch Lomond.

Planning permission has now been given for conversion of the station to a pumped storage scheme, where electricity generated elsewhere during periods of low demand and low value will be used to pump water from Loch Lomond up into Sloy, to be released for generation at times of high demand and higher value. At present, Loch Sloy does not provide sufficient head for the station to be economic at all times and an increased head will expand the capacity of the power station. There are few consequences for such a scheme for Loch Lomond except that, despite filters to be placed across the pipes through which the water will be pumped, there is a high risk that eggs of ruffe will be transported to Loch Sloy, so that the powan population there will no longer be protected and new refuges in other lakes will have to be found.

The 71 km² of Loch Lomond look tranquil, and provide a good day out for 60 per cent of the Scottish population, nearly 3 million of which live within an hour's journey, but the loch is under pressure from many sides: agriculture and population in the south, afforestation with conifers and the erosion that comes with felling in the north; damage to banks and disturbance of birds by boats; and road construction and upgrading, which has dumped spoil into the littoral zone on the west side. Pressures will increase with demand for better tourist facilities, especially as the area is now a National Park, and the unknown implications of an epidemic of introduced fish species. It is not easy to keep lakes in a good state in these crowded islands.

LOCH LEVEN

That is certainly the case at our next stop at Loch Leven in the Scottish lowlands, north of Edinburgh. Loch Leven (Fig. 168) has been studied since the 1960s, beginning with the International Biological Programme (IBP), a worldwide effort to explain the pattern of productivity in natural habitats. The British contribution was a contrast between Lake George, in Uganda, and Loch Leven, both shallow lakes of great local importance. Loch Leven remains a prime site for British limnological research and is both remarkable and unremarkable.[8] It is remarkable because its choice for work during the IBP rested almost randomly on its being the closest large loch to the Edinburgh office of the then Nature Conservancy, headed by Neville Morgan, an energetic man who pushed successfully for inclusion of the UK in the IBP. It is unremarkable because its fate is that of all lowland, and many upland, lakes in Britain and Ireland. A series

FIG 168. Loch Leven has a long cultural history. From the gardens of the seventeenth-century Kinross House, now rentable for the weekend, if you are exceptionally wealthy, the fourteenth-century Lochleven Castle, a former state prison where the sadly unfortunate, including Mary, Queen of Scots, were imprisoned, is seen on its island in the loch. (Sandy Stevenson/Tour Scotland)

of interferences with the lake by private interests has led to ramifications and damage that has been, and continues to be, paid for largely by those who have not profited from these ill-judged ventures.

From our flying carpet we look down on a largish lake, 13.3 km² in area, in a catchment that is mostly arable farmed, though with its distant edges on low hills with sheep and cattle. The streams near the lake, and the outflow, have been straightened, always a giveaway sign for ecological problems, and there are three small towns, one of them, Kinross, on the main inflow, the South Queich, very close to the lake. Drifting at the edges in sheltered bays are light green patches of surface blooms of cyanobacteria, usually another bad sign. We can conclude that this lake is strongly eutrophicated. Nonetheless it has all the official labels of what we would expect to be a high-quality habitat: National Nature Reserve, Site of Special Scientific Interest, Special Area of Conservation and RAMSAR site. Millions of pounds have been spent to remedy a slate of problems, with some improvement over its worst state in the 1970s, but, in terms of what would have been its pristine state, it is still severely damaged.

The problems began in the early nineteenth century. Water from the outflow had been used since the 1700s to drive mills for grinding corn, sawing timber, powering looms and for bleaching cloth. The local landowners, with interests in paper making in Leven where the outflow reaches the sea, saw advantages in controlling this water supply in case of dry years. One option was to dam the lake to raise the water level and storage capacity, whilst the alternative was to lower it, uncovering new land for farming at the edges, installing sluice gates to regulate the outflow so as to guarantee a supply in dry summers, and reducing the area from which water might be lost by evaporation. They chose the latter, manipulated an Act through Parliament to allow them to do this in 1831, and promised bounty in the form of 440 ha of rich, new farmland at low cost. In the event, only 265 ha were created, of poor quality, at a cost nine times greater than anticipated. The depth of the loch was reduced by 1.4 m (it is currently on average now 3.9 m) and the area was reduced by 4.5 km², the shoreline moving by 500 m in places. Two fish species disappeared soon after this conversion of the lake to a reservoir: charr for reasons unknown; and salmon because it was unable to migrate through the sluice gates. There was a decline in the value of the food fishery for trout and other species, and the local poor were prevented by new fences from reaching traditional areas for peat cutting and reed gathering. Downstream farmers also claimed compensation for land that was flooded by the management regime used.

Another pie, in which the local worthies had their fingers, was the woollen industry. Mills were built in Kinross in 1840 to spin and weave the wool from the local sheep. Wool has to be washed, which uses detergents, and the cloth is prone to infestation by the clothes moth, especially in damp houses, so that insecticides were also used. The result was a progressive discharge into the loch of both pesticide and detergent phosphate-rich effluent. By the 1980s, the woollen mills were contributing about a third of the total load of phosphate (6.4 tonnes per year, compared with 5.3 from the sewage works, 8.1 from farming and very small amounts from direct rainfall and the pinkfooted geese that graze in the fields and swim on the loch). The mills were using some fairly noxious insecticides including aldrin and dieldrin, chlorphenylid and flucofenwon, which were detectable in the zooplankton and fish and probably led to a decline in water fleas. In turn this was associated with reduced grazing on the blooming algae. The combination of high nutrients and low grazing led to some spectacular algal growths in the 1990s.

A third finger in the pie came with the fishery on the loch. It had been famous for a particular race of brown trout with dark colouring and deep pink flesh, and was valued first as a food source and later for recreational angling. Daniel Defoe, in 1723, remarked upon it as being especially rich. The new railways in the nineteenth century helped exports to the cities and brought in anglers from about 1844. The rod fishery income was substantial by 1859, so that the notion arose of stocking even more fish from a hatchery. The concept of carrying capacity was not widely understood at the time.

Putting more fish in simply means that more fish are eliminated by competition for food. By the 1930s the hatchery had closed, but it was reopened in 1983, following catastrophic declines in the fish stock as a result of the increasing eutrophication problem. The peak catches had been in the 1960s when anglers landed about 50,000 fish per year and expectations were of catches of 0.2 to 0.6 fish per boat per hour. They have declined to a few thousand in the twenty-first century and an angler might expect to spend anything up to 20 hours for a catch. The fish are slightly bigger though!

The more resilient, but alien rainbow trout were introduced, between 1993 and 2005, in an attempt to counter the annual losses of about £100,000 being incurred in managing the fishery. That was not a good idea; the rainbow trout reduced the *Daphnia* population, which had begun to recover following the voluntary abandonment of the use of insecticides in 1988 by the woollen mills, and thus contributed to an increase in algae, and attracted a flock of cormorants. Rainbow trout did not breed in the loch and appear to have more or less disappeared by now.

In the 1990s, the effluent from the woollen mill became less damaging as phosphate-free detergents were used, and phosphorus stripping was installed at the two main sewage treatment works. The phosphorus input has been reduced overall from around 20 tonnes per year to around 8 and is now dominated by the diffuse load from the farmland. The lake has shown some recovery in terms of reduced phosphorus concentrations (from about 0.09 mg/L in 1968, though it may previously have risen higher, to about 0.03 now). The transparency has increased so that water plants, confined to a depth of 1.5 m in 1968, now grow down to 4.3 m. The algal chlorophyll has declined to about 25 micrograms from a peak of at least 90, and the diversities of invertebrates on the bottom and of plants have increased.

The process has taken 20 years because of release of phosphorus from the stores in the sediments, and the costs, born largely by the general public, have been very great. Even so, there are still problems because the diffuse sources from farming of both phosphorus and nitrogen are still high. There is little chance of the formerly occurring isoetids returning, and current conditions are not so good for the trout fishery as they were. Cyanobacterial blooms, which are potentially toxic, though local authorities tend to overestimate the risk and overreact, are still common. One intense bloom of microcystin-containing *Anabaena flos-aquae* in the summer of 1992 was linked with a major fish kill and led to the cancellation of an international angling championship match. 'Scum Saturday' was estimated to have cost the local economy up to £1 million in lost revenue that year and caused considerable longer-term damage to the reputation of the fishery. A long-term practice of removal of pike to reduce predation on young perch may also be self-defeating, for lack of predators on small zooplanktivorous fish, like perch, in turn means more predation on daphnids and larger algal growths.

The Loch Leven reservoir has been meddled with for two centuries and will now have to be interfered with in different ways forever to maintain a status quo that is far inferior to what it could have been if left well alone, with proper management from the outset of the inevitable effluents of the local population. It has also been a highly privileged lake. By the accident of its position, it has received much more attention, both in research and restoration management, than most lakes will ever receive. We should celebrate the partial rescue but not be misled into thinking that this is the norm.

IRELAND

It is time now to cross the North Channel and see what is happening in Ireland, culturally and geologically a land with greater similarities to Scotland than to England. Ireland is like a saucer. There are uplands of metamorphic rocks, granite and basalt to the north, east and west, and of sandstone in the south, and lowlands of carboniferous limestone in the centre. Superimposed is a very wet climate, especially in the west, so that, irrespective of the rock, leaching of the surface soils has been so intense that acid peats have been able to form almost everywhere in the west and centre. On the uplands they have merged into blanket bogs; in the lowlands they have also formed in depressions in the limestone that now bear the domed surfaces of raised bogs. The magic carpet is fortunately equipped with large umbrellas and a waterproof underlay.

Most of the Irish lakes were formed by ice, those in the mountains being generally small, with the larger and generally shallow ones in the lowlands. Flushing rates are high and water is often retained for only weeks or months, whilst the windy westerly climate and the modest depths mean that stratification is rarely strong or stable and hypolimnia depleted of oxygen are rare. Characteristic is Lough Neagh,[9] unmissable from the air (Fig. 21), being large (383 km²) but shallow (mean depth 8.6 m). Its fisheries (Chapter 8) are important, but nowadays, despite efforts to treat the effluents that run into it from small towns and villages, the intensification of agriculture, particularly dairying, in the catchment, and the

FIG 169. Lough Furnace is visible to the top right across this classic view of the drumlin-strewn Clew Bay. (Matt Middleton)

abundant supplies of phosphorus stored by now in the sediments, leave it as yet another heavily eutrophicated, shallow lake, also affected by past lowering of its water level and with many of the same lessons as Loch Leven.

We fly on towards Sligo and Mayo, in the remote northwest and the astonishing Clew Bay (Fig. 169) with hundreds of low, sensuously rounded islands and a hinterland like a huge basket of eggs, the drumlins left when one lot of ice deposited clay then another ran over it to mould it into rounded ridges and dumplings. We glimpse the common seals, hauled out on the shingle shores below the green turfy tops of the islands, and turn northwards inland to look at a whole catchment, that of Burrishoole. Our first landing, close to the sea, is at an extraordinarily shaped lake, an almost psychedelic pattern of swirls, for its form is determined by the low land among the drumlins. This is Lough Furnace and it lies just slightly above mean sea level. In its time it has been an estuary and is now a meromictic lake.

A meromictic lake is permanently stratified because the layers at the bottom are much denser (through their chemistry) than those at the top, and the winds cannot shift them. Meromictic lakes often develop in hot regions where temperature stratification might persist year round for a time, allowing salts from decomposition to accumulate in the hypolimnion and increase its density. Freshwater from the inflows layers on the top and the contrast becomes stronger and stronger. The origin of meromixis was different in Lough Furnace. It was seawater that formed the lower layer, and as sea levels fluctuated following the main glaciation and the irregular rebound of the land, freshwater layered on top. The process began about 4,300 years ago and the stratification was so stable by 3,400 years ago that the bottom waters had permanently lost all their oxygen.[10]

We know this from an analysis of the sediments. Iron and manganese, derived from soil minerals, are abundant in most sediments, but when deoxygenation sets in, their salts become very soluble and they diffuse out and the sediments become depleted. We can also trace a rising salinity (Fig. 170) in the surface waters from changes in the diatoms in the sediments and a loss of the spicules of freshwater sponges. Lough Furnace now has a salinity varying, in the top 3–4 m, from fresh to about 5 ppt, and from 18 to 20 ppt in the monimolimnion, the deep salt layer, which reaches down to the maximum depth of over 21 m. A small weir separates the lake from the sea, but this is topped by the higher tides, which shoot some salt water in. A plentiful supply of freshwater from the rainy catchment then flushes the sea from the surface layers.

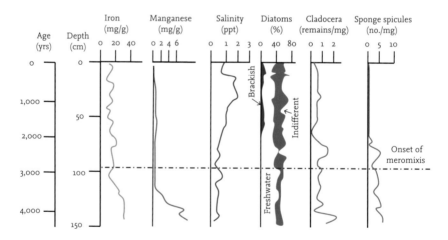

FIG 170. Some data from cores taken in Lough Furnace. The dotted line indicates when the lough is believed to have become permanently meromictic. Decline in iron and manganese in the sediments indicates their loss from a monimolimnion that had become anaerobic. Salinity increased as sea levels rose and freshwater diatoms, cladocerans and freshwater sponges became less abundant, unable to compete with brackish water species. Based on Cassina et al., 2013.

Lough Furnace has a brackish water flora and fauna in its top four metres, but nothing but bacteria and protozoa in the anaerobic salty layer. The relict mysid species *Neomysis integer*, the isopods *Jaera albifrons, J. ischiosetosa* and *J. nordmanni* and two rare amphipods (*Lembos longipes* and *Leptocheirus pilosus*) are found in the surface and it is ringed by a narrow swamp of common reed and common club-rush, with small patches of great fen-sedge and bottle sedge. Submerged are both Irish species of tasselweed (*Ruppia maritima* and *R. cirrhosa*), but they do not grow very deeply because the water is very brown and light does not penetrate much beyond a metre and a half.

The reason for the cold-tea brownness is the nature of the catchment. Organic compounds leached from the blanket bogs provide from 50 to over 100 mg/L of organic matter (a lake in a catchment lacking peat might have up to 5) and these feature in most of the lakes in the Burrishoole catchment.[11] Most of the catchment is blanket bog, a mosaic of brown, ochre, pinkish and reddish colours given to the land by the nonetheless photosynthesising *Sphagnum*, its greens hidden by red pigments. Where the Burishoole catchment is not brownish, it is dull green from the conifer forest planted several decades ago and now covering a fifth of its area. Sometimes we look down on patches with straight lines etched in where past domestic peat cutting has dug trenches, which quickly refilled with bog vegetation, and do no permanent harm. They contrast with the devastation caused over most of the huge drained area of Irish bog, particularly in the central lowlands, by machines that strip the vegetation then mine long sausages of peat for burning in power stations or manufacture of garden composts.

Before reaching the upper western parts of the catchment in the Nephin Beg mountains, we pass over the narrow strip of land that separates Lough Furnace from the rather bigger Lough Feeagh, 14 m above sea level and flowing into Lough Furnace, but too high to have any seawater injection. Feeagh is a lake with a more conventional shape, formed as the glaciers slid down its valley from the mountains. It is deeper (43 m), low in salts and naturally only a little acid (conductivity 80–90 microSiemens per cm, pH 6.3–7). The lakes of this catchment, despite their bog coverage and largely underlying resistant Precambrian metamorphic rocks of schist, gneiss and quartzite, are influenced by some limestone, an ancient dolomite that provides just enough buffering capacity to have protected them, with their westerly location, from the industrial gases and acidification of the more easterly regions.

Lake Bunaveela, a small lake high in the Burrishoole catchment, is the most buffered because of the dolomite, and has *Gammarus duebeni* and molluscs in contrast to the more acid Feeagh. There is a small corrie lake high on Nephin Beg that has a rocky basin, and a variety of small peaty loughs make this an intensely varied catchment for a limnologist. It has some other important features too. On the peninsula of land that separates Loughs Feeagh and Furnace is a station of the Irish Marine Institute, which now owns the catchment. For some decades it has specialised in studies on Atlantic salmon, trout and eels and indeed maintains a hatchery for rearing salmon smolts for release here and elsewhere.

Salmon is perhaps the best-known fish in Britain and Ireland; formerly we ate lots of it. We still do but almost all of it is farmed in riverside hatcheries, and pens in shallow coastal seas off Ireland and Scotland. Wild salmon numbers have declined very greatly in recent decades; the reasons are many and their importance differs in different places. Prime are the ruination of the rivers, where salmon formerly spawned, by silting of the gravel beds through which oxygenated water easily poured and in which the eggs were buried by the female after fertilisation. Silt clogs the beds and kills the eggs. Next is alteration of the hydrology by dams that either block the passage of the adult fish or alter the pattern and intensity of river flows needed to attract the fish up the rivers on their spawning runs. At sea, where the smolts move to mature as predators, overfishing and then, in the estuaries, poaching have not helped and there are suggestions now that climate change, in altering ocean currents, may be confusing the fish in their movements back towards the rivers where they spawned.

There is worse. Millions of fish escape from the salmon farms and these are not the same as the wild fish, which are genetically very varied and exist in many local races specific to particular river systems, but which are all selected for survival and completion of their life cycle. Cultured fish are bred to grow rapidly but not to survive, for they are culled young and breeding is managed artificially. Cultured fish, when they escape as parr into rivers, compete with wild parr because they grow rapidly and are voracious feeders. This then reduces the number of wild smolts running to the sea. Cultured escapees, if they manage to run into the rivers and mate, introduce genes that are selected against, but again displace wild fish. Treatment of eggs under high pressure (9,500 psi for five minutes) in hatcheries can do something about this problem for pressure induces changes in the chromosomes of the eggs. It results in retention (triploidy) of an extra set of chromosomes that make these fish sterile and also interferes with their ability to navigate from the sea into rivers.

The problems of habitat change in the river systems are less easily dealt with. Even in the Burrishoole catchment there are disturbances. Planting trees and, even more, felling them, disturbs the peat and causes erosion that not only clogs the gravels of the rivers but also results in more algal growth, because nutrients are released by the erosion. Phosphorus concentrations, normally around 0.006 mg/L in undisturbed catchments, may reach over 0.4 just after felling and the effects may persist for four or more years.¹² Overstocking with sheep, especially when headage payments were made in the 1980s by the European Union, also caused serious erosion. Rain runs rapidly off this saturated land with soggy peats and impermeable rocks, so the rivers rise quickly and flow rapidly, carrying the eroded soils fast down river and into the loughs. Lough Feagh has been filling in at a rate of 0.6 to 1.7 cm per year in recent decades compared with only a millimetre or two formerly. Seeding the cut plantations with grass can reduce the problem but not eliminate it.

CARRA, MASK AND CORRIB

A little further southwards in Mayo, the crystalline rocks meet the limestone and the divide is straddled by three of the most prized loughs, for their fishing at least, in western Ireland: Carra, Mask (Fig. 171) and Corrib. As we fly in, the outline of the most northerly, Carra, shows up as very irregular. The length of shoreline is about five times what it would be for a circular lake of the same area and this gives us a clue as to the origin of this lake. Its basin was scraped by the ice, and the hardness of the limestone left jagged promontories, sharpened by

FIG 171. Lough Mask is a marl lake and one of a group well known for fly-fishing, in which artificial flies, including the green drake (inset) mimic local caddis and mayfly species. (Brian Nelson)

later solution. Mask and Corrib were formed in the same way, but whereas Carra lies entirely on the limestone, the geological divide runs under the basins of Mask and Corrib, so that the streams to their west run off the ancient hard rocks of the Partry and Maumturk mountains, whereas those from the east drain the more populated lowlands on the richer farming country of the limestone.

From above we see that the basins – especially of Carra, the shallower of the three – are covered with white marl sediment (Chapter 5). There are extensive bare areas, even in water shallow enough to bear rooted plants. This is typical of undisturbed marl lakes and may be a result of a strong tying up of phosphate in complexes with the marl, which makes root development difficult. The same plants are found in Mask and Corrib, but the marl formation is less intense because the acid water from the west limits its formation and leads to a different water chemistry in the western basins of Mask and the northern one in Corrib and thence to a different flora with isoetids, including shoreweed and lobelia, and the peculiar pipewort with its strangely ribbed roots. The nutrient loads entering these three loughs are not uninfluenced by human activity, but they are relatively modest, so, with the influence of the marl in binding phosphorus, the algal crops are low and light penetrates for several metres into the water column. Nonetheless there are already problems with extensive development of Canadian pondweed in Corrib.

The conductivities of these loughs are three or four times those found in Feeagh, with its almost entirely crystalline rock catchment; they have substantial bicarbonate concentrations and pH higher than 8. The invertebrate communities are rich in molluscs and crustaceans, particularly ten species of snails, several bivalves and three species of *Gammarus: duebeni, lacustris* and *pulex*. Mayflies include Baetidae, *Caenis luctuosa, Centroptilum luteolum* and *Ephemera danica* and it is these, and the many species of caddis, that inspire the flies used to catch the trout for which these loughs are famous.

The remoter western Irish lakes, not least Lough Melvin, already mentioned in Chapter 4, retain a fish community that is less altered by introductions than in many lakes in Britain. They are primarily salmonid lakes, with salmon where there is a connection with the sea, as in Corrib, but not Mask and Carra, which discharge to Corrib through underground caverns not surface streams. There are charr in Carra and brown trout in all three, the latter showing genetic differences in different tributary streams of Corrib that may represent particularly fine adaptation to details of local conditions. Pike and perch have been introduced, and pike are generally culled in the management of the fisheries.

The edges of all three lakes show rocky outcrops of limestone, there are many islands and there is a great variety of depth among the several sub-basins.

Stretches of reedswamp with reed, common clubrush, shoreweed, white water lily, and bog bean, alternate with shingle and rock shores. What perhaps we do not realise when we take this bird's eye view is the perception of anglers, wading or fishing from boats, around the lakes. They see a geography far more detailed perhaps than a limnologist, who takes in the lake as a whole, and though they may be unable to find rational explanations, have a lore that is based on experience of what artificial flies are best for fishing at different times of year and in different sections of the lough. I quote for Lough Mask: [13]

> There is excellent wet-fly fishing, and dapping the mayfly in late May and June is most productive. Dapping the natural grasshopper takes a lot of good fish in August–September. Dry fly fishing with a lightly dressed Green Drake [Fig. 171] works well when the trout are feeding on mayfly and shore fishing is possible in a number of places. One such place is the mouth of the canal, where dry sedges are fished off the shore, and Olive Spinners will take good trout in the summer evenings along many of the bays on the eastern shore.

There are other reasons for visiting these loughs. They lie in what has been the home of some of the poorest people in Europe, a wet and sodden land, capable of raising sheep and cattle but not grain, so that the potato has historically been a major staple. Between 1845 and 1855, 40 per cent of the population of western Ireland died or emigrated to Britain or the USA. A disease of potatoes, introduced from Mexico, blighted the crop on which the Irish depended. It did not help that it was largely of one poorly resistant potato variety. The land was to a large extent abandoned and so the diffuse loadings of nutrients, hitherto not great (the manuring by cattle and, towards the sea the dressings of seaweed, had not led to huge productivity), became even lower. The record is there in the sediments of Lough Carra.[14] Dated cores show a fall in phosphorus, nitrogen and organic matter in the sediments around 1845, then a rise as the population recovered a little, and finally a later eutrophication of the loch as the smaller farms were amalgamated into bigger units farmed more intensively, especially from 1950 onwards.

The balance of production in Lough Carra, during the Famine, is shown by the levels of [13]carbon to shift towards organic matter coming in from the catchment as production declined in the lake, and there are linked changes in the diatom remains. The lough is now more productive than before the Famine. The total load of P has increased from about 1.7 tonnes per year in the mid-nineteenth century to around 2.1 now, not a huge rise, but the proportions from different sources have changed dramatically. Crops, formerly making up 26 per cent, now contribute only 1; stock and the grassland on which it depends formerly contributed 22 per cent and now 84 per cent, whilst the human contribution is down from 52 per cent to 15 per cent. The depopulation of the Famine has never been entirely replaced but the farms are larger now and carry more stock, leading to increase in eutrophication problems. But if the effects of the Famine on the limnology were short-lived, a small blip in the graphs of data, the consequences for Irish society and British and American politics were profound.

One million deaths, 2 million emigrants and a further 2.6 million forced into workhouses, where 200,000 died, are historical facts not to be ignored. The land was owned by landlords living in England and subletting to local tenants who then let to the farmers. The peasant farmers had no power and no security. Their civil rights were eliminated by penal laws, passed in 1690, which forbade the Catholic Irish to enter the professions or to own land, and indirectly led to production of large families as the only possible economic security, even if such large numbers could not easily be fed. A Free Trade mentality in London meant that there was little sympathy for the plight of the Irish poor and all over western Ireland are small plots of land bearing the graves of the victims.[15] Landlords took the opportunity of the Famine to evict tenants and consolidate their holdings.

The English were universally hated in western Ireland and there can be little doubt that the rebellion of Ireland and its bloody gaining of independence had its thickest roots in the Famine. Some of the leaders of the Easter Rising of 1916 had families affected by it. And closely associated with our last visit to the Irish lakes was a poet whose haunting verse contributed greatly to the Irish spirit at the time of rebellion. It was W. B. Yeats who wrote the stirring words: '*A terrible beauty is born*' at the end of each verse of his poem, 'Easter 1916'. He also wrote the line: '*All changed, changed utterly*'. And it is change that stirred him to write of *The Wild Swans at Coole*, whence we now fly, across the county boundary of Galway.

TURLOUGHS AND THE SWANS AT COOLE

Coole Lough is a special kind of Irish lake. There are over 300 of them, called turloughs, and they lie, in beautiful order, only on the purest of the limestone across several of the Irish counties.[16] Some turloughs are small, only a few hectares. One was 440 ha until it was drained in 1846 as part of a scheme to provide work for the starving farmers in the Famine, but the largest now, Rahasane (Fig. 172), is 267 ha. Most are small, and all are very shallow, a few metres at most, 1.5 on average. What groups them together is that they are lakes

FIG 172. Rhasane is the largest turlough remaining in Ireland, and is seen here as the water begins to recede in spring.

from autumn to spring, and then become damp grazing meadows floored with plants that reflect the limey soils, the disturbance of drying and flooding, and the intensity of the grazing by sheep, cattle, horses or domestic geese that are released onto them in summer. Beneath them is a labyrinth of passages and caves, holes and underground river channels, dissolved from the limestone over millions of years, the process being helped by the cracks of the bedding planes and the purity and solubility of this otherwise hard, uniform grey rock. In winter, when rainfall starts to exceed evaporation, the groundwater levels rise and fill the basins through springs and swallets. In summer the water drains away, often through the same holes, then called estavelles, sometimes leaving small residual pools, but otherwise baring the bottoms to the grazing stock.

Turloughs, the word means dry lake in Irish Gaelic, are not unique to Ireland, but they are very characteristic. There is one example, Pant-y-Llyn, in Carmarthenshire, in Wales and there are larger versions called poljes in Slovenia. There are also lakes on chalk or limestone that wet and dry on a cycle of years in the Norfolk Breckland and in Canada, but Ireland has some special claims. Across the bottoms of the basins are dry stone walls, built by farmers and colonised by the black, essentially terrestrial moss *Cinclidotus fontinaloides* on their tops and the water moss *Fontinalis antipyretica* on the lower sides.

The ground in early summer is littered with flat sheets of drying-out and stranded filamentous algae: lake paper. There is a variety of plants in summer, including shoreweed, spike rush, water purslane, fen violet and, in one turlough, the rare vernal water starwort, and trifid bur marigold where the bottom remains quite wet, and grasses and sedges where it dries out a little more. None of the plants is confined to turloughs; they are similar to those of drying shores, when water levels of more conventional lakes fall in summer. A soil invertebrate community develops, often with unusual animals reflecting the disturbed conditions and including some rare carabid beetles. The surroundings of the turloughs are often bare, with limestone pavement where the glaciers scoured off the former soils and left only thin coverings of drift, and there may be some hawthorn and buckthorn, and leached limestone heath, with ling and juniper, blue moor grass and yew.

By spring the turloughs have become lakes again, with plankton and bottom invertebrates, frogs and newts but usually no fish, which have no way of surviving the summer drying. There may be a few sticklebacks in residual pools, and eels, with their ability to cross wet meadows in rainy weather. The invertebrate communities vary greatly from year to year depending on what recolonises from resting stages, or flies or crawls in, and the drier the turlough in summer, the greater the changes from year to year in the winter community. The same is true of the winter bird populations.

And those are what attracted Yeats. Turloughs are attractive to waterfowl because the luxuriance of their summer vegetation provides abundant green matter and detritus for the grazing birds, and invertebrates on which other birds feed. There are dabblers like wigeon and teal, and divers, pochard and tufted duck, and white-fronted geese and pintail. In summer, meadow pipit, lapwing and snipe may breed so long as the grassland has been kept in the right condition by the grazing regime. Until their favoured sites were drained, a fate of half of the former turloughs, the black-necked grebe and red-necked phalarope used to nest. But what really distinguishes the turloughs is their attractiveness to whooper, Bewick's and mute swans, which bring us back to Coole.

Yeats had a penchant for the countryside, so long as he had a comfortable place in which to stay, and Coole House, close to the turlough, and the hospitality of Isabella Augusta, Lady Gregory, brought him there for many years to meet and talk with the intellectuals of the day and to write. With Lady Gregory and others he was to found the Abbey Theatre in Dublin and to revive the Irish literary tradition that had wavered in the face of the oppressions of the nineteenth century. In *The White Swans at Coole*, Yeats admires the beauty of the birds, their continuity from year to year. He sees them as unwearied, their hearts not grown cold, still attended by passion in contrast to the disappointments of his own life, which by then had seen the extremes of the First World War and the Irish Civil War and his rejection by the beautiful revolutionary, Maud Gonne. Alas, the house was demolished in 1944, but the estate remains as a nature reserve, with its turloughs conserved as any can be in an agricultural landscape. The woods of which he wrote are still there, and there can be few lakes that have had the benefit of the writings of a Nobel prize-winner for literature. One other is Lough Gill in Sligo, which Yeats wrote about in 'The Lake Isle of Innisfree':

> I will arise and go now, for always night and day
> I hear lake water lapping with low sounds by the shore;
> While I stand on the roadway, or on the pavements grey,
> I hear it in the deep heart's core.

And it is time now for us to head from the wilder landscapes of western Ireland to the tamer ones, with their grey pavements, of the British mainland. First we are off to Wales.

ANGLESEY AND SNOWDONIA

Wales has always attracted travellers and chroniclers. The remoter uplands were the refuges of Celtic tribes from the invasions of Rome and, by and large, the Welsh, like the Scots and Irish, have maintained more distinctive cultures than the English, who have been continually disturbed by new invasions from the mainland. One of the first travellers to record his observations of Wales was a Norman cleric, Gerald (1146–1223), who travelled with Archbishop Baldwin in 1182 to raise funds for the crusades, and gave us possibly the first record of a surface algal bloom, in Llangorse Lake, a shallow body of water still affected by eutrophication, a Welsh Loch Leven, in Breconshire:[17]

> The lake also (according to the testimony of the inhabitants) is celebrated for its miracles; for, as we have before observed, it sometimes assumed a greenish hue, so in our days it has appeared to be tinged with red, not universally, but as if blood flowed partially through certain veins and small channels.

Gerald faithfully recorded the lore of the local people, but it is not always clear whether he believed it or not. He continues about Llangorse lake:

Moreover it is sometimes seen by the inhabitants covered and adorned with buildings, pastures, gardens and orchards. In the winter, when it is frozen over, and the surface of the water is converted into a shell of ice, it emits a horrible sound resembling the moans of many animals collected together; but this, perhaps, may be occasioned by the sudden bursting of the shell, and the gradual ebullition of the air through imperceptible channels.

When the party reached North Wales, he continued to hover between reality and legend:

On the highest parts of these mountains are two lakes worthy of admiration. The one has a floating island in it, which is often driven from one side to the other by the force of the winds; and the shepherds behold with astonishment their cattle, whilst feeding, carried to the distant parts of the lake. A part of the bank naturally bound together by the roots of willows and other shrubs may have been broken off, and increased by the alluvion of the earth from the shore; and being continually agitated by the winds, which in so elevated a situation blow with great violence, it cannot reunite itself firmly with the banks. The other lake is noted for a wonderful and singular miracle. It contains three sorts of fish – eels, trout, and perch, all of which have only one eye, the left being wanting; but if the curious reader should demand of me the explanation of so extraordinary a circumstance, I cannot presume to satisfy him.

Another well-known traveller in North Wales was the colourful George Borrow,[18] much impressed in his book, *Wild Wales* (1862) by the mountains, after an upbringing in the flatness of Norfolk. Close to Llyn Cwellyn, to the southwest of Yr Wyddfa, the proper name for Snowdon, he came across an old man who had already seen the attractions of the area for an increasing number of tourists, and introduced himself as the Snowdon ranger:

'I suppose you are acquainted with all the secrets of the hills?'
'Trust the old ranger for that, your honour. I would show your honour the black lake in the frightful hollow in which the fishes have monstrous heads and little bodies, the lake on which neither swan, duck nor any kind of wildfowl was ever seen to light. Then I would show your honour the fountain of the hopping creatures ...'

The truths of these places are no less interesting than the stories that Gerald and Borrow relate. We fly in over Anglesey and then hover around the mountains of Eryri, or Snowdonia, which merge to the south with the less craggy uplands of mid-Wales, before reaching the lowlands of South West Wales. Anglesey, separated from the mainland by the fault that the sea has eroded to create the Menai Strait, has a particularly complex geology with many sedimentary rocks, including limestone, that give the catchments the gift of fertile farmland, and many of its 100 or so shallow lakes the scourge of excess nutrients.[19] Conductivities are of the order of 200 to 450 µS/cm, and their pH values are distinctly alkaline for the most part.

Their origins are as natural glacial rock or moraine-dammed basins (about a quarter of them), reservoirs, quarry or mine pools, relict river channels, subsidence lakes, coastal lagoons and artificial fish ponds. *Llynnoedd* (the Welsh plural of lake, 'llyn') Cadarn, Llwydiarth and tarns on Mynydd Bodafon have formed in rock basins. Deposits of boulder clay retain Llynnoedd Llygeirian and Hafadol. Maelog, Rhos Ddu and Coron are dammed by sand. The largest lakes on Anglesey are reservoirs, Alaw and Cefni, and the largest natural Lake, Llyn Traffwll, is also used for water supply.

Anglesey also holds volcanic rocks with metal deposits, and the Parys Mountain Mine (Fig. 173) was once the world's largest producer of copper.

Oxidation of the exposed sulphide minerals in the spoil heaps produces iron-rich waters and sulphuric acid, with high concentrations of toxic metals, and precipitation of red-orange ochre (iron oxide/hydroxide) in the streams draining the workings. The water of Llyn Llaethdy, which receives drainage from Parys Mountain, is coloured red, has a pH of 3.2 and is devoid of fish. Small ponds, close by, may have pH 2.2, and conductivities of over 4000 µS/cm, but these waters are not sterile. Apart from bacteria, they may have algae such as *Euglena*, growing in otherwise lethal concentrations of copper of 400 mg/L.

FIG 173. Water draining from Parys Mountain in Anglesey, an old copper mine surrounded by mounds of colourful mining waste, is highly acid and influences pools and small lakes in the area.

It is the northern massif of the Welsh mainland that attracts the most attention, however. The 400 lakes of Snowdonia are grouped, like those of the Cumbrian Lake District, in ice-deepened valleys, radiating from the highest points of Yr Wyddfa, the Glyders and Tryffan. There are Cwellyn, Peris, Padarn and Ogwen, in the northwest, Gwynant and Dinas in the southwest and Eigiau, Cowlyd, Crafnant and Geirionydd in the northeast. They are higher, cooler and less well known than the English Lakes and it is said that one visits the English Lake District for the lakes and Snowdonia for the mountains. It is true that the Snowdonia lakes are more uniform – limnologically that is. The geology is varied, but largely of hard igneous and metamorphic rocks that all weather slowly and give soft water of slightly acid pH, low conductivity and broadly similar ecological communities.[20]

The core geology is of compressed volcanic ash, hard and poorly weathered, with craggy ridges. It is flanked by Cambrian, Ordovician and Silurian sediments, many of them squeezed and baked by the past volcanic activity into hard slates. The communities of plants in the lakes are largely isoetids, the plankton, diatoms and desmids, and the fish, trout, with a few remnants of charr, called torgoch. It is claimed that the torgoch is genetically distinct from charr elsewhere, and varies even among the four lakes, Padarn, Cwellyn, Mymbyr and Bodlyn, where it naturally occurs. It is undoubtedly true, but is not a distinctive Welsh phenomenon. It is a tendency of many fish in the circumstances of isolation that a lake gives.

The Welsh lakes appeal more for their aesthetic qualities; their framing against the mountains, irregularity of shape and long association with Welsh myths and literature give them a mystique not enjoyed by the cosy regularities and foot-of-the-mountain comfort of the better-known English ones. George Borrow again:

Manifold were the objects which we saw from the brow of Snowdon ... but of all the objects we saw, those which filled us with most delight and admiration, were numerous lakes and lagoons which like ice of polished silver, lay reflecting the rays of the sun in deep valleys at our feet.

Their very names add an aura, in their original language or in translation. Llyn Caseg Fraith is the lake of the dappled mare, Llyn Crafnant that of the garlic hollow and Llyn y Dywarchen that of the floating island, which Gerald first described, and to which the Astronomer Royal, Edmund Halley (of the comet), swam out to establish that it really was floating in 1698. There are commemorations of past events, for which history and mythology inseparably merge. Llyn Teyrn, a small corrie lake below the peak of Snowdon, is the Lake of the King, and like Llyn Ogwen, more prosaically the Lake of the Pig, is associated with Arthur. Llyn Morwynion is the Lake of the Maidens, where Bloduedd and her sisters from

Ardudwy drowned when fleeing the nefarious attentions of the men of Gwynedd (various Blodueddai meet sticky ends in Welsh legend). Llyn Perfeddau is the Lake of Entrails, but Llyn Mwyngil is the Lake of the Pleasant Retreat.

Cultural associations are strong also in the more recent industrial past. These rocky landscapes owe not a little to piles of mining and quarry debris, some of them quite enormous. Mining and quarrying began early, but their main effects were in the nineteenth century. Slate was quarried to roof the Roman garrison at Caernarfon and the valley, Cwm Peris, that runs to the northeast of Snowdon was the site of a productive copper and lead mine. Mining also took place around Llynoedd Glaslyn and Llydaw, well known now to many walkers who take the Miners' Track up Snowdon, but in the nineteenth century places of brutal hard work, from which the crushed ore was carried in sacks for many miles until it could be loaded onto carts at the nearest road. Ravens now circle over the deserted workings and smelter. The mine was closed in 1915, after the level of Lydaw was lowered by 4 m to ease the work, and water is still fed from Llyn Llydaw down to Cwm Dyli, the oldest power station in Britain and Ireland, where electricity has been generated since 1906 in a building more reminiscent of a chapel than a factory.

Evidence of industry is everywhere in Eryri and there is some sort of modification to almost every lake. Most prominent are slate workings (Fig. 174).

FIG 174. Slate waste and the engineering of water needed for preparation of the slates is common all over Snowdonia; part of one of the few remaining quarries, at Bethesda.

Slate quarrying does not poison the water, as heavy metal mining did for a time, but it needs water to power and cool the saws used in fashioning the slates, and to wash away the fine debris, so many of the lakes were dammed to create greater stores. The slate industry blossomed in the eighteenth and nineteenth centuries with the flurry of house building in the industrial towns in Britain. There were huge quarries at Penrhyn in Bethesda, Dinorwic, the Nantlle Valley and Blaenau Festiniog. The best slate comes from Cambrian rocks and was quarried at Penrhyn and Dinorwic, but less brittle and more easily workable by machine, is the Ordovician slate of Blaenau Festiniog and Corris, close to Cader Idris to the south near Macynlleth.

Slate production in North Wales reached 450,000 tons per year in the 1870s (with the rest of Britain producing only a tenth as much). It dominated the economy of North Wales and was as significant to Wales as coal; but quarrying slate needs a large labour force and this disappeared following the First World War. Most of the quarries had closed by the 1960s and 1970s, with production down to 22,000 tons and unable to compete with cheaper plastic slates, cement slabs and ceramic tiles. But the industry left three important legacies. One was cultural. The quarrymen had little formal education, but they created, in the cabans where they ate their midday meal, vital discussion groups that ultimately improved working conditions for the largely Welsh-speaking, nonconformist and liberal workers, in confrontation with the English-speaking, Anglican and Tory owners and managers. Discourse strengthened the bases of Welsh culture and attitudes to the environment that are even now more sympathetic than those of the piratical English. In the *Dictionary of Welsh Biography*, 50 entries started life as slate workers, only four as owners.

FIG 175. View of Snowdon from Llyn Nantle Uchaf.

FIG 176. Painting (in the Walker Art Gallery, Liverpool) by Richard Wilson made around 1766 of Snowdon, showing two lakes, Nantle Uchaf, in the background, and Nantle Isaf, in the foreground. The latter was later drained to facilitate slate working around the Dorothea Quarry and thus does not appear in the modern picture (Fig. 175).

The second was the modification of the landscape by the huge piles of inert rock waste that both dramatise and disfigure many of the hillsides. One ton of finished slate leaves 30 tons of waste. But there was extensive modification to the streams and lakes also. Llyn Nantle Uchaf appears on maps close to the Dorothea Quarry and beyond which a splendid panorama of the peak of Snowdon can be seen (Fig. 175). But *uchaf,* meaning high is usually matched by a sister lake *isaf,* meaning low. There is a nineteenth-century painting of this panorama in the Walker Art Gallery in Liverpool by Richard Wilson (Fig. 176), in which a narrow promontory separates two bodies of water. Llyn Nantle Isaf did exist, but it interfered with the quarry workings and was drained to a wet meadow.

The third legacy lies in the development of water power for the industry and in a prominent alteration to one of the most dramatic lakes of Snowdonia, Llyn Peris, and in the creation of the largest (or second largest; measurements vary) lake in Wales, the Trawsfynnyd Reservoir. Llyn Peris, close to Llanberis, was once a single lake with Llyn Padarn, but the delta of a side stream, the Afon Hwch, cut the lake into two. On the land which now separates the lakes are the romantic ruins of Dolbadarn Castle and, more prosaically, the sewage treatment works for Llanberis, a popular small town for walkers and the start of the small railway that climbs Snowdon for those unwilling or unable to walk up it. Llyn Padarn suffered algal problems, peculiarly of a desmid, *Staurastrum planktonicum*, which coloured the lake like paint in 1992 and led to a legal case against the lake managers by a local angling club. Phosphorus stripping was installed at the works in 1995, but is not particularly efficient and the bloom problem is still there, now caused by cyanobacteria. In 2009 the lake was closed to recreation for a time and its appearance has done nothing to improve the economy of the town.

Alterations to Llyn Peris have been more dramatic. The Afon Nant Peris used to be the main inflow to Peris and then Padarn. It is now diverted through a tunnel direct to Padarn, thus isolating Peris, whose level has been lowered by about 2 m. This was to modify the lake as part of a pumped storage hydroelectric scheme. Deep inside the mountain to the north of the lake, under the old workings of the Dinorwig slate quarry, a huge cavern has been excavated to accommodate the machinery. The head of water comes from an artificial reservoir, Llyn Marchlyn Mawr, high above on the moorland. Water is pumped up from Peris to this reservoir when there is surplus capacity on the National Grid. The scheme was originally conceived to accommodate a surplus from proposed nuclear power stations, whose power generation cannot be switched off, as it can be in a hydroelectric or fossil fuel-burning station. New nuclear power stations have not been built so the power to pump up the water is taken from the grid when general demand is low and prices cheap. As at Loch Lomond, the water is used to generate power when prices are high. The scheme has been well disguised and the lake is less disfigured by it than by the slate workings. There has been a small bonus in that lowering the level has exposed, in what were the shallows, some exquisite ice-scratched rocks, now preserved as a Site of Special Scientific Interest.

TRAWSFYNYDD AND THE DEE REGULATION SCHEME

The putative nuclear power stations, planned for Wales, were heralded by the Trawsfynnyd nuclear power station, which operated from 1965 to 1991 (when necessary repairs were found to be uneconomic). Lake Trawsfynedd, which had been created in the late 1920s as a head for hydroelectric power generation at a station at Maentwrog on the coast, was used as cooling water for the nuclear

FIG 177. Llyn Tegid.

station after the dam had been raised, though it is shallow and needed baffles to be built linking some of its islands to ensure the circulation of the water.

The creation of Trawsfynydd lake passed with little complaint but that was not the case for our next stop, around the headwaters of the River Dee and Llyn Tegid (Bala Lake). To the southeast of Snowdonia, Llyn Tegid (Fig. 177), the largest natural lake in Wales, is not far from the English border. It was formed by the ice along a fault whose weakness allowed gouging to some depth, around 43 m. Like most lakes, Llyn Tegid has some star species, much vaunted as flagships by the conservation organisations: the gwyniad, the same species as the powan of Loch Lomond and the schelly of the English Lake District, the glutinous snail and the floating water plantain, which crops up in some of the more sheltered bays. Llyn Tegid is attractively set, and from the small railway that runs along its southern shore, brightly coloured yachts set off the hills from which its waters come. There have been some algal blooms which have exercised the tourist industry, which nonetheless attracts the tourists that provide the nutrients, and several fish introductions including ruffe, but with apparently little effect on the gwyniad. Deep down, however, the hypolimnion is probably becoming more deoxygenated than formerly and the gwyniad may be squeezed in summer between a warm epilimnion that it has always shunned and the cooler waters whose high concentrations of oxygen provide a refuge.

Llyn Tegid, however, has had a greater role to play. It is now the main reservoir for a scheme that makes the Dee, its outflow, perhaps the most regulated and controlled river of Europe, and the water supply for much of industrial North Wales and Merseyside. The Dee flows through Corwen and Llangollen to its meandering course, alas now embanked, on the Cheshire plain, eventually to Chester. It is then insulted by a straightened channel, built in the eighteenth century in a failed attempt to maintain Chester as a port, which takes it out to its now silted estuary separating the Wirral from North Wales.

In the early nineteenth century, Thomas Telford put sluices on the outflow of Llyn Tegid so that more water could be stored to support his new Shropshire Union Canal, which began at the Horseshoe Falls, close to Llangollen. From 1826, water was withdrawn from the lower Dee, above the tidal limit inland of Chester, to supply the city. A reservoir, Llyn Alwen, was built in the Dee catchment in the 1920s, to supply Birkenhead on the Wirral. Then in the 1950s, more ambitious schemes were conceived by the then Dee and Clwyd River Board to control flooding in the lowlands and guarantee a supply of water for abstraction.

In 1956 the Tegid outlet was lowered by 2 m and sluice gates built so that more water could be stored or drawn off; the Afon Tryweryn, which joined the Dee downstream of Llyn Tegid, was sluiced so that Tryweryn water could be diverted into Tegid and stored, or allowed downstream in dry summers. This enabled continuous abstraction from the River Dee of 235,000 cubic metres per day for drinking water and by the British Waterways Board for its canals.

Demand for water in Liverpool and the Wirral then increased and plans were made to create a reservoir on the course of the River Tryweryn. This required a parliamentary bill, which, once passed, gave Liverpool City Council a compulsory purchase order to buy the land of Cwm Celyn Valley. A dam was built across the valley and a village was evacuated and drowned. It was an entirely Welsh-speaking community, with a chapel and cemetery, school, post office and 12 farms. Llyn Celyn was completed in 1967, enabling abstractions of 327,000 cubic metres per day, together with additional flood control storage. The scheme could then increase by threefold the dry-weather flow for most of the length of the river and could even allow discharges to be made to enable white water rafting.

Llyn Brenig, a new reservoir, was added to the scheme in 1979, increasing the potential abstraction from the Dee to nearly 900,000 cubic metres per day with a flow of at least 364,000 cubic metres per day in the river at Chester, except in the more extreme of droughts. This allows salmon to pass up river, though the numbers are now small, and prevents tidal salt water from reaching the water supply intakes above Chester. A third of the total run-off of a catchment

FIG 178. Llyn Celyn at low level (right), with ruins of a wall destroyed in the flooding of the lake appearing (photo by Oosoom); the Rev. R. S. Thomas around the time he wrote his poem 'Reservoirs'; and a painted wall, south of Aberystwyth, exhorting us to 'Remember Tryweryn'.

of 1,816 km² is now under control of the water engineers. In very dry conditions the flow of the river would otherwise be only 0.3 m³ per second, compared with the regulated flow, which can usually be kept to at least 4.2. Overall, the Dee Regulation scheme might be seen as of all-round positive benefit, but there is a downside, which might seem small but which has had great political significance and will continue to reverberate. It has been the consequences of flooding of the village of Tryweryn to create Llyn Celyn (Fig. 178).

The scheme was opposed by most of the Welsh Members of Parliament when the Bill was presented in 1957, but they could not stop the development because the government was determined to push the Bill through Parliament. The local authorities had no voice in the decision and this caused great resentment. Many people opposed the scheme with demonstrations and petitions. The Tryweryn Defence Committee included some of Wales' most prominent and revered personalities, including Ifan ab Owen Edwards, Megan Lloyd George, T. I. Ellis, and Lord Ogmore, and although opposition to the scheme did not come only from Welsh nationalists, the issue inspired Plaid Cymru, and provided an impetus to its campaigns.

The Lord Mayor of Cardiff, Alderman J. H. Morgan, called a 'Save Tryweryn' meeting in October 1956, when over 300 representatives from local government and trade unions, and ten MPs were present. It was decided to send a delegation to Liverpool to appeal for a change of heart but the entreaties failed. In November 1956, a procession, led by Gwynfor Evans, leader of Plaid Cymru, and including 70 of the villagers, walked through Liverpool to oppose the reservoir, and in August 1957 Gwynfor Evans proposed that Meirionnydd County Council could build a reservoir in Cwm Croes, where only one farm would be affected, and sell the water from the reservoir to Liverpool Corporation.

On three occasions in 1962 and 1963 there were attempts to sabotage the building of the reservoir. But the sentiments were strongly anti-English in every part of Welsh society. One of its most famous poets, R. S. Thomas (Fig. 178), contributed a bitter poem called 'Reservoirs':

> There are places in Wales I don't go:
> Reservoirs that are the subconscious
> of a people, troubled far down
> with gravestones, chapels, villages even;
> The serenity of their expression revolts me,
> it is a pose for strangers, a watercolour's appeal
> to the mass, instead of the poem's harsher conditions ...

Liverpool Corporation was forced to call the reservoir Llyn Celyn, dropping the planned name Tryweryn, of the flooded village. The dam's opening ceremony, on 28 October 1965, lasted only a few minutes before it was disrupted by a riot. In 2005, the Liverpool City Council offered an apology for its former insensitivity, no doubt with an eye to future relations with what is now a semi-independent country providing much of the city's water supply. Resentment over reservoir schemes in Wales has undoubtedly contributed greatly to the Welsh Nationalist Movement and the political changes that may ultimately result in the break-up of the United Kingdom into separate countries.

When our carpet next flies, southwards towards Pembrokeshire, we will pass over the village of Llanyrhystud, south of Aberystwyth, and there, by the side of the main road to Cardigan, a wall (Fig. 178) has been painted in large letters with the words 'Cofiwch Dryweryn'. I have passed it many times in the last 40 years. When the paint fades, it is always renewed. It means 'Remember Tryweryn'.

PEMBROKESHIRE

Pembrokeshire, in southwest Wales, is justly famous in university geology departments for the variety of its rocks, and among marine biologists for the richness of its seas as they roar through the passages among the islands of its exposed coast. The glaciation was at its limits here, leaving, as the Gwaun Valley, a deep trough eroded by the water draining from ice-bound lakes to the north, and a famous ria in Milford Haven where the rising seas drowned the valley of the River Cleddau to provide a deep-water harbour, now importing oil and natural gas. There are no high mountains, just the low hills of Preseli, but there is a wonderful contrast, both geological and cultural, between the hard Ordovician metamorphic rocks of the north, with igneous intrusions, one of them famous as the source of the Sarsen stones at Stonehenge, and the sedimentary rocks of the south, where, in patterns of parallel bands, the folded coal measures, millstone grit, carboniferous limestone and old red sandstone are laid out.

Pembrokeshire provides poor pickings for limnologists. There are no natural lakes. But there is a reflection of the powerful north–south divide in the three artificial ones. In the north are two drinking water reservoirs, Rosebush and Llys-y-Fran on the Afon Syfynwy. The former is the older water supply reservoir, the latter created when it was predicted that the oil port around Milford Haven would lead to burgeoning industry. It didn't. Rosebush has developed swamps of sedge; Llys-y-Fran has uninteresting edges for its sides are steep and the littoral is spare, but that means it has a useful role for damage-free canoeing, kayaking and sailing, and angling for stocked rainbow and brown trout. To the south, on the limestone, is the much more interesting Bosherston Lake, or rather the Bosherston Lily Ponds (Fig. 179) of long local tradition.[21] They were distinguished in name as a lake only when the area was made a National Nature Reserve and a degree of pompous officialdom was imposed. The lily ponds are also artificial, but much older, and with a story that reflects the cultural history of the county.

The Normans moved into Pembrokeshire with alacrity, pushing the Welsh northwards onto the poorer, hilly land, still a stronghold of the Welsh language, its villages with chapels or simple churches, and its attitudes, at least until very recently, serious and austere. The richer land of the south, which the Normans had grabbed, was defended by a line of castles following a divide, the Landsker, that is much older and follows the geology.[22] The lingua franca is English, the churches with castellated watchtowers and the living easier. Gerald of Wales was born in one of the additional coastal castles, at Manorbier, and waxes lyrical about the richness of the land.

FIG 179. The eight-arch bridge on the eastern arm, looking northwards, of the Bosherston Lily Ponds. The former site of Stackpole Court is upstream to the right.

William of Normandy gave a large portion, the slice of limestone that occupies the south coast of Pembrokeshire, to Elidyr de Stacpole. The Manor passed to the Vernons, the Stanleys and, in the seventeenth century, to the Lorts, one of whom, Elizabeth, heiress to the property, married Alexander Campbell of Cawdor (shades of *Macbeth*) in 1689. Stackpole Court was then fortified and solid, rather than elegant, but was rebuilt much larger by their son in the 1730s in the Palladian style. The mediaeval village of Stackpole, sited across a stream, and facing the house, was moved to its present position so as not to taint the view. The grandson, John Campbell (1755–1827), who inherited in 1777, then began a major project of landscaping. More funds had come in when he inherited the Cardiganshire estate of his mother's family.

At that time the house overlooked the wet meadow floodplain of a small stream that shortly became an estuary, opening out to the coast at Broadhaven. Three years later, Campbell had dammed the upper part of the estuary to form a freshwater lake, and by 1797 had built an elegant eight-arch bridge (Fig. 179), with a weir at its foot to facilitate draining and removal of silt, and a single-arch bridge upstream on the approach to the house. He also included silt-trapping ponds on the tributaries. Campbell and his son then expanded the house, built a stable block, brewery and dairy and dammed two further tributaries of the original main stream with causeways that allow a flow through narrow gaps midway along each. In 1789 John Campbell had married Isabella Caroline, eldest daughter of Frederick Howard, 5th Earl of Carlisle. One cannot but wonder at the motivation for creation of the lily ponds. Was it a gift to impress a new young wife; was it just to conform to the fashion of the time for taming the landscape; was it her idea to enhance the status of the family? Lancelot (Capability) Brown had by then set a fashion for English country estates to have lakes close to them, mirroring the house on still days. It was certainly not inexpensive.

It is likely that the former estuary was blocked and unblocked regularly by sand blow so the lily ponds were completed in 1914 with a final dam, now buried under sand, at the mouth of the former estuary, so that the Ponds radiate in three arms (Fig. 180) from a central basin closest to the sea. Stackpole was by then an almost self-contained estate of several thousand acres and remained prosperous until, in 1938, the War Office compulsorily purchased 6,000 acres for army tank-training grounds and, without the revenue, the estate never recovered. The Campbells retreated to their house in Scotland; Stackpole Court was demolished in 1963, and in 1976 the remaining estate was broken up and sold. Part of it passed to the National Trust and the lily ponds, coast, dunes and woodlands became a National Nature Reserve. All that remains of the House is a stone plaque, with the family motto '*Be Mindful*', set at the top of steps that start the descent to the water below.

Of the three arms of the ponds, the easternmost, above which the Court stood, is the longest and is supplied by a stream that comes from the west from Merrion, where stand the buildings of the army camp that manages the tank ranges. Effluent from there, and originally effluent from the sewage works that serves Stackpole village, entered the eastern arm and raised the nutrient levels.

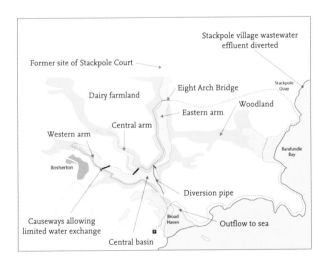

FIG 180. The Bosherston Lily Ponds

The Stackpole stream also drains old red sandstone, with seeded pastures and some arable land and plantations on the slopes, whose soils erode readily. The effluent from Stackpole was diverted to the sea in 1984, but the arm remains nutrient rich from the diffuse sources. A large dairy farm occupies many of the surrounding fields.

There are vigorous populations of curly and sago pondweeds, and spiked water milfoil, characteristic of nutrient-rich sites, skeins of filamentous green algae, and sometimes cyanobacterial blooms in the eastern arm. The western and central arms lie entirely on limestone. The western arm is also somewhat enriched. Its main water source is through groundwater springs, but it drains the village of Bosherston and there is the possibility of numerous small nutrient sources, but it bears populations of the white water lilies and charophytes for which the ponds are well known. The middle arm, fed by springs from the limestone, has probably best preserved the original state of the water. It is always crystal clear, with a dense bed of bristly stonewort and other charophytes, and broad bands of lilies, stretching off into the distance, as one stands on the causeway and looks upstream.

The central portion, bordered by reeds on the east and a steep rocky shore backed by woodland to the west, is in varying condition. Its plant populations are probably declining owing to nutrients coming in from the eastern and western arms. More would come in from the east but, in 1992, a pipe, buried in the sediment and controlled by a sluice within the causeway dam, was installed. The pipe takes eastern arm water directly to the outlet, bypassing the central basin. The contrasts between the arms rest mostly on the differences in nutrient supply and the balance between surface water and groundwater, which give the pools their varied character, a not inconsiderable diversity of dragonflies (some 21 species) and a panoply of ten species of bats, including greater and lesser horseshoe, feeding partly on the insects that emerge from the marly sediments.

THE NOT-SO-DEEP SOUTH

Southwards from Pembrokeshire, across the Severn Estuary, our carpet reaches the southern coasts of England. The south of England is not notable for its natural lakes. The rocks are largely sedimentary and porous, and of chalk in places, so that even streams disappear underground or dry up, but there are lakes on the coast. Eroded by the sea, rock fragments are rolled and rounded by the waves and deposited in shingle ridges around the high tide level. Storms may heighten these beaches by throwing the stones inland, and in time a barrier may be formed, which, if it is across a stream, will dam a lake. In Kent, the enormous amount of shingle piled up at Dungeness originated the Romney marshes, formerly with myriad small lakes and wetlands, but these are now largely drained, leaving just two small natural lakes, the Open Pools amid the shingle, though there is a much greater area of water (around 12 per cent of the Ness) created by gravel extraction. Westwards, the Fleet behind Chesil Beach could well have become a freshwater lake, but its connection to the sea near Weymouth and Portland has been kept open and it remains an estuary. The Little Sea, near Studland in Dorset, is a large slack in a sand dune system, that started as a stream dammed by the blown sand. On the southwestern peninsula are a few small lakes, or ex-lakes, formed by barrier-beach damming. One, at Porlock in Somerset, was largely a freshwater marsh until a storm in 1996 breached the barrier and returned it to being an estuary with salt marshes, but in Cornwall, Loe Pool, downstream of Helston, the Swanpool at Falmouth and, in Devon, Slapton Ley, where we are hovering, remain.

The Ley (Fig. 26) is surrounded by rich farmlands on Devonian slates, shales and sandstones, with low rounded hills, deep valleys, green pastures and lots of cows. A long shingle ridge, the Slapton Line, runs from Start Point in the south, to Blackpool (not *the* Blackpool but a hamlet where the ridge once dammed back the now drained black pool) in the north. The central part of the shingle is called Slapton Sands, 100–150 m in width and 6–11 m deep, though there is little sand (the material is gravel and pebbles, up to 5 cm in size), which have dammed the Stokely Stream, the Start Stream and the River Gara to form what were once probably two, maybe three, separate lakes. With the meddling so characteristic of human endeavour these have been combined into one by the diversion of the River Gara and a connection made at Slapton Bridge between what are now called the Higher Ley and the Lower Ley.

Both basins are shallow, with mean depths around 1.5 m, and the Higher Ley is now swamp, with a stream channel flowing between partly floating rafts of reed; it is accumulating eroded soil from the pastures of the catchment rather rapidly. This, however, saves the Lower Ley from filling in so quickly, but does not prevent a eutrophication problem, first noticed in the 1970s, but accelerating since 1945, and now mostly from the nutrients excreted by the stock kept on the catchment farms. Mains sewerage for the villages was installed in 1953, but people contribute only about 14 per cent of the phosphorus and 2 per cent of the nitrogen. As so frequently elsewhere, the increased nutrients have converted a relatively clear lake, floored by a diversity of plants, into one with much larger algal populations, more turbid water, and only a residual plant community dominated by the very tolerant hornwort. Dating of sediments shows the Lower Ley to have been an estuary until

FIG 181. The road running along the shingle ridge that dams Slapton Ley was damaged in storms in 2001. (Nick Slinger)

about 3,000 years ago when it became fresh as the barrier beach, moving inland with the rising sea level, finally closed, but there have been some brief periods (though they could have been decades) when the sea reinvaded, leaving deposits of clay and the shells of marine molluscs. Freshwater has prevailed for perhaps the last 1,000 years. We are here, however, not so much for any particular peculiarity of the limnology, but for two other reasons: the history and future of the shingle ridge that is crucial to maintenance of the lake, and for the significance of the lake in the practice of publishing scientific information.

The findings from the bottom deposits that this is by no means a permanent freshwater system give a background to the winter of 2000/2001 when the shingle ridge was greatly disturbed in storms, and a section of the road that runs along it was destroyed (Fig. 181). Over about a kilometre stretch, about 5 m of a total height of 6m of the ridge were washed away. The road was built in 1856 and is important for tourism in the area. Slapton Sands are popular, not least for the warm Devon climate and the pubs and restaurants at Torcross and in Slapton Village, but are visited also because of their wartime significance. In 1943, several villages in the area were evacuated so that the beach and hinterland could be used as a rehearsal area for the D-Day landings of the British and American armies on the French coast. A monument in the centre of the ridge commemorates that, and deaths during the practice manoeuvres. The roads inland of the Ley are narrow and winding and there is no access for buses and coaches through Slapton village.

In 2001, following the damage and closure of the road, different groups of people wanted different things to happen. One group wanted immediate reinstatement of the road, creation of a sea wall, or other substantial fortifications, to prevent the shingle ridge from possible breaching, and protection of the tourist assets at whatever cost. Another would have preferred creation of new and wider roads inland of the Ley. This acknowledged that shingle ridges are not permanent. The village of Hallsands, to the south of the Ley, was irretrievably damaged in storms in 1903, following excavations of gravel offshore for the building of the dockyards at Devonport and this illustrated the consequences of interfering with local natural features.

Slapton Sands are steadily rolling landwards as the seas erode shingle from the front of the ridge and throw it backwards over the crest. This process would undermine a sea wall or sheet piling. The shingle exposed on the ridge is part of a much bigger system under the water that cannot be controlled. In any case the costs of major fortifications or new roads would be very great and not justifiable by the relatively small economy associated with the road. The compromise was to rebuild the damaged 200 m part of the existing road 20 m further inland, taking areas from what is now a National Nature Reserve, and creating an awkward precedent. The policy is to maintain the road as long as is feasible; it probably has a future life, if kept repaired, of 50 or a 100 years, though perhaps much less as sea levels rise and the frequency of extreme weather increases. But eventually it is likely that, as at Porlock, the barrier will be breached irreparably and the local economy will simply have to adjust.

So also will the local nature conservation (Fig. 182). What is now a freshwater lake will become a saline lagoon. The reeds that support populations of Cetti's (7 per cent of the British breeding population), sedge and reed warblers will disappear. The only location in Britain and Ireland for a tiny plant of the pink family, the strapwort, which grows on wet gravel on the western side of the lower

FIG 182. When the shingle ridge at Slapton Ley is eventually breached by rising sea levels and storms, the freshwater lake, site of many field courses (left), the only British location of the tiny strapwort (top right) and one of the few locations for Cetti's warbler (lower right) will be replaced by an estuary.

Ley, will go. But there will be replacement with equally interesting brackish communities and an opportunity for study from the field centre in Slapton village. Established in a former hotel in the late 1950s it has already spawned an entire literature on the Ley and its catchment.[23] The brief summary of the limnology of the Ley, a few paragraphs ago, is possible because there are 30 or 40 papers, representing over 100 person-years of work, that contain the evidence on which those couple of hundred or so words were based.

About half of these papers come from a journal, *Field Studies*, founded by the Field Studies Council in 1959 to publish research carried out from its centres by its staff and visiting researchers. The intention was that these should be intelligibly written so that anyone could understand them and this mission was faithfully followed. Some of the papers are classics of how to carry out and record field observations on limited budgets, and how to write well. Alas, the journal had to be discontinued in 2003, simply because the flow of papers had dried up.

There were several reasons. Staff at the centres had less time for research because teaching has become more intense and directed more towards providing basic geography and ecology courses for schools whose teachers seem less willing to run their own courses than formerly (possibly a consequence of the fear of legal reprisals should someone fall over). University researchers have been under pressure to publish their work in prominent international journals, even if it is not read widely, because of restrictions on access to those unable to afford the sometimes very expensive journal subscriptions. Not only that but the standard of writing has deteriorated greatly in the last 50 years and papers are now much more pompously written and often full of unnecessary jargon.[24] Science now needs lots of money and to raise the grants and contracts needed to support it means that it must sound impressive. The work may be valuable but the communication of it is often abysmal and therefore much is wasted. *Field Studies*, and the work it contains on the Slapton area, remains something of a beacon.

THE MERES AND MOSSES

Field Studies was where a paper that really influenced me was published.[25] It was by Charles Sinker, Warden of Preston Montford Field Centre in Shropshire. It described the least well-known lake district in Britain and Ireland: the meres and mosses of the Cheshire, Shropshire and Staffordshire plain, to which we will now fly. The lakes are hidden among farmland, private estates and golf courses, in countryside where public paths are scarce or grossly overgrown, and scattered over an area so large that their existence as a lake district is not obvious on the

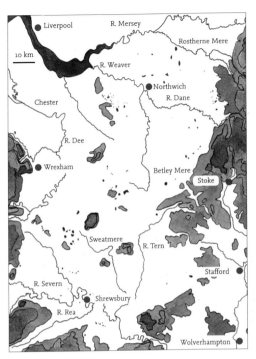

FIG 183. The meres lie on the northwest Midland plain and are the small blue dots on this map. Land over 50 m is shown in green and over 100 m in brown. The Welsh Hills lie to the left (west), the Mersey estuary to the north, the Pennines to the right (east) and the South Shropshire Hills to the lower edge of the map.

maps (Fig. 183). In 1961, when I attended, as a sixth-former, a course given by Charles on the meres and mosses and contributed some of the data in a diagram eventually to appear in the paper, I did not know that, 30 years later, it was to become one of my own research areas.

Imagine the Devensian ice sheet, hundreds of metres thick, melting back from its limit, somewhere in the Midlands. As the ice melts back, great chunks, sometimes a couple of kilometres across, break off and crash down. From under the sheet, torrents of meltwater gush out, bringing with them the debris of clay, sand, gravel and rock that the ice had scraped from the land as it moved forward. The noise is terrific as the water pours out, spreads over the land, slows its flow and drops its load of debris in temporary lakes and mudflows. In winter, the melting slows, so that bigger piles of debris accumulate as moraines at the foot of the cliff of ice. In summer the melting accelerates, and this is when icebergs topple from the glacier edge and fall into the wet, soft deposits below, and become buried in more debris that insulates them for a time. Push ice cubes into wet sand in a tray in a warm room and you get the effect. When the ice melts, a hole remains and becomes full of melt water.

FIG 184. Charles Sinker's drawings of Sweatmere, with its fringing carrs (upper) and Clarepool Moss, with its raised bog (lower) and residual mere at the centre, are somehow far more evocative of the feel of these places than any photograph could be. From Sinker, 1962.

The icebergs varied in size and the resultant basins consequently are big and small, shallow and deep. The setting is the great wet and flat theatre of the northwest Midland plain, rimmed by the Welsh hills to the west, the Shropshire Hills to the south and the Pennines to the east. To the north, across the River Mersey, it continues between the coast and the Pennines into Lancashire and to the feet of the Cumbrian Mountains. The deeper basins remain as meres, fringed with wetlands (Fig. 184), the shallower have succeeded to raised bogs, the mosses. In some small steep-sided basins, as at Black Mere, Chartley Moss and Clarepool Moss (Fig. 184), reed crossed over the lake as a floating mat and bog formed on that, leaving a small area of open water in the middle, and giving a surface that quakes like a water bed if you walk on it (but don't, it is easily damaged).

One mere and moss complex that was obliterated now underlies the precinct of the University of Liverpool. The Moss Lake was a large expanse of bog and water, in its time sufficiently large to force a diversion for travellers entering the city. Two streams emerging from it provided water-mill power and supplied tanners and dyers with clean water, and were regulated by flood gates to serve as a means of cleansing the Pool, the first harbour around which Liverpool was built. But in the early nineteenth century, Moss Lake was drained, and the construction of the Georgian Quarter around Abercromby Square, now the centre of the University, began. When later construction re-exposed the underlying peat deposits, the doyen of palaeoecology, Harry Godwin, tipped off by A. N. Burgess, the University's Professor of Botany at the time, took the opportunity to study the deposits and pollen sequence in them.[26] He revealed a splendid and classic sequence of development of a raised bog in a lake basin formed by melting of an ice block that I, as a successor professor of botany, would have greatly valued at the centre of the University instead of the rather boring garden which now occupies the only unbuilt part of the site.

The icebergs were dropped randomly; sometimes the basins were isolated from streams so that the meres are fed entirely by groundwater and rain; sometimes they were in what turned out to be stream valleys and have surface inflows and outflows. But there is also something of a pattern that has never been fully explained, in that the meres tend to fall into distinct groups, with tracts of country where there are few or none among the groups (Fig. 183). In all there are around 60 remaining meres and perhaps 200 mosses south of the Mersey, though many of the latter have been drained for agriculture or cut for peat to make garden compost and bulb fibre. Rarely, archaeological remains turn up during cutting, as at Lindow Moss, near Wilmslow, where the 2,000-year-old body of a young Celt, ritually sacrificed at a time of great upheaval as the Romans marched northwards, was exposed.[27] Many of the meres are probably naturally quite fertile; Oakmere, in Cheshire is an exception, for it is embedded in sand, but most of the meres are surrounded by fertile glacial drift. As elsewhere, the lakes are troubled by diffuse nutrients from the land and sometimes sewage effluents, discharged to their inflowing streams, for example at Aqualate Mere and Cop Mere, have artificially increased their productivity.

FIG 185. The Moss Lake has been replaced in Liverpool by houses and a garden, Abercrombie Square at the heart of the University of Liverpool.

There is a evidence of early algal blooms caused by cyanobacteria pre-dating the major intensification of agriculture following the Second World War.[28] This comes from direct observations from the late nineteenth century, and from the remains of algal pigments that can be extracted from dated sediment cores. Whitemere shows an abundance, at depths dated to about 6,400 years ago, of cyanobacterial carotenoids.

There is also a folk tradition of algal blooms. Mary Webb published, in 1924, a classic romantic novel, set in the early nineteenth century, called *Precious Bane*, whose heroine, Prudence Sarn, has a harelip, a birth defect now easily corrected by minor surgery but then feared as a sign of witchcraft. Prudence believes that if she bathes, dressed in a white smock and in full public view, in the local mere (probably Mary Webb had Bomere Pool in mind, since she lived close to it) during the time that the waters broke, she would be cured. The breaking of the waters was the appearance of cyanobacteria at the surface during calm conditions, when they float upwards and are not mixed back downwards. The analogy was made with the breaking of the yeast scum to the surface in the brewing of beer. The cure did not work, but Prudence was rescued by one Kester Woodseaves, a progressive man for his time, who rode in to pluck her to safety before the villagers could burn her. But that is to trivialise a work that embodies universal themes of suffering, the strength of individual spirit, the tension between spiritual and material values, good and evil, love and lust, and written with a deep knowledge and feeling for rural life and country prejudice.

The early occurrence of cyanobacterial blooms may be linked to another feature of the deeper meres. They have unusually high concentrations of phosphorus compounds, sometimes around a milligram of P per litre and much of it in organic and available form. Lakes elsewhere, in their undisturbed state, have lower than 0.015 mg/L, even in fertile areas (Chapter 2), and at most 0.1 or 0.2, even when heavily eutrophicated, and most of the phosphorus is then in combined form in the biomass and debris. These deeper meres tend also to have low nitrogen concentrations, despite agricultural catchments, and the growth of phytoplankton in them is limited by availability of nitrogen rather than by the more common cases elsewhere of limitation by phosphorus or both phosphorus and nitrogen.[29] Cyanobacteria as a group tend to be favoured by low ratios of nitrogen to phosphorus in the water, partly because some of them can fix their own nitrogen from the atmosphere.

The shallower meres do not necessarily have these features. They currently often have high algal growths but this is linked with eutrophication of the streams that flow into them carrying sewage effluent and farm and field drainage. The peculiarity lies with the deep meres, fed by groundwater, not surface streams. One suggestion has been that the local groundwater receives very high phosphorus concentrations from a mineral called apatite which is common in the glacial drift, but analysis of groundwater does not show particularly high concentrations except in a very few springs. The key to the high phosphorus levels may be that the deeper meres stratify in summer and have deoxygenated hypolimnia. This means that phosphate will be released from the sediments when iron compounds, which otherwise bind it, are reduced. The retention times of these meres are probably long because groundwater moves much more slowly than surface water, so that there is much less washout to remove the phosphate.

When the lake overturns and the water again becomes oxygenated we should expect that the phosphate would re-precipitate and indeed some does. However, a state appears to have been reached in which the steady small supply of phosphorus in the groundwater, accumulating over many years, is too much for the iron supply to cope with, and so a surplus remains in the water. At the same time the nitrogen supply from the catchment, also entering slowly, is vulnerable to denitrification in the soggy soils of the wetlands it must pass through at the edges of the meres, and becomes quite scarce. Some of the meres that fall into this category are: Hatchmere, Mere Mere, Crosemere, Betton Pool, Tatton Mere, Colemere, Combermere, Berrington Pool, Whitemere, Bomere Pool and Rostherne Mere, though the latter was influenced by a stream bearing sewage effluent until the mid-1990s. They provide interesting problems for water managers who see phosphorus reduction alone as the key to restoring damaged lakes.

The meres do not exhaust the range of lakes on the northwestern plains. As we fly northwards towards the Cumbrian Lake District, we will reach the flashes of Cheshire and Lancashire and the remnants of floodplain lakes set in the valleys of rivers draining from the east Pennine moors to the sea in Lancashire. These are our next stops.

THE FLASHES OF CHESHIRE AND LANCASHIRE

Flash is a local name for lake in the northwest, and has a 'flash in the pan' feel, if not origin, to it. The flashes were formed by the collapse of underground mines: for salt in Cheshire, for coal in Lancashire, and they tended to appear suddenly as the ground beneath caved in, and sometimes disappeared equally rapidly as further movements drained the water away. When they formed, they caused chaos to roads and buildings. The M62 Motorway between Manchester and Liverpool is distinctly bumpy in places, and one hopes that the signs saying 'Mining Subsidence' are just informants of history not portents of the future. The mines have now been made stable, we hope.

FIG 186. Salt mining undermined parts of Cheshire and gave rise to the flashes. Modern techniques are more brutal, but there is more attention given to support of the roof.

The deep salt beds of Cheshire are themselves 220-million-year-old lake deposits. When the continents briefly merged to form Pangaea around 300 million years ago, the interior of the huge land mass, where Britain and Ireland were squeezed, was very dry, just as the deep interiors of the continents are often dry now. The continuing turmoil in the land brought floodings of seawater to form huge salt lakes in the desert, as cracks opened and closed and the evaporation of this water led to the halite beds set among the sand dunes that became the New Red Sandstones of the Triassic period. The flashes are miniscule resurrections of these lakes, for they are flooded in Cheshire with salt water. There are not many of them, and most have been formed since 1897, around Winsford, the current centre of the salt industry, Sandbach, Northwich, Nantwich and Middlewich.

Salt has been mined from Roman times, at first for preserving food, but from the seventeenth century onwards as a raw material for the chemical industry that originated along the River Weaver, especially where it merged with the Mersey and its cargoes of coal from upstream in Lancashire. At first, salt was mined dry (Fig. 186) and pillars of salt were left to support the roofs of the galleries. For surety about 30 per cent of the salt should have been left for support, but the greed of the nineteenth-century owners sometimes reduced the pillars to 5 per cent. From the 1850s, the development of steam pumps meant that it was possible to get much more salt faster to the surface by flooding the mines, dissolving the salt and pumping the brine to the surface. The fresh water dissolved the old mine support pillars causing the massive and spectacular subsidence that created the flashes. It also opened up salt springs and, together with some dumping of chemical waste rich in lime and gypsum from processes that used salt to make sodium carbonate and sodium hydroxide, gave us the only inland salt lakes in Britain and Ireland. Salt lakes are characteristic of just under half of the world's land mass, where climates are arid, but they do not form naturally in a wet climate.

The flashes are unstable, changing in size and salinity as brine is deliberately pumped in or river floods dilute it, and the meadows bearing small patches of salt marsh are vulnerable to drainage, but they bear an interesting biological community that resembles that of brackish lagoons on the coast, but is generally poorer in species.[30] The Winsford Flashes (Top Flash, Middle Flash and Bottom Flash) are the town's most notable geographical feature, extending over 80 hectares and first appearing between 1845 and 1872, when they became popular with working-class day-trippers from the nearby industrial centres of Manchester and the Staffordshire Potteries for boating, picnicking and sightseeing. They still support sailing and angling.

The best investigated flash is near Sandbach, at Watch Lane (about 11 ha, originating in 1925), and lies among cattle pastures. Its catchment includes a series of brine springs, giving salinities between 4 and 32 per cent of seawater, with the largest values in summer when evaporation is greater than incoming water supply. It has been continually affected by attempts to stabilise its level by weirs at the outflow, and by piping in waste salt water, and remains a widely fluctuating lake habitat, with a range of tolerant freshwater animals, particularly snails and corixids and including several exotic crustaceans that have entered probably through water pumped originally from the local canal system (*Corophium curvispinum, Gammarus zaddachi, Gammarus tigrinus*). The number of species detectable is greatest when the salt is most diluted. The salinity of the flashes is generally more variable than that of the inland salt marshes, which are usually fed by springs of more constant composition, so there is a contrast between what is a brackish community in the water and a marine community on the marshes.

THE LANCASHIRE FLASHES

Across the Mersey, the Lancashire Flashes are somewhat different. The Wigan Flashes, eight shallow areas totalling 240 hectares to the south of the town, and formed through coal mining subsidence, were, by the 1970s, a horrible reminder of Wigan's industrial past. Heavily polluted with iron, sometimes with water bright orange in colour, and by overflow sewage in wet weather, they were fringed with colliery waste tips and household refuse. Few plants grew and no birds sang. The site had little value to the local people, in an area of high unemployment and many social problems. Yet the Wigan Flashes, and a similar site, Pennington Flash, near Leigh, have now been transformed to lakes still of only modest water quality, but far more attractive and widely used and valued by birds and people alike.

Restoration of colliery wastes, using sewage sludge for nitrogen fertilisation, can re-establish soils on which vegetation, including woodlands, will grow, and diversion of industrial water pipes through the wastewater treatment works can make a great deal of difference to water quality. Removal of rubbish, re-landscaping and capping of inert rubble with soil, exposure of previous soils, clearance of willow scrub, and planting of reeds and other emergent plants can stimulate colonisation by more species and eventually a rich bird community. Redshank, snipe, lapwing, pochard, gadwall, little ringed plover, garganey, willow tit, long-eared owl and reed bunting now all breed around the Wigan Flashes. Birds are fortunately both attractive to people, visible and valued, but also tolerant of modest-quality water. Ditches can be dug to protect nesting areas and create more habitat for water plants and invertebrates. Pike, tench and roach, the tolerant fish of lowland waters, now grow well.

Rejuvenated bodies of water in such areas are crucial for recreation such as walking, cycling, water sports, fishing and bird watching. They need co-operation, leadership and money, alas rarely provided by those who caused the damage in the first place, but coming variously. In this case, the Wigan Metropolitan Borough Council, the Wigan Flashes Conservation and Community Group, Lancashire Wildlife Trust, the Royal Society for the Protection of Birds, English Nature and the Environment Agency were all involved. In the end, what can be restored is of immense value; about 100,000 people visit and use the Flashes now each year. There are openings for voluntary work and local employment and a site that was depressing has become one of pride and stimulation for the local community. Diverse ecological communities (Fig. 187) boost morale.

FIG 187. The dereliction left by the coal industry in Lancashire can be remedied to create habitats of high social and conservation value, as at the Wigan Flashes.

RESTORATION OF A SORT: MARTIN MERE

A final visit in the lowlands of Lancashire takes in the tiny remnant of Martin Mere, once one of the country's largest lakes, 8 km across and 30 km around, but obliterated by drainage from about 1697 onwards. It lay in the very flat floodplain of the River Douglas, downstream from the Wigan Flashes, and an area regarded, like most floodplains, as wasteland in the past, and heavily abused. Some 5,000 years ago, the sea penetrated far inland on the Lancashire coast, but as coastal sand dunes and salt marshes formed, the estuaries became more restricted and the freshwater rivers, the Alt, the Crossens Stream and the Douglas, a tributary of the Ribble, spread out over a plain that acquired lakes, marshes and mosslands for several thousands of years. Virtually none of those remain.

Martin Mere is thought to have been a lake created by a melting ice block and there is a depression in the glacial drift to support that, but it must have been remoulded many times by the natural floods of the rivers and was part of a system of other shallow lakes in the area, like Gettern Mere and White Otter Mere, of which even less remains.[31] The water was an important local fishery and there were extensive rights of turbary (peat cutting) over the mosslands. Martin Mere was bordered by the estates of several landowners, who collectively valued the potential land on its bed more than the water above it. In 1694, Thomas Fleetwood of Bretherton obtained the right, from the other landowners, to drain it. With a workforce of 2,000 men, he directed the digging of a ditch, only a little over 2 km long, to the sea at Crossens, and drained the mere in a matter of days, though the land was not kept really dry until after a system of subsidiary drains had been created over the next two centuries. It was not plain sailing because the highest spring tides were above the level of the bottom of the ditch, so sluice gates had to be built and a large pumping station now occupies the site. By 1714 squabbles had broken out among the landowners as to which proportions of the bottom of the former mere they each owned and led to legal proceedings.

But the mere had gone. Its former existence can be traced partly from its sediments, though these have been much disturbed by ploughing, a wave-cut cliff near Holmeswood Hall that is a former shoreline, the pattern of field boundaries that formerly fenced the edge, place names like Boathouse field where a patch of sandy drift gave a secure haul out, and some low mounds. These are the remains of islands, the Peels, where lights were maintained to guide travellers and fishermen in the black darkness of nights where clouds blocked out the moon and stars.

The squabbles over land had replaced equally bitter disputes over fishing rights, wildfowl shooting and the collection of eggs. Martin Mere had been rich

FIG 188. Nothing lake-like remains of Martin Mere, only a re-excavated few hectares now managed as a bird reserve.

in wildfowl: swans, teal, coot, mallard and moorhen were taken. There was a duck decoy at Wet Holsome near Scarisbrick on the former western shore, and reed cutting was a useful source of income for the estates. There are many records indicating that Martin Mere was managed and valued by the local people for the goods and services it provided.

One small corner of the former lake, about 146 ha, near Burscough, has been taken over following the founding of the Wildfowl and Wetlands Trust by Peter Scott, who had watched pink-footed geese grazing on Holcroft's Farm in the late 1960s, and bought the land. The newly dug mere is only 8 ha, little more than a pond, but blocking of the drains has created a bigger area of marsh, and birds are attracted by management of the land using cattle and sheep grazing to keep a sward that geese favour. The birds are fed surplus potatoes close to the hides, and it is possible to see spectacular numbers (Fig. 188) in water that is consequently highly polluted with guano. This creates a problem for the stream, or rather ditch system to which the reserve drains, though water quality there is already compromised by intensive arable farming. The birds also cause erosion of the banks and there are problems of preventing the open water from rapidly filling in.

What remains of Martin Mere is largely the name and a muddy duckpond; it is an undignified reminder of what was once an important and valuable lake; and it is beset by continued disputes with wildfowlers outside the reserve boundaries, who may shoot geese and ducks, though not swans, and farmers who cannot be compensated for the damage the birds do to young crops in winter and spring. But it is better than nothing and one small delight is to see, from the railway that links the coast with Wigan and Manchester, groups of Whooper swans standing out brightly white as they devastate wheat fields made tastelessly bright green by excessive nitrogen fertilisation.

THE CUMBRIAN LAKE DISTRICT

Our journey now takes us briefly northwards to the Cumbrian Lake District: briefly because we have visited it several times before in this book, but a grand tour around the lakes of Britain and Ireland would be unthinkable without such a visit. It is not the largest lake district in Britain and Ireland, but it is the most researched and, giving its name to a National Park, it is perhaps the best known.[32]

For a limnologist, it is bijou: compact, almost circular, with the resistant rocks of the central mountains holding the rocky upland tarns and giving birth through their former glaciers to a neat radiation of long thin lakes. In the north and centre, these lakes are very leer in nutrients, but they become naturally quite fertile in the sedimentary rock lowlands to the south: the classic series of W.H. Pearsall (Chapter 2), first scientifically documented in the 1920s, but doubtless known to local people for millennia. The Lake District proper is surrounded by a halo of limestone, with fewer but marl lakes, including Hawes Water, Sunbiggin Tarn, Semer Water and Malham Tarn.[33]

The Cumbrian Lake District lakes are not immune to the hands of man. Water is abstracted from them, lake levels are often regulated, and the effluent from the attractive stone-built towns and villages has been causing eutrophication problems since the area first became popular with the writings of the lake poets in the nineteenth century, and the tourists flocked in, for ill as well as good. The remote and grandly bleak Wastwater (Fig. 19), with its rocky screes falling into the lake, is the least, and the lakes of the Windermere catchment the most influenced, but all the main lakes are much cherished by visitors and walkers and their names are loved and well known: Ennerdale Water, Wastwater, Coniston Water, Esthwaite, Windermere, Grasmere, Rydal Water, Thirlmere, Haweswater, Ullswater, Derwent Water, Bassenthwaite Lake (Fig. 189), Buttermere, Crummock Water and Loweswater.

Not surprisingly, the Cumbrian Lake District is being proposed for listing as a World Heritage Site. Its landscapes combine the influences of geology and

FIG 189. Bassenthwaite Lake is seriously influenced by human activities. Its catchment contains farmland, the town of Keswick, old mines and extensive forestry plantations. Siltation is a problem for the spawning of vendace, which were once common, and there is still a high nutrient load, though phosphorus stripping has been installed at the Keswick sewage works.

glaciation with traditional farming of sheep on the uplands and the associated details of dry stone walls, small fields and picturesque farmsteads at the feet of the hills. There is a historic tradition of mining; some of the streams are still contaminated with heavy metals from seventeenth- and eighteenth-century mine waste. There is even a graphite mine in Borrowdale, the provider, once, of an essential component for gunpowder, and later for the pencils made in Keswick.

In the public paths of the Lake District, and its sister park in the Peak District, lie the links that united a major movement for access to land in the twentieth century, and began to break the unjustified privileges that landowners had seized with the Norman conquest. You can be sure that a public path in the uplands will be open and well maintained, whilst that is increasingly not the case in any lowland of Britain. There are even strong associations with the well-loved small and beautifully illustrated children's books of Beatrix Potter, a woman who took her inspiration from the wild and domestic animals of the Lake District: Peter Rabbit, Jemimah Puddleduck, Jeremy Fisher and Mr Tod, the fox, whilst farming there herself close to Esthwaite Water and rebelling successfully against a Victorian tradition that had relegated women to domestic oblivion.

Why then can there be opposition to a proposal to list the Lake District as a World Heritage Site? It would seem to meet all the necessary criteria. But there is, and it rests in a deeper understanding of the landscape and a consideration for the future. World Heritage Sites include outstanding buildings, and such status protects them from removal or intrusive surrounding development. They include largely undisturbed landscapes that should be protected from prospecting and mining, building and roads, and that is only right. And they do include cultural landscapes like the Lake District. But the problem is that despite the often valued open nature of the fells that surround the lakes, these are grossly damaged lands, severely overgrazed in the past so that they have lost most of the diversity they would have had when woodland was much more extensive, and the lakes better protected from the diffuse nutrients that now influence them. Designation as a World Heritage Site would fossilise these characteristics, making it difficult to change the historic patterns of abuse. The essence of a cultural landscape is that it reflects change, preserving some features but acquiring others. Our deepening understanding is that loss of forests and wetlands to agriculture is not quite the bonus that it has been held up to be.

THE ENGLISH MANMADE LAKES

Northwestwards of the Cumbrian Lake District is Kielder Water, something of a controversial white elephant and the start of the last, southward leg of this journey. It takes us to a series of manmade lakes, some only decades old, others, the Broads, 1,000 years, and the final one about 300. Manmade lakes are the most common lake type in southern and eastern England (even if ponds are not considered). There are around 350 constructed reservoirs in England, around 230 in Scotland, 150 in Northern Ireland, 70 or so in Wales and an undetermined number in the Irish Republic; they have some peculiarities.

Most have been made to guarantee drinking water supplies, some for floodwater storage on rivers with prominent towns rather unwisely built in river floodplains; and Kielder Water, like Lys-y-Fran in Pembrokeshire, for the supply of industry that never materialised.[34] Back in the 1960s and for ten years afterwards until 1974, there was an organisation called the Water Resources Board. It has been called a body for the self-governance of water engineers by water engineers and it was seduced by what dam engineering could do. It made self-serving projections of increasing population and the burgeoning of heavy industry that were substantial overestimates, and convinced itself that our use of water would expand to rival that of the USA. Kielder is one of its children, by British standards a very large lake (11 km²), standing in an even larger and somewhat gloomy land of conifer plantations. It was built on the River Tyne to guarantee water for the supposedly expanding industries of Teeside and for transfer of water to the rivers Wear and Tees, but any need for it was disappearing even before its construction began. Kielder has a role now in providing recreation but the cool and windy northeast is attractive only to hardy tourists, and the early summer midges are a problem.

A little to the south, the much smaller Cow Green reservoir was created to regulate flow in the Tees and was controversial for the different reason that on the surrounding moorlands was a very unusual flora of relict Arcto-alpine plants, including the Teesdale violet, spring gentian and alpine bistort, on a rock formation known as sugar limestone from the way the parent rock weathers into a white coarse sand. Ten per cent of this habitat was flooded by the reservoir and it was feared that the warming effect of a large body of water would change the local microclimate unfavourably for this specialist flora. So far the flora has survived but the fortunes of plants are settled over periods of decades and it is yet too early to judge the effects.

FIG 190. Spring gentian (*Gentiana verna*) was potentially threatened by the change in microclimate due to the creation of Cow Green reservoir, but has survived.

Further south, in the East Midlands and East Anglia, is a clutch of reservoirs built partly to store water, partly to improve its quality for the refinement of drinking water, and partly for flood regulation in the generally flat landscapes. Some of these reservoirs, at least, really are needed, for crop irrigation is locally necessary, and the weather is much drier than in the north and west. Close to Cambridge is Graffham Water, to which water is pumped through pipes from the River Great Ouse, but Graffham, although attractive to winter wildfowl, is a mundane body of water, shallow and valued for sailing and trout fishing. For its water-company owners, it is a bread-and-butter sort of water, surrounded by intensively farmed low mounds with small woodland copses in an open landscape that preserves none of the feeling of mystique or grandeur that comes with a natural glacial lake. Reservoirs are icons of control rather than of freedom.

The problem for pumped storage reservoirs in eastern and southern England is that they are always heavily eutrophicated. They are needed because the rivers are slow and sluggish, not dammable in their floodplain reaches, and with upper-reach tributaries that are small and unyielding of much supply. The solution for regional water supply is to build a reservoir on a tributary, where at least the lie of the land will accommodate a dam, but to fill it with water pumped from the lower reaches of the rivers. Storage in the reservoir allows silt and phosphorus to settle into the bottom, and nitrate, often present in near toxic levels in the river water, to denitrify and make treatment for the public supply easier and cheaper. Nonetheless, a panoply of devices for mixing of the water, filtration, treatment with ozone and cleaning through charcoal is necessary to clear it of the algae, particularly cyanobacteria that dominate water enriched from a largely agricultural catchment.

Rutland Water in Leicestershire (though it occupies much of the former tiny county of Rutland) is the epitome of such reservoirs and illustrates many of their features. It stores water from the Welland and Nene (Fig. 140), major rivers of The Wash, draining hugely cultivated and fertilised arable lands. It too was a child of the Water Resources Board and its building was contested in the 1960s by all the local authorities, but their arguments were hampered by lack of cash and expertise compared with a long-prepared and aggressive engineering profession. The reservoir was full by around 1980, but probably would not have been considered necessary were modern measures of economic growth and water need available at the time.

The lake has a shape like the two joined antlers of a deer, with a long peninsula separating them in an east–west direction. The dam was built across the River Gwash, a tributary of the Welland, from clay scraped from what is now the bed, pushed into a long heap, 35 m high and faced with stone. The lake deepens to about 29 m close to the dam and stratifies in summer, but rarely becomes anoxic because the stratification, in the open landscape, is often disturbed by wind and by the incoming water, which is brought in through jets angled at 22.5 degrees to create the maximum turbulence. Twelve aerators (Helixor air guns) have also been installed close to the dam to mix the water, prevent deoxygenation and discourage cyanobacterial growth.

The builders, conscious of the controversy of flooding almost an entire county, were careful to create also an amenity with a nature reserve at the eastern end, a trout fishery, and walking and cycling paths. The water companies are not especially known for charitable endeavour and the expectation was that the fishery in particular would produce extra revenue. Dame Sylvia Crowe, a well-known landscape architect who had encouraged the Forestry Commission to stop planting conifers in rectangular blocks and to respect the shape of the land and its contours, was brought in to advise on landscaping. She was concerned with the ugly drawdown zone left in reservoirs during summer, when their levels fall and expose bare sand and rock, so she recommended the planting of goat willow, alder and tolerant grasses so as to provide cover during drawdown (Fig. 191).

She also organised wetlands around some former fish ponds at the western end and a series of lagoons, which form the core of the nature reserve and are very attractive to ducks and grebes. Osprey have been introduced, and, as at other

FIG 191. Normanton Church, now a museum, escaped the flooding that created Rutland Water and now stands above the bare drawdown zone that robs reservoirs of a functional littoral zone.

sites in England and Wales, much is made of their nesting as a tourist attraction. The original fish community was removed to make way for a fishery for rainbow trout and a fish hatchery was built. Engineers have faith that everything can be controlled. Most of the native fish species have now recolonised from the sources by which they originally entered the new lake, and the fishery, though popular, has not met expectations, a parallel situation to the overenthusiastic forecast of water need and the directive approach of an authoritarian commercial organisation.

Rutland Water went through an early phase of high biological production, with plagues of midges as the food supply provided by the rotting of flooded vegetation was consumed, and nutrients released from the flooded soils were used by algae. This early high production is very common in new reservoirs the world over. Usually the production then declines as the initial bounty is used up and the early nutrient-rich water is replaced by much less fertile water from the inflows. That was not the case for Rutland Water because the pumped water is very rich in nutrients and it remains a lake frequently suffering from algal blooms. There was a notable incident in the dry summer of 1989 where sheep and dogs, which had drunk water with windrowed algae at the lake edge, died, promoting a flurry of fuss even in Parliament where, during debates, a considerable talent for lengthy rhetoric was demonstrated,[35] but it gave a fillip to the new National Rivers Authority (now replaced by the Environment Agency) a year after its creation. In September 2012 a charity swim had to be cancelled because of the continuing algal problems.

Management of the nature reserve at the western end is directed particularly towards birds; the plant communities are those of eutrophicated sites and not particularly notable though the devastation rendered to wetlands in Britain has been so great that even run-of-the-mill sites are now designated as Sites of Special Scientific Interest. The lagoon water levels can be regulated to create bare mud for waders, and woodlands and fields owned by the water company at the edges of the reservoir are only lightly farmed to create pastures attractive to birds. More lagoons were built in 2008 to compensate for more intensified water management. The reserve is one of the most important inland sites in Great Britain for passage waders and among damsel and dragonflies, emperor, broad-bodied and four-spot chasers, two species of darters, emerald damselfly and black-tailed skimmer are all regularly seen uncommon species.

Rutland Water is an interesting place: highly managed for water, conservation and recreation with a balance more biased towards the latter two than would have been the case if projections for water need when the reservoir was built had been realistic. For me the highly organised pathways and signposts, visitor centres and tourist facilities, management plans to expand the catalogue of birds, and drying edges, *pace* Dame Sylvia, are alien, but there is no doubt that thousands of visitors gain a great deal of enjoyment from it. I only wish that the more natural lakes and wetlands now drained from the English lowlands were still available alternatives. But then I have never been much enchanted by authority and control.

THE BROADS

The Broads are our next stop: manmade lakes, but old and unintended. One of the classic research stories is about how the botanist, Joyce Lambert, with the help of a geomorphologist, Joe Jennings, a historical geographer, Clifford Smith, an archaeologist, Charles Green, and John Hutchinson, a civil engineer, brilliantly challenged the traditional view that the Broads were former estuaries dammed by tidal clay. Lambert made a series of borings though the deposits of the Norfolk valleys that, with historical information, showed incontrovertibly that the Broads were pits dug out of the peat for fuel between the ninth and the thirteenth centuries.

The thirteenth century was generally nasty, a time of the Black Death, failed crops and miserably wet weather, such that the pits, separated from the rivers only by narrow spits of remaining peat, were breached and flooded, thus creating a series of lakes in the river valleys. These lakes, the Broads, persist amid a floodplain that contains reedswamp, fens and alder carr beyond the point where the salt tides reach, whilst in the lower reaches the floodplains and most of the former estuary have been embanked and drained to form level grazing marshes that dominate the area. It was what Noël Coward had in mind in his play, *Blithe Spirit*: 'Very flat, Norfolk'.

The Broads Authority, now responsible for much of the area, was created in 1978, and fully established in 1988, in the mode of a national park authority, but not legally such for navigation lobbies were powerful enough to prevent such an authority gaining the control of navigation that it would have elsewhere, in the Lake District National Park, for example. The Authority immediately found itself confronting several issues: first was water quality, with sewage effluent and agricultural drainage having led to severe loss of aquatic plants. Second was the loss of traditional management of the fens, in which regular cutting for reed and sedge had prevented succession to alder carr until labour become expensive and unwilling, following the World Wars; and, thirdly, there was a perpetual struggle with demands that rivers and Broads be dredged to keep open navigations that had been established for industrial purposes in the nineteenth century but on which a tourist boating industry had thrived since paid holidays had become mandatory after the emancipations of the First World War. Soon a further problem emerged as the arrangements of the Common Agricultural Policy made it more profitable to deep drain and plough grazing marshes for growing wheat rather than raising cattle, and thus threatened to destroy perhaps the most characteristic landscape of Broadland. These issues have already been recounted in an earlier book on *The Broads* in the New Naturalist series, in 2001.[36] What has happened to the Broads since then?

The answer is a lot and a little.[37] There have been successive five-yearly Broads Plans, numerous action plans, strategies, meetings and reports, surveys and pontifications; there have been improvements made to eroded banks, creation of new small areas of reedswamp and much better provision for tourism, but rather little has changed in the Broads themselves. Central and largely insoluble is the problem of nutrients. By 2001 a number of wastewater treatment works had been modified to remove phosphate, but little had been done to curb the still large amounts of phosphate and huge quantities of nitrate draining from the land. Those problems are now talked about much more, but so long as the Broads Authority's executive area is confined to the river valleys and does not include the much larger area of catchment from which the water comes, there is little it can do beyond cheer-leading for better nutrient control. Even had it got jurisdiction over the entire catchment, there is only a limited amount of nutrient control that is possible without removing a great deal of land from agriculture.

The Authority tries hard, by encouraging farmers to leave 2 m buffers between ploughed land and streams, for example, but that will never do much. Most of the nutrients enter during heavy rain that purges through such scanty buffers like food poisoning through the guts. It has tried a variety of restoration projects within the Broads. Attempts to prevent release of phosphorus from the sediments by adding iron salts have failed; new attempts using lanthanum salts may prove more effective in Broads isolated from the catchments by thick bands of fen and reedswamp, but can be no more than palliatives for the Broads open to the rivers. Biomanipulation has worked well in Ormesby Broad, where the eutrophication problem was relatively small because of the small agricultural catchment, and behind barriers constructed in Barton Broad kept fish-free by repeated removal. The main part of Barton Broad, despite treatment of effluent and extensive dredging of sediment, remains resistant to re-establishment of the rich beds of water plants it had until the Second World War.

For a time in 2008 and 2009, Hickling Broad became clear and developed swards of rare charophytes, despite no management intervention at all, but then reverted to turbid water and lost its plants for reasons that remain mysterious.

FIG 192. Nineteenth-century wind pumps add great charm to the reed-edged rivers and Broads, but severe ecological problems remain.

The Trinity Broads, linked with Ormesby Broad (but not Filby Broad), have also become relatively clear in recent years because their fish move to Ormesby Broad in winter and were removed by biomanipulation then, but may well revert to algal dominance given the still very high concentrations of nutrients. Ranked for the Water Framework Directive (see Chapter 10), all of the Broads are considered to be in poor or sometimes moderate ecological condition, and there are new problems of invasive species, including an Asiatic clam, killer shrimps, alien crayfish, New Zealand pygmy weed and floating water pennywort, to add to the zebra mussels and mink previously present.[38]

Dredging has become increasingly popular, because of pressures from the navigation lobby and indeed there are large amounts of soil being eroded from the land and some from the banks. Sailors do not much value water plants either, for they interfere with races and caused a furore in Hickling Broad when they returned. The Broads Authority has changed its priorities from restoring water quality and plants, in its early Plans, to a much more nebulous approach to maintaining biodiversity, creating tourist opportunities and involving the local populace in its latest one.[39] It now puts emphasis on planning for the long-term future in response to climate change and sea level rise, which will re-establish an estuary where now there are grazing marshes. The flood embankments must eventually fail or be overtopped. It concentrates on '*promoting understanding, enjoyment and wellbeing, tourism, recreation and access*'.

It is all very laudable but the Authority has little choice. Its administrative area is too small, its powers too weak, its funds have been cut and, despite a plethora of politely conducted liaison committees, the old divides among conservation, farming and navigation remain deeply embedded. The tradition of experimental research in Broadland during the 1970s and 1980s, which led to some fundamental shifts in understanding that were uncomfortable for the local interests, but firmly established what the problems in the lakes really were, has been replaced by a more bureaucratic, safe approach of listing and recording what remains, to see if it is holding, or still in decline. The Authority is now promoting, with local businesses, a 'Broads Brand', with a vocabulary replete with empty managerial phrases like 'key messages', 'sustainable tourism strategy', 'consistent and coherent messages' and 'maximising engagement'. It has a slogan, coined originally by local naturalist and broadcaster, Ted Ellis: '*a resting place for the cure of souls*'. Maybe, but no longer for mine; we leave, with not a little frustration, on my part at least, what could be the most fascinating lake system in Britain and Ireland, and still one rich in habitats and species, traditional practices, cultural history (Fig. 192) and human foibles, and make our final landing in the middle of London, by the Serpentine Lake in Hyde Park.

THE SERPENTINE

But why the Serpentine? If we have to come to London, why not the large pumped storage reservoirs, the Queen Mary, Queen Mother, King George VI and Queen Elizabeth II, along the Thames west of Heathrow Airport, where a tradition of experimental limnology, now long gone since drinking water provision was privatised, produced fascinating data on how algal growths might be mitigated by grazing or mixing? The Thames in summer largely comprises the sewage effluent of numerous upstream towns: a rich medium for algae. These reservoirs also threw light on why the algal populations were not even bigger. It was because their essentially concrete bowls provided little littoral spawning terrain for fish, thus restricting fish stocks and allowing large *Daphnia* to persist in quantity and graze some of the algae, particularly the diatoms that thrive in the waters of large rivers and reservoirs that have short retention times.

The reason is simply that the Serpentine (Fig. 193), in Hyde Park, is the best-known, publicly accessible lake in the capital: manmade by royal command,

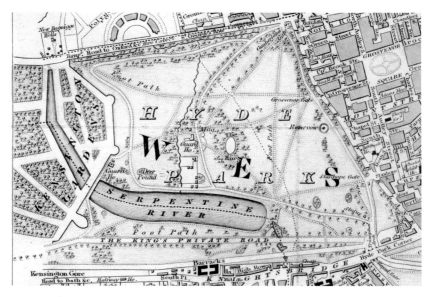

FIG 193. The Serpentine in Hyde Park, London, on a map of 1833.

with a fascinatingly murky past, and with water now even more controlled than that of the East Anglian reservoirs for its appearance and economic value. It is the epitome of the values that large cities represent. Hyde Park has figured prominently in English history. It was once part of a monastic estate, running from Westminster to Kensington, owned by the monks of Westminster Abbey and purloined by Henry VIII in 1536 for private hunting lands of open woodland with deer and wild boar. Henry fenced in the park, organised hunts for the court and foreign legations, and had the Westbourne Stream, which flowed through it, dammed to provide drinking ponds for the deer.

It remained restricted until the accession of James I and, in 1637, his son, Charles I opened it completely to the public and began to build driveways and paths. During the Civil War of 1642–9, Parliamentary troops built earthworks there for the defence of Westminster against the King. On the restoration of the monarchy, in 1660, Charles II replaced the wooden fence around the area with a brick wall and restocked the park with deer. People camped in it in 1665, hoping to avoid the Plague and, in the late seventeenth century, William III, having moved the court to Kensington Palace, had a route across the Park to St James lit by oil lamps and so created the Route de Roi, now Rotten Row.

A few years later, in 1728–30, it was the wife of George II, Queen Caroline, who, with her gardener, Charles Bridgeman, began the process of turning a semi-natural landscape into a huge garden. She took 300 acres to the west for the royal gardens at Kensington Palace, separating the two areas by a long ha-ha, and had the Westbourne Stream dammed in the east to create an 11.3 ha lake, the Serpentine. It was something of a revolution in landscape gardening on landed estates, for it was curved, not straight, and designed to look natural. Strictly the Serpentine is the eastern part of the lake, and the western end, separated by a bridge and carriageway, is the Long Water, but together these waters then formed the centrepiece of the park and, like all lakes, acted as a focus and magnet for visits.

On their banks, fireworks were organised to mark the end of the Napoleonic Wars (in 1814), the Great Exhibition was held in 1851 in the Crystal Palace and a Silver Jubilee Exhibition was held in honour of Queen Elizabeth II's 25 years on the throne. Since 1872, people have been allowed to spout at Speaker's Corner on any subject they wish. In the 1820s, George IV employed Decimus Burton to remodel the park, building lodges, screens and gates, replacing the walls with railings and building the West Carriage Drive across the lake, and left the park more or less as it is now seen, with only some monuments added in the last two centuries.

Once the Park was open, the public was versatile in its use of it. Few houses had piped water, and 'bathing' was only possible in lakes and ponds. The Serpentine was described as 'the only public bath in London'. A parliamentary answer in 1859 suggested a quarter of a million bathers each year, with the total number of accidents to bathers, 377, of which 348 were saved, and 29 drowned and 273 suicide attempts of which 88 ended fatally. The Royal Humane Society was established in 1774 to rescue people who got into difficulties whilst bathing and built a 'receiving house' alongside the Serpentine, with two recovery rooms, and equipment for resuscitation. It was permanently manned with medical staff, lookouts, boats and grappling hooks. In winter people fell through the ice when skating, and sleds and ladders were used to rescue them. The bottom of the lake had a sticky sludge in which people panicked and mouthfuls of the water could easily lead to waterborne diseases.

The Serpentine was never a very salubrious lake. It is shallow (maximum 5.3 m) and with one bend, not exactly serpentine. The Westbourne Stream, whose flow was slight, entering from the northwest, was also known as the Ranelegh Sewer, though formerly the name sewer did not have its modern connotations and the dumping of waste in the sewers was, at least theoretically, forbidden. With the invention of water closets, however, there came the problem of disposing of much grey water, instead of the semi-solid night soil that had been the previous problem. The rivers and streams of London became increasingly polluted with diluted raw sewage from 1815 and, by 1844, the water companies had successfully lobbied the government to make disposal of the grey water to the rivers (rather than the streets) mandatory. In 1834, water was pumped into the Serpentine from the Thames to attempt to counteract the rather noxious Ranelegh Sewer, but the quality was not hugely better. The outflow was diverted into a culvert and a waterfall, the Dell, where the stream emerged, was so often dry that recirculating pumps were installed to maintain the illusion.

The Act of 1844 had made it illegal to construct a house in London that was not connected to the public sewers, provided that there was one within 100 feet. Covered main sewers, intercepting the surface drains, were constructed rather randomly as the century wore on, until Joseph Bazalgette in the 1860s and 1870s properly ordered the network. One sewer ran along the Bayswater Road, intercepting the Westbourne Stream with a weir that allowed the Bayswater Sewer to overflow into the Serpentine in storm conditions. Although this topped up the Serpentine with rainwater, it was now the sewer overflow. In droughts water was bought, at huge expense, from the Grand Junction Waterworks Company and pumped in to alleviate the smell of the lake.

By 1848 the Serpentine, despite its location in a popular Royal Park, was a national disgrace. Public meetings were called, and after one of these, in July 1859, a deputation visited with some fervour, the newly appointed Commissioner for the Royal Parks, Henry Fitzroy MP. Fitzroy obtained permission to spend £16,500 from the Treasury to solve the problem, using the advice of Thomas Hawksley, who was pilloried for his solution. Hawksley proposed to install filters at the western end and recirculate water from the eastern outflow through them to create a 'pellucid' cascade, with the entire lake filtered once per month. He would also treat the shores with quicklime to kill the conferva, an old name for algae and filamentous bacteria. *The Times* derided the plan, demanding new sources of clean water, and wondered how the 25 weekly cartloads of filtered filth would be disposed of. Hawksley countered that all the available water had been polluted with sewage or diverted by the canal companies, and that the local wells were unreliable.

Nonetheless the work was begun, supported by the famous engineer, Robert Stephenson, and a company founded by James Watt that was to supply the pumps. Stephenson and Fitzroy died later that year and a new Commissioner, W. F. Cowper MP, backed by a Parliamentary Select Committee, suspended the work in March 1860. Cowper wanted a new source of water to be found and the ever-exuberant Hawksley claimed, within a month, to have found it in the form of local springs to be tapped by a borehole. He also proposed that his filter beds, which had by then been constructed, be used as ornamental water gardens or fish pools, or for construction of a glass-roofed, steam-heated Crystal Winter Garden to shelter the public on inclement days. The filters remain as ornamental ponds and a borehole was sunk, but the Serpentine remained a problem. Hawksley waived his professional fees but critical letters continued to be published in *The Times*.

The improvements made to the sewerage system in the early twentieth century and the development of treatment works took some of the pressure off the Serpentine and it even became popular for swimming again in the 1930s when the Lido on the southern shore was established, with a cordoned-off area for swimming and changing rooms. Members of the Serpentine Swimming Club (founded in 1864) bathe daily, no matter what the water temperature, and run special races on Christmas Day for a cup given by Sir James Barrie, author of *Peter Pan*. But it was the stimulus of hosting the Triathlon and Marathon swimming events of the 2012 Olympic Games that finally prompted a solution to the quality of the Serpentine. Its waters did not before that meet with modern standards for bathing.

Water is now pumped from three boreholes penetrating the upper chalk in Hyde Park, the most recent being commissioned in May 2012. The retention time of the lake has been reduced to a few months, compared with ten years formerly. There has been some sediment treatment with lanthanum salts, and aeration pumps have been installed for use in warm periods when oxygen levels may fall sufficiently to cause fish kills. There has been some biomanipulation to remove large bream and carp and help minimise disturbance of the bottom. The lake continues to have relatively high nutrient levels supporting algal blooms that will thrive on the nutrients still emerging from the sediments but also running in from the fertilised flower beds and grassed areas, and the droppings of geese. The Serpentine is no longer a disgrace; but where lakes are concerned, the Celts still have the best of it, by a long chalk.

CHAPTER 10

The Future of the Lakes of Britain and Ireland

ENVIRONMENTAL SCULPTURES HAVE BECOME POPULAR. Sometimes they are made with natural materials that will meld back into nature with time (Fig. 194) and contrast with the monumental brass works of the great, intended to celebrate a power that has not always been to the good. Occasionally they draw attention permanently to the damage we do so cavalierly to our environment. Across the width of the Alexandersgarten, a shopping street close to the harbour in Helsinki, are set four strips of copper at different angles, inscribed with the scientific names of freshwater and brackish water animals and plants: *Phragmites australis, Bithynia tentaculata, Myriophyllum sibiricum, Asellus aquaticus* and 20 or so more (Fig. 195). Few passers-by notice them and fewer realise their significance, but the strips mark the edges of a small bay of the Baltic Sea that was filled in as part of the harbour development in the nineteenth century. The names are of those of the former inhabitants, long made refugees in the name of progress.

FIG 194. 'Ban an t-ishka, Woman of the Water' made by Alannah Robins in 1995 and one of the best known of the sculptures in Grizedale Forest, Cumbria. The stream has been channelled through pipes supported by a woman so that it cascades over the head and body of a man.

But was it really progress or just the illusion of it in a world that is educated increasingly only to value the acquisition of wealth in the short term, even if that acquisition cannot continue forever because it undermines the very systems that maintain the conditions we all need to survive (Chapter 3)? It will not have escaped you that not a single British or Irish lake visited in Chapter 9 was untouched by significant human activity. My task now is to look to the future of our lakes and to place it into a wider context. The pressures are more likely to increase than decrease as we contemplate further impacts of climate and weather change. Somewhat grandly, lakes have been described as sentinels, integrators and regulators of climate change.[1] What that means, respectively, is that the symptoms of climate change are seen early in lakes, that their sediments (Chapter 7) contain a record of climate changes and that lakes and wetlands, in receiving organic compounds washed in from their catchments (Chapter 2), as

FIG 195. Set in the pavement of the Aleksanderinkatu (Alexandersgarten) in Helsinki are four 8.5 cm copper bands recording the former Kluuvinlahti Bay of the Baltic Sea that was filled in when the city was developed in the early nineteenth century. It is little known even to native Finns, but was made in 2003 by Tuula Närhinen and called Kluuvinlahti Fossils. It lists the names of 25 animals and plants that formerly grew in the bay. The work is complemented by cast-iron manhole covers with pictures of some of the animals and plants.

well as producing more within the lake, are important parts of the system that controls the carbon cycle on Earth.[2]

We have also to take into account a dense and rising population in Britain and Ireland, mostly as people live longer and increase in biomass with obesity, rather than through immigration and reproduction, the conventional determinants of increasing animal populations. These have become relatively unimportant in Britain and Ireland. Expectations of comfortable lifestyles mean increased demands for safe and clean domestic water. People are also increasingly expansive in their aspirations for a variety of food and housing that puts pressures on catchments. Most, rightly, expect a pleasant environment. There is thus a tension between desires for improved water quality and attractive landscapes, and the increasing detriment to them from a more demanding people, increasingly insulated from an understanding that all these things ultimately depend on natural ecosystems. Government propaganda, *dirigiste* education, electronic enslavement and fears for personal economic security do not bode well for our future.

British and Irish limnologists belong to an international community that contributes understanding, and attempts to influence government policy (though not very extensively or effectively) to ameliorate our mounting problems.[3] Britain and Ireland constitute only 0.2 per cent of the world's land area and house only 0.95 per cent of its population, but both have greatly impacted on world history, and are still politically influential. How Britain and Ireland care for their lakes and landscapes will therefore be noticed on the world stage. Not least, as members of the European Community, Britain and Ireland subscribe to a positive, if often grudging, approach to environmental improvement. The question we have to ask is what the net direction of a yet uncontrolled climate change plus increasing pressures from other human activities and an increasingly firm approach on the part of the European Community to improving habitat quality will be. Will it be uphill or downhill?

CLIMATE CHANGE

Climate is changing rapidly the world over, and there is virtual certainty that this is being caused by human activities, primarily the increased burning of coal, oil and gas in the last two centuries. The carbon dioxide concentration in the atmosphere has now passed 400 ppm compared with a pre-industrial 260 ppm (we know this from analysis of the bubbles of air trapped in accumulating Antarctic ice) and is now higher than it has been in the past 100,000 years or more. The average temperature of the atmosphere has risen by about 0.8°C since 1850. That may not sound much, but represents a colossal amount of extra energy stored in the Earth's envelope of atmosphere, land and oceans. The temperature has risen much more in polar latitudes (by up to 10°C) and the current trends suggest that on average the rise could be by several degrees by the end of this century.[4] Mountain glaciers, and even the Greenland glacier, are melting rapidly, sea levels have already risen by 20 cm, and the extent of ice in the Arctic Ocean in summer has declined to an unprecedentedly small area. Rainfall patterns are changing with a tendency for more rain, especially in winter for already moist areas, and increasing summer drought in the more arid regions. As the atmosphere is forced continually to adjust, extreme weather events: storms, typhoons, floods and droughts, are becoming more frequent.[5]

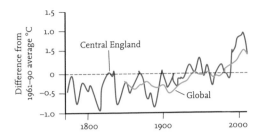

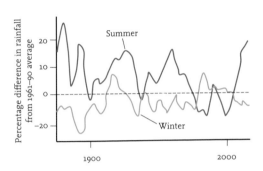

FIG 196. Trends in mean temperature and rainfall in central England, measured as deviations from the long-term 1961–90 average. Based on Meteorological Office data.

In Britain and Ireland, the trends have been slightly greater than the world average (Fig. 196). Since the 1970s, temperature in central England has risen by about 1°C, and in Scotland and Northern Ireland by about 0.8°C. Total rainfall has not yet changed, but has increased by about 20 per cent of the long-term mean in winter and decreased by about the same amount in summer, but with quite wide swings over the period. Of the 14 years on record (since absolutely standardised records began in 1910) with mean daily maximum temperature greater than 13°C, 12 have occurred since 2000. All regions have had more rain in short heavy storms in winter, and severe windstorms have recently become more frequent. Sea-surface temperatures in British waters have risen by about 0.7°C in the last 30 years and sea levels have risen by about 1 mm per year in the twentieth century and somewhat faster in the last 20 years.[6]

The effects on lakes have been widely noted.[7] As temperature rises, the period of ice cover in winter becomes much less long and the stability of summer stratification becomes greater. In turn this means that hypolimnia are less disturbed by summer winds and deoxygenation in them becomes more intense. Cyanobacterial blooms increase in amount and frequency because such conditions favour them. The increased winter rainfall may flush the lake out more rapidly, but in summer the reduced rainfall increases the retention time, allowing bigger crops of algae to build up. Fish that require cold oxygenated

FIG 197. Changes in the timing of events such as flowering, peak population size, first reproduction and arrival on migration among British plants and animals since 1970. Data are given as days earlier per decade.

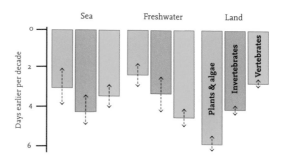

water, such as the charr and whitefish, find themselves squeezed between the warm surface waters and the deoxygenating hypolimnion.[8] Growth seasons of algae, invertebrates and fish start earlier[9] and may end later, but the effect varies in extent among different species so that there may be irregular changes in what were predictable patterns (Fig. 197).

The symptoms of eutrophication become more intense with warming (Fig. 198) so that solving the problem becomes more difficult.[10] Invasive species find it easier to gain a toehold because the flow of new species tends to be from warmer regions with higher biodiversity. Southerly species are tending to move northwards, rapidly in the cases of winged insects like dragonflies and

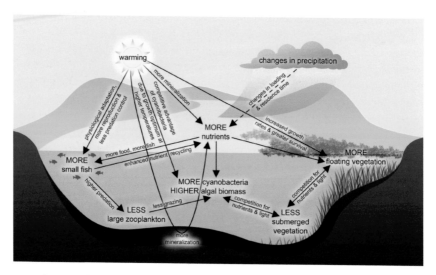

FIG 198. Some changes now established that link climate change with increasing symptoms of eutrophication. From Moss *et al.*, 2011.

FIG 199. The common darter has moved its range northwards by about 340 km in Britain in recent decades. (L. B. Tettenborn)

damselflies (Fig. 199).[11] Lake communities are changing in unpredictable ways; there are even evolutionary processes at work, with rapid development of clones of some zooplankters that are tolerant of increased temperatures.[12] The rules about how communities are made up are in turmoil.

Projections for the future have been made using many different models of global climate. They indicate temperature rises of several degrees by 2100 and, although some politicians consider a 2°C rise manageable, the indications are increasingly of a much larger rise than this because there has been no progress in reducing world carbon dioxide emissions into the atmosphere. On a recent trip down the Yangtze River to inspect the massive Three Gorges Hydroelectric Scheme in China, by far the most abundant of the many boats I saw were barges carrying coal to conventional power stations.

CHANGES IN LAW

Meanwhile, there have been developments in water legislation. The European Union has passed a series of Directives over the past 30 years with the intention of dealing with high nitrate levels from farming, proper treatment of sewage and reduction of nutrient levels in wastewater effluents, and the bacteriological quality of bathing and shellfish waters. In 2000 it began a process of consolidating this legislation with the passing of the Water Framework Directive.[13] At the time I believed this was revolutionary legislation and potentially it still is. It covers all of fresh, estuarine and coastal waters, and has three important themes. First is that the catchment ('river basin' is the term used in the Directive) should be the unit for management; secondly, that standards should be set not just for chemical water quality, which has been the traditional approach, but for ecological quality; and, thirdly, that the standards should be referenced to an absolute standard of high ecological quality, defined as not or negligibly affected by human influence. Each of these provisions has resulted in complications.

Europe has been divided into major river catchments, and collective catchments including groups of smaller rivers (with 20 such basins in Britain and Ireland), but unfortunately the legislation does not directly regulate land use and farming practices, so that successful management of whole river basins is impossible. The previous Urban Wastewaters Treatment Directive regulates wastewater effluents, but even that has been treated with different degrees of seriousness in different countries. It requires removal of nitrogen and phosphorus at treatment works, but only those serving more than 10,000 person-equivalents (pe) and then only when the receiving waters are at risk of eutrophication.

Some countries have quite rightly defined their entire land area as at risk; others, including Britain and Ireland, have taken a very restricted view and installed such treatment only where the water is being used for the domestic supply or where there has been sufficient clamour from conservation organisations worried about particular lakes or rivers. Works serving fewer than 10,000 pe, are excluded, so that five small works in an area, each with 2,000 pe would not be required to have nutrient stripping installed, whereas one works for 10,000 would. Some countries, Denmark and the Netherlands, for example, have attempted to restrict the amounts of diffuse nutrients coming from farms by regulating fertiliser usage, but the restrictions are relatively liberal. Countries like Britain and Ireland have relied on voluntary compliance, with yet negligible results.

The move to measuring ecological quality rather than just water quality was a major step of the Water Framework Directive. Previously there had been chemical standards for effluents from wastewater treatment works and industries, but no real check on whether such standards made much difference to the receiving waters. The new Directive concerns itself with the effects in the receiving waters and its Annex 5 is quite specific as to what ecological features should be measured. For lakes these include the phytoplankton, bottom algae, aquatic plants, bottom invertebrates and fish communities, as well as a range of chemical substances (nutrients, oxygen, pH and more) and the degree to which the structure (of the shoreline, for example) and the natural hydrology (through weirs, dams and irrigation) have been changed.

The approach is first to create a classification of types of different sorts of lakes, based on relatively fixed geographical features such as size, depth, altitude and local geology, and then for each type to establish what the features of the water chemistry, the structure, the hydrology and the various biological communities are, in comparison with reference sites where human influence is, at most, negligible. This can be done by finding high-quality reference lakes, by reconstructing conditions from sediment analyses, or through expert opinion, or some combination of these. The problem is that no such reference conditions now exist in Britain and Ireland, all of whose landscapes are strongly influenced

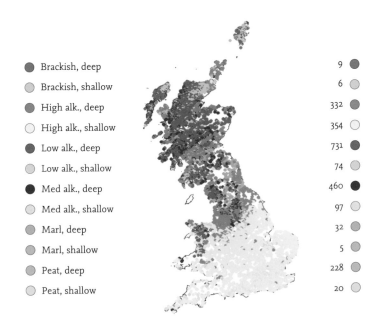

● Brackish, deep	9 ●
○ Brackish, shallow	6 ○
● High alk., deep	332 ●
○ High alk., shallow	354 ○
● Low alk., deep	731 ●
○ Low alk., shallow	74 ○
● Med alk., deep	460 ●
○ Med alk., shallow	97 ○
● Marl, deep	32 ●
● Marl, shallow	5 ●
● Peat, deep	228 ●
○ Peat, shallow	20 ○

FIG 200. Classification of lakes used in the United Kingdom for assessment under the Water Framework Directive. Each dot represents a lake greater than 1 ha in area, so most ponds are excluded and no distinction is made here by altitude. There are thus 12 categories (6 geological x 2 depth) and the number of lakes in each is shown on the right. The predominant types are deep (>3 m) lakes with low and moderate alkalinity (see text) in the uplands of the north and west, and lakes with high alkalinity in the south and east. Peaty lakes are prominent in the Pennines and northern Scotland and there is a band of low alkalinity shallow lakes across southern England, coinciding with sandstone rocks.

by people, even in the remotest parts of Scotland, though the Irish and Scottish Environment Protection Agencies have convinced themselves that the effects of man have been negligible in some areas, despite a near complete removal of the former natural vegetation. Palaeolimnology, despite its current sophistication (Chapter 7), is unable to reconstruct most features of a habitat, and expert opinion has been thought to be too subjective. The obvious approach would have been to find negligibly influenced equivalent sites in North America and Russia, but attitudes have been parochial and such data have not been used.

The least controversial aspect has been in establishing the classification system for lake types. In Britain and Ireland it rests on the understanding related in Chapter 2. Figure 200 shows the distribution of lakes in the categories used. The first criterion depends on geology of the catchment, and five categories are recognised – peat; low and medium alkalinity (this is a measure largely of bicarbonate) waters with siliceous solid geology; high alkalinity calcareous waters; and brackish waters. Low, medium and high alkalinity waters have <0.2, 0.2–1.0 and >1.0 milliequivalents/ L, or conductivities of <70, 71–250 and 251–1,000 µS/cm. Brackish waters have >1,000 µS/cm. A sixth category has been created by distinguishing marl lakes in the high alkalinity category, where more than 65 per cent of the catchment is made up of limestone. There are then two categories for depth (<3 or >3 m; <4, >4 m in the Irish Republic) and three altitude categories (<200 m, 200–800 m and >800 m). This gives a total (6 × 2 × 3) of 36 potential types. Potentially a further category of size (1–9 ha, 10–49 ha and >50 ha) can be used but has not been so far. The Directive does not require lakes smaller than 50 ha to be considered, so the quality of the multitudes of ponds in Britain and Ireland is not being assessed.

CLASSIFICATION SCHEMES

Once reference standards have been drawn up for each lake type, a classification scheme for ecological quality must be established in which successive standards for good, moderate, poor and bad quality are defined relative to the gold standard of high quality in the reference sites. The Directive defines good quality as differing only slightly from high quality, but is unhelpful as to what it means by moderate, poor and bad, and a compiler of dictionaries would be amazed at the extent to which the word 'slightly' has been stretched. The key boundary is that between good and moderate because the Directive says that all habitats must be restored to good quality by 2015 (or failing that 2021 or 2027). However, the standards that have generally been set for that boundary are really quite low, especially when criteria for high quality have also been set low as well.[14] Some countries consider (amazingly) that a catchment with 50 per cent of its land in intensive agriculture can be considered to support high quality.

Setting standards for chemistry is conceptually easy because single substances are involved; it is also relatively easy for measures of total phytoplankton such as chlorophyll *a*; but doing it for most of the biology is more difficult because communities of many species are involved. The Directive requires that some measure be determined for high quality and then that numerical proportions of this measure (ecological quality ratios) be set for the subsequent classes of quality. The difficulties are in determining measures and proportions that mean something, and are not just arbitrary for the different qualities. Some countries use the presence or absence of particular species, others the proportions of particular families or genera, but there is little consensus and some hundreds of biological measures are in use.[15]

For British lakes, standards have been set for total phosphorus and chlorophyll and there are schemes for determining the plant community and the diatoms growing on rocks, but they are not yet widely used and essentially assessments are being made mostly on phosphorus and chlorophyll. This falls far short of the intentions of the Directive, which were to create a picture of what high-quality conditions would be like from at least 40 features, with some sort of concept of the system as a whole. Instead, there has been a reluctance to move from the old principles of setting chemical standards, because even where biological measures are being used they have been calibrated against expectations of chemistry, particularly total phosphorus. What the biology is giving therefore is simply another (and cruder, for the relationships are far from exact) measure of water chemistry.

What has been done, however, is to recognise firmly the role of phosphorus and eutrophication, which was not a feature of the former British system for assessing water quality. In lakes, nitrogen has been ignored, it being argued that not enough is known for standards to be set. That is nonsense; nitrogen standards have been set for estuaries and coastal waters, but not rivers and lakes. The real reason is that controlling nitrogen would cause problems for farmers and landowners and these groups are politically very influential in Britain and are very loath to change their current practices. Legislation on water quality is very much politically manipulated.

In 2003, before the first assessments under the Directive were made, the state of British rivers (lakes were not much considered then) was trumpeted as the best for 200 years; in 2004 the Secretary of State for Environment was forced to admit that standards might be improving, but that most British waters were

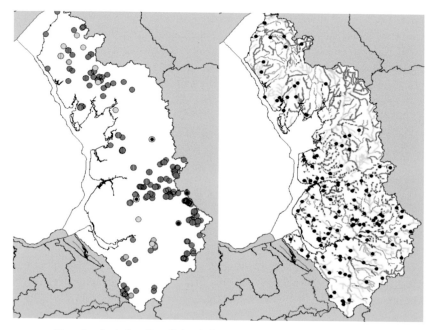

FIG 201. Map of ecological quality of lakes (left) and rivers (right) in the North West region of England. Grey symbols indicate lakes where the Environment Agency considered there were too few data to be sure at the time of drawing up the River Basin Management Plans in 2009. Emphasis in the UK had previously been mostly on rivers so there were few 'official' data on lakes. There are no high-quality waters shown. They would be coloured in blue according to the standard scheme. Good quality is indicated by green, moderate by yellow, poor by orange and bad by red. Black dots indicate sites where the water fails a chemical assessment because it is contaminated by one or more from a list of priority pollutants, including, for example, lead and mercury, dioxins and polychlorinated pesticides. In such cases the site is considered worse than bad.

unlikely to meet the 'good' standard required under the Water Framework Directive. Former assessments really only measured the degree of gross organic pollution, the levels of some particularly toxic heavy metals, ammonia and pH (which together at high values could be toxic to fish). The new assessments have forced the environment agencies in Britain and Ireland to acknowledge the importance of eutrophication, and in rivers also the detrimental effects of engineering for drainage and flood control.

Nonetheless, doubtless under considerable political pressure, the agencies have undermined the spirit of the Directive to a high degree. Even with liberal

TABLE 19. The current ecological quality of surface waters in the UK, the Republic of Ireland and the European Union, as reported under the provisions of the Water Framework Directive The numbers are the percentages of the total number of sites (lakes and rivers) assessed using the methods developed in each country. Many ecologists would see this as an overoptimistic estimate of the true situation.

	High	Good	Moderate	Poor	Bad
UK	5.8	35.4	41.4	13.8	3.5
Ireland	17.9	36.5	26.2	14.5	5
EU lakes	15	42	27	10	6

standards, most locations in England and Wales and Northern Ireland currently fail to meet good quality (Fig. 201, Table 19) though this is not helped by a principle known as 'one-out-all-out'. A site is assessed on its worst failing, not on the overall assessment of several features, which would ecologically be much more sensible. Even pristine sites sometimes show temporary oddities. In the UK, we have now reached the stage that where assessments of ecological quality of lakes using chlorophyll, and those using total phosphorus, give different answers, there has been an attempt to adjust the scales of one or the other to give similar answers. This shows a profound misunderstanding of ecology by water managers. The proposed use of many variables in the Water Framework Directive recognised that different measures would indicate different things. To attempt to harmonise them all to give the same answer is ultimately to measure only one thing, and that of questionable value.

The deep problem is that ecological quality is not being assessed. What is being assessed is still chemistry, with the chemist's rather rigid view of what happens in a simple reaction system, not an immensely complicated ecological one. There will doubtless be some improvements made to lakes as a result of the Directive, but they will fall far short of what might have been the outcome had the spirit of the Directive been respected. When the first River Basin Plans were published in 2009, it was clear that there would be negligible progress in Britain and Ireland by 2015. What was more disappointing, however, were the diagrams for each region (Fig. 202) showing the projected improvements by 2021 and 2027. In every region all or most sites were shown to have achieved good status by 2027. They had to; the Directive says so! And in every case the proportion achieving good status by 2021 was exactly half way between 2015 and 2027. In other words these were simply presumptions, drawn in to tick boxes and not based on definite plans.

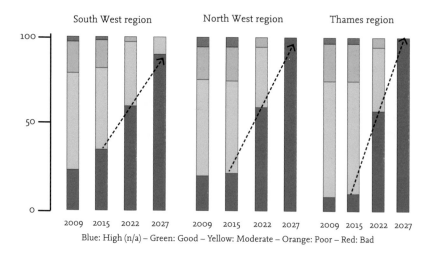

South West region   North West region   Thames region

Blue: High (n/a) – Green: Good – Yellow: Moderate – Orange: Poor – Red: Bad

FIG 202. Expected trends of improvement in British freshwaters given in the River Basin Management Plans. The standard colouring scheme described for Fig. 201 is used. The arrows suggest that expected future trends are calculated more on presumption than planning.

THE DIRECTIVE AND THE FUTURE

The European Community is clearly not happy with progress in implementing the Directive, despite the diplomatic language of its documents, nor are external organisations.[16] A group of non-governmental organisations, assessing progress after ten years, found the Directive to have been reduced to a 'toothless tiger'. The quality of the River Basin Management Plans for England and Wales was legally challenged by the Anglers Alliance and the Worldwide Fund for Nature, though the case never went to Court because the government suddenly found some extra money ostensibly to make improvements. The agencies responsible for enactment of the Directive are struggling. The Environment Agency, Natural Resources Wales, the Environment Agency of Northern Ireland, the Scottish Environmental Protection Agency and the Irish Environment Agency are all kept very short of funds by governments that see no further than the next election.

In 2009, the British government spent over £100 billion shoring up a group of banks that had been operating irresponsible policies; in the same year the entire spending on environment in the UK was around 7 per cent of this and there has been little protest from the management boards of environmental and conservation agencies. Ministers appoint all of their members, and ministers do not favour radical thought. In 2013, of the collective 54 members of the boards of these organisations, politicians and administrators made up 16.7 per cent, people with accounting, financial or economics backgrounds, 14.8 per cent, and company directors 16.7 per cent. With another 13 per cent farmers and land managers, 14.9 per cent miscellaneous professionals including lawyers, medics and vets, a cleric and an architect, and 7.4 per cent engineers, that leaves only 11.1 per cent administrators of conservation or environmental organisations and a mere 5.6 per cent professional ecologists. The Irish Environment Agency does not give enough details to be certain, but there would seem to be vanishingly small numbers of ecologists in its executive or advisory board either. The British agencies are no longer permitted to express opinions that might conflict with those of ministers, most of whom are themselves rank amateurs with little expertise when it comes to environmental problems. That reflects also the nature of heads of state. Of 194 such leaders in 2009, 75 per cent came from law, economics and finance, business and politics, engineering and the military. Only one had any sort of environmental qualification and that was not particularly advanced.[17] The best-known environment in Whitehall is cloud-cuckoo land.

CONSERVATION IN THE FUTURE

Conservation thinking, in Britain and Ireland, developed in the early twentieth century in landscapes that were already broken up, fenced and boundaried so that natural connections were not apparent. The assumption was then made that this was normal and therefore that these remnants could be conserved. But it is not normal and in the long term, they can't. It is as if a doctor treating a patient saw each organ as completely separate and ignored the fact of the bloodstream. The freshwater system is the bloodstream of our landscapes and to manage or assess it in isolation betokens a profound ignorance of its significance.

Conservation agencies in Britain and Ireland have a remit for the entire countryside but have even less control over the catchments of the lakes they are attempting to manage than the environment agencies. Few designated conservation sites were established with sensible natural boundaries and no organisation can manage a lake without control of the catchment. It can only be managed to encourage or save particular species, often at the expense of others. The results have been a steady decline in the quality of habitats and the number of species.[18] Repeatedly, reports have been produced, even by the statutory organisations themselves, that document decline over the past 50 years.

The reasons are not mysterious: increasing urbanisation, more intensive farming, acidification and eutrophication, drainage and an increasing invasion of alien species, but UK governments have never been more than lukewarm about conservation.[19] It is not surprising that only a very small percentage of lakes fall into the categories of good and high for the Water Framework Directive, and then only because the standards set have betrayed the intentions of the Directive. There are, of course, species action plans and drives to improve or increase the areas of particular habitats, particularly under the EU Habitats Directive, but all of them succeed, when they do, only because there has been local, intensive and expensive treatment of the symptoms of a problem. Little has been done about the causes, and therefore treatment has to be more or less continuous.

So far in nature conservation, we have stumbled along, winning an occasional battle in a losing war, but the end game may soon be approaching and our present tactics are looking puny. A fragmented approach, with treatment of the symptoms of human-caused problems, can only work for a limited time and to a small extent. It is necessary to maintain the freshwater bloodstream and the organs of the land as an intact system and to do it in climatic circumstances that are changing rapidly and may be irreversible in the foreseeable future. Some idea of what is really needed can be obtained from a consideration of the Earth's carbon cycle.

THE CARBON CYCLE AND FUTURE CONSERVATION AND RESTORATION

The changing carbon budget for the Earth, over the past 50 years, is shown in Table 20.[20] It shows the balance between releases of carbon (mostly as carbon dioxide) to the atmosphere, and storage of carbon as calcium carbonate in the oceans, or as organic matter in peats, soils and sediments mostly in wetlands, forests and freshwaters.[21] The emissions from fossil fuel burning and cement manufacture have steadily increased, and those from forest felling and burning, especially in the tropics, have decreased slightly but are still high. Meanwhile, as a result of fertilisation with carbon dioxide there has been a doubling of storage in the ocean and about a 50 per cent increase on land. The net effect of all of these processes is still an annual increase in carbon in the atmosphere and this lies behind our current changes in climate. One misconception is that all we need to do to reduce the pace of climate change, or halt it, is to reduce our carbon emissions. That will not be enough, but so far we have even failed to do that. Although in Europe we may appear to be reducing our emissions,

TABLE 20. Changes in the global carbon budget between 1960 and 2011. Values are in gigatonnes (petagrams) carbon per year ±1 standard deviation (a measure of the uncertainty in the estimate). Fuel burning, cement manufacture, land use change and net increase in the atmosphere are all determined from empirical data. Ocean sinks are based on biogeochemical calculations. Land sinks are determined by difference. Based on Le Quéré et al., 2012.

	1960–9	1970–9	1980–9	1990–9	2000–11
Emissions					
Fuel burning & cement manufacture	3.1±0.2	4.7±0.2	5.5±0.3	6.4±0.3	8.1±0.4
Land use change (including burning)	1.5±0.5	1.3±0.5	1.4±0.5	1.6±0.5	1.0±0.5
Sinks					
Ocean	1.2±0.5	1.5±0.5	1.9±0.5	2.2±0.4	2.5±0.5
Land	1.7±0.7	1.7±0.8	1.6±0.8	2.7±0.8	2.5±0.8
Net increase in atmosphere	**1.7±0.7**	**2.8±0.1**	**3.4±0.1**	**3.1±0.1**	**4.2±0.1**

this is not quite an honest position because we buy increasing amounts of goods and services from the Far East and effectively therefore simply export the responsibility for our carbon emissions.

Just reducing emissions will not halt climate change. Emissions have to be reduced to the point where they are balanced by storages. We have been fortunate so far that storages have increased (though there is uncertainty as to whether the land storages have really increased, because the numbers are obtained by difference rather than by direct measurement). The ocean storage may now be reducing because the pH of the ocean is decreasing as carbon dioxide is injected and this makes calcium carbonate precipitation less easy. The land storages depend on natural vegetation; there is virtually no storage in agricultural land and as the organic matter in its soils has decreased through more intensive ploughing, it may have become a net emitter. We have lost up to 75 per cent of our natural land biomes to agriculture and we continue to remove forest.[22] Experiments using wetland ecosystems in tanks have shown that, as temperatures increase, the balance between photosynthesis and respiration increasingly favours respiration, so the extensive stores of carbon in lake sediments and as peat in the tundra and boggy Boreal forests may already be becoming sources rather than stores.[23]

It follows that we should not only be reducing emissions as fast as possible but also restoring the storages. There is little that can be done to increase the ocean sink. Fertilising the seas to increase photosynthesis might help but there is no guarantee that the extra photosynthesis might not be respired back;[24] there would be an energy cost in obtaining and distributing the fertiliser (iron is particularly favoured for some parts of the ocean); the additional phytoplankton would absorb more heat radiation; and the scale of the oceans is so great, two thirds of the Earth's surface, that, because of dilution, such attempts could only have a very minor effect at the scale at which they would be feasible.

The natural land biomes are a better bet, though it will still be a formidable task to increase their area. It is worth taking a look at what would be involved because, if we are to maintain a comfortable and civilised world, we may have no choice. The first question is to what extent; the second is how should we go about it. If we assume that we stabilise current carbon emissions at their present levels, halt current forest destruction, and maintain the current ocean sink, all of which are optimistic assumptions, we would need to create storage for about 2.9 gigatonnes of carbon per year. This is a little more than a doubling of the current land storage. In round numbers we would need to double the present area of land biome by restoring agricultural land to fully functioning ecosystems. At present about 25 per cent of the former natural biome area is left so this would mean re-creating a further 25 per cent or, in other words, reducing the world's agricultural land by about a third.

This will be difficult with a still increasing population, but desperate circumstances mean desperate measures. Some of the geo-engineering alternatives to averting climate change, such as suspending aerosols at the top of the atmosphere, are equally desperate but are likely to cause further problems. Restoring biomes is at least to use a mechanism that has worked well for millions of years and carries other benefits. Restoring forest in hot regions, for example, appears to increase rainfall and minimise the risk of drought.[25] Our present agriculture and food businesses are very efficient at making money for the companies concerned, but very inefficient at using what is grown. Estimates vary, but with rejection of crops on cosmetic grounds by supermarkets, packaging strategies that avoid small portions to minimise handling costs, processing of food into higher value prepared meals, or even just packets of pre-chopped vegetables, overbuying as a result of advertising persuasion and waste on the plate, as much as half of the food we grow may be wasted in developed countries.

Peoples in less fortunate countries are much more frugal but similar proportions are wasted through pests and poor storage. Food availability is also reduced because of crops grown as monocultures, often to produce fuel for cars and to be sold for hard currency. There is discouragement of traditional cultivation methods in favour of those that appear efficient under western conditions but are inappropriate in warm climates, and introduction of high-yielding varieties that are much less pest-resistant under circumstances where expensive pesticides are unaffordable. In the end people in developed countries will have to accept a more spartan diet but that may have great benefits; many diseases are now caused by over-consumption. Obesity is an affliction often imposed by ruthless marketing of highly profitable but unhealthy food. Everyone bar a number of multinational corporations and unprincipled politicians and businessmen will benefit from more basic diets.

RESTORING BIOMES

How do we go about extending the remaining biomes? The simple answer is to allocate the land and allow natural processes to take over with minimal management. This is alien to traditional conservationists in the UK, at least, whose approach is that of agricultural land managers, manipulating nature reserves to favour particular, often charismatic species. But such an approach is failing; it is essentially a symptom treatment. In any case the creation and maintenance of biodiversity does not lead to ecological quality; it is the establishment of suitable habitat conditions that leads to development of appropriate biodiversity.

Natural processes, left alone, will establish appropriate systems for a given climate regime and geology. The obvious places to start extension are at the edges of existing tracts of natural biome, because these provide sources of species for colonisation. Isolated patches can be restored but not so quickly. In all cases what has to be done is to re-establish the three fundamental characteristics of independent self-sustaining systems (Fig. 203). All else follows from these.

The first is that nutrients like phosphorus and nitrogen be mainly present within the biomass and not as freely soluble inorganic compounds that can easily be washed out of soils and into the freshwater system. Low levels of such available nutrients are always associated with high biodiversity and high biodiversity gives an insurance policy to a system, by which it can maintain its functions, even if there are local extinctions of some species. Natural systems are extremely good at recycling nutrients using a variety of biological mechanisms and hence persist on a small capital of these nutrients.

Crops need fertilisation because they have no means of recirculating nutrients within an established and permanent biomass, and systems of animal

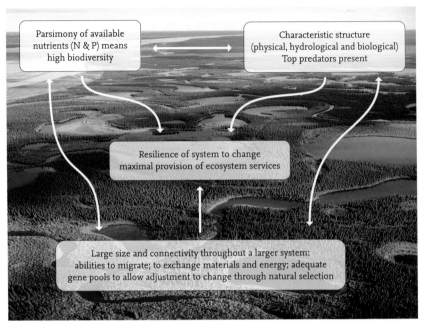

Parsimony of available
nutrients (N & P) means
high biodiversity

Characteristic structure
(physical, hydrological and biological)
Top predators present

Resilience of system to change
maximal provision of ecosystem services

Large size and connectivity throughout a larger system:
abilities to migrate; to exchange materials and energy; adequate
gene pools to allow adjustment to change through natural selection

FIG 203. Characteristics of self-sustaining biomes.

husbandry generally need food bringing in from elsewhere and that also brings
in excess nutrients. Land that will be restored to biome systems may thus at first
have far too much nutrient, and will become dominated by rank and competitive
plants, but, given time, these nutrients will be leached out and end up in the deep
oceans as sediments, or be denitrified. The land will go through successional
processes that lead to a climax vegetation type: some sort of forest in the moister
parts of the world, with a high-quality freshwater system permeating it.

The second principle is that natural biomes in particular places have
characteristic structures. This means, for example, that the hydrological regime
is not interfered with by dams or abstraction, that where dead trees fall down
onto forest floors or collapse into rivers and streams, they are not cleared, that
soils are not disturbed and that complete food webs are able to establish. Top
predators (tigers, lions, wolves, salmonid fish, sharks and the like) are essential to
the continued maintenance of self-sustaining ecosystems.[26] They must colonise
and persist for they prevent grazing animals from becoming so abundant that the
vegetation structure is simplified or destroyed, as happens when forest is cleared
for cattle to graze.

And the third essential is that the systems be large and interconnected. This is an insurance policy against disturbance in one section that allows recolonisation from another. It maintains enough territory for large animals to have sufficient breeding populations to avoid inbreeding, and to maintain gene pools on which natural selection can act to keep adjusting the community to change. Above all it guarantees the functioning of the freshwater systems that form the bloodstream of the land. The isolation of rivers into embanked channels and the destruction of the floodplains and lakes that connected them with the drier systems to landwards have been among our greatest errors. Such isolation may have created more agricultural and urban land, but it destroyed services like flood storage and maintenance of high water quality and has led to high costs of damage when the rivers have overtopped the embankments and reclaimed their original bed.

The initial stages of development of new biomes will not please the tidy minds of orthodox conservationists, who want fast results, an increase in numbers of a particular species and a reserve that has the cared-for look of a garden. Current conservation, like farming and gardening, is essentially about control. Such an approach is fine for small amenity reserves in the middle of towns and will still be needed there, for there is no reason that they should be alien places in which to live. But it is inadequate for solving the Earth's current problems. The advantages to restoration of biome areas on a large scale are many. It costs little; the essence is to leave nature to re-establish its own self-regulating systems, and not to interfere. There will be additional storage of water in the wetlands and floodplains of such systems and the water running out from them will be of high quality, and appropriate amounts can be taken for the domestic supply.

FIG 204. The dragon fountain in the restored lake at Llandrindod Wells (see Chapter 8).

FIG 205. The Oostvardesplassen in the Netherlands is a 61 km² tract of land that has been restocked with large herbivores, either native (red deer) or resembling former native species (Hecht cattle, Konic ponies). Other species, including many birds, have colonised but until there is general acceptance for the reintroduction of native predators like wolves, there is some culling of diseased or weakened cattle and ponies to prevent overpopulation. The land is not otherwise managed.

This process has been tentatively discussed in the UK under the name 'rewilding', but we have been too timid and have done nothing significant about it.[27] Our approach to conservation remains that of fussy gardeners, tidying, planting, weeding and sometimes installing the equivalents of garden gnomes on a somewhat bigger scale (Fig. 204). There is a more ambitious scheme at the Oostvardesplassen in the Netherlands,where more than 60 square kilometres of what was intended to be agricultural and urban land, in a polder reclaimed from the Zuider Zee, have been restocked with large mammals (though not yet the natural top predators) and now sport a hugely diverse system (Fig. 205).[28] Britain and Ireland are too small to make much absolute difference to phenomena like the carbon cycle on a world scale, but we are influential and need to show a willingness to do this so that other, larger countries do not have the excuse that they are shouldering a burden alone. Rewilded biomes in much of Scotland and western Ireland and the uplands of northern England and Wales will offer also tourist and inspirational value. Some people will still be needed for protection of these areas, and to service an appropriate tourist industry, but the suitable areas will in general be remote, and depopulation of them over a few decades would be manageable.

In the remaining developed land, which will still cover half of the continents, food distribution will need to be much less wasteful and urban living conditions must be improved for a greater population density. We have the talents, and collectively the money, to do these things; indeed we will have to do them. Our greatest mistake, as human populations have developed new tools and overwhelming confidence, has been to think that we can do whatever we like with our patches of land and water. Not surprisingly we now have, almost universally, lakes and rivers of poor quality, increasingly defiled landscapes and associated social problems; violence to nature is invariably accompanied by disregard, even brutality, to people. Lakes have indeed been the sentinels in which the changes show up earlier than on the land, and their sediments have recorded the changes. Their abilities to regulate the changes have been severely impaired as they have become modified, but if we learn the lessons that they tell us, we may have a future that can be viewed with optimism rather than dismay.

A grand strategy to save our civilisation will not come easily, but it will have to come.[29] Our political institutions are not well suited and will have to change. In the UK, the policy of allocating different responsibilities for functions: planning, transport, housing, waste disposal, agriculture and conservation, to different bodies so that they conflict eternally with one another, needs reform. Single unified catchment bodies, with their loyalties to the wise management of their catchment, rather than to sectional interests, would be a useful start.[30] The Water Framework Directive could still be saved from emasculation.

The message is that lakes do not exist as separate, distinct entities; they are cogs in the endless machine of the water cycle. The cogs remain functioning only when the whole machine is in good order. In the UK and Ireland we have been among the leaders in understanding these things, as well as prominent in overexploiting the world's resources, but we have lagged yet as leaders in finding solutions. It is time that we pulled up our socks.

Notes

CHAPTER ONE

1. Crannogs are wholly or partly artificial circular or oval islands built in lakes. They were made of dumped layers of timbers, brushwood and peat, stone and soil and originally surrounded by a wooden palisade, partly for defence, partly to hold the material in place. About 1,200 are known in Irish lakes (O'Sullivan, 2000), the earliest from the Mesolithic (7000–4000bc) but most from the early Mediaeval (ad500–1200). There may be many thousands more than currently known: sunken below the water or buried in peat and sediment, they are not obvious. Many are described from Scotland, eighteen in Loch Tay alone and were built slightly earlier, with a peak from the third to the fifth centuries ad. They were used for simple domestic occupation, industry (iron smelting) or ceremonial and governmental use. In one crannog in Loch Tay, Oakbank, there were found abundant and well-preserved plant remains suggesting a society with rich arable and pastoral agriculture. Opium poppy and remains of spelt wheat imply trade and high status, whilst cloudberry pips suggest long-range gathering, possibly during seasonal movements (Miller *et al.*, 1998). The one crannog known from Wales, in Llangorse Lake, may have been occupied by a regional king and court (Campbell & Lane 1989). Crannogs may also have had spiritual significance and been part of a widespread lake culture in Scotland lasting until the sixteenth century.

2. In 1893, Arthur Bulleid, an amateur archaeologist eventually forced by his would-be father-in-law to become a medical doctor so as to be able to support a wife, discovered a site with low mounds amid the wetlands of the Somerset Levels. Excavation rewarded him with two of the most famous archaeological sites in the world: Glastonbury and Meare lake villages, the latter probably a temporary market site, but the former a self-contained settlement of 40 houses formed on floors of brushwood and clay, plus sheds and barns, stone and gravel hearths, evidence of spinning and weaving, glass and pottery making, and a dock for canoes.

   Occupied from 250bc to 50bc, they sat among shallow lakes in the floodplain of the River Brue, connected to the uplands by trackways across the wetlands as well as through open water and channels. A huge variety of remains of animals and plants has come from them. Birds include the now locally extinct pelican and white-tailed sea eagle among many that are still common in England. Among fish, roach, trout, shad, perch and pike were caught and mammals included both wild and domesticated species providing bone or antlers for implements or food and included wild boar, wild cat and beaver. Bulleid's findings are summarised in Minnit and Coles (2006). A wide survey of lake and wetland archaeology is Coles and Coles (1989).

3. Freshwaters figure in some way in the cultures of all peoples. For Canadians and Americans, Scandinavians and Russians it is through the tradition of having a holiday cottage on the edge of a lake in the swathe of the Boreal forest that girdles North America and northern Eurasia, where the last glaciation left the basins of many millions of lakes. Elsewhere it is through the importance of inland fisheries for providing food.

   In Britain and Ireland, the linkage is less prosaic. The lake poets, William Wordsworth, Samuel Taylor Coleridge and Robert Southey, living and writing in the Cumbrian (English)

Lake District at the turn of the nineteenth century, drew inspiration from the land and waterscapes. The lake poet tradition has been continued by Norman Nicholson in the English Lake District, Norman MacCaig in the Scottish Highlands and Seamus Heaney and George Moore with the lakes of Ireland. In the nineteenth century, Walter Scott's novels romanticised the highlands and lochs and his poem 'The Lady of the Lake', brought Loch Katrine and the Trossachs into prominence and stimulated tourism and consequent hotel building in nearby Callender.

John Betjeman, perhaps the best-loved, certainly the most approachable poet of modern times, found inspiration from his visits to Norfolk and the Broads. Many people know of the Norfolk Broads and the English Lake District from Arthur Ransome's *Swallows and Amazons* (1930) and *Coot Club* (1934), whilst the natural history of the Lake District manifests itself in Beatrix Potter's well-loved characters. The fascination with lakes, and the landscapes they focus, can be traced throughout English art (Dimbleby, 2005) and literature (Hahn & Robins, 2008). It is no doubt there also in Welsh, Gallic and Gaelic, though alas these riches are not immediately available to most of us.

4. In fields outside science, biographies, autobiographies and obituaries abound. Scientists seem more inclined to cover their tracks, perhaps because their emphasis is less self-indulgent. Personality cults are not greatly admired. T. T. Macan and Barton Worthington have left little for the historian. There is an obituary for Macan (1911–85), written by Worthington (1985), but it is short and bare. He was educated at Wellington College and Christ's College, Cambridge, taught by Ernest Saunders, and wrote a PhD thesis on starfish, based on his membership of the John Murray expedition to the Indian Ocean in 1933–4. He joined the Freshwater Biological Association staff in 1935, worked as an army major on malaria in Iraq, Iran, India and Burma, wrote five books and numerous papers, and became Deputy Director of the FBA until his retirement in 1976. For 15 years he was General Secretary Treasurer of the International Society for Limnology. Macan was a keen sailor and did good service for the local scout movement, wildlife trust and National Trust. There is little else about the man, bar that he was careful and meticulous, and my only insight into his sense of humour was a warning to me to beware of publishers and tax collectors.

I can trace no obituary of Worthington. He had a brief Cambridge lectureship, carried out research in East Africa (which resulted in a very well-written book, *Inland Waters of Africa*, 1933, with his wife, Stella, as senior author), and was an executive member of a government survey in Africa in 1933–7 and Director of the Freshwater Biological Association from 1937–46. Worthington then became scientific adviser to a government mission concerned, towards the end of the War and after it, with the state of knowledge about the Middle East, and simultaneously development and scientific adviser to the Governor of Uganda and later to the East African Federation. His reports were classics for their integration of ecological with economic and development issues and led to a brief period with an international Conseil Scientifique pour l'Afrique, then seven years as Deputy Director-General (Scientific) of the UK Nature Conservancy. Thereafter he was Scientific Director of the International Biological Programme (an attempt to look widely at the productivity of habitats and the limitations on it). He wrote a book (*The Ecological Century: A Personal Appraisal*, 1983) whose title promised great insight, but which I reviewed with deep disappointment. His was the book of the detached, discrete and distant civil servant, almost the bare Minutes of the official meetings, the diplomatic veneer. We could have learned so much about how decisions are made, the complexities of dealing with environmental problems, the compromises, fudges and mistakes and sometimes the triumphs; but alas, we learn nothing of deep value.

5. Antonie Philips van Leeuwenhoek (1632–1723) was a tradesman and scientist from Delft in the Netherlands, and was the first microbiologist. He developed a new way of making very small lenses that did not involve tedious grinding and polishing but depended on casting of spheres from a rod of glass melted at the tip. Mounted on brass frames, the lenses were powerful enough to allow him to see single-celled animals and bacteria, spermatozoa and the flow of blood cells in the capillaries of frog skin. The microorganisms he was seeing were without precedent and occasioned the Royal Society, to which he had submitted an account of his findings, to send a delegation of clerics and doctors to Delft to be convinced. They were. Leeuwenhoek was made a Fellow and the fundaments of how life was perceived began to change forever. Microorganisms dominate the ecological processes on Earth, and the biosphere could

not function without them, whereas a living planet could probably persist without any of the myriad of larger organisms that are perceived to be more important.

6. In 1887 Stephen Forbes, then State Entomologist of Illinois, gave a talk, later to be published as his now famous paper on 'The lake as a microcosm' (Forbes, 1887) to a meeting of the Peoria Scientific Association. The paper made a major advance and had a major misconception but laid the foundations of modern limnology. The advance was to see the links among the environmental features and the nature and behaviours of the organisms in the lake. The limitation was in seeing the lake as isolated and self-contained: a microcosm. He was wrong about that. The unit that limnologists now have to consider is not the lake but the catchment, river basin, or watershed, to use the synonyms, respectively, of the UK, Europe and North America (Chapter 2). Nonetheless, Forbes should be anything but derided. He foresaw later work on food webs, population and community ecology, and the ecosystem concept, and he understood the prime ecological importance of natural selection, then a very new idea. His misconception stimulated further work and his insight reminds us that perception, whether of human investigators or organisms living in the lake, is important in determining how we 'see' the habitat and how organisms see it.

7. The National Library of Scotland maintains a web site on the bathymetrical survey (http://maps.nls.uk/bathymetric/index.html), including digitised versions of the maps.

8. Herbert Spencer (1820–1903) was a philosopher, biologist, sociologist and political theorist. He viewed evolution as a common basis for development of the physical world, biological organisms, the human mind, and human culture and societies. It was he who articulated the idea of the 'survival of the fittest', in *Principles of Biology* (1864), after reading Charles Darwin's *On the Origin of Species* and thus contributed to what is now the fundamental basis of all ecology.

9. There is a description (Gurney & Gurney, 1908) of the Sutton Broad laboratory, at Longmoor Point near Stalham in Norfolk, advertising it for use free of charge. The building still stands as a private house.

10. Fellows of the Royal Society are treated to obituaries. Those for W. H. Pearsall by A. R. Clapham (1971), Patrick Buxton by V. B. Wigglesworth (1956) and Felix Fritsch by E. J.

Salisbury (1954) are particularly detailed with interesting insights.

11. Robert Gurney left a series of diaries (now in the Castle Museum, Norwich) in which he bound letters he had received and sometimes copies of those he had sent. From this correspondence, some of the difficulties in getting the Freshwater Biological Association founded can be deduced and light thrown on attitudes to science at the time (Moss, 1991).

12. Women have been undervalued in freshwater science, as in other areas. Slowly this is being dealt with, but it was rife in the early years. Lund & Monaghan (2000) show the major contributions made by Penelope Jenkin that were largely ignored in the early days of the FBA, and in his review of Worthington's book, *The Ecological Century*, Colinvaux (1984) is scathing about the treatment of one very distinguished FBA palaeoecologist.

13. At the outbreak of the Second World War, Barton Worthington wondered how the FBA might help the war effort and thought that freshwater fish might be used as food. He started a trapping programme for perch in Windermere, which still continues, for monitoring the population changes of the fish, its rate of reproduction and relationships with other fish (Le Cren, 2001) particularly its predator, the pike. In 1941 perch were sent to Leeds to be canned in Yorkshire relish and tomato ketchup and sold as *'Perchines – Lakeland perch, Britain's most lovely and tasty freshwater fish'*. Apparently they sold quite well, not needing many ration coupons to buy them.

14. The history of conservation in Britain has been long and thorny. See Shoard (1980, 1987), Sheail (1998) and Marren (2002).

15. The Water Framework Directive, passed in 2000, was lauded as a revolution in water management in Europe and is discussed in more detail in Chapter 10. The documentation is extensive but the river basin plans for England and Wales can be viewed at www.environment-agency.gov.uk/research/planning/33106.aspx, for Scotland at www.sepa.org.uk/water/river_basin_planning.aspx, for Northern Ireland at www.doeni.gov.uk/niea/water-home/wfd.htm and for Ireland at www.wfdireland.ie/links.html.

16. Jack Talling (2004) has summarised the considerable British achievements in freshwater ecology in the twentieth century. The recent decline in the UK in investment and people in freshwater research is discussed and evidenced in Hildrew (1993) and Battarbee *et al.* (2005).

17. This can be found on pp. 77–80 of Macan (1973).

CHAPTER TWO

1. A readable book on the geology of Britain and Ireland is Fortey (1993).

2. Ireland and the Outer Hebrides became isolated from mainland Europe by the seas, around 12,000 years ago, but England, the rest of Scotland and Wales not until about 7,000 years ago (Gibbard & Woodcock, 2012).

3. George Evelyn Hutchinson was a professor at Yale for 43 years, with wide interests embracing the humanities as well as the sciences. He was primarily a limnologist, but, like other limnologists since, made significant contributions to the foundations of all ecology, particularly in community and population ecology. His papers on the nature of the ecological niche, and his book, *The Ecological Theater and the Evolutionary Play* (1965), have been widely appreciated. Hutchinson was at home with artists, writers and musicians, and worked with oceanographers, geochemists, anthropologists, paleontologists, sociologists and behaviourists.

   Born of a junior lecturer, later Professor of Mineralogy at Cambridge University, and an Italian mother, from a noble family forced in the eighteenth century to leave Italy on account of a duel. He showed an early interest in natural history and his first publication, at age 15, was a note on swimming grasshoppers, observed at Wicken Fen in Cambridgeshire, and written whilst he was at Gresham's School, in Holt, Norfolk. He graduated from Emmanuel College, Cambridge, took a Rockefeller Fellowship in Naples and worked on octopus hormones. The work did not progress well as the octopi were scarce, because, he said, they were good to eat. Whilst at Naples he applied for a lectureship in zoology at the University of Witwatersrand in Johannesburg and accepted an appointment against parental advice because it was under H. B. Fantham, who had a reputation for being unreasonable. Fantham dismissed Hutchinson from his teaching duties for alleged incompetence, so Hutchinson used his time to research the ecology of the seasonally dry lakes (pans) of South Africa, with his first wife, Grace Pickford.

   He was appointed to a junior lectureship in zoology at Yale University and in 1932 went on an expedition to India with a geologist, Helmutt de Terra, and studied the chemistry and biology of the high-altitude lakes in Ladakh. Hutchinson was particularly valuable because he knew how to skin mammals, a skill learned as a boy. Whilst in India he also became immersed in culture and religion and published a book on the subject, *The Clear Mirror*, in 1936.

   His later work at Yale was seminal in the development of limnology; he was the first to use radioactive phosphorus to study phosphorus cycling, and effectively founded the fields of radioecology and later, palaeolimnology. Lakes that had implications for archaeology and history fascinated Hutchinson, and his study of the palaeolimnology of the volcanic Lago di Monterosi, near Rome, where Aeneas is supposed to have descended into the underworld, is a little-known classic. Many ideas of modern ecology can be traced back to his writings and at least 22 species of organisms are named after him. The biography of a fascinating man can be found in Slack (2011).

4. See Hutchinson (1957, 1967, 1975, 1993)

5. Hutchinson based some of his classification of lake origins on a chapter (Peach and Horne, 1910) in Murray and Pullar (1910).

6. Turloughs illustrate very well the continuity of habitats. They are limestone basins that fill with water in autumn and winter and then support a freshwater community, but drain naturally through swallets in summer and become damp or wet grasslands or fens (Chapter 9).

7. Ponds may seem isolated but they are not, for they are connected into the whole by groundwater movements even if no stream is visible. But as small lakes they do have an appeal and approachability, history and cultural significance that have been greatly underemphasised. Their significance is celebrated in Andrews & Kinsman (1990), which deals with the importance of worked-out gravel pits for creating new standing water habitats, Moore (2002), who documented the creation of his own pond on retirement from a distinguished career in nature conservation research, and Williams *et al.* (2010), who offer a manual for management and creation of ponds.

8. Moss (2001).

9. Reynolds (1995).

10. There is no shortage of literature on stream and river ecology. See Allan & Castillo (2009).

Important papers include Vannote *et al.* (1980) which originated our current views on how material falling in from the forests of the land drives the functioning of headwater streams and Baxter *et al.* (2005) on linkages between the stream and the land.

11. The new view of lakes as heterotrophic systems is summarised in Reynolds (2008) and can be traced through Cole *et al.* (2007) and Cole (2013).

12. Loch Ness is discussed in Chapter 9. Some of the species of zooplankton in the lake depend up to 40 per cent on food energy that washes in from the catchment (Jones *et al.*, 1998; Grey *et al.*, 2001).

13. Upland walkers will be familiar with the brownish tinge of water in streams that is easily seen when water cascades over waterfalls. In lakes surrounded by bogs the water can look like cold tea (without milk). The brown substances are decomposition products of lignin and cellulose and many are long-chain fatty acids. In soils they form part of the humus; in limnology they have variously been called yellow substances or *gelbstoff*. They are difficult to break down and persist for a long time, so that they have major effects on light penetration, being especially absorbent of blue light.

14. A classic experiment was carried out in the 1960s in the White Mountains of New Hampshire, USA, when the catchments of some tributaries of a river were clear felled whilst others were left intact as controls. The work is discussed in Likens (1992).

CHAPTER THREE

1. Techniques for examining microorganisms and their activities are changing rapidly. Zinger *et al.* (2012) was the current view when the text was written.

2. Our view of the biosphere was revolutionised by earth system science, started by James Lovelock with his book in 1979. Our previous understanding was that the biosphere was essentially superimposed on a chemistry of the Earth's surface determined by physical processes and geology. Lovelock's revolution was to point out that the composition of the atmosphere, soils and oceans of the biosphere was far from the equilibrium state towards which physical processes would tend. The biosphere is kept in a highly unlikely non-equilibrium state by the combined activities of living organisms. An equilibrium state would leave Earth with an atmosphere that would be in line with those of Venus and Mars, our neighbours in the solar system, with virtually no free oxygen, huge amounts of carbon dioxide, only a trace of free nitrogen and a temperature close to 300 °C, and hence no liquid water. Liquid water is essential for living organisms.

By maintaining a slightly higher level of photosynthesis compared with respiration of the entire biological community, the system stores carbon, and keeps a surplus of oxygen in an atmosphere that is relatively sparse in carbon dioxide. In turn this maintains an equable mean temperature around 13 °C, at which liquid water can persist. There is much controversy about how this situation, known as the Gaia hypothesis, can be maintained by what appears to be co-operation among organisms, but the fact is that they do maintain it and that it is essential for the persistence of life on Earth. Lakes are very important as major stores of carbon in their sediments and the surrounding wetlands for storage of carbon in peat.

For most of Earth's history, equable conditions have been maintained solely by microorganisms. Currently larger plants also have a significant role but plants would be unable to function were it not for the microbial activity that maintains in circulation the essential nutrients that they need. Animals have a very minor role. See Lenton & Watson (2011) and Moss (2012) for detailed discussion.

3. Lynn Margulis began, or at least revived, another revolution in biology with her 1970 book. Since then the idea of endosymbiosis has changed from wild idea to conventional wisdom, virtually universally accepted with the new evidence that molecular studies have given. We walk around with each of our cells ultimately a collection of co-operating bacteria! See Archibald (2011) for a reasonably readable account of the current understanding.

4. The Archaea were first distinguished in 1977, with the position strengthened in Woese *et al.*, 1990. A useful book is Howland (2000), but the field is fast moving. Brochier-Armanet *et al.* (2011) includes material on sequencing of genomes that was not available only ten years previously.

5. Speculation about the origin of the structure of the eukaryotic cell, beyond the understanding that plastids originated from symbiotic eubacteria and cyanobacteria, is rife and inconclusive. The whimsical title of Forterre (2011) is indicative.

6. Weisse (2006) gives a clear review of how perceptions of bacterial communities in lakes have changed in the past two decades, including problems of knowing what is there, how to classify it and the meaning of 'species' in prokaryotes.

7. Bacteria have long been known to colonise much more extreme habitats, in terms of temperature, salinity, deoxygenation and acidity, than eukaryotes, but even they find the conditions of the exceptionally dry Atacama Desert in Chile challenging. Nonetheless though it is too dry for them to grow in the moister atmosphere under translucent grains of quartz, as they do in the Negev and other deserts, a few cyanobacteria grow within salt crystals whose hygroscopic properties are able to extract water from the atmosphere in tiny but sufficient amounts, resulting in a very saline habitat, but nonetheless one where liquid water, the *sine qua non* for active organisms, can be found. See Wierzchos *et al.* (2006).

8. It is possible to use a huge variety of techniques to measure growth and activity in natural bacterial populations. So far it is fair to say that little really new ecological insight has emerged, but the techniques are in their infancy and the communities are complex. Many things are happening simultaneously and it is difficult to separate them. Comte & Del Giorgio (2009) give a flavour of the techniques and the difficulties.

9. The paper by Whittaker (1969) is now out of date but at the time represented the first radically new thinking on the kingdoms of organisms for half a century.

10. A good review of the current classification of supergroups (kingdoms) and phyla is Walker *et al.* (2011). Be prepared for an enormous number of unfamiliar names.

11. The green algae come in a wonderful variety of forms. See Leliaert *et al.* (2011) for a good overview.

12. The word 'bloom' has become overused to describe large or even moderate populations of algae in the sea or freshwaters. Its original and more precise use was to refer to aggregations of cyanobacteria that sometimes form at the surfaces of lakes on calm summer days. There is a long folk tradition of their occurrence in the Northwest Midland meres (see Chapter 9).

13. Falkowski *et al.* (2004) attempt a rationalisation, but the question is still open (Finazzi *et al.*, 2010).

14. Priest Pot has been studied for many years. A general account is given in Finlay and Maberly (2000), and more specialist treatment in Esteban *et al.* (2012).

15. The distribution of microorganisms and the ubiquity or not of their species are discussed in Fenchel and Finlay (2004). Issues of biodiversity, ecosystem function and the importance of microorganisms are discussed in Finlay *et al.* (1997).

CHAPTER FOUR

1. No one knows exactly how many species there are. The most recent estimate of 8.7 million is given by Mora *et al.* (2011), based on projections from the number of species per genus, family or higher levels, known in well-studied groups, to groups that are not so well studied. It is likely to be an underestimate because of the difficulties of distinguishing what a species is in the prokaryotes and the fact that even well-studied groups have not been comprehensively described in some parts of the world. Other estimates vary from just over the present number (around 3 million) to ten times as many. Numbers of freshwater species are given in a series of 60 papers in the journal *Hydrobiologia*, volume 595. See Balian *et al.* (2008) for an overview. Estimates of numbers for Britain and Ireland are based on Dobson *et al.* (2012), supplemented by more specialist works.

2. An account of the problems that freshwater organisms have overcome is given in Pennak (1985). Evidence that freshwater invertebrates are often readily transferred between water bodies in the guts or on the feathers or feet of birds includes Frisch *et al.* (2007) and Van Leeuwen *et al.* (2012).

3. Features of the recent glaciation are discussed in Chapter 2. A review of the lakes (proglacial lakes) ponded up at the foot of the British glaciers is given by Murton & Murton (2012). The lake basins can be deduced from relict features such as wave-cut shorelines and well-sorted clay and sand deposits.

4. The history of the British flora, with a comprehensive listing of species from previous interglacials, is given in Godwin (1975). Evidence comes from pollen, seeds and plant fragments preserved in sediments and peat.

5. Analyses of the base sequences of nucleic acids are showing the relationships among different races in a species, even when these are not distinct in appearance, and allow more reliable conclusions about movements

and origins. The work on the bullhead (miller's thumb) is given in Hänfling *et al.* (2002). Other molecular studies that suggest that many species may have been able to persist in southern England, despite the proximity of the glacier, include McKeown *et al.* (2010). Møbjerg *et al.* (2011) point out just how resilient tardigrades (water bears) are, based on physiological studies that show that they can survive extremes of heat and cold by greatly reducing their water content. Tardigrades could easily have survived close to the glaciers.

6. See Murton & Murton (2012).

7. The most extreme lakes are those in the Antarctic interior, which lie close to glaciers and freeze over for most of the year. However, despite this, and their isolation, they are not devoid of invertebrates, but have no vertebrates. Laybourn-Parry *et al.* (2012) give a review of them. No matter how cold the region, wherever there is liquid water, for at least part of the year, some sort of ecosystem will develop (Anesio & Laybourn-Parry, 2011).

8. Reynoldson (1983) is an excellent account of his work on the commoner triclads and is exemplary in its use of experiments to find the reasons for their current distributions. Statistical methods for handling huge amounts of observational data are now very sophisticated, and elaborate maps can be plotted of distributions, which, through geographical information systems, can be compared with maps of environmental factors such as rainfall and temperature. These allow hypotheses to be drawn but can never provide a mechanistic explanation. Only experiments can reveal mechanisms and, alas, Reynoldson's is the only study on the British freshwater fauna that has been so thorough. Reynoldson & Young (2000) provide an update and increased detail on other of the triclad species.

9. See Kottelat (1997).

10. Lough Melvin is only one of a number of Irish and Scottish lakes showing coexistence of different sub-species of trout, but it is one of the best studied. See McKeown *et al.* (2010) for an account. The importance of these findings of great variety in common species is in showing that adequate conservation of the species cannot be confined to a limited number of sites.

11. Changes in range are normal responses to natural climate changes. The warming, after the ice retreated, led to what might be seen as mass invasion. Introductions by wealthy estate owners have been made over several centuries and to these we owe the Canada goose, Egyptian geese, the wels, pikeperch and several other fish. The common carp was brought in possibly by the Romans. There appears now to be a wave of new invasions. One the one hand, global warming is allowing many southern species to push northwards (see Hickling *et al.* (2005, 2006); Hassall *et al.* (2007); and Parmesan (2006)). On the other, increased international trade and travel is introducing many new species. See Chapter 8.

12. Dawkins (1976).

13. Cormorant numbers have increased on inland lakes in the last few decades (Kirby *et al.*, 1995), perhaps because of scarcity of food due to commercial overfishing at sea. New breeding colonies have established inland and may still be increasing in number. Adult cormorants eat up to a kilogram of fresh fish each day and may bring about major changes in small lakes by allowing zooplankton populations, previously fed on by fish, to increase and graze phytoplankton, thus clarifying the water (Leah *et al.*, 1980). Fishery managers often allege that cormorants are taking large numbers of fish and this may be true where the fish community is not diverse or comprises heavily stocked, open-water fish such as rainbow trout for angling. Cormorants are top predators and feed mostly in the open water rather than in the littoral zone. Predation may thus be high where the underwater structure (plant beds, woody debris) that provides refuges for the fish has been lost, or, as in reservoirs, is lacking because of severe water level changes. Heavy predation by cormorants is much less the case where the littoral zone is well developed, with plants among which many fish find refuge, and where the fish community is diverse (Harris *et al.*, 2008; Doucette *et al.*, 2011; Ostman *et al.*, 2012).

14. Work carried out by the Game Conservancy at a set of flooded gravel pits in the 1970s and 1980s (Giles, 1992) showed that fish and ducks both fed on chironomid larvae and other invertebrates and competed, so that removal of fish increased duck numbers. Large pike also fed on ducklings, illustrating that determination of population fluctuations of both birds and fish needs consideration of what is happening to both groups.

15. There are good examples of guanotrophication by both black-headed gulls and geese. The first purported example in the UK was at Rostherne Mere, in Cheshire

(Brinkhurst & Walsh, 1967), but later nutrient budgeting made it unlikely that gulls were a major source. However, much better evidence was produced for Hickling Broad, in Norfolk (Moss & Leah, 1982), where build-up of migratory gull numbers in winter was associated with their moving inland, feeding on a local waste tip and roosting on the Broad, which, in tandem with increases in salinity from land drainage, suffered a loss of its once famous submerged plant communities. Geese, particularly Canada geese, which are now very abundant, produce large quantities of faeces and are likely to have significant effects on small lakes, especially in municipal parks. Chaichana et al. (2010) studied a small lake at Brown Moss in Shropshire, where birds provided a large proportion of the nutrients entering the lake.

16. See Naiman et al. (2002) and Helfield & Naiman (2006).

17. A paper summarising major lines of evidence that vertebrates have major effects on the structures of the ecosystems is Estes et al. (2011).

CHAPTER FIVE

1. Cook (1999).

2. Opinions vary as to where to draw the line between an aquatic plant and a terrestrial one. Chambers et al. (2008) include all plants that are rooted in soils that are saturated with water for most of the year. Other definitions (Preston & Croft, 1997) demand that part of the photosynthetic structure be submerged. I have taken the wider view for it embraces the reality that freshwaters are not separate but are parts of a continuous series of ecosystems on the surface of the planet.

3. This does not stop attempts to classify vegetation into rigid schemes. Palmer et al. (1992) is widely used in Britain and Ireland, but, although the classification stands up in some places, it has generally to be tweaked to cope with many local deviations.

4. See Braendle & Crawford (1999) for a review of how plants cope with flooding.

5. Plant and algal biomass in freshwaters is eventually limited by the availability of nutrients, generally nitrogen or phosphorus, but the rate of growth may be limited by light or sometimes carbon. Often the two concepts of biomass accumulation (= growth) and rate of production (also sometimes = growth) are confused.

6. Smolders et al. (2002).

7. See Moss (1973) and Maberly et al. (2009).

8. Carbon dioxide is a polar compound and reacts with water molecules to form an acid, bicarbonic acid (H_2CO_3). This then splits apart to form hydrogen ions (H^+) and bicarbonate ions (HCO_3^-) to an extent determined by the pH of the water. If pH is low (abundant hydrogen ions) the dissociation is limited and most of the carbon dioxide remains as free carbon dioxide or undissociated bicarbonic acid. If the water is more alkaline (high pH, low concentrations of hydrogen ions), the dissociation is favoured and bicarbonic acid dissociates to give hydrogen ions and bicarbonate to an extent that is regulated by the pH. pH is determined by other reactions that produce hydrogen ions, including entry of acid or alkaline water from the catchment, so that a natural water's carbon dioxide availability will be determined by a range of circumstances. Photosynthesis will result in withdrawal of carbon dioxide and a rise in pH. The rise in pH will itself then reset the proportions of carbon dioxide and bicarbonate, resulting in a rise in the proportion of bicarbonate ions but a reduction in the total amount of inorganic carbon (carbon dioxide, bicarbonic acid and bicarbonate) present in the water.

   Many plants and algae can take up bicarbonate, using an enzyme called carbonic anhydrase to release carbon dioxide from bicarbonate at the surfaces of the leaves or cells. This then reduces the bicarbonate concentrations in the water, causing again a reassociation of hydrogen ions and a rise in pH, which then resets the proportions at a lower total carbon concentration. Below pH 4.5, very little bicarbonate is present, but between 4.5 and 8.4, there are increasing proportions of bicarbonate. Free carbon dioxide will then be quite scarce, but that will be immaterial to plants that can take up bicarbonate. Such uptake will push the pH even higher and above 8.4, carbonate, which is not available to photosynthesisers, will increasingly be formed and bicarbonate proportions will fall. pH may rise to 10 or 11, when concentrations of free carbon dioxide are essentially zero and of bicarbonate very small so that photosynthesis stops until more carbon dioxide enters overnight from the atmosphere.

9. Ranunculus aquatilis, for example, can produce three very different types of leaves, depending on photoperiod and degree of submergence (Cook, 1969).

10. Representative sampling is always difficult in natural habitats. Samples need to be taken randomly and they need to be repeated (replicated) many times to give a fair measure of what is present. No method perfectly samples all plants or animals and several different approaches are usually needed. Macan (1977a) illustrates this well with different sorts of samples from a small lake.

11. Plastic plants can be used to investigate the influence of plant architecture on the nature of the invertebrate community as well as to provide convenient sample units. For example, Hinojoso-Garro et al. (2010) showed a greater diversity of species on fine dissected leaves compared with flat plate-like floating leaves, but not a difference in total biomass.

12. A general account of Llyn Idwal is Duigan et al. (1998).

13. Sphagnum appears to be interlinked with many sorts of fungi and algae and only recently has the huge diversity of partners been revealed. Stenroosa et al. (2010) give some interesting examples.

14. See Moss (1973) for an exploration of desmid physiology in relation to pH and carbon availability.

15. The testae of dead amoebae are often preserved in peats and sediments and knowledge of their current ecology is needed for interpretation of species changes in historical deposits. There are very many species and Mitchell et al. (2000) give an introduction to the problem of separating their ecologies.

16. See Ings et al. (2012) for studies of the house and garden of the caddis, Tinodes waeneri.

17. Architecture and life forms of the many species of algae are as varied as in flowering plants, but on a microscopic scale. It is just as misleading in understanding the ecology of lakes to lump 'diatoms' together as it would be to consider the many species of plants just as 'plants'. Lowe (2011) will begin to convince you of this.

18. Details of Martham Broad's invertebrates are given in Mason & Bryant (1975).

19. Jones et al. (2000a).

20. Barker et al. (2010).

21. Timms & Moss (1984).

22. Macan (1977b) is an early review, still valuable, of the effects of predation in shaping animal communities. The topic is particularly important in plankton and is considered in Chapter 6.

23. Bronmark (1985).

24. This paper (Hutchinson, 1959) is one of the most cited papers in ecology. Part of the title is 'Homage to Santa Rosalia'. The pond with the corixids was close to a church dedicated to Santa Rosalia in rural Sicily. Hutchinson had interests in many subjects and was not afraid to acknowledge it. The traditions of scientific writing now, in an age of league tables and managerialism, are much more prosaic.

25. Jones et al. (2000b).

26. Eminson & Moss (1980).

27. A quite extensive literature now shows that fish often compete successfully for invertebrate food with water birds. Elmberg et al. (2010) showed that lakes lacking fish had more teal and goldeneye and considered predation on ducklings by pike to be the reason. Bigger ducks, like mallard, were unaffected. Other studies suggest that it is competition for invertebrate food that results in reduced numbers of ducks when fish are abundant (e.g. Väänänen et al., 2012; Winfield & Winfield, 1974).

28. Comin & Hurlbert (2012) introduce a series of papers on 'ornitholimnology' and make the point that holistic studies, in which birds are examined as parts of ecosystems, rather than as curiosities or ends in themselves, are much lacking. See also Steinmetz et al. (2003).

29. Birds have often been shown to be severe grazers on aquatic vegetation (Chaichana et al. 2011), but generally where the birds were introduced or maintained in artificially high numbers, or during periods of moult (Matuszak et al., 2012).

CHAPTER SIX

1. Molecular studies now allow differences to be identified in populations of algae that appear visually to be the same. A common diatom, Asterionella formosa, in Lake Maarsseveen in the Netherlands had seven distinct genotypes in the same population (Gsell et al., 2012).

2. Lehman & Scavia (1982).

3. Recent reviews of the roles of kairomones and other substances used in chemical signalling between organisms are Van Donk et al. (2011) and Bronmark & Hansson, (2012).

4. G. E. Hutchinson (1961) pointed out the 'paradox of the plankton', the existence at the same time of many species in what appears to be a uniform mass of water. Since then much work has centred on how this might be explained. The different pigment compositions of different species in a varying light climate provides one way of dividing the habitat (Striebel *et al.*, 2009) as do motility and size (Reynolds, 1980; Reynolds *et al.*, 2002). A recent paper on mixotrophy in the plankton, which gives an entry to the previous literature, is Hiltunen *et al.* (2012). The British contribution to phytoplankton ecology has been significant in terms of concepts and ideas (Talling, 2012).

5. Pace & Orcutt (1981) showed that in at least one lake, for which there is no reason to think that it was odd, ciliates dominated the numbers of zooplankton and constituted 15–62 per cent of the biomass.

6. Boyd (1970).

7. Mackerewicz & Likens (1975).

8. See Wilson (1998) for leads into the subject of personality in fish.

9. It is rare for several forms of predation to be measured simultaneously and usually it is assumed that fish are more effective predators on zooplankton than invertebrates. This may, however, not always be the case (Bunnell *et al.*, 2011).

10. Vertical migration over the 24-hour day has been long known for zooplankton (Hays, 2003), but the chemical mechanisms controlling it are not clear.

11. It is difficult to obtain good estimates of fish biomass because fish are not uniformly distributed in a lake. They move rapidly and can detect nets and traps, and different species require different techniques. New approaches include use of underwater sonar in which radio beams are reflected back from individual fish or shoals, but these have to be calibrated against actual catches. Most fish statistics are relative not absolute and based on catch per unit effort (for example, for a net of specified length and mesh size, set for one night) rather than biomass per unit area. Precise estimates of the latter are only possible when a lake or pond can be drained down and all the fish removed. However, with a variety of methods, less precise estimates, probably within the right order of magnitude, are possible. The data used here are judged on estimates from what are likely to be upper

limits of fish biomass from fertile lakes in East Anglia (Perrow *et al.*, 1999).

12. There is a large literature on coregonids because they are important food fish in North America and mainland Europe. Their plasticity has also stimulated studies on evolution and adaptation (Kahilainen *et al.*, 2011; Mehner *et al.*, 2012).

13. The British freshwater fish fauna is limited, but has been well investigated. Maitland (2004) is a comprehensive key with distribution maps and many references. Maitland and Campbell (1992) give more information on ecology, whilst Varley (1967) is still useful on wider aspects of British fish biology, such as physiology.

14. Charr in Loch Rannoch are described in Fraser *et al.* (2007), and in Wales, where the fish is sometimes called the torgoch, by McCarthy (2006). The plasticity of charr is illustrated by Eloranta *et al.* (2013) and controversies over its existence as one or fifteen species in Britain and Ireland are discussed by Adams & Maitland (2007).

15. The three-spined stickleback is so versatile, amenable and interesting a fish as to have been used in thousands of studies of physiology, behaviour and ecology. A comprehensive summary is Östlung-Nilsson *et al.* (2007).

16. The literature on the effects of birds has been already referred to in Chapters 4 and 5. See also Notes 17 (Chapter 4) and 29 (Chapter 5).

17. A review of the growth of cyanobacteria (then usually called blue-green algae) and the formation of water blooms is Reynolds & Walsby (1975). In that paper, surface scums were seen as terminal. Subsequently evidence emerged that they might aid in obtaining carbon dioxide (Paerl & Ustach, 1982) or nitrogen for fixation (Lewis, 1983).

18. The general course of seasonal changes in the open water of north-temperate lakes was neatly summarised in the Plankton Ecology Group Model in 1986, updated by Sommer *et al.* (2012).

19. The role of organic matter in lakes has been discussed in Chapter 2 and there is now an extensive literature (Duarte & Prairie, 2005). One instance of a net heterotrophic plankton community is Loch Lomond (Bass *et al.*, 2010), but the phenomenon is likely to be very widespread. In experiments carried out on field courses in spring at Slapton Ley in

Devon, a lake with plentiful phytoplankton populations, I consistently showed that respiration over 24 hours was greater than the gross photosynthesis by day, despite the many things that can undermine any experiment carried out by first-year students.

20. The evolutionary play is increasingly studied in the ecological theatre and rapid evolution of many organisms in response to environmental change is well established (Post & Palkovacs, 2009).

21. Mesocosm experiments have been useful in determining the underlying mechanisms that operate in both the plankton and the littoral, though they are most useful for the latter since mesocosms are most conveniently placed in shallow water. Little Mere in Cheshire has been a useful lake for mesocosm experiments and some important findings have been made there. These include: Beklioglu & Moss (1996), who looked at the mutual effects of fish, nutrients, sediment and plants on the plankton communities; Williams *et al.* (2002) who showed how the effects of fish can be manifested through both predation on the zooplankton and release of nutrients through excretion and disturbance of the bottom sediments; Moss *et al.* (1998) who demonstrated experimentally the role of water lily cover in reducing predation by perch on zooplankters; and, in a *tour de force*, Moss *et al.* (2004) who co-ordinated a set of similar mesocosm experiments in Finland, Sweden, the UK, the Netherlands and Spain to investigate the effects of different latitudes on processes in the plankton and littoral. Mesocosm experiments can also be done in experimental ponds, for example created in the ditches of wetlands by damming them with wooden dams. Key experiments in understanding changes in shallow lakes and the roles of nutrients and fish were done by Irvine *et al.* (1989) and Balls *et al.* (1989) in ditches in Woodbastwick fen in Norfolk.

Making the link between a mesocosm and a whole lake remains a problem. Mesocosms offer control and replication but reduced reality. A whole-lake experiment means little control and no replication. Jumping from the laboratory to the lake is even more unreliable. In laboratory systems using rotifer populations and algae, Yoshida *et al.* (2003) showed strong top-down effects of grazing by the rotifer *Brachionus calyciflorus* on an alga, *Chlorella vulgaris*, when just a single clone of algae was used, with clear alternating rises and falls in rotifer and algal numbers. But when several different clones of *Chlorella* were used, as would

be found in a natural lake, the fluctuations were much more muted as different clones of different susceptibility to grazing compensated for one another.

22. Carpenter *et al.* (1987).

23. Schindler (1998) provides a vigorous argument in favour of whole-lake studies and against the relevance of mesocosm experiments. Spivak *et al.* (2011) argue for their relevance and extrapolation to whole lakes. Whole-lake manipulations have been uncommon in Britain and Ireland, with restoration attempts at Esthwaite, Windermere, Loch Leven and in the Norfolk Broads most prominent. These are discussed in Chapters 8 and 9.

24. Lund & Reynolds (1982), Leah *et al.* (1978) and Moss (1981).

25. I have deliberately avoided using specialist terms in this book, but you may wonder why I do not refer to oligotrophic and eutrophic lakes as these are well-known terms. I avoid them because they imply two distinctly different sorts of lakes, the first rich in nutrients, the second poor in them, but the reality is that conditions in lakes form continuous series rather than discrete categories. Though the terms are widely bandied about, not least in official conservation circles, there is no agreed definition of exactly what they mean.

26. Many people think that a productive lake must have the greatest diversity; others think that where nutrients are scarce and production is low, there will be the greatest number of species. Yet others place the greatest diversity at an intermediate stage. The views held often depend on whether diversity is measured for just one or several groups of organisms, the thoroughness of the sampling and the skills of the identifiers. Post *et al.* (2000) throw a different and more profound light on the problem. They measured the length of the food chains in around 60 lakes of greatly differing area and phosphorus content, using the range of contents of ^{15}N in the organisms to establish the number of steps in the chains and found that the longest chains (and hence potentially the greatest number of steps) were found in the biggest lakes. There was no link with production. The reason appears to be that the bigger the system, the greater variety of niches it can provide.

27. Strong links are found within different parts of lakes through fish movements and feeding. Van der Zanden *et al.* (2011) used stable

isotope data to calculate the dependence of fish on littoral and bottom animals and found that up to 65 per cent of the food came from the bottom and edges. Limnology has traditionally concentrated on the open water and the plankton, and that may have given a biased understanding. The open water seems to be highly dependent on both the littoral and the catchment. In a way it represents the end of a line, not the hub on which everything turns.

CHAPTER SEVEN

1. Animals bigger than a millimetre or two are confined to the surface layers of sediment, where there is some oxygen. They continually work it over, a process called bioturbation. It causes changes to the sediment and to some extent homogenises the sediments reaching the bottom over a few years. With sedimentation rates naturally lower than about a millimetre a year (Pennington, 1974), this period might be up to five or ten years, but where sedimentation rates are high (where catchments are eroding rapidly or production in the lake has been stimulated by eutrophication, for example) it could be less than a year before the sediment can be considered to have entered permanent storage, in which it will undergo little further change.

2. Ralph Brinkhurst compiled a notable book on the benthos of lakes in 1974, in which he was able to make little reference to the benthos of British lakes and none at all to Irish. Humphries (1936) carried out a survey of the benthos of Windermere; she found comparatively few animals (about 30 per m^2) in the deep water, but this may be because she used too coarse a sieve to sort the animals from the sediment.

3. See Jonasson (1972), Jonasson & Thorhauge (1976) and Holopainen & Jonasson (1989).

4. McLachlan et al. (1979).

5. Much of the work on methane has been British-based (Jones and Grey, 2011).

6. Molongoski & Klug (1980).

7. Kelly et al. (2004). See McElhone (1982) for one of the few examples of a detailed study of the invertebrate benthos in British lakes.

8. Solomon et al. (2008).

9. Johnson & Brinkhurst (1971).

10. See Brinkhurst (1974) and Moss et al. (1994) for discussions on lake types and the replacement of the idea of types by that of continua.

11. Pennington (1973, 1974).

12. The palaeolimnological scientific community in Britain has been a co-operative one, prone to celebrating the achievements of its leading lights by special issues of journals that begin with appreciative articles that can give excellent insight into the circumstances of the research. Battarbee et al. (2008), Birks and Birks (2007), Brooks et al. (2011), Oldfield (2010) and Birks & Smol (2013) are worth reading for the insights they give.

13. Pennington (1947) with an update in Pennington (1973).

14. Round (1957, 1961), Mackereth (1965, 1966), Haworth (1969).

15. The original description of the Mackereth corer is Mackereth (1958). There are several other types of corer in use. The Livingstone corer works by pushing an open tube past a piston. Various borers move sediment sideways using the same principle as the Jenkin corer and many peat borers. The soft sediment at the surface is often a problem as it is too fluid to stay in the corers. However, it can be sampled by using a device that is a box with a flat surface. The box is filled with solid carbon dioxide and then inserted into the surface ooze. The sediment freezes onto the flat surface and can be removed in an orderly way, as ice, when the apparatus is retrieved after a few minutes.

16. Pearsall & Pennington (1947).

17. See Oldfield (2010) for a general account of the development of 210lead dating.

18. Oldfield (2013).

19. The recent development of palaeolimnology in Britain and Ireland has moved along three lines. First has been more quantitative use of a variety of biological features of the cores, developed some time ago (for example Moss, 1979, Stansfield et al., 1989). These include photosynthetic pigments (e.g. McGowan et al., 1999), remains of chironomids (Langdon et al., 2004), aquatic plants (Davidson et al. (2005), zooplankton (Davidson et al., 2007) and potentially fish (Davidson et al., 2003). Last & Smol (2001) is a comprehensive account of methods available. Secondly, a variety of specialist chemical techniques (for example for detecting faecal substances (Vane et al., 2010) and those using stable isotopes) has become available. See Leng & Henderson (2013) for a review of isotope methods. Isotopes allow studies on temperature reconstruction (Batarbee, 2000; Marshall

et al., 2002), different sources of organic matter (Diefendorf *et al.,* 2008) and lake levels (Jones *et al.,* 2011). The third trend has been development of statistical methods for reconstructing past environmental features, such as temperature, pH, salinity, total phosphorus and total nitrogen. There are now at least ten methods available but the sophistication of the mathematics is often greater than the quality of the core data, because of limitations in the sediment record and inappropriate use of training sets from other areas. Early enthusiasm (Anderson *et al.,* 1993; Brooks *et al.,* 2001) has sobered as different methods have given different results, the calculations have not matched up to contemporary measurements or have given the 'right' trend but concentrations that were inherently very unlikely (Birks & Birks, 2006; Juggins *et al.,* 2013). There has been a tendency to use single cores to reconstruct recent events, yet single cores are representative only in very small basins. The approaches of Pennington (1943) and Moss (1980, 1988) of using many cores are being revived (Engstrom & Rose, 2013). There is also renewed concern that diatom preservation may not be as good as is usually presumed (Ryves *et al.,* 2013). Nonetheless, palaeolimnology remains a hugely valuable tool in interpreting lake ecology.

20. Flower *et al.* (1987); Battarbee *et al.* (2007).

CHAPTER EIGHT

1. A general account of the former Holderness lakes is Sheppard (1957) and the most recent work at Star Carr is given in Milner *et al.* (2013).

2. Hoskins (1955) is a classic and very readable work, updated by Prior (2010) on the history of the British landscape.

3. Bogaard *et al.* (2013).

4. Johnes (1996) pioneered techniques of detailed export coefficient modelling for rivers in southern England and Johnes and Moss & Phillips (1996) use it to trace the changing sources of nutrient loading to a representative set of rural English catchments since the 1930s. The contribution by stock was surprisingly high.

5. An account of mediaeval fisheries in Norman times is given in the Domesday Book (www.nationalarchives.gov.uk/domesday); Aston (1988) surveys what is known from modern archaeology and Lucas (1998) describes the fisheries of Whittlesea Mere.

6. Celia Fiennes (1662–1741) travelled throughout England on horseback between 1694 and 1712, and kept a detailed diary. Her notes were eventually published (Fiennes, 1888) and give a vivid account of the landscape of the time. She comments on Windermere (*'Wiandermer'*) and its charr fishery, Martin Mere (*'I avoided going by the famous Mer Call'd Martin mer that as ye proverb sayes has parted many a man and his mare'*), Ullswater, one of the Cheshire Meres near Nantwich, and Dozmary (*Dosenmeer*) Pool, in Cornwall, but that is about the limit of her limnological interests. She was far more interested in the towns, the houses of the landed gentry and in mining; she owned a valuable salt deposit in Cheshire.

7. The classic works on the fens and their drainage are Godwin (1978) and Darby (1983).

8. Gregory (2000) documents the diatomite workings at Kentmere.

9. Ormerod *et al.* (1991) and Schindler (1988) discuss the effects of acidification on freshwater communities. NEGTAP (2001) is a survey of the emissions causing acidification at the start of the twenty-first century and discusses concepts like critical loads (the amount of acidity a landscape can bear without showing symptoms). Davies *et al.* (2005) show how water chemistry has been improving in the uplands since sulphur emissions were reduced, but Kwalik *et al.* (2007) and Ormerod & Durance (2009) note the effects of acid episodes still in retarding biological recovery. Weatherly (1988) tells of the negative effects of liming, which was sometimes used to mitigate acidification in lakes, on catchment vegetation.

10. Newman (1997).

11. Jorgensen (2010) looks at early sewage disposal in Coventry and York; Cooper (2001) gives an account of the historical development of sewage treatment.

12. Moss (2001).

13. The literature on eutrophication is large and the main principles and remedies were established long ago; many modern publications are simply more detailed case studies. Phosphate precipitation has had a revival recently with the use of lanthanum compounds. Spears *et al.* (2013) have tested a variety of products in the laboratory and Cooke *et al.* (2005) give examples of longer-term use of aluminium and industrial compounds in a general manual of lake restoration. Biomanipulation as a

restoration technique is discussed in Moss *et al.* (1996). Much modern palaeolimnology has concentrated on documenting recent increases in eutrophication (Davidson & Jeppesen, 2013) and current emphasis is on the difficulties of controlling diffuse pollution from farming (e.g. Mainstone & Parr, 2002; Jennings *et al.*, 2013).

14. Reports by the European Community and by national governments are always amusing for the positive spin that they apply to limited achievements. The latest assessments of progress on the Urban Wastewaters Treatment Directive are Dept of the Environment, Food and Rural Affairs (DEFRA, 2012) and European Commission (2013).

15. Catchment Sensitive Farming Evidence Team (2011).

16. Foy *et al.* (1995).

17. A splendid example of a long government report documenting complete ineffectiveness, concerns the Nitrates Directive in the UK (Johnson *et al.*, 2011). Burt *et al.* (2011) show how nitrate levels in British rivers are no longer increasing but remain exceptionally high compared with pristine waters.

18. See McGowan *et al.* (2012) and Pickering (2001).

19. Pimental *et al.* (2005) estimate that alien species in the United States cause damage and losses of almost US$120 billion per year, with approximately 50,000 foreign species present, and believe that about 42 per cent of the species on the threatened or endangered species lists are at risk primarily because of alien-invasive species. Much of the damage is due to crop weeds and diseases, cats and rats. Oeska and Aldridge (2011) give much more modest costs for freshwater problems in the UK. Britton *et al.* (2007) discuss the recent invasion of top mouth gudgeon in the UK and Winfield *et al.* (2008) the effects of introduction of a native fish species to a wider range within Britain.

20. Carvalho & Moss (2005) show that many freshwater Sites of Special Scientific Interest in England and Wales have been damaged by introduction of common carp.

21. There is a small lake at Llandrindod Wells in mid-Wales. It was created in 1873 by the damming of a small stream for the amenity of visitors to this never-very-prosperous but nonetheless charming small town. The lake is fed by streams from the surrounding hills and until around 1950 had clear water, an extensive littoral zone with aquatic plants and was used as source of gudgeon for live bait used in the trout fishery on the nearby River Wye. The lake owners, the local council, meddled somewhat in the early part of the twentieth century because they did not like the plants and did various things to try to discourage their growth, including addition of a large amount of phosphate to stimulate algal growth in an attempt to shade them out – a deliberate eutrophication. Various fish were stocked: at first trout, then coarse fish including bream, roach, bitterling (an exotic) and perch, and eventually carp. In the 1950s the lake began to become turbid in summer with cyanobacteria. Sailing was banned because of this in 1989.

Meanwhile the lake was prized as a carp fishery but in the 1990s, with the lever of the possibly poisonous algal blooms, the local council decided the lake should be restored. The inflow water was relatively low in nutrients, but levels of phosphorus rose greatly in summer because phosphorus was mobilised from the sediments by the carp activity and this underlay the large algal crops. A lack of piscivores meant there were also many small zooplanktivorous bream in the lake, and thus only a small population of zooplankton capable of grazing the algae. The solution was to biomanipulate the lake, removing carp and bream, planting in native plants and then restoring a community of native fish, including some piscivores. The local angling club was not pleased at the potential loss of their carp so a plan was made to include just a few (helped by the fact that carp do not usually breed successfully in the wild at British temperatures), but the council considered the amenity value of the lake should take precedence over the fishery. Carp are valuable fish to fishing clubs and it was intended to sell most of the fish for stocking elsewhere.

The plans went awry when it was discovered that the carp were infected with an exotic parasite, a flatworm carried by oligochaete worms that had been imported as bait from eastern Europe or Russia. This meant that the fish were not marketable and the fish stock was never fully removed, though the carp population was reduced. Fish removal had been helped by the fact that the lake could be drained, but there were concerns for the breeding toad population, which meant that there was always a residual pool of water in which fish persisted. Plants were stocked, but instead of the modestly growing native species recommended, more aggressive species and some horticultural cultivars of lilies were put in. The result, after the water levels had been restored, was a rampant growth of plants in much clearer water. The Chamber of Commerce was not pleased, despite the installation also of a fountain in the form of a large Welsh dragon in the middle of the lake (Fig. 204). Responsibility for the lake then changed because of local government reorganisation from Radnorshire District Council to Powys County Council.

The new owners brought in a fisheries consultant, a carp enthusiast, who recommended use of herbicides to remove the plants, stocking of more carp and a promotion of a carp fishery. The wheel had turned full circle, fuelled by the expenditure of some hundreds of thousands of pounds. The paper written on this saga (Moss et al., 2002) was justifiably entitled 'a restoration comedy'. In 2006 in a dry, warm summer, the chickens came home to roost. There were extensive algal blooms and a major fish kill, even of the carp. Oxygen and additional water were pumped into the lake as a temporary measure. The next year a 'restoration' programme costing several hundred thousand more pounds was begun. Sediment was dredged from the bed and formed into bunds at the edge, which were then planted with reed and other emergent plants. This deepened the water and may have exposed sediment to more oxidising conditions, but the carp population is still present. For the moment, the fuss has died down but we await the next hot dry summer for a further instalment of this saga.

22. Table 1 is based on Pretty et al. (2003) and Dodds et al. (2009).

23. Ritvo (2009).

24. Papers covering aspects of pond conservation are: Biggs et al. (2005), Raebel et al. (2012) and Wood et al. (2003).

25. Collar (1996) gives an account of Red Data books.

26. Andrews & Kinsman (1990).

27. Brown (2012).

28. Hewlett et al. (2009).

29. http://uknea.unep-wcmc.org/

30. Ecological goods and services are seen to be a possible salvation for nature conservation, especially among economists. Ecologists generally are more sceptical. The Department of the Environment, Food and Rural Affairs produced a useful guide (DEFRA, 2007). Costanza et al. (1997) was the first major attempt to value ecosystem goods and services

on a global scale and determined that they were annually worth about three times the total GDP of all nations combined, but this is now seen as a major underestimate. One problem with the approach is that most economists treat agricultural systems as ecosystems (agroecosystems) and include the value of food produced from them. This biases thinking because agroecosystems are not truly ecosystems and cultivation of food is not an ecological service. Valuations of the total goods and services rendered by pristine systems consistently seem to be greater than when they are cultivated or otherwise developed (Balmford et al., 2002). Keniger et al. (2013) summarises the benefits to people from contact with nature, without, perhaps wisely, trying to put cash values on these.

31. Knight et al. (2005).

CHAPTER NINE

1. General works, on the waters of Scotland, Ireland and Wales, respectively are Maitland et al. (1994), Reynolds (1998) and Jones (2002).

2. The excursion is documented by Tansley (1911) and some interesting insights from its visit to the Norfolk Broads concerning Marietta Pallis and the suppression of women in science at the time are discussed, a century later, in Cameron & Matless (2011).

3. See International Centre for Island Technology (2004) for an overview. The report can be downloaded from the web site of Scottish Natural Heritage.

4. Holdway et al. (1978).

5. Jones et al. (2001) and Grey et al. (2001) summarise evidence for the role of external organic matter in Loch Ness.

6. Two ways of calculating the size of the monster population are given in Sheldon & Kerr (1972) and Scheider & Wallis (1973). A symposium on the loch was published in The Scottish Naturalist in 1988 with an account of sonar investigations (Shine & Martin 1988), which does not mention the monster, but makes it clear that there isn't one.

7. Murphy et al. (1994); Tippett (1994).

8. May & Spears (2012a,b) enfold a series of papers in Hydrobiologia celebrating the work done at Loch Leven over the past 50 years. Dudley et al. (2012) summarise current water quality in the loch.

9. There is a large literature on Lough Neagh,

ranging from the first palaeolimnological study noting its increasing eutrophication (Battarbee, 1978) to a recent paper showing a decline in the number of water birds because attempts to reduce its nutrients and production have been partly successful (Tománková *et al.*, 2013).

10. Cassina *et al.* (2013).

11. Drinan *et al.* (2013).

12. Rodgers *et al.* (2010) document the loss of phosphorus from Irish forest felling, and McGinnity *et al.* (2003) the genetic problems caused by escaped cultured salmon.

13. National Tourism Development Authority, The Great Fishing Houses of Ireland web site (http://irelandflyfishing.com/loughs/lough-mask). Krause & King (1994) describe Lough Corrib, and McGarrigle & Champ (1999) Lough Mask, but may be outdated. The past 20 years have seen major increases in nutrient flows in agricultural areas.

14. Donohue *et al.* (2010) and King & Champ (2000) document the past and present of Lough Carra.

15. Robinson (2008) is an evocative account of the landscape of bogs and lakes of Mayo and Galway. He even touches on the arguments among the ecologists of the International Phytogeographical Excursion about how to view plant communities as they meandered over the Roundstone Bog.

16. Sheehy-Skeffington *et al.* (2006).

17. Gerald of Wales (1191–1194). Duigan *et al.* (1999) is a more considered account.

18. Borrow (1862).

19. Duigan *et al.* (1996).

20. Liddle *et al.* (1979).

21. Haycock & Ellis (2010)

22. Lockley (1969) is an old book, but contains rich details of contrasts between the north and south of Pembrokeshire that are still there in geology, buildings, culture and natural history but seem to be less celebrated in more recent tourist guides that place more emphasis on beach quality, shopping, theme parks and other trivia.

23. The literature on Slapton Ley can be accessed through Johnes & Wilson (1996). The future of the barrier beach is discussed by Trudgill (2009) and Watson (2011). All the papers published in Field Studies can be freely downloaded from the publications section of the Field Studies Council's web site. *Floreat!*

24. See Moss (2013).

25. Sinker (1962).

26. Godwin (1959). There is an irony to the loss of this lake. In the 1960s, when a wave of new universities was being built, the landscape architects often incorporated a lake at the centre of the new campuses. At Stirling, there was already a natural loch, but elsewhere the basins had to be dug. At the University of East Anglia, in Norwich, a rather deep-sided, uncharacteristic basin for the region was excavated for gravel, used to construct a nearby by-pass road, but the lake is not unpleasing. At York, and University College, Dublin, horrible, concrete-sided sumps are now plagued by the droppings of Canada geese, and the pools at Warwick University are monuments to severe eutrophication in the Midlands.

27. See Stead *et al.* (1986) and Brothwell (1986). Lindow Man is now preserved, but dwarfed, in a small space in the British Museum in London. He would be much better honoured in the museums of Liverpool or Manchester, close to his home.

28. The general limnology of the meres is reviewed in Reynolds (1971, 1979) and Moss *et al.* (1997). Demonstration of early peaks in cyanobacterial growths through preserved pigments is given in McGowan *et al.* (1999) and early historical references are in Phillips (1884).

29. See Moss *et al.* (1997), Moss *et al.* (1994), Hameed *et al.* (1999), Kilinc & Moss (2002) and James *et al.* (2003).

30. Lee (1977) describes the inland salt marshes and Savage (2000) changes in Watch Lane Flash.

31. Coney (1992) gives a history of Martin Mere and Wisniewski (1993), the creation of the wildfowl reserve.

32. Many references have been given in previous chapters to the Cumbrian lakes, but none yet to Bassenthwaite Lake. See Thackeray *et al.* (2006) and Winfield *et al.* (2011).

33. Malham Tarn has been well studied. Holmes (1965) gives a general account and Talling & Parker (2002) more recent information. Pigott & Pigott (1963) describe the history of the site.

34. McCulloch (2006).

35. See Hansard 1990, 5 August, 170, 1369–76.

In 1982, a symposium was held assessing the history of the reservoir, its limnology and wildlife. Harper (1982) is the scene-setting introduction to a series of papers in *Hydrobiologia*, 88.

36. Moss (2001).

37. There have been few significant papers produced on the Broads in the last ten years to supplement the account given in Moss (2001). Some interesting data emerged from sediment cores suggesting that use of tributyl tin compounds in boat anti-fouling paints may have been linked to loss of grazing zooplankters in Hickling Broad (Sayer *et al.* (2006). However, the ability of the sediments to support plant communities with abundant zooplankters in the overlying water, in experiments in tanks with Hickling sediment and water (Barker *et al.*, 2007) makes this likely to be a correlation rather than a causative mechanism. Madgwick *et al.* (2012) is an interesting compilation of historical data on the history of Barton Broad.

38. Kelly (2013).

39. Broads Authority (2011).

CHAPTER TEN

1. Williamson *et al.* (2009).

2. About 2.7 gigatonnes of carbon enter lakes and wetlands each year from the land; 0.6 is stored in sediments, 1.2 is respired back to the atmosphere and 0.9 is washed through to the ocean. Lakes and wetlands are responsible for about one quarter of the storage of carbon on the continents, though they occupy less than 2 per cent of the total area.

3. A survey of American ecologists found that a surprisingly small proportion involved itself in environmental advocacy or activism (Reiners *et al.*, 2013).

4. There are concerns that current estimates of the changes to come may be too conservative. See Anderson and Bows (2011).

5. Intergovernmental Panel on Climate Change (2013).

6. The UK meteorological office web site has many data. Summaries have been prepared for precipitation, temperature and sea level by the Department of Energy and Climate Change and are available on its web site.

7. A useful general reference is Kernan *et al.* (2010). The literature is large but see Adrian *et al.* (2009), Feuchtmayr *et al.* (2009), George

(2010), Gyllstrom *et al.* (2008), George *et al.* (2004), McKee *et al.* (2003) and Magnusson *et al.* (2000).

8. Winfield *et al.* (2008).

9. Thackeray *et al.* (2010), using over 25,000 sets of records from British amateur naturalists and professional sources, show that life cycle events in plants, invertebrates and vertebrates have become earlier by between seven and seventeen days since 1975, during which time temperatures have increased by about 1°C in the UK. The patterns differ among freshwater, marine and land environments and among the groups of organisms and there is no understanding of why.

10. Moss *et al.* (2011).

11. Hickling *et al.* (2005), using records from amateur odonatologists found that, in the 25 years between 1960–70 and 1985–95, many southern British dragonflies and damselflies shifted their range northwards. *Coenagrion puella, Ischnura elegans* and *Enallagma cyathigerum* changed their ranges by around 170 km; *Sympetrum striolatum* moved northwards by 346 km. The mean northward movement of 37 species, for which there were good data, was 74 km.

12. Hairston *et al.* (1999), Van Doorslaer *et al.* (2007, 2010). Even fish may evolve very rapidly (Hendry *et al.*, 2000).

13. European Union (2000).

14. See Leira *et al.* (2006) for an account of the process by which the Irish government has used low standards for determining high status sites.

15. Birk *et al.* (2002) review the problems of using nearly 300 ways of assessing ecological quality in the European member states.

16. See Moss (2008) for a critique of the whole approach taken in the Water Framework Directive, Demars *et al.* (2012) for a demolishing of some of its detailed approaches, European Commission (2012) for a diplomatic treatment of its limited effects so far, Hering *et al.* (2010) for a more optimistic scientists' view on the grounds that a great many new data have been gathered, and European Environmental Bureau (2010) for arguments that it has been a toothless tiger.

17. Moss (2012).

18. There are numerous reports documenting the progressive decline of British wildlife. A recent selection includes Natural England

(2010), Royal Society for the Protection of Birds (2013) and Wildlife & Countryside Link (2013).

19. Sheail (1998) and Marren (2002) give honest accounts of how conservation has developed and been bureaucratised and rebuffed in Britain, but nonetheless has managed to win a few battles.

20. Le Quéré et al. (2012); Oliver et al. (2013).

21. For stimulating, and sometimes radical, views of the carbon cycle, see Lovelock (1979), Cole et al. (2007) and Cole (2013).

22. Millennial Ecosystem Assessment Board (2005).

23. See Moss (2010) and Yvon-Durocher et al. (2010) for accounts of experiments to measure effects of increased temperature on respiration to photosynthesis ratios in shallow lake systems. Increases of 2–3°C gave a rise in ratio of 18 per cent, and of 4°C, 35 per cent. Extrapolated to a world scale such changes would release a frightening amount of carbon dioxide into the atmosphere. See also Walter et al. (2006) for a discussion of how warming may release large amounts of methane from these systems.

24. Lampitt et al. (2008).

25. Sheil & Murdiyarso (2009).

26. Estes et al. (2011).

27. Taylor (2005).

28. Wigbels (1980).

29. Ehrlich & Ehrlich (2013). See also Diamond (2005).

30. Carvalho & Moss (1995).

References

Adams, C. E. & Maitland, P. S. (2007). Arctic charr in Britain and Ireland – 15 species or one? *Ecology of Freshwater Fish* 16, 20–8.

Adrian, R. and others (2009). Lakes as sentinels of current climate change. *Limnology & Oceanography* 54, 2283–97.

Ahlgren, J., Yang, X., Hansson, L.-A. & Brönmark, C. (2013). Camouflaged or tanned: plasticity in freshwater snail pigmentation. *Biology Letters* 9: 20130464. http://dx.doi.org/10.1098/rsbl.2013.0464.

Allen, J. D. & Castillo, M. M. (2009). *Stream Ecology. Structure and Function of Running Waters.* 2nd Edition. Springer, The Netherlands.

Anderson, K. & Bows, A. (2011). Beyond 'dangerous' climate change: emission scenarios for a new world. *Philosophical Transactions of the Royal Society A* 369, 20–44.

Anderson, N. J., Rippey, B. & Gibson, C. E. (1993). A comparison of sedimentary and diatom-inferred phosphorus profiles: implications for defining pre-disturbance nutrient conditions. *Hydrobiologia* 253, 357–66.

Andrews, J. & Kinsman, D. (1990). *Gravel Pit Restoration for Wildlife.* Royal Society for the Protection of Birds, Sandy.

Anesio, A. & Laybourn-Parry, J. (2011). Glaciers and ice sheets as a biome. *Trends in Ecology and Evolution* 27, 219–25.

Archibald, J. M. (2011). Origins of eukaryotic cells: 40 years on. *Symbiosis* 54, 69–86.

Aston, S. (1988). *Mediaeval Fish, Fisheries and Fishponds in England.* British Archaeological Research British Series 182, Oxford.

Balian, E. V., Segers, H., Lévêque, C. & Martens, K. (2008). The Freshwater Animal Diversity Assessment (FADA) project: an overview of the results. *Hydrobiologia* 595, 627–37.

Balls, H., Moss, B. & Irvine, K. (1989). The loss of submerged plants with eutrophication. I. Experimental design, water chemistry, aquatic plant and phytoplankton biomass in experiments carried out in ponds in the Norfolk Broadland. *Freshwater Biology* 22, 71–87.

Balmford, A. and others (2002) Ecology – Economic reasons for conserving wild nature. *Science* 297, 950–3.

Barker, T. and others (2007) Control of ecosystem state in a shallow, brackish lake: implications for the conservation of stonewort communities. *Aquatic Conservation* 18, 221–40.

Barker, T., Irfanullah, H. M. & Moss, B. (2010). Micro-scale structure in the chemistry and biology of a shallow lake. *Freshwater Biology* 55, 1145–63.

Barnett, A. J., Finlay, K. & Beisner, B. E. (2007). Functional diversity of crustacean zooplankton communities: towards a trait-based classification. *Freshwater Biology* 52, 796–813.

Bass, A. M., Waldron, S., Preston, T. & Adams, C. E. (2010). Net pelagic heterotrophy in mesotrophic and oligotrophic basins of a large, temperate lake. *Hydrobiologia* 652, 363–75.

Battarbee, R. W. (1978). Observations on the recent history of Lough Neagh and its drainage basin. *Philosophical Transactions of the Royal Society* B 281, 303–44.

Battarbee, R. W. (2000). Palaeolimnological approaches to climate change, with special regard to the biological record. *Quaternary Science Reviews* 19, 107–24.

Battarbee, R. W. and others (2005). *A Review of Freshwater Ecology in the UK.* Freshwater Biological Association, Ambleside.

Battarbee, R. W. and others (2008) Frank Oldfield and his contributions to environmental change research. *The Holocene* 18, 3–17.

Battarbee, R. W., Curtis, C. J. & Shilland, E. M. (2011). The Round Loch of Glenhead: recovery from acidification, climate change monitoring and future threats. *Scottish Natural Heritage Commissioned Report* no. 469.

Baxter, C. V., Fausch, K. D. & Saunders, W. C. (2005). Tangled webs: reciprocal flows of invertebrate prey link streams and riparian zones. *Freshwater Biology* 50, 201–20.

Beklioglu, M. & Moss, B. (1996). Mesocosm experiments on the interaction of sediment influence, fish predation and aquatic plants with the structure of phytoplankton and zooplankton communities. *Freshwater Biology* 36, 315–25.

Bennion, H., Harriman, R. & Battarbee, R. (1997). A chemical survey of standing waters in southeast England, with reference to acidification and eutrophication. *Freshwater Forum* 8, 28–44.

Biggs, J. and others (2005). 15 years of pond assessment in Britain: results and lessons learned from the work of Pond Conservation. *Aquatic Conservation: Marine and Freshwater Ecosystems* 15, 693–714.

Birk, S. and others (2012). Three hundred ways to assess Europe's surface waters: an almost complete overview of biological methods to implement the Water Framework Directive. *Ecological Indicators* 18, 31–41.

Birks, H. J. B. & Birks, H. H. (2006). Multi-proxy studies in palaeolimnology. *Vegetation History and Archaeobotany* 15, 235–51.

Birks, H. J. B. & Birks, H. H. (2007) Winifred Tutin. *Journal of Paleolimnology* 38, 601–5.

Birks, H. J. B. & Smol, J. P. (2013). Rick Battarbee and his many contributions to palaeolimnology. *Journal of Paleolimnology* 49, 313–32.

Bogaard, A. and others (2013). Crop manuring and intensive land management by Europe's first farmers. *Prcoceedings of the National Academy of Sciences.* Early edition www.pnas.org/cgi/doi/10.1073/pnas.1305918110.

Borrow, G. (1862). *Wild Wales: Its People, Language and Scenery.* John Murray, London.

Bowes, M. I., Hilton, J., Irons, G. P. & Hornby, D . D. (2005). The relative contribution of sewage and diffuse phosphorus sources in the River Avon catchment, southern England: implications for nutrient management. *Science of the Total Environment* 344, 67–81.

Boyd C. M. (1970). Selection of particle sizes by filter-feeding copepods: a plea for reason. *Limnology & Oceanography* 21, 175–80.

Braendle, R. & Crawford, R. M. M. (1999). Plants as amphibians. *Perspectives in Plant Ecology, Evolution and Systematics* 2, 56–78.

Brinkhurst, R. O. (1974). *The Benthos of Lakes* (reprinted 2003). Blackburn Press, New Jersey), Macmillan, London.

Brinkhurst, R. O. & Walsh, B. (1967). Rostherne Mere, England, a further instance of guanotrophy. *Journal of the Fisheries Research Board of Canada* 24, 1299–309.

Britton, J. R., Davies, G. D., Brazier, M. & Pinder, A. C. (2007). A case study on the population ecology of a topmouth gudgeon (Pseudorasbora parva) population in the UK and the implications for native fish communities. *Aquatic Conservation: Marine & Freshwater Ecosystems* 17, 749–59.

Broads Authority (2011). *A Strategic Plan to Manage the Norfolk and Suffolk Broads.* www.broads-plan.co.uk.

Brochier-Armanet, C., Forterre, P. & Gribaldo, S. (2011). Phylogeny and evolution of the Archaea: one hundred genomes later. *Current Opinion in Microbiology* 14, 274–81.

Bronmark, C. (1985). Interactions between macrophytes, epiphytes and herbivores: an experimental approach. *Oikos* 45, 26–30.

Bronmark, C. & Hansson, L.-A. (Eds) (2012). *Chemical Ecology in Aquatic Systems.* Oxford University Press, Oxford.

Brooks, A. S. , Lund, J. W. G. & Talling, J. F. (2011). Clifford Hiley Mortimer. 27 February 1911–11 May 2010. *Biographical Memoirs of Fellows of the Royal Society* 57, 291–314.

Brooks, S. J., Bennion, H. & Birks, H. J. B. (2001). Tracing lake trophic history with a chironomid-total phosphorus inference model. *Freshwater Biology* 46, 513–33.

Brothwell, D. (1986). *The Bog Man and the Archaeology of People.* British Museum Publications, London.

Brown, A. (2012). *National Angling Survey.* Environment Agency, Bristol.

Bulleid, A. (1924, revised 1958). *The Lake-Villages of Somerset.* Glastonbury Antiquarian Society.

Bunnell, D. B., Davis, B. M., Warner, D. M., Chriscinske, M. A. & Roseman, E. F. (2011). Planktivory in the changing Lake Huron zooplankton community: *Bythotrephes* consumption exceeds that of *Mysis* and fish. *Freshwater Biology* 56, 1281–96.

Burt, T. P., Howden, N. J. K., Worrall, F., Whelan, M. J. & Bieroza, M. (2011). Nitrate in United Kingdom rivers: policy and its outcomes since 1970. *Environmental Science & Technology* 45, 175–181.

Burton, A. W. & Aherne, J. (2012). Changes in the chemistry of small Irish lakes. *Ambio* 41, 170–9.

Cameron, L. & Matless, D. (2011). Translocal ecologies; the Norfolk Broads, the 'natural' and the International Phytogeographical Excursion, 1911. *Journal of the History of Biology* 44, 15–41.

Campbell, E. & Lane, A. (1989). Llangorse: a tenth century royal crannog in Wales. *Antiquity* 63, 675–81.

Carpenter, S. R. and others (1987). Regulation of lake primary productivity by food web structure. *Ecology* 68, 1863–76.

Carvalho, L. & Moss, B. (1995). The current status of a sample of English Sites of Special Scientific Interest subject to eutrophication. *Aquatic Conservation: Marine and Freshwater Ecosystems* 5, 191–204.

Cassina, F., Dalton, C., Dillane, M., de Eyto, E., Poole, R. & Sparber, K. (2013). A multi-proxy palaeolimnological study to reconstruct the evolution of a coastal brackish lake (Lough Furnace, Ireland) during the late Holocene. *Palaeography, Palaeoclimatology, Palaeoecology* 383/384, 1–15.

Catchment Sensitive Farming Evidence Team. (2011). Catchment sensitive farming. England Catchment Sensitive Framing Delivery Initiative, Phase 1 and 2 Full Evaluation Report. Natural England, Environment Agency and DEFRA.

Chaichana, R., Leah, R. T. & Moss, B. (2010). Birds as eutrophicating agents: a nutrient budget for a small lake in a protected area. *Hydrobiologia* 646, 111–21.

Chaichana, R., Leah, R. & Moss, B. (2011). Seasonal impact of waterfowl on communities of macrophytes in a shallow lake. *Aquatic Botany* 95, 39–44.

Chambers, P.A., Lacoul, P., Murphy, K.J. & Thomaz, S.M. (2008). Global diversity of aquatic macrophytes in freshwater. *Hydrobiologia* 595, 9–26.

Chapman, P. J., Edwards, A. C. & Cresser, M. S. (2001). The nitrogen composition of streams in upland Scotland: some regional and seasonal differences. *Science of the Total Environment* 265, 65–83.

Clapham, A. R. (1971). William Harold Pearsall. 1891–1964. *Biographical Memoirs of Fellows of the Royal Society* 17, 511–40.

Cole, J.J. (2013). *Freshwater Ecosystems and the Carbon Cycle.* Excellence in Ecology, 18, International Ecology Institute, Oldendorf/Luhe, Germany.

Cole, J., Prairie, Y. T., Caraco, N. F., McDowell, W. H., Tranvik L. J., Striegl, R. G., Duarte, C. M., Kortelainen, P., Downing, J. A., Middelburg, J. J. & Melack, J. (2007). Plumbing the global carbon cycle: integrating inland waters into the terrestrial carbon budget. *Ecosystems* 10, 171–84.

Coles, B. & Coles, J. (1989). *People of the Wetlands: Bogs, Bodies and Lake Dwellers.* Thames and Hudson, London.

Colinvaux, P.A. (1984). Our man in Africa (Review of Worthington, E. B. The Ecological Century): A Personal Appraisal. *Nature* 308, 385–6.

Collar, N.J. (1996). The reasons for Red Data Books. *Oryx* 30, 121–30.

Comin, F.A. & Hurlbert S. H. (2012). Preface: perspectives on progress in ornitholimnology. *Hydrobiologia* 697, 1–4.

Comte, J. & Del Giorgio, P.A. (2009). Links between resources, C metabolism and the major components of bacterioplankton community structure across a range of freshwater ecosystems. *Environmental Microbiology* 11, 1704–16.

Coney, A. (1992). Fish, fowl and fen: landscape and economy on seventeenth-century Martin Mere. *Landscape History* 14, 51–64.

Cook, C. D. K. (1969). On the determination of leaf form in Ranunculus aquatilis. *New Phytologist* 68, 469–80.

Cook, C. D. K. (1999). The number and kinds of embryo-bearing plants which have become aquatic: a survey. *Perspectives in Plant Ecology, Evolution and Systematics* 2, 79–102.

Cook, J, Chubb, J. C. & Veltkamp, C. J. (1998). Epibionts of Asellus aquaticus (L.) (Crustacea, Isopoda): and SEM study. *Freshwater Biology* 39, 423–38.

Cooke, G. D., Welch, E. B., Peterson, S. A. & Nichols, S. A. (2005). *Restoration and Management of Lakes and Reservoirs.* 3rd Edn, Taylor & Francis, New York.

Cooper, P. F. (2001). Historical aspects of wastewater treatment. In: *Decentralised Sanitation and Reuse: Concepts, Systems and Implementation.* (Eds Lens, P., Zeeman, G. & Lettinga, G.) IWA Publishing, London.

Costanza, R. and others (1997). The value of the world's ecosystem services and natural capital. *Nature* 387, 253–60.

Darby, H. C. (1983). *The Changing Fenland.* Cambridge University Press, UK.

Davidson, T. A. & Jeppesen, E. (2013). The role of palaeolimnology in assessing eutrophication and its impact on lakes. *Journal of Palaeolimnology* 49, 391–410.

Davidson, T. A., Sayer, C. D., Perrow, M. R. & Tomlinson, M. L. (2003). Representation of fish communities by scale sub-fossils in shallow lakes: implications for inferring percid–cyprinid shifts. *Journal of Palaeolimnology* 30, 441–9.

Davidson, T. A. and others (2005). A 250 year comparison of historical, macrofossil and pollen records of aquatic plants in a shallow lake. *Freshwater Biology* 50, 1671–86.

Davidson, T. A. and others (2007). Are the controls of species composition similar for contemporary and sub-fossil cladoceran assemblages? A study of 39 shallow lakes of contrasting trophic status. *Journal of Paleolimnology* 38, 117–34.

Davies, H. & Neal, C. (2007). Estimating nutrient concentrations from catchment characteristics across the UK. *Hydrology and Earth System Sciences* 11, 550–8.

Davies, J. J. L. and others (2005). Trends in surface water chemistry of acidified UK freshwaters, 1988–2002. *Environmental Pollution* 137, 27–39.

Dawkins, R. (1976). *The Selfish Gene.* Oxford University Press, Oxford.

DEFRA (Department of the Environment, Food and Rural Affairs) (2007). *An Introductory Guide to Valuing Ecosystem Services.* DEFRA, London.

DEFRA (Department of the Environment, Food and Rural Affairs) (2012). *Waste Water Treatment in the United Kingdom – 2012. Implementation of the European Union Urban Waste Water Treatment Directive – 91/271/EEC.* DEFRA, London.

Demars, B. O. L., Potts, J. M., Tremolieres, M., Thiebaut, G., Gougelin, N., Nordmann, V. (2012). River macrophyte indices: not the Holy Grail! *Freshwater Biology* 57, 1745–59.

Diamond, J. (2005). *Collapse: How Societies Choose to Fail or Succeed.* Viking Press, New York.

Diefendorf, A. F., Patterson, W. P., Holmden, C. & Mullins, H. T. (2008). Carbon isotopes of marl and lake sediment organic matter reflect terrestrial landscape change during the late Glacial and early Holocene (16,800 to 5,540 cal yr BP): a multiproxy study of lacustrine sediments at Lough Inchiquin, western Ireland. *Journal of Paleolimnology* 39, 101–15.

Dimbleby, D. (2005). *A Picture of Britain.* Tate Publishing, London.

Dobson, M., Pawley, S., Fletcher, M. & Powell, A. (2012). *Guide to Freshwater Invertebrates.* Freshwater Biological Association Scientific Publication 68.

Dodds, W. K., Bouska, W. W., Eitzmann, J. L., Pilger, T. J., Pitts, K. L., Riley, A. J., Schloesser, J. T. & Thornbrugh, D. J. (2009). Eutrophication of US freshwaters: analysis of potential economic damages. *Environmental Science and Technology* 43, 12–19.

Donohue, I. and others. (2010). Rapid ecosystem recovery from diffuse pollution after the great Irish famine. *Ecological Applications* 20, 1733–43.

Doucette, J. L., Wissel, B. & Somers, C. M. (2011). Cormorant-fisheries conflicts: stable isotopes reveal a consistent niche for avian piscivores in diverse food webs. *Ecological Applications* 21, 2987–3001.

Drinan, T. J., O'Halloran, J. & Harrison, S. S. C. (2013). Variation in the physico-chemical and biologicial characteristics between upland and lowland (Atlantic) blanket bog lakes in Western Ireland. *Proceedings of the Royal Irish Academy* 113B, 67–91.

Duarte, C. M. & Prairie, Y. T. (2005). Prevalence of heterotrophy and atmospheric CO_2 emisssions from aquatic ecosystems. *Ecosystems* 8, 862–70.

Dudley, B. J., Spears, B. M., Carvalho, L., Gunn, I. D. M. & May, L. (2012). Water quality monitoring at Loch Leven 2008–2010 – Report of results. *Scottish Natural Heritage Commissioned Report* no. 511.

Duigan, C. A. and others (1998). The ecology and conservation of Llyn Idwal and Llyn Cwellyn (Snowdonia National Park, North Wales, UK) – two lakes proposed as Special Areas of Conservation in Europe. *Aquatic Conservation, Marine and Freshwater Ecosystems* 8, 325–60.

Duigan, C. A. and others (1996). The Anglesey lakes, Wales, UK – a conservation resource. *Aquatic Conservation: Marine and Freshwater Systems* 6, 31–55.

Duigan, C. A and others. (1999). The past, present and future of Llangorse lake – a shallow nutrient-rich lake in the Brecon Beacons National Park, Wales, UK. *Aquatic Conservation: Marine and Freshwater Ecosystems* 9, 329–41.

Ehrlich, P. R. & Ehrlich, A. H. (2013). Can a collapse of global civilization be avoided? *Proceedings of the Royal Society B* 280, 2012–45.

Elmberg, J., Dessborn, L. & Englund, G. (2010). Presence of fish affects lake use and breeding success in ducks. *Hydrobiologia* 641, 215–23.

Eloranta, A. P., Knudsen, R. & Amundsen, P.-A. (2013). Niche segregation of coexisting Arctic charr (*Salvelinus alpinus*) and brown trout (*Salmo trutta*) constrains food web coupling in subarctic lakes. *Freshwater Biology* 58, 207–21.

Eloranta, A. P., Siwertsson, A., Knudsen, R. & Amundsen, P.-A. (2011). Dietary plasticity of Arctic charr (*Salvelinus alpinus*) facilitates coexistence with competitively superior European whitefish (*Coregonus lavaretus*). *Ecology of Freshwater Fish* 20, 558–68.

Eminson, D. F. & Moss, B. (1980). The composition and ecology of periphyton communities in freshwaters. 1. The influence of host type and external environment on community composition. *British Phycological Journal* 15, 429–36.

Engstrom, D. R. & Rose, N. L. (2013). A whole-basin, mass balance approach to paleolimnology. *Journal of Paleolimnology* 49, 333–47.

Esteban, G. F., Finlay, B. J. & Clarke, K. J. (2012). Priest Pot in the English Lake District: a showcase of microbial diversity. *Freshwater Biology* 57, 321–30.

Estes, J. A. and others (2011). Trophic downgrading of Planet Earth. *Science* 333, 301–6.

European Commission (2012a). *Commission Staff Working Documents: European Overview and Individual reports for Ireland and for the UK Accompanying the document: Report from the Commission to the European Parliament and the Council on the Implementation of the Water Framework Directive (2000/60/EC) River Basin Management Plans.* European Union, Brussels.

European Commission (2012b). *River Basin Management Plans: Report on the Implementation*

of the Water Framework Directive 2000/60/EC. COM(2012) 670 final. Brussels.

European Commission (2013). *Seventh Report on the Implementation of the Urban Waste Water Treatment Directive (91/271/EEC).* Brussels.

European Environmental Bureau (2010). *10 years of the Water Framework Directive: A Toothless Tiger? A snapshot assessment of EU environmental ambitions.* Brussels.

European Union (2000). Directive 2000/60/EC of the European Parliament and of the Council of 23 October 2000 establishing a framework for community action in the field of water policy. *Official Journal of the European Communities,* L327, 1–73.

Evans, C. D. & Jenkins, A. (2000). Surface water acidification in the South Pennines II. Temporal trends. *Environmental Pollution* 109, 21–34.

Falkowski, P. G. and others (2004). The origin of modern eukaryotic phytoplankton. 305, 354–60.

Fenchel, T. & Finlay, B. J. (2004). The ubiquity of small species: patterns of local and global diversity. *BioScience* 54, 777–84.

Feuchtmayr, H. and others (2009). Global warming and eutrophication: effects on water chemistry and autotrophic communities in experimental, hypertrophic, shallow lake mesocosms. *Journal of Applied Ecology* 46, 713–23.

Fiennes, C. (1888) *Through England on a Side Saddle in the Time of William and Mary being the Diary of Celia Fiennes.* Field and Tuer, The Leadenhall Press, London. Available online at http://digital. library.upenn.edu/women/fiennes/saddle/ saddle.html

Finazzi, G., Moreau, H. & Bowler, C. (2010). Genomic insights into photosynthesis in eukaryotic phytoplankton. *Trends in Plant Science* 15, 565–72.

Finlay B. J. & Maberly S. C. (2000). *Microbial Diversity in Priest Pot. A Productive Pond in the English Lake District.* Freshwater Biological Association, Ambleside.

Finlay, B. J., Maberly, S. C. & Cooper, J. I. (1997). Microbial diversity and ecosystem function. *Oikos* 80, 209–13.

Flower, R. J., Battarbee, R. W. & Appleby, P. G. (1987). The recent palaeolimnology of acid lakes in Galloway, Southwest Scotland: diatom analysis, pH trends, and the role of afforestation. *Journal of Ecology* 75, 797–823.

Forbes, S. (1887). The lake as a microcosm. *Bulletin of the Scientific Association (Peoria, IL)* 1887, 77–87.

Forterre, P. (2011). A new fusion hypothesis for the origin of Eukarya: better than previous ones, but probably also wrong. *Research in Microbiology* 162, 77–91.

Fortey, R. (1993). *The Hidden Landscape*. Random House, London.

Foy, R. H., Smith, R. V., Jordan, C., and Lennox, S. D. (1995). Upward trend in soluble phosphorus loadings to Lough Neagh despite phosphorus reduction at sewage treatment works. *Water Research* 29, 1051–63.

Fraser, D., Huntingford, F. A. & Adams, C. E. (2007). Foraging specialisms, prey size and life-history patterns: a test of predictions using sympatric polymorphic Arctic charr (*Salvelinus alpinus*). *Ecology of Freshwater Fish* 17, 1–9.

Frisch, D., Green, A. J. & Figuerola, J. (2007). High dispersal capacity of a broad spectrum of aquatic invertebrates via waterbirds. *Aquatic Sciences* 69, 568–74.

George D. G. (Ed). (2010). *The Impact of Climate Change on European Lakes*. Springer, Dordrecht.

George D. G., Maberly, S. C. & Hewitt, D. P. (2004). The influence of the North Atlantic Oscillation on the physics, chemistry and biology of four lakes in the English Lake District. *Freshwater Biology* 49, 760–74.

Gerald of Wales (1191/1194). *The Journey through Wales/The Description of Wales*. In translation 1978, Penguin Books , London.

Gibbard, P. L. & Woodcock, N. H. (2012). The Quaternary: History of an Ice Age. In *Geological History of Britain and Ireland* (Eds Woodcock, N. & Strachan, R.) Wiley-Blackwell, Chichester.

Gibson, C. E., Wu, Y., Smith, S. J. & Wolfe-Murphy, A. (1995). Synoptic limnology of a diverse geological region: catchment and water chemistry. *Hydrobiologia* 306, 213–27.

Giles, N. (1992). *Wildlife after Gravel: Twenty Years of Practical Research by the Game Conservancy and ARC*. Game Conservancy, Fordingbridge.

Godwin, H. (1959). Studies of the post-glacial history of British vegetation. XIV. Late-glacial deposits at Moss Lake, Liverpool. *Proceedings of the Royal Society B* 242, 127–40.

Godwin, H. (1975). *History of the British Flora. Second Edition*. Cambridge University Press, Cambridge.

Godwin, H. (1978) *Fenland: its ancient past and uncertain future*. Cambridge University Press, UK.

Gregory, C. (2000). The extractive industries of Kentmere: lead – slate – diatomite. *The Occasional Papers of the Staveley and District History Society* 14, 1–12.

Grey, J., Jones, R. I. & Sleep, D. (2001). Seasonal changes in the importance of the source of organic matter to the diet of zooplankton in Loch Ness, as indicated by stable isotope analysis. *Limnology & Oceanography* 46, 505–13.

Gsell, A. S. and others (2012). Genotype-by-temperature interactions may help to maintain clonal diversity in *Asterionella formosa* (Bacillariophyceae). *Journal of Phycology* 48, 1197–208.

Gurney, E. & Gurney, R. (1908). The Sutton Broad Freshwater Laboratory. *Annales Biologie lacustré* 3, 1–12.

Gyllstrom, M. and others (2005). The role of climate in shaping zooplankton communities of shallow lakes. *Limnology & Oceanography* 50, 2008–21.

Hahn, D. & Robins, N. (Eds) (2008). *The Oxford Guide to Literary Britain and Ireland. Third Edition*. Oxford University Press, Oxford.

Hairston Jr, N. G. and others (1999). Rapid evolution revealed by dormant eggs. *Nature* 401, 446.

Hameed, H. A., Kilinc, S., McGowan, S. & Moss, B. (1999) Physiological tests and bioassays – aids or superfluities to the diagnosis of phytoplankton nutrient limitation? A comparative study in the Broads and Meres of England. *European Phycological Journal* 34, 253–70.

Hänfling, B., Hellemans, B., Volckaert, F. A. M. & Carvalho, G. R. (2002). Late glacial history of the cold-adapted freshwater fish *Cottus gobio*, revealed by microsatellites. *Molecular Ecology* 11, 1717–29.

Harper, D. M. (1982). Introduction – Rutland water 1970–1981. *Hydrobiologia* 88, 1–5.

Harriman, R. & Pugh K. B. (1994). *Water chemistry*. In: *The Fresh Waters of Scotland* (Eds Maitland, P. S., Boon P. J. & McLusky D. S.). Wiley, Chichester.

Harris, C. M., Calladine, J. R., Wernham, C. V. & Park, K. J. (2008). Impacts of piscivorous birds on salmonid populations and game fisheries in Scotland: a review. *Wildlife Biology* 14, 395–411.

Hassall, C., Thompson, D. J., French, G. C., & Harvey, I. F. (2007). Historical changes in the phenology of British Odonata are related to climate. *Global Change Biology* 13, 933–41.

Haworth, E. Y. (1969). The diatoms of a sediment core from Blea Tarn, Langdale. *Journal of Ecology* 57, 429–39.

Haycock, B. & Ellis, R. (2002). *Bosherston Lakes – An Introduction to their Ecology and Management.* The National Trust and the Countryside Council for Wales, Bangor.

Hays, G. C. (2003). A review of the adaptive significance and ecosystem consequences of zooplankton diel vertical migrations. *Hydrobiologia* 503, 163–70.

Helfield, J. M. & Naiman, R. J. (2006). Keystone interactions: salmon and bear in riparian forests of Alaska. *Ecosystems* 9, 167–80.

Hendry, A. P. and others (2000). Rapid evolution of reproductive isolation in the wild: evidence from introduced salmon. *Science* 290, 516–18.

Hering, D. and others (2010). The European Water Framework Directive at the age of ten; a critical review of the achievements with recommendations for the future. *Science of the Total Environment* 408, 4007–19.

Hessen, D. O. & Van Donk, E. (1993). Morphological changes in Scenedesmus induced by substances released from Daphnia. *Archiv fur Hydrobiologie* 127, 129–40.

Hewlett, N. R., Snow, J. & Britton, J. R. (2009). The role of management practices in fish kills in recreational lake fisheries in England and Wales. *Fisheries Management & Ecology* 16, 248–54.

Hickling, R., Roy, D. B., Hill, J. K. & Thomas, C. D. (2005). A northward shift of range margins in British Odonata. *Global Change Biology* 11, 502–6.

Hickling, R. and others (2006). The distributions of a wide range of taxonomic groups are expanding polewards. *Global Change Biology* 12, 1–6.

Hildrew, A. G. (1993). Freshwater ecology in Britain – a case of decline? *Freshwater Forum* 3, 237–42.

Hiltunen, T., Barreiro, A. & Hairston Jr, N. G. (2012). Mixotrophy and the toxicity of Ochromonas in pelagic food webs. *Freshwater Biology* 57, 2262–71.

Hinojoso-Garro, D., Mason, C. F. & Underwood, G. J. C. (2010). Influence of macrophyte spatial architecture on periphyton and macroinvertebrate community structure in shallow water bodies under contrasting land management. *Fundamental & Applied Limnology* 177, 19–37.

Holdway, P. A., Watson, R. A. & Moss, B. (1978). Aspects of the ecology of Prymnesium parvum (Haptophyta) and water chemistry in the Norfolk Broads, England. *Freshwater Biology* 8, 295–311.

Holmes, P. F. (1965). Malham Tarn: a background for ecologists. *Field Studies* 2, 48–57.

Holopainen, I. J. & Jonasson, P. (1989). Bathymetric distribution and abundance of Pisidium (Bivalvia: Sphaeriidae) in Lake Esrom, Denmark, from 1954–1988. *Oikos* 55, 324–34.

Hoskins, W. G. (1955). *The Making of the English Landscape.* Republished 2013, with an introduction by William Boyd. Little Toller Books, Dorchester.

Howland, J. L. (2000). *The Surprising Archaea.* Oxford University Press, Oxford.

Humphries, C. F. (1936). An investigation of the profundal and sub-littoral fauna of Windermere. *Journal of Animal Ecology* 5, 29–52.

Hutchinson, G. E. (1957). *A Treatise on Limnology, Vol 1. Geography, Physics and Chemistry.* Wiley, Chichester.

Hutchinson, G. E. (1959). Homage to Santa Rosalia or why are there so many kinds of animals. *American Naturalist* 93, 145–59.

Hutchinson, G. E. (1961). The paradox of the plankton. *American Naturalist* 95, 37–45.

Hutchinson, G. E. (1965). *The Ecological Theater and the Evolutionary Play.* Yale University Press, New Haven.

Hutchinson, G. E. (1967). *A Treatise on Limnology, Vol 2. Introduction to Lake Biology and the Limnoplankton.* Wiley, Chichester.

Hutchinson, G. E. (1975). *A Treatise on Limnology, Vol 3. Limnological Botany.* Wiley, Chichester.

Hutchinson, G. E. (1993). *A Treatise on Limnology, Vol. 4. The Zoobenthos* (Ed. by Edmonson Y.H.), Wiley, Chichester.

Ings, N. I., Hildrew, A. G. & Grey, J. (2012). House and garden: larval galleries enhance resource availability for a sedentary cadddisfly. *Freshwater Biology* 57, 2526–38.

Intergovernmental Panel on Climate Change (IPCC) (2013). *Climate Change Working Group I Contribution to the IPCC Fifth Assessment Report Climate Change: The Physical Science Basis. Summary for Policymakers.* IPCC, Geneva.

International Centre for Island Technology (2004). *Factors influencing the condition of Loch of Stenness marine candidate Special Area of Conservation – summary report.* Scottish Natural Heritage Commissioned Report No. 066.

Irvine, K., Moss, B. & Balls, H. R. (1989). The loss of submerged plants with eutrophication. II Relationships between fish and zooplankton in a set of experimental ponds, and conclusions. *Freshwater Biology* 22, 89–107.

James, C. Fisher, J. & Moss, B. (2003). Nitrogen driven lakes: the Shropshire and Cheshire Meres? *Archiv für Hydrobiologie* 158, 249–66.

Jennings, E. and others (2013). Drivers of long-term trends and seasonal changes in total phosphorus loads to a mesotrophic lake in the west of Ireland. *Marine & Freshwater Research* 64, 413–22.

Johnes P. J. (1996). Evaluation and management of the impact of land use change on the nitrogen and phosphorus load delivered to surface waters: the export coefficient modelling approach. *Journal of Hydrology* 183, 323–49

Johnes, P. J. & Wilson, H. M. (1996). The limnology of Slapton Ley. *Field Studies* 8, 586–612.

Johnes, P., Moss, B. & Phillips, G. (1996). The determination of total nitrogen and total phosphorus concentrations in freshwaters from land use, stock headage and population data: testing of a model for use in conservation and water quality management. *Freshwater Biology* 36, 451–73.

Johnson, D. and others (2011). *Nitrates Directive Consultation Document: The evidence base for assessing the impacts of the NVZ Action Programme on water quality across England and Wales.* ADAS, Wolverhampton.

Johnson, M. G. & Brinkhurst, R. O. (1971). Benthic community metabolism in Bay of Quinte and Lake Ontario. *Journal of the Fisheries Research Board of Canada* 28, 1715–25.

Jonasson, P. M. (1972). Ecology and production of the profundal benthos in relation to phytoplankton in Lake Esrom. *Oikos*, suppl 14, 1–148.

Jonasson, P. M. & Thorhauge, F. (1976). Population dynamics of Potamothrix hammoniensis in the profundal of lake Esrom with special reference to environmental and competitive factors. *Oikos* 27, 193–203.

Jones, J. (2002). *The Lakes of North Wales.* Y Lolfa, Talybont.

Jones, J. I. & Waldron, S. (2003). Combined stable isotope and gut contents analysis of food webs in plant-dominated, shallow lakes. *Freshwater Biology* 48, 1396–407.

Jones J. I., Eaton J. W. & Hardwick K. (2000a). The influence of periphyton on boundary layer pH conditions: a microelectrode investigation. *Aquatic Botany* 67, 191–206.

Jones, J. I., Moss, B., Eaton, J. W. & Young, J. O. (2000b). Do submerged aquatic plants influence periphyton community composition for the benefit of invertebrate mutualists? *Freshwater Biology* 43, 591–604.

Jones, R. I. & Grey J. (2011). Biogenic methane in freshwater food webs. *Freshwater Biology* 56, 213–29.

Jones, R. I, Grey, J., Quarmby, C. & Sleep, D. (1998). An assessment using stable isotopes of the importance of allochthonous organic carbon sources to the pelagic food web in Loch Ness. *Proceedings of the Royal Society of London B* 265, 105–11.

Jones, R. I., Grey, J., Quarmby, C. & Sleep, D. (2001). Sources and fluxes of inorganic carbon in a deep, oligotrophic lake (Loch Ness, Scotland). *Global Biogeochemical Cycles* 15, 863–70.

Jones, R. T. and others (2011). Controls on lake level in the early to mid Holocene, Hawes Water, Lancashire, UK. *The Holocene* 21, 1061–72.

Jones, V. J., Stevenson, A. C. & Battarbee, R. W. (1989). Acidification of lakes in Galloway, south west Scotland: a diatom and pollen study of the post-glacial history of the Round Loch of Glenhead. *Journal of Ecology* 77, 1–23.

Jordan, C. (1997). Mapping of rainfall chemistry in Ireland 1972–1994. *Biology and Environment: Proceedings of the Royal Irish Academy* 97B, 53–73.

Jorgensen, D. (2010). What to do with waste? The challenges of waste disposal in two late mediaeval towns. In *Living Cities* (Eds Lilja, S. and Ligne, M.). Swedish Research Council, Stockholm.

Juggins, S. and others (2013). Reconstructing epilimnetic total phosphorus using diatoms: statistical and ecological constraints. *Journal of Paleolimnogy* 49, 373–90.

Kahilainen, K. K. and others (2011). The role of gill raker number variability in adaptive radiation of coregonid fish. *Evolutionary Ecology* 25, 573–88.

Kelly, A. (2013). *Status and Lake Management Activity in The Broads. Broads Authority Report.* Norwich, UK.

Kelly, R. I., Jones, R. I. & Grey, T. (2004). Stable isotope analysis provides fresh insights into dietary separation between Chironomus anthracinus and C. plumosus. *Journal of the North American Benthological Society* 23, 287–96.

Keniger, L. E., Gaston, K. J., Irvine, K. N. & Fuller, R. A. (2013). What are the benefits of interacting with nature? *International Journal of Environmental Research and Public Health* 10, 913–35.

Kernan, M., Battarbee, R. W. & Moss, B. (2010). *Climate Change Impacts on Freshwater Ecosystems.* Wiley-Blackwell, Chichester.

Kilinc, S. & Moss, B. (2002). Whitemere, a lake that defies some conventions about nutrients. *Freshwater Biology* 47, 207–18.

King, J. T. & Champ, W. S. T. (2000). Baseline water quality investigations on Lough Carra, Western Ireland, with reference to water chemistry, phytoplankton and aquatic plants. *Proceedings of the Royal Irish Academy. Biology and Environment* 100B, 13–25.

Kirby R. S., Gilburn A. S. & Sellers R. M. (1995). Status, distribution and habitat use by cormorants *Phalacrocorax carbo* wintering in Britain. *Ardea* 83, 93–102.

Kloskowski, J., Nieoczym, M., Polak, M. & Pitucha, P. (2010). Habitat selection by breeding waterbirds at ponds with size-structured fish populations. *Naturwissenschaften* 97, 673–82.

Knight, T. M. and others (2005). Trophic cascades across ecosystems. *Nature* 437, 880–3.

Kottelat, M. (1997). European freshwater fishes: an heuristic checklist of the freshwater fishes of Europe (exclusive of former USSR), with an introduction for non-systematists and comments on nomenclature and conservation. *Biologia* 52 (suppl. 5), 1–271.

Krause, W. & King, J. J. (1994). The ecological status of Lough Corrib, Ireland, as indicated by physiographic factors, water chemistry and macrophytic flora. *Vegetatio* 110, 149–61.

Kwalik, R. A. and others (2007) Acidic episodes retard the biological recovery of upland British streams from chronic acidification. *Global Change Biology* 13, 2439–52.

Lampitt, R. S. and others (2008). Ocean fertilization: a potential means of geoengineering? *Philosophical Transactions of the Royal Society* A 366, 3919–45.

Langdon, P. G., Barber, K. E. & Lomas-Clarke, S. H. (2004). Reconstructing climate and environmental change in northern England through chironomid and pollen analyses: evidence from Talkin Tarn, Cumbria. *Journal of Paleolimnology* 32, 197–213.

Last, W. M. & Smol, J. P. (Eds) (2001). *Tracking Environmental Change Using Lake Sediments*. Vols 1–4. Kluwer, Dordrecht.

Laybourn-Parry, J., Tranter, M. & Hodson, A. J. (2012). *The Ecology of Snow and Ice Environments*. Oxford University Press, Oxford.

Le Cren, D. (2001). The Windermere perch and pike project: an historical review. *Freshwater Forum* 15, 3–34.

Le Quéré, C. and others (2012). The global carbon budget 1959–2011. *Earth System Science Data* 5, 1107–57.

Leah, R. T., Moss, B., & Forrest, D. E. (1978). Experiments with large enclosures in a fertile shallow brackish lake, Hickling Broad, United Kingdom. *Internationale Revue der Gesamten Hydrobiologie* 63, 291–310.

Leah, R. T., Moss, B. & Forrest, D. E. (1980). The role of predation in causing major changes in the limnology of a hypereutrophicated lake. *Internationale Revue der Gesamten Hydrobiologie* 62, 223–53.

Lee, J. A. (1977). The vegetation of British inland salt marshes. *Journal of Ecology*, 65, 673–98.

Lehman, J. T. & Scavia, D. (1982). Microscale patchiness of nutrients in plankton communities. *Science* 216, 729–30.

Leira, M. and others (2006). Assessing the ecological status of candidate reference lakes in Ireland using palaeolimnology. *Journal of Applied Ecology* 43, 816–27.

Leliaert, F., Verbruggen, H. & Zechman, F. W. (2011). Into the deep: new discoveries at the base of the green plant phylogeny. *Bioessays* 33, 683–92.

Leng, M. J & Henderson, A. C. G. (2013). Recent advances in isotopes as palaeolimnological proxies. *Journal of Paleolimnology* 49, 481–96.

Lenton, T. & Watson, A. (2011). *Revolutions That Made the Earth*. Oxford University Press, Oxford.

Lewis, W. M. (1983). Interception of atmospheric fixed nitrogen as an adaptive advantage of scum formation in blue-green algae. *Journal of Phycology* 19, 534–6.

Likens, G. E. (1992). *The Ecosystem Approach: its Use and Abuse*. Ecology Institute, Oberdorf-Luhe, Germany.

Lindegaard, C. (1992) Zoobenthos ecology of Thingvallavatn: vertical distribution, abundance, population dynamics and production. *Oikos* 64, 257–304.

Lockley, R. M. (1969) *Pembrokeshire*. The Regional Books. Robert Hale, London.

Lovelock, J. (1979). *Gaia: A new Look at Life on Earth*. Oxford University Press, Oxford.

Lowe, R. L. (2011). The importance of scale in understanding the natural history of diatom communities. In *The Diatom World* (Eds Seckbach, J. & Kociolek, J. P.), 293–311. Springer, Dordrecht.

Lucas, G. (1998). A mediaeval fishery on Whittlesea Mere, Cambridgeshire. *Mediaeval Archaeology* 42, 19–44.

Lund, J. W. G. & Monaghan, E. B. (2000). Dr P.M. Jenkin (1902–1994) and the earliest days of the FBA's laboratory at Wray Castle. *Freshwater Forum* 13, 2–15.

Lund, J. W. G. & Reynolds, C. S. (1982). The development and operation of large limnetic enclosures in Blelham Tarn, and their contribution to phytoplankton ecology. *Progress in Phycological Research* 1, 1–65.

Maberly, S. C., Ball, L. A., Raven, J. A. & Sültemeyer, D. (2009). Inorganic carbon acquisition by chrysophytes. *Journal of Phycology* 45, 1052–61.

Macan, T. T. (1973). *Ponds and Lakes*. Allen & Unwin, London.

Macan T. T. (1977a). The fauna in the vegetation of a moorland fishpond as revealed by different methods of collecting. *Hydrobiologia* 55, 3–15.

Macan, T. T. (1977b). The influence of predation on the composition of fresh-water animal communities. *Biological Reviews* 52, 45–70.

Mackarewicz, J. & Likens, G. E. (1975). Niche analysis of a zooplankton community. *Science* 190, 1000–3.

Mackereth, F. J. H. (1958). A portable core sampler for lake deposits. *Limnology & Oceanography* 3, 181–91.

Mackereth, F. J. H. (1965). Chemical investigations of lake sediments & their interpretation. *Proceedings of the Royal Society (B)* 161, 293–375.

Mackereth, F . J . H . (1966). Some chemical observations on post-glacial lake sediments. *Philosophical Transactions of the Royal Society B* 250, 165–213.

Madgwick, G. and others (2012). Centennial-scale changes to the aquatic vegetation structure of a shallow freshwater lake and implications for restoration. *Freshwater Biology* 56, 2620–36.

Magnuson, J. J. and others (2000). Historical trends in lake and river ice cover in the Northern Hemisphere. *Science.* 289, 1743–6.

Mainstone, C. & Parr, W. (2002). Phosphorus in rivers: ecology and management. *Science of the Total Environment* 282/3, 25–47.

Maitland, P. S. (2004). *Keys to the Freshwater Fish of Britain and Ireland, with notes on their distribution and ecology.* Freshwater Biological Association Scientific Publication 62.

Maitland, P. S. & Campbell, R. N. (1992). *Freshwater Fishes.* HarperCollins New Naturalist, London.

Maitland, P. S., Boon, P. J. & McLusky, D. S. (Eds) (1994). *The Fresh Waters of Scotland.* Wiley, Chichester.

Margulis, L. (1970). *Origin of Eukaryotic Cells.* Yale University Press, New Haven.

Marren, P. (2002). *Nature Conservation: A Review of the Conservation of Wildlife in Britain 1950–2001.* Collins New Naturalist, London.

Marshall, J. D. and others (2002). A high resolution late-glacial isotopic record from Hawes Water, northwest England: climatic oscillations: calibration and comparison of palaeotemperature proxies. *Palaeography, Palaeoclimatology, Palaeoecology* 185, 25–40.

Mason, C. F. & Bryant, R. J. (1975). Changes in the ecology of the Norfolk Broads. *Freshwater Biology* 5, 257–70.

Matuszak, A., Mortl, M., Quillfeldt, P. & Bauer, H.-G. (2012). Exclosure study on the exploitation of macrophytes by summering and moulting waterbirds at lower lake Constance. *Hydrobiologia* 697, 31–44.

May, L. & Spears, B. M. (2012a). A history of scientific research at Loch Leven, Kinross, Scotland. *Hydrobiologia* 681, 3–9.

May, L. & Spears, B. M. (2012b). Managing ecosystem services at Loch Leven, Scotland, UK: actions, impacts and unintended consequences. *Hydrobiologia* 681, 117–30.

McCarthy, I. D. (2006). The Welsh torgoch (*Salvelinus alpinus*): a short review of its distribution and ecology. *Ecology of Freshwater Fish* 16, 34–40.

McCulloch, C. S. (2006). The Kielder Water scheme: the last of its kind? In *Improvements in Reservoir Construction, Operation And Maintenance.* (Ed. Hewlett, H.), 196–210. Thomas Telford, London.

McElhone, M. J. (1982). The distribution of Naididae (Oligochaeta) in the littoral zone of selected lakes in North Wales and Shropshire. *Freshwater Biology* 12, 421–5.

McGarrigle, M. L. & Champ, W. S. T. (1999). Keeping pristine lakes clean; loughs Conn and Mask, Western Ireland. *Hydrobiologia* 395/6, 455–69.

McGinnity, P. and others (2003). Fitness reduction and potential extinction of wild populations of Atlantic salmon, Salmo salar, as a result of interactions with escaped farm salmon. *Proceedings of the Royal Society B* 270, 2443–50.

McGowan, S., Britton, G., Haworth, E. & Moss, B. (1999). Ancient blue-green blooms. *Limnology & Oceanography* 44, 436–9.

McGowan, S. and others (2012). Humans and climate as drivers of algal community change in Windermere since 1850. *Freshwater Biology* 57, 260–77.

McKee, D. and others (2003). Response of freshwater microcosm communities to nutrients, fish, and elevated temperature during winter and summer. *Limnology & Oceanography* 48, 707–22.

McKeown, N. J. and others (2010). Phylogeographic structure of brown trout *Salmo trutta* in Britain and Ireland: glacial refugia, postglacial colonization and origins of sympatric populations. *Journal of Fish Biology* 76, 319–47.

McLachlan, A. J., Pearce, L. J. & Smith, J. A. (1979) Feeding interactions and cycling of peat in a bog lake. *Journal of Animal Ecology* 48, 851–61.

Mehner, T. and others. (2012). Ecological commonalities among pelagic fishes: comparison of freshwater ciscoes and marine herring and sprat. *Marine Biology* 159, 2583–603.

Millennial Ecosystem Assessment Board (2005). *Millennial Ecosystem Assessment Synthesis Report.* United Nations Environment Programme, New York.

Milner, N., Taylor, B., Conneller, C. & Schadia-Hall, T. (2013). *Star Carr: Life in Britain after the Ice Age.* Council for British Archaeology.

Minnit, S. & Coles, J. (2006). *The Lake Villages of Somerset.* Glastonbury Antiquarian Society and Somerset Levels Project, Somerset County Council Heritage Service, Taunton.

Mitchell, E. A. D. and others (2000). Relationships among testate amoebae (Protozoa), vegetation and water chemistry in five Sphagnum-dominated peatlands in Europe. *New Phytologist* 145, 95–106.

Møbjerg, N. and others (2011). Survival in extreme environments – on the current knowledge of adaptations in tardigrades. *Acta Physiologia* 202, 409–20.

Mojzsis, S. J. (2001). Life and the evolution of Earth's atmosphere. In: *Earth Inside and Out* (Ed Mathez, E.), 32–9. New Press, New York.

Molongoski, J. & Klug, M. J. (1980). Anaerobic metabolism of particulate organic matter in the sediments of a hypereutrophic lake. *Freshwater Biology* 10, 507–18.

Moore, N. W. (2002). *Oaks, Dragonflies and People.* Harley Books, Colchester.

Mora, C. and others (2011). How many species are there on Earth and in the Ocean? *PloS Biology* 9 (8) e1001127. doi: 10.1371/journal.pbio.1001127.

Moss, B. (1969). Vertical heterogeneity in the water column of Abbot's Pond: The influence of physical and chemical conditions on the spatial and temporal distribution of the phytoplankton and of a community of epipelic algae. *Journal of Ecology* 57, 397–414.

Moss, B. (1973). The influence of environmental factors on the distribution of freshwater algae: an experimental study. 2. The role of pH and the carbon dioxide-bicarbonate system. *Journal of Ecology* 61, 157–177.

Moss, B. (1979). Algal and other fossil evidence for major changes in Strumpshaw Broad, Norfolk, England in the last two centuries. *British Phycological Journal* 14, 256–73.

Moss, B. (1980) Further studies on the palaeolimnology and changes in the phosphorus budget of Barton Broad, Norfolk. *Freshwater Biology* 10, 261–79.

Moss, B. (1981). The composition and ecology of periphyton communities in freshwaters. 2. Inter-relationships between water chemistry, phytoplankton populations and periphyton populations in a shallow lake and associated experimental reservoirs (Lund Tubes). *British Phycological Journal* 16, 59–76.

Moss, B. (1983). The Norfolk Broadland: experiments in the restoration of a complex wetland. *Biological Reviews* 58, 521–61.

Moss, B. (1988) The palaeolimnology of Hoveton Great Broad, Norfolk: Clues to the spoiling and restoration of Broadland. In: *The Exploitation of Wetlands*, Symposia of the Association for Environmental Archaeology, 163–91.

Moss, B. (1991). Robert Gurney and the founding of the Freshwater Biological Association. *Freshwater Forum* 1, 20–4.

Moss, B. (2001). *The Broads: The People's Wetland.* HarperCollins New Naturalist, London.

Moss, B. (2008). The Water Framework Directive: total environment or political compromise. *Science of the Total Environment* 400, 32–41.

Moss B. (2010). Climate change, nutrient pollution and the bargain of Dr Faustus. *Freshwater Biology* 55, 171–83.

Moss, B. (2012). *Liberation Ecology: The Reconciliation of Natural and Human Cultures.* Excellence in Ecology 24, International Ecology Institute, Oldendorf/Luhe, Germany.

Moss, B. (2013). Something is rotten in the state of our writing. *SILNews* 63, 6–9. (Available at www.limnology.org)

Moss, B. and others (1997). Vertically-challenged limnology; contrasts between deep and shallow lakes. *Hydrobiologia* 342/343, 257–67.

Moss, B. and others (2004). Continental-scale patterns of nutrients and fish effects on shallow lakes: synthesis of a pan-European mesocosm experiment. *Freshwater Biology* 49, 1633–49.

Moss, B. and others (2011) Allied attack: climate change and eutrophication. *Inland Waters* 1, 101–105.

Moss, B., Carvalho, L. & Plewes, J. (2002) The Lake at Llandrindod Wells – a restoration comedy? *Aquatic Conservation: Marine & Freshwater* 12, 229–45.

Moss, B. & Leah, R. T. (1982). Changes in the ecosystem of a guanotrophic and brackish shallow lake in Eastern England: potential problems in its restoration. *Internationale Revue der Gesamten Hydrobiologie* 67, 625–9.

Moss, B., Johnes, P. & Phillips, G. (1994a) August Thienemann and Loch Lomond – an approach to the design of a system for monitoring the state of north-temperate standing waters. *Hydrobiologia* 290, 1–12.

Moss, B., Kornijow, R. & Measey, G. J. (1998). The effects of nymphaeid (*Nuphar lutea* L.) density and predation by perch (*Perca fluviatilis* L.) on the zooplankton communities in a shallow lake. *Freshwater Biology* 39, 689–97.

Moss, B., Madgwick, J. & Phillips, G. (1996) *A Guide to the Restoration of Nutrient-Enriched Shallow Lakes.* Environment Agency, Broads Authority & European Union Life Programme, Norwich.

Moss, B., McGowan, S. & Carvalho, L. (1994b). Determination of phytoplankton crops by top-down and bottom-up mechanisms in a group of English Lakes, the West Midland Meres. *Limnology & Oceanography* 39, 1020–9.

Murphy, K. J., Beveridge, M. C. M. & Tippett, R. (Eds) (1994). *The Ecology of Loch Lomond.* Kluwer Academic Publishers. Also published as *Hydrobiologia* 290.

Murray, J. & Pullar, L. (Eds) (1910). *Bathymetrical Survey of the Freshwater Lochs of Scotland, Vol 1.* Challenger Office, Edinburgh.

Murton, D. K. & Murton, J. B. (2012). Middle and Late Pleistocene glacial lakes of lowland Britain and the southern North Sea Basin. *Quaternary International* 260, 115–42.

Naiman, R. J., Bilby, R. E., Schindler, D. E. & Helfield, J. M. (2002). Pacific salmon, nutrients, and the dynamics of freshwater and riparian ecosystems. *Ecosystems* 5, 399–417.

National Expert Group on Transboundary Air Pollution (NEGTAP) (2001) *Transboundary Air Pollution: Acidification, Eutrophication and Ground level ozone in the UK.* DEFRA, London.

Natural England (2010). *Lost Life: England's Lost and Threatened Species.* Natural England, Sheffield.

Neal, C., Jarvie, H. P., Neal, M., Hill, L. & Wickham, H. (2006). Nitrate concentrations in river waters of the upper Thames and its tributaries. *Science of the Total Environment* 365, 15–32.

Newman, E. I. (1997). Phosphorus balance of contrasting farming systems, past and present. Can food production be sustainable? *Journal of Applied Ecology* 34, 1334–47.

O'Sullivan, A. (2000). *Crannogs. Lake-dwellings of Early Ireland.* Town and Country House, Dublin.

Oeska, M. P. J. & Aldridge, D. C. (2011). Estimating the financial costs of freshwater invasive species in Great Britain: a standardized approach to invasive species costing. *Biological Invasions* 13, 305–19.

Oldfield, F. (2010). Palaeolimnology: personal reflections and early UK contributions. *Journal of Paleolimnology* 44, 505–10.

Oldfield, F. (2013). Mud and magnetism: records of late Pleistocene and Holocene environmental change recorded by magnetic measurements. *Journal of Paleolimnology* 49, 465–80.

Oliver J. G. J., Janssens-Maenhout, G., Muntean, M. & Peters, J. A. H. W. (2013). *Trends in Global CO₂ Emissions; 2013 Report,* The Hague: PBL Netherlands Environmental Assessment Agency; Ispra: Joint Research Centre.

Ormerod, S. J. & Durance, I. (2009). Restoration and recovery from acidification in upland Welsh streams over 25 years. *Journal of Applied Ecology* 46, 164–74.

Ormerod, S. J. and others (1991). The ecology of dippers Cinclus cinclus in relation to stream acidity in upland Wales: breeding performance, calcium physiology and nestling growth. *Journal of Applied Ecology* 28, 419–33.

Östlund-Nilsson, S., Mayer, I. & Huntingford, F. A. (Eds) (2007). *Biology of the Three-Spined Stickleback*. CRC Press, Boca Raton.

Ostman, O., Bergenius, M., Bostrom, M. K., & Lunneryd, S. G. (2012). Do cormorant colonies affect local fish communities in the Baltic Sea? *Canadian Journal of Fisheries and Aquatic Sciences* 69, 1047–55.

Pace, M. L. & Orcutt, J. D. (1981). The relative importance of protozoans, rotifers, and crustaceans in a freshwater plankton community. *Limnology & Oceanography* 26, 822–30.

Paerl, H. W. & Ustach, J. F. (1982). Blue-green algal scums-an explanation for their occurrence during freshwater blooms. *Limnology & Oceanography* 27, 212–17.

Palmer, M. A, Bell, S. L. & Butterfield, I. (1992). A botanical classification of standing waters in Great Britain: applications for conservation and monitoring. *Aquatic Conservation: Marine & Freshwater Ecosystems* 2, 125–43.

Parmesan, C. (2006). Ecological and evolutionary responses to recent climate change. *Annual Review of Ecology, Evolution and Systematics* 37, 637–69.

Peach, B. N & Horne, J. (1910). The Scottish lakes in relation to the geological features of the country. In: *Bathymetrical Survey of the Freshwater Lochs of Scotland* (Eds Murray, J. & Pullar, L.). Challenger Office, Edinburgh.

Pearsall, W. H. & Pennington, W. (1947). Ecological history of the English Lake District. *Journal of Ecology* 34, 137–48.

Pennak, R. W. (1985). The fresh-water invertebrate fauna: problems and solutions for evolutionary success. *American Zoologist* 25, 671–87.

Pennington, W. (1943). Lake sediments: The bottom deposits of the North Basin of Windermere, with special reference to the diatom succession. *New Phytologist* 42, 1–27.

Pennington, W. (1973). The recent sediments of Windermere. *Freshwater Biology* 3, 363–82.

Pennington, W. (1974). Seston and sediment formation in five Lake District lakes. *Journal of Ecology* 62, 215–51.

Perrow, M. R. and others (1999). The stability of fish communities in shallow lakes undergoing restoration: expectations and experiences from the Norfolk Broads (UK). *Hydrobiologia* 408/9, 85–100.

Phillips, W. (1884). The breaking of the Shropshire meres. *Transactions of the Shropshire Archaeological and Natural History Society* 7, 277–300.

Pickering, A. D. (2001). *Windermere: Restoring the Health of England's Largest Lake*. Freshwater Biological Association, Ambleside.

Pigott, C. D. & Pigott, M. E. (1963). Late Glacial and Post-Glacial deposits at Malham Tarn, Yorkshire. *New Phytologist* 62, 317–34.

Pimental, D., Zuniga, R. & Morrison, D. (2005). Update on the environmental and economic costs associated with alien-invasive species in the United States. *Ecological Economics* 52, 273–88.

Pomeroy, P. P. (1994). Zooplankton in Loch Lomond: perspectives, predation and powan. *Hydrobiologia* 290, 75–90.

Post, D. M. & Palkovacs, E. P. (2009). Eco-evolutionary feedbacks in community and ecosystem ecology: interactions between the ecological theatre and the evolutionary play. *Philosophical Transactions of the Royal Society B* 364, 1629–40.

Post, D. M., Pace, M. L. & Hairston Jr, N. G. (2000). Ecosystem size determines food-chain length in lakes. *Nature* 405, 1047–9.

Preston, C. D. & Croft, J. M. (1997). *Aquatic Plants in Britain and Ireland*. Harley Books, Colchester.

Pretty, J. N. and others (2003). Environmental costs of eutrophication in England and Wales. *Environmental Science & Technology* 37, 201–8.

Prior, F. (2010). *The Making of the British Landscape*. Allen Lane, London.

Purseglove, J. (1988). *Taming the Flood*. Oxford University Press, Oxford.

Raebel, E. M. and others (2012). Identifying high-quality pond habitats for Odonata in lowland England: implications for agri-environment schemes. *Insect Conservation and Diversity* 5, 422–32.

Reiners, D. S., Reiners, W. A. & Lockwood, J. A. (2013). The relationship between environmental advocacy, values, and science: a survey of ecological scientists' attitudes. *Ecological Applications* 23, 1226–42.

Reynolds, C. S. (1971). The ecology of the planktonic blue green algae in the North Shropshire meres, England. *Field Studies* 3, 409–32.

Reynolds, C. S. (1979). The limnology of the eutrophic meres of the Shropshire-Cheshire Plain – a review. *Field Studies* 5, 93–173.

Reynolds, C. S. (1980). Phytoplankton assemblages and their periodicity in stratifying lake systems. *Holarctic Ecology* 3, 141–59.

Reynolds C. S. (1995). River plankton: the paradigm regained. In: *The Ecological Basis for River Management* (Eds Harper, D. & Ferguson A. J. D.).Wiley: Chichester.

Reynolds, C. S. (2008). A changing paradigm of pelagic food webs. *International Review of Hydrobiology* 93, 517–31.

Reynolds, C. S. & Walsby, A. J. (1975) Water blooms. *Biological Reviews* 50, 437–81.

Reynolds, C. S. and others (2002). Towards a functional classification of freshwater phytoplankton. *Journal of Plankton Research* 24, 417–28.

Reynolds, J. D. (1998). *Ireland's Freshwaters*. The Marine Institute, Dublin.

Reynoldson, T. B. (1983). The population biology of Turbellaria with special reference to the freshwater triclads of the British Isles. *Advances in Ecological Research* 13, 235–326.

Reynoldson, T. B. & Young, J. O. (2000). *A Key to the Freshwater Triclads of Britain and Ireland with notes on their ecology*. Freshwater Biological Association Scientific Publication 58.

Ripple, W. J. & Beschta, R. L. (2011). Trophic cascades in Yellowstone: the first 15 years after wolf reintroduction. *Biological Conservation* 145, 205–13.

Ritvo, H. (2009). *The Dawn of Green: Manchester, Thirlmere, and Modern Environmentalism*. University of Chicago Press, Chicago.

Robinson, T. (2008) *Connemara: Listening to the Wind*. Penguin, London.

Rodgers, M. and others (2010). Phosphorus release from forest harvesting on an upland blanket peat catchment. *Forest Ecology and Management* 260, 2241–8.

Round, F. E. (1957). The late-glacial and post-glacial diatom succession in the Kentmere valley deposit. Part I. Introduction, methods and flora. *New Phytologist* 56, 98–126.

Round, F. E. (1961) The diatoms of a core from Esthwaite Water. *New Phytologist* 60, 43–59.

Royal Society for the Protection of Birds (2013). *State of Nature Report 2013*. Sandy.

Ryves, D. B., Anderson, N. J., Flower, R. J. & Rippey, B. (2013). Diatom taphonomy and silica cycling in two freshwater lakes and their implications for inferring past lake productivity. *Journal of Plaeolimnology* 49, 411–30.

Salisbury, E. J. (1954). Felix Eugene Fritsch 1879–1954. *Obituary Notices of Fellows of the Royal Society* 9, 130–40.

Savage, A. A. (2000). Community structure during a 27-year study of the macroinvertebrate fauna of a chemically unstable lake. *Hydrobiologia* 421, 115–27.

Sayer, C. and others (2006). TBT causes regime shift in shallow lakes. *Environmental Science and Technology* 40, 5269–75.

Scheider, W. & Wallis, P. (1973). An alternate method of calculating the population density of monsters in Loch Ness. *Limnology & Oceanography* 18, 343.

Schindler, D. W. (1988) Effects of acid rain on freshwater ecosystems. *Science* 239, 149–157.

Schindler, D. W. (1998). Replication versus realism: the need for ecosystem-scale experiments. *Ecosystems* 1, 323–34.

Sheail, J. (1998). *Nature Conservation in Britain: The Formative Years*. The Stationery Office, London.

Sheehy Skeffington and others (2006). Turloughs – Ireland's unique wetland habitat. *Biological Conservation* 133, 265–90.

Sheil, D. & Murdiyarso, D. (2009). How forests attract rain: an examination of a new hypothesis. *BioScience* 59, 341–7.

Sheldon, R. W. & Kerr, S. R. (1972). The population density of monsters in Loch Ness. *Limnology & Oceanography* 17, 796–8.

Sheppard, J. A. (1957). The mediaeval meres of Holderness. *Transactions and Papers (Institute of British Geographers)* 23, 75–86.

Shine, A. J. & Martin, D. S. (1988). Loch Ness habitats observed by sonar and underwater television. *The Scottish Naturalist* 1988, 111–19.

Shoard, M. (1980). *The Theft of the Countryside*. Maurice Temple Smith, London.

Shoard, M. (1987). *This Land is our Land*. Paladin, London.

Sinker, C. A. (1962). The North Shropshire meres and mosses; a background for ecologists. *Field Studies* 1, 101–38.

Slack, N. G. (2011). *G. Evelyn Hutchinson and the Invention of Modern Ecology*. Yale University Press, New Haven.

Smith, R. A., Alexander, R. B. & Schwartz, G. E. (2003). Natural background concentrations of nutrients in streams and rivers of the conterminous United States. *Environmental Science and Technology* 37, 3039–47.

Smolders, A. J. P., Lucassen, E. C. H. E. T. & Roelofs, J. G. M. (2002). The isoetid environment: biogeochemistry and threats. *Aquatic Botany* 73, 325–50.

Solomon, C. T., Carpenter, S. R., Cole, J. J. & Pace, M. L. (2008). Support of benthic invertebrates by detrital resources and current autochthonous primary production: results from a whole-lake ^{13}C addition. *Freshwater Biology* 53, 42–54.

Sommer, U. and others (2012). Beyond the plankton ecology group (PEG) model: mechanisms driving plankton succession. *Annual Reviews in Ecology, Evolution and Systematics* 43, 429–48.

Spears, B. M., Meis, S., Anderson, A. & Kellou, M. (2013). Comparison of phosphorus (P) removal properties of materials proposed for the control of sediment P release in UK lakes. *Science of the Total Environment* 442, 103–10.

Spivak, A. C., Vanni, M. J. & Mette, E. M. (2011). Moving on up: can results from simple aquatic mesocosm experiments be applied across broad spatial scales? *Freshwater Biology* 56, 279–91.

Stansfield, J., Moss, B. & Irvine, K. (1989). The loss of submerged plants with eutrophication III Potential role of organochlorine pesticides: a palaeoecological study. *Freshwater Biology* 22, 109–32.

Stead, I. M., Bourke, J. B. & Brothwell, D. (1986). *Lindow Man: The Body in the Bog.* British Museum Publications, London.

Steinmetz, J., Kohler, S. L. & Soluk, D. A. (2003). Birds are overlooked top predators in aquatic food webs. *Ecology* 84, 1324–28.

Stenroosa, S. and others (2009a). Carbon sequestration and stoichiometry of motile and nonmotile green algae. *Limnology & Oceanography* 54, 1746–52.

Sutcliffe, D. W. (1998). The ionic composition of surface waters in the English Lake District, related to bedrock geology, with some singular facts and speculation on the existence of mineral-rich groundwaters. *Freshwater Forum* 11, 30–51.

Syrjänen, K. & Hyvönen, J. (2010). Multiple origins of symbioses between ascomycetes and bryophytes suggested by a five-gene phylogeny. *Cladistics* 26, 281–300.

Talling, J. F. (2004). The development of freshwater science in Britain, and British contributions abroad, 1900–2000. *Freshwater Forum* 22, 22–80.

Talling, J. F. (2012). Freshwater phytoplankton ecology: the British contribution in retrospect. *Freshwater Reviews* 5, 1–20.

Talling, J. F. & Parker, J. E. (2002). Seasonal dynamics of phytoplankton and phytobenthos, and associated chemical interactions, in a shallow upland lake (Malham Tarn, northern England). *Hydrobiologia* 487, 167–71.

Tansley, A. G. (1911). The International Phytogeographical Excursion in the British Isles. *New Phytologist* 10, 271–91.

Taylor, P. (2005). *Beyond Conservation: A Wildland Strategy.* Routledge, London.

Thackeray, S., Maberly, S. C. & Winfield, I. J. (2006). The ecology of Bassenthwaite Lake (English Lake District). *Freshwater Forum* 25, 1–80.

Thackeray, S. T. and others (2010). Trophic level asynchrony in rates of phenological change for marine, freshwater and terrestrial environments. *Global Change Biology* 12, 3304–13.

Timms, R. M. & Moss, B. (1984). Prevention of growth of potentially dense phytoplankton populations by zooplankton grazing in the presence of zooplanktivorous fish, in a shallow wetland ecosystem. *Limnology & Oceanography* 29, 472–86.

Tippett, R. (1994). An introduction to Loch Lomond. *Hydrobiologia* 290, 11–15.

Tománková, I., Harrod, C., Fox, A. D. & Reid, N. (2013). Chlorophyll-a concentrations and macroinvertebrate declines coincide with the collapse of overwintering diving duck populations in a large eutrophic lake. *Freshwater Biology*, doi:10.1111/fwb.12261.

Trudgill, S. (2009). You can't resist the sea. *Geography* 94, 48–57.

Väänänen V-M. and others (2012). Fish–duck interactions in boreal lakes in Finland as reflected by abundance correlations. *Hydrobiologia* 697, 85–93.

Van Donk, E., Ianora, A. & Vos, M. (2011). Induced defences in marine and freshwater phytoplankton: a review. *Hydrobiologia* 668, 3–19.

Van Doorslaer, W., Stoks, R., Jeppesen, E. & De Meester, L. (2007). Adaptive microevolutionary responses to simulated global warming in Simocephalus vetulus: a mesocosm study. *Global Change Biology* 13, 878–86.

Van Doorslaer, W. and others (2010). Experimental thermal microevolution in community-embedded Daphnia populations. *Climate Research* 43, 81–9.

Van Duinen, G. A. and others (2006). Basal food sources for the invertebrate food web in nutrient poor and nutrient enriched raised bog pools. *Proceedings of the Netherlands Entomological Society Meetings* 17, 37–44.

Van Leeuwen, C. H. A., van der Velde, G. van Lith, B. & Klaassen, M. (2012). Experimental quantification of long distance dispersal potential of aquatic snails in the gut of migratory birds. *PloS ONE* 7 (3): e32292. doi 10.1371/journal.p.one.0032292.

Van der Zanden, M. J., Vadeboncoeur, Y. & Chandra, S. (2011). Fish reliance on littoral-benthic resources and the distribution of primary production in lakes. *Ecosystems* 14, 894–903.

Vane, C. H. and others (2010). Sedimentary records of sewage pollution using faecal markers in contrasting peri-urban shallow lakes. *Science of the Total Environment* 409, 346–56.

Vannote, R. L. and others (1980). The river continuum concept. *Canadian Journal of Fisheries and Aquatic Sciences* 37, 120–37.

Varley, M. E. (1967). *British Freshwater Fishes.* Fishing News Books Ltd, London.

Walker, G., Dorrell, R. G., Schlacht, A. and Dacks, J. B. (2011). Eukaryotic systematics: a user's guide for cell biologists and parasitologists. *Parasitology* 138, 1638–63.

Walter, K. M. and others (2006). Methane bubbling from Siberian thaw lakes as a positive feedback to climate warming. *Nature* 443, 71–5.

Watson, J. (2011). Case study of a conflict. *Geography Review,* November, 8–12.

Weatherly, N. S. (1988) Liming to mitigate acidification in freshwater ecosystems: a review of the biological consequences. *Water, Air and Soil Pollution* 39, 421–37.

Webb, M. (1924). *Precious Bane.* Jonathan Cape, London.

Weisse, T. (2006). Biodiversity of freshwater microorganisms: achievements, problems & perspectives. *Polish Journal of Ecology* 54, 630–52.

West, W. & West, G. S. (1904–22). *A Monograph of the British Desmidiaceae.* Vols. I–V. The Ray Society, London.

Whittaker, R. H. (1969). New concepts of the kingdoms of organisms. *Science* 163, 150–60.

Wierzchos, J., Ascaso, C. & McKay, C. P. (2006). Endolithic Cyanobacteria in halite rocks from the hyperarid core of the Atacama desert. *Astrobiology* 6, 415–22.

Wigbels, V. (1980). *Oostvardersplassen.* MMI Staatsbosbeheer Flevoland-Overijssel, Zwolle.

Wigglesworth, V. B. (1956). Patrick Alfred Buxton 1892–1955. *Biographical Memoirs of Fellows of the Royal Society* 2, 69–84.

Wildlife & Countryside Link (2013). *Nature Check 2013. An Analysis of the Government's Natural Environment Commitments.* Wildlife & Countryside Link, London.

Williams, A. E., Moss, B. & Eaton, J. (2002). Fish-induced macrophyte loss in shallow lakes: top-down and bottom-up processes in mesocosm experiments. *Freshwater Biology* 47, 2216–32.

Williams, P., Biggs, J., Whitfield, M., Thorne, A., Bryant, S., Fox, G., Nicolet, P. & Julian, A. M. (2010). *The Pond Book: A Guide to the Management and Creation of Ponds.* 2nd Edn. The Ponds Conservation Trust, Oxford.

Williamson C. E., Saros, J. E., Vincent, W. F., Smol, J. P. (2009). Lakes and reservoirs as sentinals, integrators, and regulators of climate change. *Limnology & Oceanography* 54, 2273–82.

Wilson, D. S. (1998). Adaptive individual differences within single populations. *Philosophical Transactions of the Royal Society B* 353, 199–205.

Winfield, D. K. & Winfield, I. J. (1974) Possible competitive interactions between overwintering tufted duck (Aythya fuligula (L.)) and fish populations of Lough Neagh, Northern Ireland: evidence from diet studies. *Hydrobiologia* 279/280, 377–86.

Winfield, I. J., Fletcher, J. M. & James, J. B. (2008). The Arctic charr (Salvelinus alpinus) populations of Windermere, UK: population trends associated with eutrophication, climate change and increased abundance of roach (*Rutilus rutilus*). *Environmental Biology of Fishes* 83, 25–35.

Winfield, I. J., Fletcher, J. M. & James, J. B. (2011). Invasive fish species in the largest lakes of Scotland, Northern Ireland, Wales and England: the collective UK experience. *Hydrobiologia* 660, 93–103.

Wisniewski, P. J. (1993). Martin Mere. *The Biologist* 40, 194–6.

Woese C. R., Kandler, O. & Wheelis, M. L. (1990). Towards a natural system of organisms: proposal for the domains Archaea, Bacteria, and Eucarya. *Proceedings National Academy of Sciences, USA* 87, 4576–9.

Wood, P. J., Greenwood, M. T. & Agnew, M. D. (2003). Pond biodiversity and habitat loss in the UK. *Area* 35, 206–16.

Worthington, E. B. (1983). *The Ecological Century; A Personal Appraisal.* Oxford University Press, Oxford.

Worthington, E. B. (1985). Obituary. Dr T.T. Macan. *Freshwater Biology* 15, 643–4.

Worthington, S. & Worthington, E. B. (1933). *Inland Waters of Africa.* Macmillan, London.

Yoshida, T. and others (2003). Rapid evolution drives ecological dynamics in a predatior-prey system. *Nature* 424, 303–6.

Yvon-Durocher, G. and others. (2010). Warming alters the metabolic balance of ecosystems. *Philosophical Transactions of the Royal Society* B 365, 2117–26.

Zinger, L., Gobet, A. & Pommiers, T. (2012). Two decades of describing the unseen majority of aquatic microbial diversity. *Molecular Ecology* 21, 1878–96.

Index

The New Naturalist Library